D1527681

Leibniz on the Problem of Evil

# Leibniz on the Problem of Evil

Paul Rateau

OXFORD
UNIVERSITY PRESS

## OXFORD
UNIVERSITY PRESS

Oxford University Press is a department of the University of Oxford. It furthers
the University's objective of excellence in research, scholarship, and education
by publishing worldwide. Oxford is a registered trade mark of Oxford University
Press in the UK and certain other countries.

Published in the United States of America by Oxford University Press
198 Madison Avenue, New York, NY 10016, United States of America.

Library of Congress Cataloging- in- Publication Data
Names: Rateau, Paul, author.
Title: Leibniz on the problem of evil / Paul Rateau.
Other titles: Question du mal chez Leibniz. English
Description: New York : Oxford University Press, 2019. |
Includes bibliographical references and index.
Identifiers: LCCN 2018050787 (print) | LCCN 2019011220 (ebook) |
ISBN 9780199996513 (updf) | ISBN 9780199350971 (online content) |
ISBN 9780190054564 (epub) | ISBN 9780199996506 (cloth : alk. paper)
Subjects: LCSH: Leibniz, Gottfried Wilhelm, Freiherr von, 1646-1716. Essais
de th?eodic?ee. | Theodicy. | Good and evil. | Free will and determinism.
Classification: LCC B2590.Z7 (ebook) | LCC B2590.Z7 R3813 2019 (print) |
DDC 231/.8—dc23
LC record available at https://lccn.loc.gov/2018050787

1 3 5 7 9 8 6 4 2

Printed by Sheridan Books, Inc., United States of America

# CONTENTS

# ACKNOWLEDGMENTS

I would like to express my deep gratitude to Todd Ryan for his very careful translation, helpful advice, and comments. This work would not have been possible without his continuing commitment and friendly support.

I would also like to thank Mark Kulstad who first had the idea for this project and Samuel Newlands who warmly welcomed and supported it. Finally, I am grateful to the John Templeton Foundation who generously granted their financial support.

# ABBREVIATIONS

## ABBREVIATIONS FOR LEIBNIZ'S WORKS

| | |
|---|---|
| A | *Leibniz: Sämtliche Schriften und Briefe*. Edited by Prussian Academy, then Berlin-Brandenburg Academy, and Academy of Göttingen. Darmstadt, then Leipzig and Berlin, 1923–. Cited by series, volume, and page number. |
| AG | *Philosophical Essays*. Translated by Roger Ariew and Daniel Garber. Indianapolis: Hackett, 1989. |
| C | *Opuscules et fragments inédits de Leibniz. Extraits des manuscrits de la bibliothèque de Hanovre*. Edited by Louis Couturat. Paris: Alcan, 1903; repr. Hildesheim: Georg Olms, 1966. |
| *Causa Dei* | *Causa Dei asserta per Justitiam ejus, cum caeteris ejus Perfectionibus, cunctisque Actionibus conciliatam*. Cited by section number. |
| CP | *Confessio Philosophi* (*The Confession of a Philosopher*). |
| DM | *Discourse on Metaphysics*. Cited by section number. |
| Dutens | *G. G. Leibnitii Opera omnia, Nunc primum collecta. In Classes distributa, praefationibus et indicibus exornata, studio L. Dutens*. 6 vols. Geneva: 1768; repr. Hildesheim: Georg Olms, 1990. |
| FC (L) | *Lettres et Opuscules inédits de Leibniz*. Introduction by Louis-Alexandre Foucher de Careil. Paris: Ladrange, 1854; repr. Hildesheim: Georg Olms, 1975. |
| FC (NL) | *Nouvelles lettres et opuscules inédits de Leibniz*. Introduction by Louis-Alexandre Foucher de Careil. Paris: Durand, 1857; repr. Hildesheim: Georg Olms, 1971. |
| FC (O) | *Œuvres de Leibniz, publiées pour la première fois d'après les manuscrits originaux*. Notes and introduction by |

Louis-Alexandre Foucher de Careil. 7 vols. Paris: Didot, 1859–1875; repr. Hildesheim: Georg Olms, 1969.

GB  *Briefwechsel zwischen Leibniz und Christian Wolff. Aus den Handschriften der Königlichen Bibliothek zu Hannover.* Edited by C. I. Gerhardt. Halle: 1860; repr. Hildesheim: Georg Olms, 1971.

GM  *Leibnizens mathematische Schriften.* Edited by C. I. Gerhardt. 7 vols. Berlin then Halle: 1849–1863; repr. Hildesheim: Georg Olms, 1962. Cited by volume and page number.

GP  *Die philosophischen Schriften von Leibniz.* Edited by C. I. Gerhardt. 7 vols. Berlin 1875–1890; repr. Hildesheim: Georg Olms, 1960–1961. Cited by volume and page number.

Grua  *Leibniz. Textes inédits d'après les manuscrits de la Bibliothèque provinciale de Hanovre,* ed. and notes by Gaston Grua. 2 vols. Paris: PUF, 1948.

Guhrauer  *Leibniz's Deutsche Schriften.* Edited by G. E. Guhrauer. 2 vols. Berlin, 1838–1840.

Huggard  *Gottfried Wilhelm Leibniz. Theodicy. Essays on the Goodness of God, the Freedom of Man and the Origin of Evil.* Edited and with an introduction by Austin Farrer. Translated by E. M. Huggard. New Haven: Yale University Press, 1952.

Klopp  *Die Werke von Leibniz gemäss seinem handschriftlichen Nachlasse in der Königlichen Bibliothek zu Hannover.* Edited by O. Klopp. Series I. 11 vols. Hanover, 1864–1884.

L  *G. W. Leibniz. Philosophical Papers and Letters.* Edited and translated by Leroy E. Loemker. Dordrecht: Reidel, 1969.

LR  *The Leibniz-Des Bosses Correspondence.* Edited and translated by Brandon C. Look and Donald Rutherford. New Haven: Yale University Press, 2007.

Mollat  *Mittheilungen aus Leibnizens ungedruckten Schriften.* Edited by Georg Mollat. Kassel, 1887; repr. Leipzig, 1893.

NE  *New Essays on Human Understanding.* Cited by book, chapter, and section number.

Pk  *De Summa Rerum: Metaphysical Papers, 1675–1676.* Edited and translated by G. H. R. Parkinson. New Haven: Yale University Press, 1992.

PNG  *The Principles of Nature and of Grace, Based on Reason.* Cited by section number.

R       *The Political Writings of Leibniz*. Edited and translated by Patrick Riley. Cambridge: Cambridge University Press, 1972.

RB      *New Essays on Human Understanding*. Translated by Peter Remnant and Jonathan Francis Bennett. Cambridge: Cambridge University Press, 1996.

S       *Monadology and Other Philosophical Essays. Gottfried Wilhelm von Leibniz*. Translated by Paul and Anne Martin Schrecker. With an Introduction and Notes by Paul Schrecker. Indianapolis, New York, Kansas City: Bobbs-Merrill, 1965.

Sleigh    *G. W. Leibniz*. Confessio Philosophi. *Papers Concerning the Problem of Evil*, 1671–1678. Edited, translated, and with an introduction by Robert C. Sleigh, Jr. New Haven and London: Yale University Press, 2005.

SLT     *The Shorter Leibniz Texts: A Collection of New Translations*. Edited and translated by Lloyd Strickland. London: Continuum, 2006.

T       *Theodicy: Essays on the Goodness of God, the Freedom of Man and the Origin of Evil*. Cited by section number.

T ob     *Observations on the Book Concerning the Origin of Evil Published Recently in England*. Cited by section number.

T pd     *Preliminary Discourse on the Conformity of Faith with Reason*. Cited by section number.

T ref     *Reflections on the Work Published by M. Hobbes in English on Freedom, Necessity and Chance*. Cited by section number.

T s      *Summary of the Controversy reduced to Formal Arguments*.

## ABBREVIATIONS FOR OTHER PRIMARY SOURCES
### *Aquinas*

ST      *Summa Theologica*. Translated by Fathers of the English Dominican Province. New York: Benzinger Brothers, 1947.

### *Bayle*

OD      *Œuvres Diverses de Mr. Pierre Bayle*. 4 vols. The Hague: 1727–1761; repr. Hildesheim: Georg Olms, 1964–1982.

## Descartes

AT      *Œuvres de Descartes*. Edited by Charles Adam and Paul Tannery, 11 vols. (plus a vol. including biography and supplement). Paris: L. Cerf, 1897–1913. New edition: Paris: Vrin/CNRS, 1964–1974.

CSM      *The Philosophical Writings of Descartes*. Edited and translated by John Cottingham, Robert Stoothoff, and Dugald Murdoch. 2 vols. Cambridge: Cambridge University Press, 1985.

CSMK      *The Philosophical Writings of Descartes*. Volume 3: *The Correspondence*. Translated and edited by John Cottingham, Robert Stoothoff, Dugald Murdoch, and Anthony Kenny. Cambridge: Cambridge University Press, 1991.

## Hobbes

EW      *The English Works of Thomas Hobbes of Malmesbury*. Edited by William Molesworth. 11 vols. London: Bohn, Longman, Brown, Green, and Longmans, 1839–1845.

## Luther

WA      *D. Martin Luthers Werke: Kritische Gesamtausgabe* [*Weimarer Ausgabe*]. 120 vols. Weimar: H. Böhlau and H. Böhlaus Nachfolger, 1883–2009.

Leibniz on the Problem of Evil

# Introduction

## 1. THE EXISTENCE OF EVIL

Let it be said from the outset: for Gottfried Wilhelm Leibniz (1646–1716), evil is not an enigma or an "unparalleled challenge" threatening to put an end to philosophy and rational theology. Far from posing an unsolvable theoretical problem,[1] evil does not defy rational investigation. Nor does this examination lead to the denial of the reality of evil in the world—although Leibniz refuses to exaggerate its extent, with the result that he has sometimes appeared to commentators as lacking a "dramatic sense of sin"[2] and as shrugging off the "tragedy of human existence."[3] On the contrary, for Leibniz, the fact of evil is undeniable:

> [O]ne cannot deny that there is in the world physical evil (that is, suffering) and moral evil (that is, crime) and even that physical evil is not always distributed here on earth according to the proportion of moral evil, as it seems that justice demands.[4]

Evil is not a mere appearance that results from our partial understanding of things and vanishes altogether when we regard the universe from the correct point of view. Although, metaphysically speaking, evil is merely a privation, it is not a pure nothing, but that which limits perfection and being and so resists and impedes the good. The forms that evil takes (flaws, disorders, natural calamities, monsters, errors, ignorance, sin, vice and pain) are as varied as the good it limits, even if it is reduced at *Theodicy* §21 to three fundamental kinds (metaphysical, physical, and moral evil).

Leibniz neither questions nor seeks to minimize either the effects themselves or their pervasiveness—indeed, prosperity—in the world. In thinking about evil, Leibniz does not ignore experience, even if he refutes objections against providence based solely on its evidence.

Leibniz is not unaware of the evils and misfortunes of his time. On the contrary, his philosophical investigation is undertaken from a practical perspective. As Donald Rutherford has convincingly argued,[5] Leibniz's Theodicy and metaphysics are indissolubly linked to moral concerns and are wholly oriented toward the improvement of the human condition through the exercise of reason. However, his goal is not exclusively moral in the strict sense of the term, for it is also, more broadly, political and religious. In keeping with his well-known motto, *Theoria cum praxi* ("Theory with Practice"), Leibniz's philosophical reflection on evil is accompanied by a constant and relentless struggle against the concrete forms in which evil appears in the world. The various undertakings and projects he pursued during the course of his life—however various and disparate they may appear—were all born of a desire to work for the perfection and happiness of human beings, including at the material level, by relieving their misery. These efforts included attempts at reunification of the churches (both among the Protestant churches and with Rome); scientific projects (an encyclopedia of human knowledge, plans for the foundation of academies and learned societies); mathematical and technical inventions; support for the arts and literature; research relating to demographics and the economy (especially the idea of founding insurance funds and creating public storehouses permanently stocked with primary goods); proposals to reform the law and contemporary judicial procedures; and political and diplomatic missions. All of these projects and undertakings illustrate his firm conviction that intellectual activity ought not to be separated from action and "engagement" in the world in the service of neighbor and society. The just man must consider everything he does and everything for which he labors from the perspective of the "general good" and the glory of God.

Leibniz well understood the contemporary situation in Germany, which had been exhausted by the Thirty Years' War (1618–1648). He describes the suffering of this war, which saw German princes tear each other apart, and whose effects continued to be felt long after the signing of the Treaty of Westphalia.[6] In various pamphlets and manifestos, Leibniz took exception to the expansionist politics of France and denounced the disastrous consequences of the wars instigated by Louis XIV.[7] In a letter to Marshal Villars (May 1704), Leibniz expresses outrage at the terrible repression of the Protestants of Cevennes carried out by Villars under orders from Louis XIV and accuses Villars of becoming "the infamous minister of his [the king's] fury and the cruel executioner of his innocent compatriots."[8] When reading these pages in which Leibniz vigorously denounces the injustices committed by France in Europe, and the inhumanity, cruelty, and barbarism of Marshal Villars, one can almost wonder whether this is the same man who defends the existence of the best of all possible worlds! André Robinet has rightly wondered, "What is the meaning of the *Theodicy*, if Leibniz was so familiar with the existence of real and concrete evil?"[9] Is there a gap between Leibniz the metaphysician and Leibniz the pamphleteer and politician? The thesis of the best of all possible worlds does not imply the perfection of every one of its parts. In no way is this thesis the result of blindness, ignorance, or indifference to worldly affairs. It does not amount to a legitimization of the present state of things on the grounds that they cannot fail to be good, since they belong to the best of all possible worlds. Nor should it lead to resignation or inaction. On the contrary, the task of the just man is to work tirelessly for the good, despite all obstacles and setbacks, and to make the future better to the utmost of his ability by altering those things that need reform.

Thus, Leibniz is perfectly aware of the weight of evil in the world and of its consequences at every level: moral, religious (confessional divisions, intolerance), social, economic (poverty, famine), and political (war and its attendant evils). For Leibniz, the sole source of evil is man. For this reason, "it is only the will that men lack to deliver themselves from an infinity of evils."[10] Indeed, the will of some few would often suffice to bring relief to entire nations. Man is "one of the most powerful creatures and one of the most capable of causing evil." The faculty of reason with which he is endowed makes him capable of causing much evil, for which reason "one single Caligula, one Nero, has caused more evil than an earthquake. An evil man takes pleasure in causing suffering and destruction, for which there are only too many opportunities."[11] Here, forty-five years prior to the Lisbon earthquake (1755), is Leibniz's response to those who would accuse God of all the disorders of the world: no natural evil can compare to what human beings do and are capable of doing to one another.

Must we then conclude that Leibniz held a rather dim view of human beings and that behind his metaphysical "optimism" lies a certain anthropological "pessimism"? Certain texts can give this impression.[12] However, Leibniz generally avoids excessively dramatizing evil and exaggerating human misery in the manner of Augustine, Luther, or Pascal. For Leibniz, even if human beings cannot be saved without Christ, it does not follow that pagan virtue is a false virtue and that of necessity all of their actions are sinful.[13] Leibniz has little regard for those authors who take pleasure in portraying humans as wicked and contemptible, hypocritical and deceitful.[14] By emphasizing evil, such accounts only add to it and lead us to believe that it generally predominates over the good. For Leibniz, it is unjust to degrade the human condition in this way. It is even sinful to portray human beings as so evil and contemptible, since it is a failure to recognize the goodness that God has shown us.[15] In fact,

> this [moral] evil is not even so great in men as it is declared to be. It is only people of a malicious disposition or those who have become somewhat misanthropic through misfortunes, like Lucian's Timon, who find wickedness everywhere, and who poison the best actions by the interpretations they give to them.[16]

The disposition to "make an evil of everything" is fundamentally harmful to society and serves to teach human beings to be wicked.[17] Furthermore, Leibniz is wary of those who speak of the evils and faults of humans "without the slightest intention of taking effective measures to remedy them," and who prefer instead to waste their time "in impotent wishes and useless complaints."[18]

Evil exists. However, our tendency is to exaggerate it. This explains the success of those who would portray human nature as depraved and the world as full of evil. In reality, human beings pay greater attention to evil than to good and, as a consequence, are more inclined to believe that on balance the evil of the universe outweighs the good both in quantity and intensity. Like health, the good often goes unrecognized. It is less noticeable and frequently passes unobserved, whereas evil is exaggerated.

> It is only want of attention that diminishes our good, and this attention must be given to us through some admixture of evils. If we were usually sick and seldom in good health, we should be wonderfully sensible of that great good and we should be less sensible of our evils. But is it not better, notwithstanding, that health should be usual and sickness the exception?[19]

Thus, our sense that evils are greater and more numerous than goods does not prove that they really are so. On the contrary, it shows that they are not, since we notice only what is rare and pay no attention to the ordinary and habitual: "evil arouses our attention rather than good: but this same reason proves that evil is more rare."[20]

Paradoxically, the tendency to exaggerate evil can be found among theologians as well as skeptics and atheists—although for exactly opposite reasons. Evil serves as an argument for apologists as well as critics. In the case of the former, the omnipresence of evil in the world shows the need for a redeemer, the Christ. In the case of the latter, it calls into question either the existence of God or his unity and consequently his power (according to the Manichean hypothesis popularized by Pierre Bayle) or his justice. Leibniz seems to adopt a more measured approach. He does not dismiss the experience of evil; however, he treats it with caution in light of our natural tendency to exaggerate it. For Leibniz, evil cannot serve as the basis for a serious objection to the existence of God or to monotheism. On the other hand, it unquestionably poses a problem with regard to justice, which is an attribute traditionally ascribed to God. It is for this reason that a doctrine of God's justice, that is, a *théo-dicée* in the literal sense of the term, is necessary.[21] It is within the framework of this doctrine that the theoretical difficulties raised by the existence of evil can be resolved.

## 2. EVIL CONSIDERED IN RELATION TO JUSTICE

The manner in which Leibniz approaches the problem of evil is original in that it is explicitly connected with the theme of justice.[22] The first question raised by evil is not "Why does it exist?" or the traditional "Where does it come from?" (*Unde malum?*), but rather "Who is responsible for it?" The issue is, in the first instance, moral and juridical because it is the question of imputation that is at stake. Obviously, the metaphysical aspects and implications of the problem are not overlooked, but they are considered only subsequently, when the inquiry turns to the origin of evil and its essence. Why does Leibniz adopt this juridical approach? As is well known, Leibniz was a jurist. In the preface of the *Theodicy*, he takes on the role of a lawyer who pleads the cause of God.[23] As we shall see, Leibniz appeals in the defensive wing of the *Theodicy* to the rules of controversy that he set out in the *Preliminary Discourse*[24] and that are clearly inspired by judicial debates.

However, I believe that Leibniz adopts a juridical point of view for a more fundamental reason: he considers *injustice* to be the true evil. Injustice is all that violates the law (natural or positive): injustice committed (sin) as well as injustice suffered (undeserved physical pain and moral grief). For Leibniz, evil is not a scandal in and of itself. It becomes shocking when it seems to be unjustly distributed, when pain befalls one who did not deserve it, when sin is not followed by any punishment and even proves profitable to the sinner. The existence of suffering, misfortune, calamity, and the fact that there are wicked people in the world would not be so problematic if this suffering as well as these misfortunes and calamities only happened to the wicked. In this case, evil would be easily justified, since it would appear to be natural castigation for their sins. What gives rise to the problem is that the right order of things seems to have been turned upside down. We thus see that the good are persecuted and suffer, that criminals commit their crimes with impunity and even seem to be rewarded with happiness. Leibniz emphasizes this blatant contradiction between *fact* and *right*, which is felt to be intolerable under a God who is said to be good, wise, and all-powerful.[25]

Evil challenges divine justice in both its senses: as it refers to *law*, and as it refers to *perfection*. On the one hand, divine justice is the rule according to which God governs the whole universe, and in particular the republic of spirits, assigning rewards and punishments to each according to his merit. On the other hand, divine justice signifies holiness, which Leibniz defines as the highest degree of goodness.[26] In accordance with his holiness, God always wills what is good. The apparent disorder of things (for example, prosperity among some of the wicked and misfortune among many of the good) calls into question divine justice taken in the first sense and seems to overthrow the idea of *providence* in the world. God's physical and moral concurrence with evil (physical as well as moral evil) seems incompatible with justice taken in the second sense, as perfection. Every creature and every action owes its being and reality to divine omnipotence and continues to exist because of it (conservation is continuous creation). Consequently, God contributes to sins by his will and power, insofar as nothing would happen unless he made it happen and either willed or permitted it. At issue here is the problem of *predestination* and human freedom. The punishment of the "sinner" no longer appears legitimate if he could not have done otherwise (because his action would be completely predetermined) and if in fact the sin were ultimately imputable to God, as the primary cause of all things.

Considering this close link between evil and justice (taken in its two senses) and the terms in which the problem of evil is formulated, the solution can only be found in a doctrine of divine justice. This doctrine, which aims to establish God's innocence and holiness by reason, is based on two presuppositions: (1) the idea of justice is absolutely univocal, that is, it is a single notion common to all spirits (including God); (2) this notion applies to all spirits and, as a consequence, the divine right is not the result, within universal jurisprudence, of a special regime, according to which God stands above the ordinary laws of justice and is properly speaking unaccountable for his actions.

(1) As early as 1663, Leibniz criticizes the Hobbesian reduction of justice to utility and civil law on the grounds that it opens the door to fiat and tyranny.[27] However, positive and explicit affirmation of the univocity

of justice seems only to have appeared in conjunction with the systematic critique of Cartesianism that Leibniz undertook beginning in 1676. By making the good and the just depend not on the nature of things, but on the will of God, Descartes destroys divine justice and makes of God a tyrant, who cannot be the object of sincere love.[28] However, Hobbes is also a target, insofar as he identifies right with pure power, by making justice that which is pleasing to the strongest (in accordance with the formulation that Plato attributes to Thrasymachus in the *Republic*).[29] Leibniz refuses to place divine justice beyond the jurisdiction of reason, since divine right is a part of natural law, which applies universally to all spirits.

> For my part, I believe that just as God's arithmetic and geometry are the same as man's, except that they are of infinitely greater extent, so too, natural jurisprudence and every other truth is the same in heaven and on earth. It must not be thought that God is capable of doing what for men would be tyranny.[30]

Descartes and Hobbes (together with some theologians) share the view that the rules of justice are freely instituted by God without any preexisting universal idea of justice independent of the divine will. On this view, the rules of justice are the mere effect of God's will and omnipotence. For Leibniz, this is unacceptable for three reasons.

i. It renders the notion of justice completely meaningless. Justice is confounded with power and consequently signifies nothing more than its exercise (and so is nothing considered in itself): "For why praise [God] because he acts according to justice, if the notion of justice, in his case, adds nothing to that of action?."[31] Justice becomes a purely extrinsic denomination, without any foundation in things themselves, since a thing is just only because God did or willed it. In other words, whatever God wills is just by virtue of the fact that he wills it and not because it is just in itself. Furthermore, justice ceases to be an attribute by which we honor God since he is just no matter what he does, whether he performs a given action or its contrary.[32] To make power the basis of right is "a failure to distinguish between right and fact. For what one can do is one thing, what one should do, another."[33] It is likewise a failure to distinguish right (*droit*) and law (*loi*).[34]

ii. Voluntarism replaces justice with an arbitrary power whose principle—namely, that the will stands in place of a reason (*stat pro ratione voluntas*)—is the "motto of the tyrant" and offers no way of distinguishing God from the devil or from the Manichean evil principle, who must be obeyed by constraint.[35] It follows that "everything is just, if it succeeds" including crimes, murders, and punishment of the innocent since, by definition, the one who holds power is never unjust.[36] However, such a view is not only contrary to the idea of God but also harmful from a practical point of view, since it replaces enlightened and sincere love (based on recognition of the divine perfections, and, in particular, his goodness and justice) by pure fear. It is destructive of religion and encourages impiety.

iii. Voluntarism is untenable insofar as it violates the Principle of Sufficient Reason and ultimately rests on a contradiction. It presupposes a will that has no other reason than itself, which, as an absolute power to establish arbitrarily the good and the just, wills *because it wills* and not because the understanding presents it with a good to be sought. This notion places the will in a state of complete indifference with regard to any prior idea of the good and the just (which would be logically prior and to which it would incline).

> Which is very strange. For if things are good or evil only as the result of God's will, the good cannot be a motive of his will, being posterior to his will. His will, then, would be a certain absolute decree, without any reason.[37]

Voluntarism reverses the true order of things and the relation between cause and effect. Furthermore, the indifference it supposes, were it possible, would be perfectly sterile. For no decision or action could follow from it, since nothing determinate can result from the indeterminate. There could be no escape from this indifference without attributing to God the ability to will to will. However, this would involve a second error, for it would lead to an infinite regress of volitions.[38]

(2) The idea of justice is the same for all minds. However, Leibniz asserts once again that all minds are equally and without exception subject to it. Divine right is not based on a separate, particular right but is part of a single general juridical system. On this point, Leibniz stands in opposition to Lutheran theologians and to all defenders of an absolute divine right. To be sure, Luther did not deny God's "justice." However, he maintained that its rules are incomprehensible to us, at least in this life. Against the conception of justice as accessible to reason (the light of nature), Luther offered two strictly supernatural conceptions of justice, successively discovered by the light of grace and the light of glory. By this latter, God's judgment, which "crowns one ungodly man freely and apart from merits, yet damns another who may well be less, or at least not more, ungodly" will be seen to express a "most perfect and manifest righteousness," although unfathomable by our reason.[39]

For Leibniz such a distinction once again introduces an equivocation into the concept of justice, since it implies that justice is not the same for God and human beings. Luther's doctrine of triple justice is indefensible at both the theoretical and practical level. How can we attribute to God a perfection that has nothing in common with our conception of it or, in other words, of which we are ignorant? How can we praise him as just, if we cannot judge his actions according to any known rule of justice?

> Thus if someone wishes to maintain that the justice and the goodness of God have entirely different rules than those of men, he must recognize at the same time that these are two different notions, and that it is either voluntary equivocation or gross self-deception to attribute justice to both. Choosing, then, which of the two notions must be taken for that of justice, it will follow that either there is no true justice in God or that there is none in men, or perhaps that there is none in either, and that in the end one doesn't know what he is saying when speaking of justice—but this would destroy it, in fact, and leave nothing but the name. As do those also who make it arbitrary and dependent on the good pleasure of a judge or of a powerful person, since the same action will appear to be just or unjust to different judges.[40]

Now to defend equivocity with regard to divine justice leads to a violation of the Principle of Contradiction, by affirming both that God is just and that he is not just, according to our ordinary understanding of the term. Thus, we cannot attribute to God a right that would exempt him from the principles of natural law without thereby affirming that he is not just and destroying the notion of a universal republic of spirits whose members (from rational creatures to God), because they differ only by degree of perfection and not by nature, are subject to the same laws.

Consequently, God possesses no right with regard to his creatures by which he may do with them as he pleases, even including damnation of the innocent. God's omnipotence, our creaturely condition, and our perpetual dependence on him are not a sufficient basis for the absolute right advocated by Hobbes, Bradwardin, Pierre d'Ailly, Theodore Beza, Amyrault, and others.[41] It is true that God is not subject to the law of any superior to whom he is accountable for his actions. Nevertheless, he is not unaccountable (*anupeuthunos*). For it is false to claim that God has no obligations[42] and that therefore no one could ever be justified in making a complaint against him, were he to break a promise or condemn an innocent person.

For Leibniz, God's justice does not consist in any such impunity or absence of responsibility. Although God has no superior, his absolute supremacy does not place him above the law. Therefore, it would be perfectly legitimate to lodge a complaint against him were he to make tyrannical use of his power.

> Thus, the damnation of an innocent man, the breaking of a divine promise, etc. would not be in conformity with justice, because such a way of acting would be completely contrary to the goodness and wisdom of God. And if, consequently, by virtue of this definition of justice, one wishes to call *a right* (albeit imperfect) *that which an individual* (with or without recourse) *can rightly expect, and, which having failed to obtain, he can justly demand*, it can be said that man also has to some extent a right with regard to God, as for example the right, based on divine promise, to what God has promised, the right, based on innocence, in the case where someone is innocent before God, not to be punished, etc.[43]

No complaint against God is inadmissible *in principle* (even if, *as a matter of fact*, such claims are always baseless, as Leibniz will demonstrate) or can be rejected simply on the grounds that God is omnipotent and has no obligations to anyone.[44] To indict God and put him on "trial" before the tribunal of reason is possible. Whence the possibility and, indeed, the necessity—in order to respond to objections based on the existence of evil—of a Theodicy. To be sure God is subordinate to no one and owes nothing to human beings. However, "he cannot fail to satisfy himself"; he is obliged "to justify himself to himself as a wise sovereign."[45] His wisdom obligates him and demands justification of him. What he owes to wisdom (or owes to himself) is nothing other than what he owes to every spirit who consults reason.

## 3. A VOCATION: TO DEFEND GOD'S JUSTICE

"We will renounce the use of reason when God ceases to be wise or man to be rational."[46] For one who maintains—as Leibniz does—that God's conduct is wise and that his actions must conform to the laws of universal jurisprudence, the defense of divine justice is not merely a legitimate undertaking, but a demand of reason. As Gaston Grua has observed, "throughout his whole life . . . with the fervor of a *vocation*, [Leibniz] defended divine justice."[47] He defended it not only against those who would question or deny it, but also against those who would form a false notion of it by portraying it as arbitrary or based on incomprehensible laws. Under various names and in different forms ("Catholic Demonstrations," defense [*vindicatio*[48]], "quasi kind of science" or doctrine of God's justice, pleading the cause of God, apology[49]), the project of Theodicy was long-standing and continuous, given that Leibniz explicitly relates it to questions that had already occupied him when he was a student at the University of Leipzig (1661–1663). In a letter to Jablonski (1700), he writes:

> However, from the age of sixteen, by a particular destiny [appointed by] God, it seems, I found myself drawn to an investigation in itself rather difficult and to all appearances rather disagreeable; however, I have not been fully satisfied until just a few years ago, when I truly discovered the reasons for contingency [*rationes contingentiae*], since prior to this I could not reply as fully as I would have liked to the arguments of Hobbes and Spinoza in favor of the absolute necessity of everything that occurs [*pro absoluta omnium, quae fiunt, necessitate*]. At that time I had formed the plan of writing a *Theodicy* in which I would defend [*vindiciren*] the goodness, wisdom and justice of God, as well as his supreme power and irresistible influence. However, this plan would greatly benefit if one day God were to give me the grace to develop properly these thoughts (of which you have seen only small samples) in oral conversation with excellent persons, in order to win over minds and promote the union of Protestant churches. However, that requires favorable circumstances.[50]

Three years earlier in a letter to Thomas Burnett,[51] Leibniz had expressed his desire for the leisure and freedom from care "to deliver on [his] promises, made more than thirty years ago, to contribute to piety and the instruction of the public, concerning the most important subject of all," that is, the problems of theology. The phrase "more than thirty years" refers to the period in which Leibniz was finishing his legal studies (1664–1666). Elsewhere, in a letter to Jaquelot, Leibniz speaks of the period beginning with his earliest reading (1661) up to his encounter with Arnauld in Paris (1672) as the time during which he became convinced that "one could offer a solid treatment of those points of theology that serve *to free God from the imputation of evil* and those of revealed religion that relieve us of the need to ascribe absolute damnation prior to any relation with sin."[52]

It is true that these autobiographical accounts involve a certain amount of reconstruction, or even dramatization, especially where the vocation is said to have been directly inspired by God, as in the letter to Jablonski cited above. Nevertheless, they all agree in emphasizing the precociousness and careful preparation of a plan conceived well before his reading of Bayle's *Historical and Critical Dictionary*. This plan, which was long in the making, was nurtured by much reading, meditation, and conversation with representatives of various confessions. For this reason, Leibniz feels justified in declaring that "there are perhaps few persons who have toiled more than I on this topic"[53] or again that "since I have been thinking about this topic from the time of my youth, I claim to have treated it in depth."[54] The project of Theodicy has two practical aims. Its goal is to inculcate "true piety" (based on true knowledge of the divine perfections[55]) and to contribute to the reunification of the Protestant and Catholic churches.[56] For God's justice is one of the major points of doctrinal disagreement between the various religious confessions, insofar as it relates to the delicate and highly controversial question of predestination.

This dual practical aim seems to have informed Leibniz's thinking from the time of his earliest writings. However, this should not cause us to overlook the theoretical evolution and conceptual shifts which his work also manifests. Rather, we ought to look with suspicion on those autobiographical references meant to suggest complete continuity of doctrine from his earliest writings to the *Essays of Theodicy*. To speak, as Leibniz does, of the project of Theodicy as long-standing is ambiguous and perhaps even misleading. There is no reason to doubt the claim that defending God's justice was a project Leibniz had pursued from the time of his youth. On the other hand, there is room for serious doubt as to whether the concepts used and the theses advanced in conjunction with this defense remained the same throughout his career, whatever Leibniz himself may claim. Leibniz suggests for example that at the time of his stay in Paris (1672–1676), he had already shown in a Latin dialogue sent to Arnauld that

> God, having chosen the most perfect of all possible worlds, had been prompted
> by his wisdom to permit the evil which was bound up with it, but which still did
> not prevent this world from being, all things considered, the best that could be
> chosen.[57]

However, it would seem that this thesis concerning God's choice of the best possible world does not appear as such before the mid-1680s. In fact, the solution to the problem of evil that Leibniz presents during that period, in the *Confession of a Philosopher* for example, is significantly different (as we shall see).

Although the complete Academy edition of Leibniz's works—and in particular the edition of the *Theodicy* and the immediately prior and contemporaneous texts— is as yet unfinished, careful study of the available texts reveals that, from the German opuscule *On the Omnipotence and Omniscience of God and Human Freedom* (1670–1671) to the *Essays of Theodicy* (1710) the Leibnizian doctrine of evil and divine justice underwent undeniable changes and shifts (while also showing undeniable similarities). The evolution of Leibniz's thought on this subject has been largely (or even entirely) neglected by commentators.[58] Evil provides the topic for a rich and illuminating chapter in Gaston Grua's magisterial *Jurisprudence universelle et théodicée selon Leibniz*. However, in that chapter Grua offers a rather static portrayal of Leibnizian doctrine. Texts prior to the *Theodicy* are not considered in themselves but are read merely as sketches of the future synthesis.[59] Likewise, by portraying Leibniz's theory of evil as virtually unchanging,[60] Grua downplays its difficulties and internal tensions and is ultimately able to draw only the following disappointing conclusion:

> Almost all of the final formulations [of the *Theodicy*] are traditional not only to Christianity, but for the most part since Stoicism and even Plato. However, the priority of eternal truths is characteristic of the Platonic school, and the uniqueness of optimism is characteristic of Leibniz.[61]

As for what Leibniz sees as original in his work—namely, his claim to have shown not only that it is possible that our universe is better than a universe without evil, but that it also must in fact be better than any other possible world—Grua doubts whether "this represents genuine progress." In his view,

> Besides the general difficulties it raises, optimism adds the paradox that permission of sin is not only permissible for God but obligatory. The same holds true of all evil.[62]

It follows, according to Grua, that the difference (which, in any case, was "hardly clear") between being a means and being a condition disappears and the distinction between action and mere permission is eliminated. And yet, it is on this very distinction that Leibniz's whole conception of God's moral concurrence with evil is based!

The aim of the present work is to shed light on the complexity and evolution of Leibnizian thought concerning evil and God's justice. It offers an account of the genesis and foundations of Theodicy, the subject matter of Leibniz's only book of philosophy, properly speaking, to be published in his lifetime. It also aims to indicate the difficulties raised by this doctrine of divine justice, which its inventor hesitates to treat as a full-fledged science.[63] Thus, the aim of the book is to explore the originality and implications of this theoretical and apologetic undertaking by showing how it differs from earlier attempts, syntheses and projects, even as it draws on some of their results.

The book is divided into seven chapters. The first three chapters examine Leibniz's treatment of the question of evil and divine justice before the project of Theodicy had fully taken shape, which likely occurred between 1695 and 1697. The final four chapters consider the genesis of the *Theodicy* properly speaking—the arguments and theses that Leibniz develops as part of its two main wings (what I call the *defensive* wing and the *doctrinal* wing).

Chapter 1 casts doubt on the notion of a "voluntarist" phase of the young Leibniz, while acknowledging certain points of contact with Luther and Hobbes. It shows that the opuscule, *On the Omnipotence and Omniscience of God and Human Freedom*, while maintaining that God is just, suggests that he is the author of evil. Chapter 2 offers an interpretation of *The Confession of a Philosopher* showing that this first completed attempt at justifying God rests on a form of necessitarianism that makes God the reason (rather than the author) of evil and the first member of the universal series of things. It emphasizes the limits of Leibniz's appropriation of the distinction between two kinds of necessity (*per se/ex hypothesi*) to be found in the text. Chapter 3 traces the doctrinal evolution that occurs following the *Confession of a Philosopher* in response to unresolved theoretical difficulties raised in that work. This evolution leads to a new conception of God (and of his relation to the world), a redefinition of the notion of the possible, and a reformulation of the doctrine of God's physical and moral concurrence.

Chapter 4 examines the manner in which the project of Theodicy is developed, with regard to its apologetic and scientific aims and the context in which it is carried out. In particular, it focuses on analyzing the arguments used by Leibniz as part of the properly defensive wing of Theodicy. This wing is itself composed of two kinds of defense: a "negative" defense and a "supererogatory" defense. Chapter 5 shows how Leibniz seeks to establish the thesis of the best of all possible worlds and examines the meaning, presuppositions, and implications of the thesis. It considers whether God's choice of this world is absolutely necessary and explicates Leibniz's "final" doctrine of the permission of sin. Chapter 6 considers God's physical concurrence with evil, the privative nature of evil, and the problems arising from its division into *metaphysical, physical*, and *moral*. It calls attention to two different and irreconcilable conceptions of evil to be found in Leibniz. According to the first, evil is a real defect that contributes to universal harmony, while according to the second, evil is merely an appearance, which vanishes upon considering the universe from the correct point of view. Finally, Chapter 7 shows how freedom can be reconciled with determinism, the truth of future contingents, and God's foreknowledge. In addition, it shows the sense in which human freedom is ideally (*idealiter*) prior to the exercise of divine freedom. It explains the principles of moral action in a universe in which every rational creature is called upon to act *as if* both its own salvation and the glory of God depended solely on its efforts.

# NOTES

1. See Ricœur, *Le mal*, 13 and 38–39.
2. The phrase is from Gaston Grua, JUT, 521.
3. Naërt, *Leibniz et la querelle du pur amour*, 63 note 53. Jacques Jalabert maintains that "Leibniz does not feel, in the same way as, for example Saint Bonaventure, what I have called the misery of sin; he lacks the anguish of a Pascal in the face of the drama of the human condition" (*Le Dieu de Leibniz*, 207).
4. T pd §43; GP VI, 75; Huggard, 98. See also T s I; GP VI; 376–377; Huggard, 378: "one must confess that there is evil in this world which God has made, and that it would have been possible to make a world without evil or even not to create any world, since its creation depended upon the free will of God."
5. Rutherford, *Leibniz and the Rational Order of Nature*, 2–3 and 62–63.
6. "In fact, the two sides were at opposite extremes: they pursued one another with iron and fire, they treated one another as heretics, idolaters, as excommunicated and damned. Germany was inundated with blood, not to mention the other countries of Europe; there was an infinity of murders, conflagrations, sackings, sacrilegious acts, rapes, and other horrific evils, the greatest of which was the loss of millions of souls redeemed by the blood of Jesus Christ, as a result of these disturbances" (*Ingrédients d'une Relation pour la Cour Impériale* [late November-early December, 1700], A I, 19, 240, §4).
7. See in particular *Mars Christianissimus, ou Apologie des Armes du Roy tres Chrestien contre les Chrestiens* [*Most Christian War-God*, 1683], A IV, 2, 498–499; *Mars Christianissimus ou Réflexions sur la déclaration de la guerre, que la France fait à l'Empire* (Autumn 1688–1689), A IV, 3, 97–98.
8. Baruzi, *Leibniz*, 211.
9. Robinet, *G. W. Leibniz*, 251.
10. Leibniz to the Abbé Saint-Pierre (February 7, 1715), FC (O), IV, 325.
11. T §26; GP VI, 118; Huggard, 138.
12. See, for example, T §105; GP VI, 160; Huggard, 180 "It may be that fundamentally all men are equally bad, and consequently incapable of being distinguished the one from the other through their good or less bad natural qualities; but they are not all bad in the same way" and *Causa Dei*, §138.
13. See, for example, T §283. On this point, see my article "Leibniz, Bayle et la figure de l'athée vertueux," in *Leibniz et Bayle: Confrontation et dialogue*, 301–329.
14. Cf. T §15, §220, and §258.
15. *Réflexions sur l'Art de connaître les hommes* (September 25, 1708), FC (L), 132.
16. T §220; GP VI, 249; Huggard, 264–265.
17. Cf. *Réflexions sur l'Art de connaître les hommes* (September 25, 1708), FC (L), 133.
18. *Memoir for Enlightened Persons of Good Intention* (circa 1692), A IV, 4, (7), 614; R 104.
19. T §13; GP VI, 109; Huggard, 130.
20. T §258; GP VI, 269; Huggard, 284.
21. As is well-known, Leibniz coined the neologism *Théodicée* from two Greek words: *théos* (God) and *diké* (justice).
22. See for example: *On the Omnipotence and Omniscience of God*, §§1–3, A VI, 1, 537; (Sleigh, 5–7); CP, A VI, 3, 116 (Sleigh, 27). In *Of Liberty, Fate and God's Grace*, A VI, 4-B, 1596–1597, the demonstration of the proposition: "God is not the

cause of evil or sin" directly follows the demonstration of the proposition: "God is supremely just."

23. See GP VI, 38.

24. See in particular §58 and §72 to §79.

25. See, for instance, *On the Omnipotence and Omniscience of God* (§2, A VI, 1, 537) "how divine predestination can exist in conjunction with the present misery of the pious and the good fortune of the malicious" (Sleigh, 5).

26. See T §151; *Causa Dei* §50.

27. See Leibniz to Jacob Thomasius (September 2, 1663), A II, 1, 5.

28. See Leibniz to Honoré Fabri (beginning of 1677), A II, 1, 463; Discussion with Arnold Eckhard (May 1677), A II, 1, 534; Leibniz to Christian Philipp (early January 1680), A II, 1, 787–788.

29. See, for example, DM §2.

30. Leibniz to Landgrave Ernst von Hessen-Rheinfels (September 14, 1690), A II, 2, 341. See also Leibniz to Electress Sophie (August 1696?), Grua, 379; T pd §35; GP VI, 70; Huggard, 94: "Universal right is the same for God and for men."

31. *Meditation on the Common Concept of Justice* (1702), Mollat, 41; R 46.

32. Cf. DM §2 (A VI, 4-B, 1532–1533), L 466: "For why praise him for what he has done if he would be equally praiseworthy in doing exactly the opposite?" and Grua, 433.

33. *Meditation on the Common Concept of Justice*, Mollat, 43; R 47.

34. Cf. *Meditation on the Common Concept of Justice*, Mollat, 43, 47; R 50: "Right cannot be unjust, that is a contradiction; but law can be. For it is power which gives and maintains law; and if this power lacks wisdom or good will, it can give and maintain quite evil laws."

35. Cf. *Meditation on the Common Concept of Justice*, Mollat, 41; Grua, 472; T Preface; GP VI, 35; T pd §37.

36. *Meditation on the Common Concept of Justice*, Mollat, 43–44.

37. Leibniz to Christian Philipp (late January 1680), A II, 1, 787; L 421. Citing a passage from the *Sixth Replies* of Descartes (§8), Leibniz draws the following consequence: "Thus we cannot promise ourselves anything with regard to God's justice, and perhaps He has done things in a way that we would call unjust, since there is no notion of justice with regard to him, and if it should happen that we are unhappy despite our piety, or if it happens to be the case that the soul perishes with the body, that would also be just" (A II, 1, 788). God's will becomes a "fiction," as does his understanding, with the result that, according to Leibniz, there is no real difference between the God of Descartes and that of Spinoza. See also *De la philosophie cartésienne* (Summer, 1683–Winter, 1684–85), A VI, 4-B, 1481.

38. On this point, see section 5.2.1. p. 202–203.

39. *On the Bondage of the Will*, 332 [WA, vol. 18, 785].

40. *Meditation on the Common Concept of Justice*, Mollat, 45–46; R 48–49.

41. See especially Grua, 430–431 and 471–472.

42. See especially Grua 252, 431, 448, and 472; *Opinion on the Principles of Pufendorf*, Dutens IV-3, 280; GP III, 30. *Anupeuthunia* is "a state of being responsible to no one for one's actions" (T §178; GP VI, 221; Huggard, 238).

43. Grua, 432.

44. Grua, 472: "That justice must be very imperfect that would obtain even if some evil demon, or the evil God of the Manicheans governed all things, against whom there would be no legal recourse, even if there were great reason for complaint." The irresistible power of an "evil demon" would not remove just grounds for

complaint: "And just reasons for complaint would remain, even if the complaints were ineffectual" (*Observations on the Principle of Law*, Dutens IV–3, §9, 272).

45. Respectively, Grua, 252 and *Meditation on the Common Concept of Justice*, Mollat, 42; R 46. See also *Opinion on the Principles of Pufendorf*, Dutens IV–3, 280; *Of Liberty, Fate and God's Grace*, A VI, 4–B, 1596.

46. *Dialogue Between a Theologian and Misosophus* (Second-half of 1678–first-half of 1679?), A VI, 4-C, 2213.

47. JUT, 8 (emphasis added).

48. See, respectively, the proposed title (probably between 1695–1697) edited by G. Grua, in Grua, 370 and Grua, 371.

49. See, respectively, Leibniz to Des Bosses (February 5, 1712), GP II, 437; T Preface; GP VI, 38; and Grua, 495. The *Causa Dei* is presented as an "apologetic treatise for the cause of God" (§1, GP VI, 439; S 114 translation modified).

50. Leibniz to D. E. Jablonski (January 23, 1700), GP VI, 3.

51. Leibniz to Thomas Burnett (February 1/11, 1697), GP III, 197.

52. Leibniz to Jaquelot (Winter 1704–1705), GP III, 481 (emphasis added).

53. T Preface; GP VI, 43; Huggard, 67.

54. Leibniz to Thomas Burnett (October 30, 1710), GP III, 321.

55. Near the end of the Preface to the *Theodicy*, Leibniz declares: "Finally, I have endeavored in all things to consider edification" (GP VI, 47; Huggard, 71). See also Grua, 499 and Leibniz to Rémond (January 10, 1714), GP III, 606.

56. "With my *Theodicy*, I tried to be of assistance in reconciling the minds of those who were inopportunely agitated" (Leibniz to Turretin, July 1712, cited by J. Baruzi in *Leibniz et l'organisation religieuse de la terre*, 196). See also Leibniz to Magliabechi (September 30, 1697), A I, 14, 520–521.

57. T Preface; GP VI, 43; Huggard, 67.

58. Thus, Foucher de Careil claims to find in *The Confession of a Philosopher* (together with a lost dialogue on the immortality of the soul and the need for a "governor" of the universe) the outline and principal arguments of the future *Theodicy* (see *Mémoire sur la philosophie de Leibniz*, 34–36). Belaval considers Foucher de Careil's view somewhat exaggerated but basically correct (*Confessio Philosophi. La profession de foi du Philosophe*, Introduction, 25–26).

59. See Grua, JUT 368.

60. With only a few exceptions (see ibid., 364).

61. Ibid., 370.

62. Ibid. See also ibid., 532.

63. Leibniz to Des Bosses (February 5, 1712), GP II, 437.

# CHAPTER 1

∾

# Difficulties Concerning the Justification of God in the Years Prior to 1673

## 1.1 EARLY READING AND THE RELATION OF JUSTICE TO POWER

### 1.1.1 The Paradoxical Reference to Luther

Leibniz's interest in questions related to evil, divine justice, and human freedom was long-standing. By the philosopher's own account, it dates to the time of his earliest reading, when as an adolescent, he passed his time in his father's library, where, hungry for knowledge, he "flitted from book to book."[1] Two books left a deep impression, "although [he] was quite aware that they had need of some mitigation":[2] *Dialogue on Free Will* by Lorenzo Valla and Luther's *On the Bondage of the Will*. The former showed the possibility of reconciling human freedom with divine foreknowledge but left unresolved the problem of predestination, and, in particular, the motives of election and damnation. The latter portrayed man as the slave of sin and incapable of doing good unaided, while at the same time portraying the omnipotent God as the author of good and evil, whose ways are impenetrable to our finite and corrupted reason. Leibniz reports having been greatly impressed, even delighted, by the two works.[3] At the same time, he was already aware that Valla did not go far enough and that Luther was immoderate and even shocking when he maintained that God could use good men to do good and wicked men to do evil, saving the one and abandoning the other, in an apparently unjust manner. Unquestionably, these texts stimulated the young man's thought, even if they could not fully satisfy him.

This tribute to Valla and Luther, which, though qualified, would be repeated in other biographical passages, allowed Leibniz to locate his own work within an illustrious theological and philosophical tradition, while at the same time pointing out the inadequacies of this tradition and the need to correct its deficiencies. For Leibniz, the *Dialogue on Free Will* and *On the Bondage of the Will* are no more than the starting point for further reflection. The *Theodicy* would conclude with a continuation of Valla's dialogue in order to "pick up where it left off"[4] with regard to the reasons of divine providence. As for the opposition between Erasmus and Luther, Leibniz claims to overcome it by showing how "free will and will in bondage are one and the same."[5] Fundamentally, the task Leibniz sets for himself is to resolve the outstanding difficulties, reconcile positions that are apparently at odds, and temper those assertions—especially Luther's—that stand in need of it. For Leibniz's admiration for the great reformer was always nuanced.[6] Leibniz laments certain unfortunate expressions to be found in Luther's work, as well as a style of writing considered "too fierce and tumultuous."[7] However, his reservations go beyond the style of the work and even beyond certain doctrinal points of secondary importance. The disagreement is far more fundamental. For this reason, his reference to Luther is somewhat paradoxical, if it is true that the theologian's "example . . . is not to be imitated."[8]

Indeed, regarding their anthropology and theology, Leibniz and Luther appear to be very far apart. To begin with, the dramatization of sin and the human condition is quite foreign to Leibniz's thought.[9] For Luther, man is a slave, whether to God or to Satan.[10] Man's inability to do good reveals his sinful nature: "free choice without the grace of God is not free at all, but immutably the captive and slave of evil, since it cannot of itself turn to the good."[11] Sin condemns man and man alone. From this point of view, there can be no question of justifying God (in the sense of defending his justice), but only of finding the means to justify man (in the theological sense of redemption). Evil is brought about by the rebellious creature, whose salvation requires faith in the redemption of Christ. The very idea of pleading the cause of God by human reason is absurd. In this sense, perhaps no theology is further removed from the Leibnizian project of Theodicy than Luther. In fact, for Luther (a) God appears as the cause of evil and the instigator of sin, (b) faith and reason are said to be at odds, and (c) divine justice is incomprehensible to the natural light of man.

(a) The comparison of the horseman and the bad horse, presented in *On the Bondage of the Will*, is well known.[12] If the horseman rides a horse with only two or three good legs, he can act in the same manner as with a healthy horse, but the bad horse will advance with difficulty, the good horse correctly. Similarly, God, who cannot perform evil by himself, does good by good men (just as the horseman goes well on a good horse) and evil by the wicked (as the horseman goes badly with the bad horse). According to Leibniz this assertion "is too harsh, because it is the horse that goes badly and not the horseman."[13] For Luther, God is the author of evil to the extent that he brings it about through us.[14] With regard to Luther himself, Leibniz is content to point out the harshness of the theologian's expressions. However, he adopts a much more critical tone with regard to the Calvinists who defend a similar thesis:

> It is obvious that Calvin himself has nevertheless made use of these expressions, which seem to suggest [that God is the author of sin] and that are difficult to excuse. In Book I of the *Institutes*, Ch. 18, n. 1, he says, "God was the author of this trial of Job, of which Satan and the thieves were the ministers . . . . God is said to be the author of everything that these critics wish to make only dependent on his inactive permission." From this it seems to follow not only that God permits sin, but that he also wills it and causes it to occur.[15]

Even when softened and considered in relation to other passages that serve to temper them, these positions of Calvin are excessive, because

> if by His [i.e. God's] willing, Calvin meant only His willing to permit, then to be sure his assertion would not be false, but in one way or another the expression would still be scandalous and offensive to pious ears, as contrary to reasonable ways of speaking, and serving not to edify, but only to destroy.[16]

Obviously, this criticism, though directed at Calvin, tells equally against Luther!

(b) The contradiction between faith and reason that Luther affirms is even more difficult to excuse. Leibniz himself must acknowledge the point: "the Reformers, and especially Luther . . . spoke at times as if they rejected philosophy and deemed it inimical to faith."[17] Leibniz maintains that Luther is offering a mere ad hominem argument in which the term *philosophy* designates only "what conforms with the ordinary course of nature, or perhaps what was taught in the schools" and which targets only those who claim to submit revealed truth to the tribunal of reason. In fact, Luther's position is much more radical, since he holds that reason is powerless and incapable of comprehending God.

> She [reason] thus measures divine things and words by the usage and concerns of men; and what can be more perverse than this, seeing that the former are heavenly and the latter earthly? So the stupid thing betrays herself, showing how she is nothing but human thoughts about God.[18]

In that sense, an attempt to provide a rational justification of God with regard to election can only lead to the opposite of what was sought:

> That is what we come to when we seek to measure God by human reason and make excuses for him, not reverencing the secrets of his majesty but insisting on prying into them. The result is that we are overwhelmed with his glory, and instead of a single excuse for him, we pour out a thousand blasphemies, quite forgetting ourselves for the time and gibbering like lunatics against both God and ourselves in the same breath, though we aspire to speak with great wisdom on behalf of both God and ourselves.[19]

(c) For Luther, reason cannot attain to God who is incomprehensible, nor can it explain his conduct. As a result, the notion of justice is equivocal; it no longer has the same sense for us and for God (contrary to what Leibniz seems always to have maintained).

> In the one case [God] pours out grace and mercy on the unworthy, in the other he pours out wrath and severity on the undeserving, and in both cases he is unprincipled and unjust by human standards, but just and true by his own.[20]

God's will is the measure of his justice, which is "foolishness" to men,[21] who are incapable of understanding it by the natural light. We must believe God

> to be righteous where he seems to us to be unjust. For if his righteousness were such that it could be judged to be righteous by human standards, it would clearly not be divine and would in no way differ from human righteousness. But since he is the one true God, and is wholly incomprehensible and inaccessible to human reason, it is proper and indeed necessary that his righteousness also should be incomprehensible.[22]

Although Leibniz attempts to moderate these declarations and to resituate them in their polemical context,[23] they are more than merely excessive. Rather, they tend to promote the notion of a hidden (*absconditus*) God contrary to the revealed (*revelatus*) God. This hidden God seems to act arbitrarily, without just motive, like a tyrant rather than a king worthy of being loved. Leibniz vigorously condemns such a conception, since it means renouncing the attempt to explain God's conduct according to his manifest will—a will that is rational—and having recourse instead to an unknown and secret will—a will that is irrational—as do the philosophers with their occult qualities.[24]

For this reason, Leibniz's attempt at moderating, which involves taking certain liberties with the texts of the reformers, is not always convincing. According to Leibniz, Luther and Calvin would not have defended the notion of an *"absolutely absolute* decree," according to which election and reprobation are without reason, either hidden or manifest, since Luther would defer our understanding of God's reasons to a future life, whereas Calvin maintains that "these reasons are just and holy, although they be unknown to us."[25] In other words, God does not act arbitrarily, or as a despot, because his reasons, once they are revealed in the next life, will appear to us as just.[26] It is true that the *Bondage of the Will* evokes the "light of glory" that will show us that "the God whose judgment here is one of incomprehensible righteousness is a God of most perfect and manifest righteousness."[27] Must we therefore conclude that, for Luther, the notion of justice is univocal? Nothing is less certain. The blessed, enlightened by the light of glory, can indeed admire God's "justice." However, it will have nothing in common with the idea of justice we have in this life. Moreover, is there anything more foreign to Leibnizian love than Luther's "height of love," which consists in "lov[ing] Him who to flesh and blood appears so unlovable, so harsh toward the unfortunate and so ready to condemn, and to condemn for evils in which he appears to be the cause or accessary, at least in the eyes of those who allow themselves to be dazzled by false reasons"?[28]

Other interpretations of Luther suggested by Leibniz, and, in particular those regarding human freedom, seem equally questionable. It is far from certain that the phrase "bondage of the will" was chosen to avoid the term "necessity"[29] or that in denying freedom Luther meant only indifference, in accordance with the mistaken Scholastic definitions of his time.[30]

In short, Leibniz's invocation of Luther in the preface to the *Theodicy* is surprising to say the least given the apparent incompatibility of the positions of the reformer with the project of providing a rational justification of divine action. To be sure, so great a name could hardly be omitted by one who belonged to the Protestant tradition and who always had in view the reunification of the churches (and above all the Lutheran and Calvinist churches). Luther is an "example not to be imitated," but he is an example nonetheless. Indeed, he is an unavoidable example given the profound impact *On the Bondage of the Will* had had on theological controversies concerning human freedom, evil, and God's justice.

Ultimately, Luther and Valla have something in common: their writings raise more questions than they answer. Both understand divine foreknowledge not as a mere vision without participation (as did Boethius and Erasmus), but as based on an efficacious divine concurrence whose reasons are unknown to us. As a result, they fall into the same trap: in attempting to safeguard God's foreknowledge and defending the infinite and unfathomable depths of his wisdom, they end up making God both unjust, since he seems arbitrarily to predestine some for beatitude and others for damnation, and the ultimate cause of sin.[31] The problem of reconciling God's omniscience, omnipotence, and goodness with the existence of evil, to which no satisfying solution had heretofore been found, must therefore be taken up again.

As I have observed, the reference to Luther was unavoidable for a "protestant" who set out to discuss evil and freedom. However, it also offers valuable insight into a period in Leibniz's career that some commentators have characterized as "voluntarist."

### 1.1.2  A Voluntarist Period?

For Luther, God's will is the measure of divine right, which human reason cannot comprehend:

> He is God, and for his will there is no cause or reason that can be laid down as a rule or measure for it, since there is nothing equal or superior to it, but it is itself the rule of all things. For if there were any rule or standard for it, it could no longer be the will of God. For it is not because he is or was obliged so to will that what he wills is right, but on the contrary, because he himself so wills, therefore what happens must be right. Cause and reason can be assigned for a creature's will, but not for the will of the Creator, unless you set up over him another Creator.[32]

Did Leibniz adopt this thesis? His reading of *On the Bondage of the Will* together with the works of Hobbes might be taken to confirm the notion of a "voluntarist" phase, which André Robinet labels ($\varphi^1$), or "archaic architectonic,"[33] and which covers the period 1663–1670. Notes taken by Leibniz in conjunction with other readings seem to confirm the suggestion. Annotating the *Summary of Metaphysics* (*Compendium Metaphysicae*, Table XI) of Stahl, Leibniz takes up the Scholastic distinction between moral and physical causes of evil: "the physical cause is that from which the effect flows forth [*Causa Physica est quae influit*]: the Moral Cause that which wills [*intendit*]. Every moral cause is physical, and not the reverse."[34] From this he concludes, "Sin flows forth from God, but God does not will sin. Therefore he is not the moral cause of sin." Leibniz follows this with a syllogism:

> Therefore, I say that 1. The moral cause is only in moral actions, that is to say,
> of the order of the Law; 2. Only he to whom the law is given is a moral cause.
> From this it appears that God cannot be a moral cause, since the Law is not given
> to God.[35]

At first glance, this conception of the law and its foundation seems indeed to amount to a voluntarist doctrine. The law, as such, does not pre-exist the will that establishes it. It presupposes the existence of a superior being from whom it issues and who enforces it. It can only be given to subordinates. Therefore, God is above all law. He gives it, but he does not receive it. He is the source of obligation but is not himself obliged to anything or anyone.

Is Leibniz here defending, as Robinet believes, a conception of God "whose omnipotence is absolute, exempt from all law and all contracted obligation"?[36] Does Leibniz adhere to the principle that the will stands in place of a reason (*stat pro ratione voluntas*—which he would later come to reject) and is he therefore "more Hobbesian than follower of his professor," Jakob Thomasius? [37] Certainly not. In fact, it was rather common, at least after Suarez,[38] to conceive of law as the prescription of a superior, without thereby committing oneself to the view that the whole of law derives from power, as though the rules of justice were merely the effect of an arbitrary will. To trace the law to a divine commandment is not to render it arbitrary, since it can require actions that are intrinsically good and reasonable, as Suarez maintained.[39] To assert that God cannot be subject to this law is merely to reiterate a traditional theological position, namely God's absolute independence, which does not automatically and necessarily place him above reason and wisdom.[40]

The real problem that these notes on Stahl present lies elsewhere, namely in a syllogism that, I believe, proves too much. For the demonstration that God is not the moral cause of sin rests on the thesis that *God is not, properly speaking, a moral cause*. This implies that he is neither the moral cause of sin nor the moral cause of good. In which case, the conclusion is not that almighty God acts and wills independently of all law, but rather that he is reduced to a merely physical cause—that is, to a "mechanistic God" (*Deus mechanicus*), a "first mover," the author only of *influxus*, but never of *intentio*. On this showing, the young Leibniz would be leaning not toward voluntarism—a theology according to which the divine will establishes good and evil and the laws of justice—but towards a necessitarianism very close to that of Spinoza, according to which God is equated with a pure, indifferent, and blind power—that is, to causation without will. It is significant, in this regard, that the autobiographical references found in Leibniz's texts never speak of an adherence to the principle *stat pro ratione voluntas*, which would render God's justice the effect of his omnipotence or will. Rather, they suggest a necessitarian period:

> For my part, during the period in which I held that nothing occurs by chance or by accident except in relation to certain particular substances, that fortune as distinct from destiny is only a meaningless name, and that nothing exists except when the particular requisites are posited (it follows from these requisites, when they are conjoined together, that the thing exists); I was not far from the opinion of those who think that everything is absolutely necessary and who hold that it is enough that freedom be preserved from constraint although subject to necessity, and who do not distinguish between the necessary and the infallible, that is to say, between the true when it is known and certainty.[41]

Likewise, Leibniz confesses: "you know that I once strayed a little too far in another direction, and began to incline to the Spinozists," with whom he shared the idea of ascribing "infinite power" to God by deriving everything from "brute necessity"[42]. An analysis of the notes and texts from 1663–1670 confirms, I believe, this orientation.

The supposed indications of voluntarism that André Robinet claims also to have uncovered in the annotations of the *Practical Philosophy* (*Philosophia Practica*, Table XXV: *Of Law*) of Jakob Thomasius are scarcely more convincing. It must be observed in the first place that among the five distinctions established between natural law and legitimate (that is, positive) law, Leibniz's opposition to his professor concerns only a single feature of the second distinction. In fact, Leibniz grants the following four propositions: "1. natural law [*jus*] has its origin in God and Nature," "3. the natural law is made known to us by our natural knowledge, legitimate law by promulgation," "4. the natural law is one and the same throughout the entire world, legitimate law is as varied as there are different republics," "5. the natural law binds all men; legitimate law binds only citizens of the same republic." Leibniz accepts proposition 2, according to which the obligation of legitimate law is "extrinsic and changeable" and that the obligation of natural law is "internal to itself." However, he refuses to characterize the latter as immutable (*immutabilis*).[43] Leibniz adds the following commentary:

On the contrary, God can change [*mutare*]: 1) because he can change being into non-being. 2) The necessity is either absolute or hypothetical. If there is no such necessity, all law [*jus*] is voluntary. If it is absolute, then there is no contradiction. 3) It is permissible to change as a result of human will: by prescription, necessity and war. Thus, the Egyptian augurs.[44]

Three remarks are in order:

i. Leibniz's criticism concerns the immutable character of *obligation* and not of natural law itself. The assertion "God can change" means that his conduct can change, that he can act against the rules of natural law, but not, strictly speaking, that he can change this law.

ii. The point once again is to call attention to divine omnipotence, or the absolute power to create and annihilate, not to extend the characteristics of positive law (which results from the will and is changeable) to natural law, as if Leibniz "applied to its domain [the domain of natural law] the voluntarist effects that Thomasius reserved for positive law."[45] Because he is all powerful, God can change, but for superior motives (prescription, necessity, war). To do so is to act neither arbitrarily nor capriciously, but for a reason.

iii. To be sure, the alternative that Leibniz considers (absolute necessity or hypothetical necessity) leaves open the *possibility* of an entirely voluntary law and so in a sense supports the voluntarist thesis. However, this does not amount to an endorsement of the position, since another hypothesis is equally possible, namely that everything is subject to an absolute necessity. Such a necessity would not deprive God of his power to change but would lead to avoiding voluntarism.

It seems that Leibniz prefers the latter hypothesis (even if he does not exclude the first *in abstracto*), as becomes clear when we take into account other contemporary texts in which he rejects the idea of a law whose foundations are arbitrary and that is always instituted (either by man or God). Thus, the critique of Thomasius does not seek to move the concept of law in the direction of voluntarism (as Robinet maintains) but rather toward a necessitating determinism. On this latter view acts of divine omnipotence are not without reason but in accordance with an absolutely "necessitating" reason.

From as early as 1663, the young Leibniz accepts the idea of one universal natural law, which is not founded on the irresistible power and institutional will of a superior. He follows Thomasius[46] in his opposition to Machiavelli and condemns the followers of the latter, who reduce natural law and divine laws to "agreements between private persons," "with that great audacity that is ready to overturn the right of the people, of war and peace."[47] Following once again in the footsteps of his professor,[48] Leibniz explicitly rejects the Hobbesian definition of justice as utility on the grounds that it would lead to the destruction of all law. In fact, by making the rules of justice relative to changeable utility, the rules themselves become variable and inconstant. What is worse, this conception leads to arbitrariness and despotism: "from the moment [Hobbes] confers absolute authority upon some Prince, a mere suspicion on the part of the Prince gives him the right to mete out punishment."[49]

The conception of law as emanating from a superior is not so much false as insufficient, because this emanation does not automatically ground its justice. The law is not just *because* it derives from the most powerful. "Indeed, once it is allowed that all justice is an outgrowth of civil law, there necessarily follows the destruction of all obligation and of the necessity to observe treaties among cities."[50] To reduce justice to mere positive law is to remove all morality from obligation and, by destroying natural law, to annihilate the law of nations (*jus gentium*). In that case, the law is only respected out of fear of the superior who decreed it, and international treaties are observed only so long as doing so is to our advantage, or so long as we are compelled to do so by other states.

Thus, far from being attracted to Hobbes's position, Leibniz could well have entertained the idea of setting himself up as Hobbes's opponent (*Antagonista*) in defense of the law of nature. In this connection, the hypothesis advanced by Richard Bodéüs is interesting. On his view the letter to Thomasius of September 2, 1663, written just as Leibniz was about to begin his studies of jurisprudence, shows that "this undertaking was perhaps in part an attempt (with nationalist undertones) to refute Hobbes by means of a method capable of rivaling the subtlety of his adversary."[51] The young student aspired to take advantage of the Euclidean method of E. Weigel (whose courses Leibniz took during his time in Jena) "to strive, like Pufendorf, to provide Germany with a method for defending natural law, which had come under attack by Hobbes."[52]

From this anti-voluntarist, natural law perspective, the adoption of Thrasymachus's definition[53] ("the just is what is useful to the most powerful") in the *Arithmetical Disputation of Combinations* (*Disputation Arithmetica de Complexionibus*, 1666) must not be misinterpreted. For it can be given a "correct interpretation" (the text reads *non inepte*):

For God is properly and simply the most powerful (*potentior*) of all [beings] (indeed, one man is not more powerful than another in an absolute sense (*absolute*), since no matter how robust he may be, he can always be killed by someone weaker). Moreover, utility for God consists not in benefit, but in honor. Therefore, *it is manifest that the Glory of God is the measure of all law [jus].* And whoever will consult those theologians who treat of morality and those who write on cases of conscience will find that it is on this that they ordinarily base their discussions. This certain principle having been established, the theory of the just can be treated scientifically, something that has not been done up until now.[54]

Thrasymachus's definition is correct if *potentior* is understood not as a comparative but as a superlative,[55] which can be applied only to God. In just this one case, it is true that the just is that which is useful to the most powerful, that is to the most powerful absolutely speaking (*absolute*). For other beings inferior to God, power is always relative and precarious, and so the definition does not apply strictly speaking: no man is strong enough to be perpetually dominant. The near equality of physical and intellectual strength among men prevents the definition from being applied to them. Its application must be restricted, both in fact and in right, to God. Must we then acknowledge that in the one case of God, Hobbes was correct to derive all right from power? No. For what is at issue here is power oriented toward the good, since in God the useful is indistinguishable from the honest. Utility is neither self-interest nor pure caprice, but glory, the supreme good on which the doctrine of justice is founded.

### 1.1.3  Rational Jurisprudence and the Unity of Law

Neither power nor mere will can take the place of reason. However, the notion of justice, whose definition in terms of utility (properly understood) applies to God alone, may appear equivocal. For André Robinet, the idea of a universal jurisprudence, common to both God and man, is not yet possible: "($\varphi^1$) is far from the concept of a universal jurisprudence which imposes a general rule of order on both God and man."[56] Here again, the texts seem not to confirm his reading. Whereas Thomasius defines universal justice as moral virtue and limits its exercise to civil society among citizens, as early as 1663–1664 Leibniz explicitly identifies it with piety.[57] The *Specimen of Philosophical Questions Collected from the Law* (*Specimen quaestionum philosophicarum ex jure collectarum*, 1664) repeats Ulpian's definition that "jurisprudence is the knowledge of divine and human things,"[58] and *On the Combinatorial Art* (*De Arte combinatoria*, 1666) as well as the *New Method of Learning and Teaching Jurisprudence* (*Nova Methodus discendae docendaeque Jurisprudentiae*, 1667) make of theology a branch of jurisprudence that deals with the right of God over men. It is "so to speak, a special jurisprudence," "as a doctrine of public law which obtains in the Republic of God over men."[59] It "deals with the right [*jus*] and laws that obtain in the Republic, or rather, the Kingdom of God over men."[60] Infidels are to theology what rebels are to the positive public law. The church is like the obedient subjects of the state. Holy scripture takes the place of the body of laws; "the doctrine of fundamental errors is, so to speak, the list of capital offenses . . . The doctrine of the remission of sins like that of the law of grace; the doctrine of eternal damnation is like that of capital punishment, etc."[61]

Must we consider this characterization of theology by jurisprudence as arising out of a superficial comparison and a "purely external" parallel, as Robinet maintains?[62] While the formulations in *On the Combinatorial Art* are guarded (theology is "so to speak [*quasi*] a special jurisprudence," it is "like [*velut*] the doctrine of public law"), those of the *New Method* are unambiguous and parallel to those Leibniz would later offer.[63] Paragraph 2 of the *New Method* begins with a formal comparison between theology and jurisprudence, according to which the divisions of the former are to serve as a model [64] for developing the divisions of the latter. But the point of the comparison is deeper: "Now, it was right of us to transfer the model of our divisions from theology to jurisprudence, since the similarity between the two domains is remarkable."[65] Besides the fact that both are twofold, insofar as their principles derive from reason (natural theology and jurisprudence) or from an external authority that establishes positive laws (scripture, positive law),

> It is not surprising that the same thing applied in jurisprudence should come to be applied in theology, since theology is a branch [*species*] of jurisprudence considered universally.[66]

Here we have a double transformation. Not only does the structural affinity become a relation of genus to species, but the terms of the comparison are also inverted. It is no longer jurisprudence that is compared to theology, which is taken as a model (§§2–4). Rather, it is theology that is related to jurisprudence, which is now taken as reference (§5). The change from compared to comparing reverses their relative priority, since theology no longer appears as primary but as falling under the genus "universal jurisprudence."

The definition of the just in terms of the useful and the referral of the law to the superior can now be given a broader application and can hold equally for God, the human race, and for the republic. The possibility of a common universal law derives, paradoxically, from the deepening of a definition that initially applied only to God (the most powerful whose utility is glory). Far from extending to all law the consequences of a *stat pro ratione voluntas* that prevailed—according to Robinet—in divine law, the point is to unify the notion of jurisprudence and the concept of law by means of a definition, which Leibniz hopes to make acceptable by stripping it of its voluntarist overtones. Leibniz begins by setting out the following general definitions: jurisprudence is "the science of actions insofar as they are said to be just or unjust," while "just" and "unjust" designate "everything that is publicly useful or harmful."[67] By this means, specification becomes possible according to the nature of the superior and his utility:

> *publically* [useful], that is to say, first to the world, or to God its governor, next to the human race, and finally to the republic: in a relation of subordination, such that in case of conflict, the will or utility of God, if I may be allowed to speak in this manner, is given preference over the utility of the human race, which in turn has preference to the republic, which itself has preference to self-utility. Whence arise *divine, human and civil* jurisprudence. For to speak of self-utility belongs not to *jurisprudence*, but to *politics*.[68]

The relation is at once of genus (*jurisprudence*) to species (*divine, human, and civil jurisprudence*) and of a hierarchy that rests not so much on the consideration of unequal power as on the consideration of "beings" and goods of unequal perfection. Whence the maximal extent of jurisprudence, its unity and its continuity, as well as the establishment of internal limitations of different "societies" (republic, human race, world and God), limitations that found subordination and dispensations.

The definition of Thrasymachus reappears in the exposition of the third degree of law.[69] Indeed, the third principle of law is to be found in the "will of the superior."

> The superior is such either by nature, God: and his will is once again either natural, whence *piety*, or it is the *law* [*lex*], whence *positive divine law* [*jus*]; or the superior is so by agreement, as in the case of man, whence *civil law* [*jus*].[70]

For Robinet, it follows that Leibniz's "fundamental voluntarism" is now twofold: with regard to divine law and civil laws.[71] In reality, Leibniz corrects Thrasymachus's definition, by making clear that the divine will is always governed by wisdom: "God, *because he is omniscient and wise*, confirms the pure law [*jus merum*] and equity; because he is omnipotent he puts it into effect."[72] The threefold division of faculties is already present: the under-standing determines the will, whose decrees become effective by means of power. The divine will is the source of law insofar as it ratifies and embraces what the wise understanding proposes to it (the universal good), and om-nipotence constitutes, so to speak, the "arm" that enforces it. In the same way, human will avoids capriciousness, and arbitrariness, because it is or-dered to the public good and beyond that to the good of the human species and to the perfection of the world. There is not only a hierarchy of ends and a subordination of levels of jurisprudence (divine, human, civil), but also a convergence and profound unity, from the simple animals all the way up to God:

> Hence the utility of the human race, and even the beauty and harmony of the
> world, coincide with the divine will. Now, according to this principle, it is not
> even permitted to abuse beasts or creatures.[73]

However, this coincidence of utilities, ends, and laws (the strict law and equity are only completely fulfilled in and through piety) is not necessary and, so to speak, automatic. It applies only if the existence of God is pos-ited, since the first two degrees of law (the strict law and equity) lack any physical—that is to say natural—connection (*vinculum physicum*), which might assure this coincidence and guarantee the attribution of rewards and punishments insofar as they are respected or violated.

> Moreover, God is necessary to ensure that all that is of public utility, that is to
> say useful to the human race and to the world, becomes useful to individuals;
> and consequently, that everything honest is useful, and everything shameful is
> harmful. For it is clear that God in his wisdom has reserved rewards for the just
> and punishment for the unjust; and what he has reserved he brings about by his
> omnipotence. Thus, the existence of a very wise, very powerful being, that is to
> say, God, is the ultimate foundation of the law of nature.[74]

God is at once the source of natural law (as *superior*) by virtue of his wisdom and the guarantor of its complete enforcement by virtue of his omnipotence—even as concerns our most private actions and hidden thoughts. In locating the origin of law in God, Leibniz does not fall into voluntarism, since he maintains that the divine will is enlightened by un-created reason. Thus, it is true that without God there would be no just or unjust, no good or evil. However, this is not because there would be no will to establish them, but because there would be no eternal wisdom in which the "pure and immutable" natural law resides.[75]

As for human justice, it is not only parallel to divine jurisprudence but is also directly subordinate to it, according to the distinction of the three types of jurisprudence set out in §14. There is no voluntarism to be found here either.[76] If civil law, imperfect and uncertain as it is, is grounded more in fact than in right (§70), this does not render it arbitrary or "beyond reason."[77] On the contrary, the principle of the nomothetic science is the utility of the republic (§76), whose supreme law is "the safety of the people," which is to be found in "the good of the citizens themselves as to the matter, and the conservation of the regime as to the form." Furthermore,

> the good of the regime consists in public law, and also in the creation of the remaining laws, so as to avoid change. The good of the citizens consists in happiness and autarky, or in the goods of the spirit and of fortune.[78]

Not only is the political end perfectly designated, but the means are clearly identified as well: all political ordinances must aim at the happiness and virtue of the citizens, through education, good morals, the rewards owed to virtue and the punishments befitting vice.

## 1.2 A JUST GOD, WHO IS NEVERTHELESS THE AUTHOR OF SIN?

### 1.2.1 The Need to Demonstrate the Existence of God and the Immortality of the Soul

The *New Method* orients Leibniz's thinking in two principal directions: juridical and theological.

(1) It shows the necessity of a rationalization of law, notably, civil law, which largely depends on contingent fact and history (§70). Hence the effort to reform positive law (Roman and Imperial), which requires clear formulation of the principles of natural law. The project was presented to Arnauld in the following terms: "My very position orders me to work to establish morality as well as the foundations of law and equity with a little more than the usual certainty and clarity."[79] The goal is to gather together into a coherent whole the elements of this law (both natural and positive), that lie scattered in various laws, edicts, decrees, and institutions. It is the work of a jurist (which explains Leibniz's collaboration with the counselor Lasser beginning in 1668) but also of a philosopher, since it involves not only organizing, simplifying, and systematizing the law, but also clarifying

its foundations. The goal is to establish a "rational jurisprudence," in which it can be established

> in the fewest words possible the elements of law contained in the Roman Corpus (in the manner of the old Perpetual Edict), so that one could, so to speak, finally demonstrate from them its *universal laws.*[80]

The examination of positive law, reduced to a "core" (*Nucleus*) of laws,[81] and the study of the elements of natural law (*Elementa juris naturalis*) work together, since it is Leibniz's belief that "half of the Roman law is mere natural law. And it is well known that almost all of Europe uses this law wherever it has not been distinctly invalidated by local custom."[82]

(2) A demonstration of the existence of God is necessary. This demonstration, which must attain mathematical certainty,[83] satisfies a dual requirement: first, *juridical*, since God is the foundation of the whole system of law by virtue of his wisdom and will. By his omniscience and omnipotence, he ensures respect for the rules of justice to their full extent, such that every vice that goes unpunished and every good deed that goes unrewarded here on earth will be respectively punished and rewarded in the next life. God also guarantees the coincidence of private and public interest, such that everyone can be certain that the true way to achieve one's individual good is to contribute to the general good. Failing that, justice would be, in the words of Carneades, "nothing at all or the greatest foolishness," since "to secure by one's death the salvation of one's country is stupidity, if no reward awaits us after death."[84] What is just must always be useful to the individual.[85] Thus, since Leibniz does not limit the application of natural law to human society and the terrestrial world (as do most modern jurisconsults), he must demonstrate not only the existence of God but also the immortality of the soul so that the latter can be rewarded or punished after death.

Finally, the demonstration of the existence of God also satisfies an apologetic and practical end. It must dispel once and for all "the clouds gathered around the truth by atheists"[86] and put a stop to the progress of skepticism that the improvement of the new science has encouraged. Together with the demonstration of the immortality of the soul, it forms a part of the vast project of religious unification put forward in the *Catholic Demonstrations* (1668–1671). The project is "catholic" in the sense of "universal" and therefore acceptable to all confessions. These two demonstrations are precisely the goal of the *Confession of Nature Against Atheists* (*Confessio Naturae contra Atheistas*) and constitute the first two parts of the *Plan of Catholic Demonstrations* (*Demonstrationum catholicarum Conspectus*). It should be noted—and the point is important for understanding the theology of the young Leibniz—that the demonstrations are based primarily on arguments drawn from physics. What Leibniz attempts to show in the *Confession of Nature* is that "in the ultimate analysis of bodies, nature cannot forego divine aid."[87] That is to say, nature itself, to which the Moderns seem to want to limit their investigations, is called upon as a witness and confesses that nothing in it can occur without supposing an "incorporeal being . . . the Governing Spirit of the whole world, that is to say, God."[88] Likewise, the proof of the immortality of the soul amounts to a proof that the soul is not a body,[89] in direct opposition to the principle that "every mover is a body," which Leibniz attributes to Hobbes.[90] Of the five ways of demonstrating the existence of God contained in the *Plan of Catholic Demonstrations,* three are based on motion and the nature of the body. The remaining two are based respectively on the principle of reason and on the consideration of the beauty of the world. This last proof affords only an "infinite probability, or moral certainty"[91] and so lacks the force of the others. As for the demonstrations offered by Descartes, Ward, van Hogelande, and Valerianus Magnus, they contain paralogisms and so cannot be accepted.

The Leibnizian demonstration of the existence of God rests above all on the necessity of an incorporeal first mover. Physics, as reformed by the Moderns, affords "the most adequate (*aptissima*) way of demonstrating the existence of God,"[92] since by rejecting substantial forms, it makes God alone the first cause of universal motion. To be sure, God must be wise and intelligent in view of the beauty of the world,[93] but the proof of his existence has the certainty of mathematical demonstration only because it establishes *first* and *foremost* the action of a divine watchmaker. Whence Leibniz's condemnation in this period of any inherent finality in nature: "in nature there is no wisdom and no appetite, but a beautiful order resulting from the fact that it is God's clock."[94]

The demonstration is that of a physicist. It privileges the conception of God as first cause, who regulates the clockwork of the world from the outside. Is this conception fully satisfying? Although the existence of the clockmaker is acknowledged, all phenomena must be explained independently of him in terms of the laws of motion alone. The result is somewhat paradoxical: the demonstration is based on the dispensability of any appeal to God to explain what happens in the world. For the less God needs to intervene, the more the world seems perfect and its author wise.[95]

Leibniz is aware that even if natural philosophy is able to silence the atheists, it is not enough. We are in danger of feeling the sense of disappointment that Socrates encountered in reading Anaxagoras, who having introduced two principles (matter and spirit), discussed everything exactly as if matter were the sole principle of things and it was by virtue of its necessity that the world arose out of darkness, as Democritus maintained.

Therefore morality and jurisprudence must here be added to geometry and physics, because

> the wisdom of the creator manifests itself [*eluceat*] principally in having so ordered the world's clockwork that, as a result, everything as if by necessity, conspires to produce the greatest harmony in the whole. *There is need of philosophers of nature, who not only apply geometry to physics (since there are no final causes in geometry), but also introduce a certain civil science into the science of nature.* The world itself is a great republic in which spirits take the place of either sons or of enemies, and other creatures of slaves.[96]

The principles of mechanism themselves reveal the need to appeal to God. Consideration of harmony forces us to recognize not only a skilled artificer but also a wisdom and goodness that impose both material and spiritual ends on nature. The efficient cause points up the final cause. The mechanical metaphor (that of the clock) is supplemented with a political one (the republic), and the prime mover becomes the perfect monarch. Natural philosophy is joined to jurisprudence, both divine and human. It is the same God, both architect and sovereign, who creates the world and governs it.

The project of the *Catholic Demonstrations*, and, to an even greater extent, the correspondence with Thomasius, Conring, John Frederick, Duke of Brunswick-Lüneburg, and Arnauld (especially from the end of 1670 onward) show that the young Leibniz does not consider his writings on jurisprudence, physics, and theology as separate and unrelated, but as arising out of a single rational enterprise and tending to the same end: religious reunification based on common philosophical and theological foundations. The transition from one discipline to another is continuous and uninterrupted: from geometry to the philosophy of motion and body, and from there to the science of spirits[97] and to God, who is both wise and powerful, the architect of the world and sovereign of the republic of spirits that is governed by the principles of universal law.[98] It is within this theoretical framework and on the strength of the demonstrations, definitions, and principles at which he had arrived that Leibniz wrote a short text in German, entitled *On the Omnipotence and Omniscience of God and the Freedom of Man*.[99] It represents Leibniz's earliest (surviving) attempt to resolve the difficulties to which the existence of evil under a just and good God gives rise.

## 1.2.2.  Two Sophisms Against God's Justice

This unfinished work, which was not intended for publication, is no more than a sketch or a rough draft. Nevertheless, it is an important indication of the state of Leibniz's thought in this period. Its interest lies not so much in its positive theoretical contributions as in the aporia and severe criticism of traditional solutions to the problem of evil to be found in it.

How can human freedom be reconciled with the omnipotence and omniscience of God? The question is traditional, but it interests Leibniz only as it relates to a further question, which is not merely *speculative* but also *practical*: How can punishment and reward be legitimate if God governs all things and foresees everything that man will do? Through the question of the legitimacy of sanctions, it is God's justice[100] that is called into question, and, even more radically, the very idea of providence in the world. For whatever an individual's beliefs may be, one cannot help but wonder how this world, in which so many of the just are miserable and so many of the unjust are happy, can be governed by divine providence.[101] Experience serves as the starting point for reflection. It reveals the existence of evil, both physical (the misery of the just) and moral (wickedness). It provides the image of an unjust world, in which order is overturned, and what in fact obtains contradicts what ought to obtain, a world in which virtue is often punished and vice rewarded. The ethical and religious import of the question is obvious, considering the connection between moral and juridical obligation and the existence of God, who guarantees that appropriate sanctions are enforced.[102] To call divine providence into question favors skepticism and atheism and so imperils the whole system of law and morality.

The traditional response is to maintain that the apparent disorder of the world will be corrected in another life, just as dissonance in music is later resolved in "a truly perfect harmony."[103] Justice will then be perfectly realized and order restored by an exact distribution of rewards and punishments according to merit. Leibniz judges this reply insufficient, since it merely postpones the difficulty and leads to the following question:

> [H]ow, then, can such punishments and rewards be in accordance with fairness and devoid of bias, when in fact this all-wise ruler of the world, through the wonderful distribution of gifts, brings it about that for one punishment, for another reward, or as Christians call it, salvation and damnation, cannot but follow?[104]

It must be determined whether these *post mortem* sanctions, which are supposed to correct the injustices of this life, are themselves in conformity with justice, given that by the unequal distribution of his gifts and his grace, God makes it the case that such a one shall sin and so be damned, while another shall be just and so be saved. How can God not be the author of the sin he punishes in the sinner and of the good he rewards in the pious man? God seems doubly unjust in so far as he is the author of the evil for which he holds responsible those he punishes, and in so far as he makes acception of persons (*Parteiligkeit*), predestining the one to salvation and the other to damnation for no known reason.

Notice that it is precisely on this difficulty that Lorenzo Valla's *Dialogue on Free Will* ends.[105] Valla leaves the problem unresolved on the grounds that God's judgments are incomprehensible and his ways impenetrable. Luther's position in *On the Bondage of the Will* was scarcely more satisfying. Luther allowed that God acts in an arbitrary and unjust manner (in our judgment and according to human justice) by bestowing his grace and mercy upon some who are unworthy and abandoning to his anger others who do not merit it. Thus predestination is the heart of the problem. It is the central question to which all the others—human freedom, divine providence, moral and physical concurrence with evil, divine justice—are connected.[106] Leibniz emphasizes the divisions this question has sown among men and the sometimes disastrous practical consequences that have followed (and not only among Christians):

> no comet, no earthquake, no plague has done more harm. It is here that laziness has found shelter, evil has found camouflage, and God himself has had to be a pretense for both.[107]

On the theoretical level, a number of opposing sects and factions have arisen. Scholastic terminology and distinctions have only added to the confusion. Therefore, we must abandon such talk and return to the simple language that "the poorest peasant, constrained to give his opinion on the subject, would use."[108]

For Leibniz the controversy fundamentally rests on two sophisms: one concerning foreknowledge (*Vorsehung*), that is, "God's knowledge and wisdom," and the other concerning predestination (*Versehung*), that is "the will and omnipotence of God."[109] The first consists in the claim that divine omniscience is incompatible with human freedom. If that which God foresees cannot not occur, and if God foresees that I will sin and be damned, then my sin and damnation are necessary. They cannot not occur (otherwise God would be mistaken) and will happen no matter what I do.[110] The second consists in making God the instigator of the very sin he punishes and even the true author of sin.[111] For God does not merely permit sin, as a simple "spectator," but concurs with it by his power and will by creating the circumstances and the occasions that lead to it and inciting man to commit it (by exposing him to temptation), whereas he could have prevented it— prevented everything that leads to it and all the dire consequences that follow from it.

These two sophisms call into question, each in its own way, divine justice. According to the first, if it is written from all eternity that I will sin, then I cannot escape my fate, however I may try to avoid it. Therefore, I am not free. So to punish me is unjust, since it was impossible for me to act otherwise. The necessity of the crime excuses it. It exonerates the sinner and leads to fatalism, inaction and laziness. Why seek to prevent what will occur regardless of what one does? It is for this reason that the argument, which was known to the ancients, came to be called the "Lazy sophism" or the "Lazy reason sophism."[112]

Leibniz's solution involves a distinction between the order of foreknowledge (the sin will be committed) and the order of existence, that is, the chain of events that effectively leads to the sin. The fact that the sin is foreseen by God does not render it necessary such that it will occur *whatever one does*. For it will not occur without the relevant causes nor without its author doing all that is required for it to occur, namely willing it and carrying it out. These pertain to the will and choice of the sinner; inaction itself (which is the result of following the lazy sophism!) is not without effect in determining the final outcome (salvation or damnation). Therefore, I will only be predestined to sin and damnation if I myself will it. I should blame neither God nor providence, since in fact my "predestination" depends on me.[113] As a consequence, Leibniz draws the following conclusion, "Thus, you may accuse neither predestination nor God, but yourself or your will."[114]

There is no opposition between divine foreknowledge and human freedom. On the contrary, the former is based on the decisions of the latter (decisions that are known by the omniscient spirit even before they occur). It is not because sin is foreseen that it will occur. Rather, it is because it occurs by a chain of causes that the foreknowledge is correct. The truth and certainty of the future are not the causes of the will's choices. The will alone, by virtue of its choices, brings about the event and renders it certain. The sin infallibly foreseen by God is the one freely willed by man. Consequently, it must be entirely imputed to the sinner. In this way, the conditions for moral action are restored, and with it, the legitimacy of the sanctions decreed by divine justice both in this life and the next.

Thus resolution of the first sophism consists in showing that it is the will that is responsible for sin. According to the second sophism, God, being the origin of all things, is the ultimate cause of the will and so the author of its sin. This sophism involves the problem of God's concurrence with evil and calls into question once again the justice of punishment. It gives rise to the complaint of the soul of the damned who accuses God of punishing a sin that God himself brought about and reproaches God for having created the condemned man so that he would be miserable, whereas God could have made him better, granted him a good nature, placed him in circumstances more favorable to the development of virtue, surrounded him with wise men and benevolent instructors, etc.[115]

Leibniz replies above all as a jurist:

> Punishment belongs to the evil will—no matter whence it comes. Otherwise, no misdeed would be punished. There is always a cause of the will outside of the willing subject, and yet it is the will that makes us human beings and persons—sinners, blessed, damned.[116]

Two reasons are offered here. On the one hand, justice requires that every sin be punished and every good action rewarded. On the other hand, the imputation rightly falls on the most proximate cause, in this case, the will of man, and not on more remote determining causes, nor *a fortiori* on God, the ultimate reason of things. The use of this rule is traditional.[117] In any trial, the judge must only consider two things: whether the committed act resulted from the will of the accused (that is, whether it was deliberate and unconstrained) and whether it was contrary to the law. Whether the causes that determine the will are necessary or not has no bearing on the licit or illicit (and therefore punishable[118]) character of the act. If it were necessary to take into account everything required to explain the crime, the character and history of the accused, his education, his bad company, the milieu in which he lives and once lived, the investigation would be endless. Nothing would prevent one from mounting up from cause to cause all the way to the origin of the world and to God himself. In the end, all responsibility would dissolve; the criminal would be exonerated, and justice would be at an end.

While this argument may be satisfactory from a strictly juridical point of view—and will be invoked in later works[119]—it is not so from a metaphysical point of view, since the problem of God's concurrence with sin is left untouched. For God does not simply *observe* the actions of men. He gives them being and power, and he fails to prevent their sins, as lies within his power (which makes him at least an accomplice). Worse still, he provides all the occasions and circumstances for sin. Although it may seem paradoxical in light of his future texts, Leibniz does not attempt to deny or restrict God's physical and moral concourse with evil. Even if the sinner merits punishment, it is nevertheless the case that, being all-powerful, God could have brought it about that the sin did not occur or was not so much as willed. However, God did not prevent it. Therefore, not only does he *permit* its existence, he *wills* it,[120] because he considers it to be for the best. Is God then the author of sin? How can it be denied given that he is the origin of all things and the cause of their being just as they are and not otherwise?

> It follows apparently that God himself creates and makes the sins of the world. Why do I now sin and commit murder? Because I will to do so and can do so. God gives me the ability to do so; the circumstances give me the will to do so, but in fact God created the circumstances too, along with the whole chain of causes back to the beginning of the world.[121]

### 1.2.3 Critique of Traditional Solutions to the Problem of Evil: Leibniz's Proximity to Luther and Hobbes

The Principle of Sufficient Reason demands that we ascend the series of causes that led to sin. It implies that God, the ultimate reason of everything, is the author of evil by virtue of his will and power. Against such arguments, which strike like a "battering ram,"[122] traditional responses drawn from the church fathers (especially Augustine) and taken up by the Scholastics (in particular Thomas Aquinas) are a weak rampart. These authors attempt to show that God is not the author of sin, that he offers it no concurrence, at least by his power, since sin is a mere nothing that "consists in the lack of due perfection." God is the cause only of what is real and positive in creatures, not of their imperfections and lacks. These imperfections and lacks have no need of a particular cause, since they are mere negations.

This argument is severely criticized by Leibniz, who judges it both indefensible from a theoretical point of view and pernicious from a practical point of view. Ultimately, it is an attempt to divide the indivisible by distinguishing, on the one hand, being, perfection, and the good (which come from God) and, on the other, negation, imperfection, and evil (which come from the creature). Such a procedure amounts to separating the thing or the act from itself, since no created being can be considered independently of the properties and limits that make it what it is. It is impossible to separate within the sinner the creature (good) from the vice that corrupts it and which constitutes its sinful nature, just as it is impossible to separate within the sin the pure act from its sinful nature in order to assign different causes to each. Therefore, both the imperfection and sin of the creature are as truly imputable to God as its perfection and good actions. To attempt to absolve God of responsibility for evil by alleging that he produces only the "physical" nature of an evil act (its reality and being) and not its "moral" nature (being contrary to justice) is as absurd as the claim that a bad violinist is only the cause of the motions of his bow but not of the resulting dissonance![123]

This last example is particularly interesting in that it admits of a dual interpretation. For the bad musician can represent God as well as the sinner. In the former case God is the author of creatures (represented by the movements of bow) and not of their associated imperfection (the dissonance produced). In the latter case, the sinner is the author of the action (the motions of the bow) but is not responsible for the fact that the action is criminal (the sounds are dissonant). Once again, the contradiction lies in the attempt to separate what is inseparable in the concurrence: the *material* (being, creature, act, motions of the bow) from its own limits (imperfection) and its moral character (evil character of the action, dissonance). On this showing, the bad musician (God or man) would not be responsible for what makes him a bad musician, namely, the dissonance he creates and the bad music he produces. Thus, the argument proves too much. In absolving God of responsibility for sin, it likewise cleanses the sinner of his crime, as the dual reading of the metaphor of the musician makes apparent.

> Indeed, I do not see why one holds the sinner himself to be a cause of sin; he does the deed (just as God does everything from which the deed follows), and who can do anything about the fact that this deed is not in harmony with the love of God?[124]

The error consists in limiting God's physical concurrence to being, perfection, and the good. The sin, distinct from the act itself (which alone is something real), just as the imperfection from the creature, is then considered a pure nothing that results from no cause whatsoever. The Augustinian conception of evil as nonbeing is therefore theoretically indefensible and practically dangerous, because evil with which nothing or no one concurs (given that all concurrence involves being) is simply nothing, and so neither man nor God is responsible for it.

Leibniz's condemnation is unequivocal: "of course, one says things in order to excuse God that are so lame that a defense attorney with similar arguments before a reasonable judge would be ashamed."[125] The image of a trial and an advocate who pleads the case of God appears well before the *Essays of Theodicy:* "Now these are the lovely lawyers of divine justice, who will at the same time make all sinners unpunishable. And it surprises me that the profound Descartes stumbled here too."[126] The severity of this judgment can seem surprising, given that Leibniz himself will later take up a number of these arguments. He will affirm, for example, that "every perfection in creatures comes from God, all imperfection from their own limitation"[127] and, drawing on the authority of the Platonists and Augustine, that "evil is a defect, that is, a privation or negation, and consequently, it arises from nothingness or nonbeing."[128] Has Leibniz forgotten the severe criticism that he himself had once made of these notions? Certainly not. For we shall see how, under the guise of a simple borrowing, he reinterprets these notions and gives them a new sense.[129]

Having challenged the reduction of evil to nothingness and the limitation of God's physical concurrence, Leibniz refutes, in the final paragraph of the text,[130] freedom of indifference and the doctrine of middle knowledge, which had been invented by the Jesuits (Fonseca and Molina) as a means of imputing sin solely to the human will. Ultimately, analysis of the second "sophism" (God is the author of sin) does not result in its refutation, but rather in its validation. That is, the argument is shown not to be a sophism, although on the condition that it does not lessen man's responsibility for the act of sin.

Here again the influence of Luther can be felt. Like the great reformer, Leibniz severely criticizes Scholastic theology and acknowledges that God is the author of sin, though without thereby conceding that God himself is evil or absolving the sinner of his responsibility, which remains in its entirety as has been shown in the refutation of the first sophism. On a more strictly philosophical level, there are undeniable similarities with Hobbes's thought. During this period, Leibniz prided himself on having read the majority of Hobbes's works and on having benefited from them to a degree unparalleled in his century.[131] There is in both philosophers a refutation of the lazy sophism and a rejection of the attempt to distinguish physical reality and moral character within an act. On the last point, Hobbes wrote:

> Nor find I any difference between an *action* and the *sin* of that action; as for example, between the killing of Uriah, and the sin of David in killing Uriah, nor when *one* is *cause* both of the *action* and of the *law*, how *another* can be cause of the *disagreement* between them, no more than how one man making a longer and a shorter garment, another can make the inequality that is between them.[132]

Similar arguments are also given against freedom of indifference on the grounds that it would place limits on God's omnipotence and foreknowledge, since whatsoever God hath *purposed* to bring to pass by *man*, as an instrument, or foreseeth shall come to pass; a man, if he have *liberty* . . . from *necessitation*, might frustrate, and make not to come to pass, and God should either not *foreknow* it, and not *decree* it, or he should *foreknow* such things shall be, as shall never be, and *decree* that which shall never *come to pass*.[133]

Leibniz presented the same difficulty to Magnus Wedderkopf (May 1671)[134] in the form of a dilemma: either God did not decree (*decernit*) all things, from which it follows that he is not omniscient, or God does decree all things, and he is absolutely (*absolute*) the author of all things. For, if he decreed and yet things did not conform to his decree, he would not be omnipotent.

Let us also add that the Leibnizian definitions of freedom ("a man has sufficient free will when he can do what he wills and wills what he considers good"[135]) and of the will as the effect of a complete cause[136] are also very close to those of Hobbes for whom freedom is the power to do or not do something in accordance with one's will[137] and the will is the necessary effect of a sufficient cause.[138] For both philosophers the will cannot be indifferent, because it is determined by consideration of the apparent good and by the whole of the circumstances or causes that form the series.[139] Not only would indifference require the ability to will to will (which Luther,[140] Hobbes, and Leibniz all reject), but it would represent for Leibniz, "an absolute will which does not depend upon the goodness of things," which would be "a monstrosity."[141] Such a will is not only impossible but would be dangerous, since it would be without reason and without consideration for good or evil.

However, as examination of his earliest writings has shown, Leibniz does not accept Hobbes's voluntarism. Nevertheless, as the letter to Wedderkopf makes clear, Leibniz does accept Hobbes's necessitarianism, which serves to reconcile freedom and necessity. Since nothing is without a cause, nor any effect without a sufficient cause, every action and every event is necessary: "*Fate* is the *decree of God* or the necessity of events. Those things are *fatal* which will necessarily happen."[142] Necessity applies to God himself, the most perfect spirit: "it is impossible for him not to be affected by the most perfect harmony, and so necessitated to the best by the very ideality of things."[143] This necessity must be taken in the strict sense—in the sense of *absolute*—as that whose opposite is contradictory. In so far as it determines one to the best, it is identical with freedom:

It is the highest freedom to be impelled to the best by right reason. Whoever desires any other freedom is a fool. From this it follows that whatever has happened, is happening, or will happen is best, and so necessary, but, as I have said, with a necessity which takes nothing away from freedom because it takes nothing from the will or from the use of reason.[144]

This necessitarianism does not reinstate the lazy sophism, because an action, although necessary, does not occur without any cause, that is, without the will of the agent. Rather, as in Luther and Hobbes,[145] necessitarianism leads to the rejection of divine *permission* of evil: "It follows from this that God can never consent merely to permit. It also follows that there is, in truth, no decree of God that is not absolute."[146] God wills *absolutely*, that is fully and positively—without restriction or condition—everything he wills and decrees. He never suspends judgment, as do we as a result of our ignorance. Everything is willed by him and conforms to his decree—including evil.

However, there are two important differences between Leibnizian and Hobbesian necessitarianism. For Leibniz, (1) freedom, even in God, is defined as the will to the best, since a will independent of the intrinsic goodness of things would be "monstrous"; and (2) the universal harmony, in accordance with which God chooses and creates the world, is not itself created by God.

If, as the letter to Wedderkopf indicates, God wills *absolutely*, he does not for all that will arbitrarily. The reference to an "absolute decree" (which echoes the theological debates concerning predestination between the supra- and infralapsarians) does not refer to a will that decides without reason, but on the contrary, to a will directed toward justice and the good, understood as eternal and uncreated notions. God is absolutely necessitated by consideration of the best. For Hobbes, everything—goods and evils—necessarily follows from God's omnipotence, which makes all that he does just. For Leibniz, by contrast, it is from the thought of universal harmony that the best necessarily follows. Likewise, it is from power determined by wisdom that creation of the most perfect universe follows. The relation of the good and the just to the necessary is exactly the reverse. For Hobbes, the just is grounded in the necessitating power of God, whereas for Leibniz, necessity is grounded in the best. In this latter case, things are necessary, *because* they are the best. The will is subordinate to the understanding that conceives the universal harmony:

What, then, is the ultimate reason for the divine will? The divine intellect. For God wills the things He understands to be best and most harmonious, and He selects them, so to speak, from an infinite number of all possibilities. The reason for the divine intellect? The harmony of things. The reason for the harmony of things? Nothing.[147]

Harmony, which is uncreated and derives from no higher reason, is indistinguishable from the divine essence.[148] It refers to the nature of things and their reciprocal relations, which do not depend upon the divine will.

> For the essences of things are like numbers, as it were, and contain the possibility of beings which God does not make as he does existence, these possibilities or ideas of things coincide rather with God himself.[149]

God cannot be the author of the possibility of things (that is, he cannot be their reason by virtue of his will), because he cannot be the reason of his own being. His essence does not depend on his will. He does not determine their possibility, but only their existence. By his understanding he is their raison d'être as *possibles*, and by his will and power, their raison d'être as existents.

However, we must not be misled. The possibility at issue here is not that which is opposed to necessity, nor should it be understood as synonymous with contingency. Rather, it signifies the *condition of the possibility* of the thing, that is to say, its nature. Possibility in this sense concerns essence, or the Idea that renders the thing possible, non-contradictory in itself and clearly conceivable,[150] able to be brought into existence (in conformity with its Idea) in the same way that the definition of a circle renders it possible by showing its non-contradictoriness and the manner of its construction. In this sense, the invocation of the infinite number of possibles in the letter to Wedderkopf is not meant to establish the contingency of the world and of divine choice, nor even to put forward the idea of an infinite number of possibles worlds. Rather, it is intended, from a Platonist perspective, to indicate the location of the Essences or Ideas (the divine understanding) in conformity with which God created the world.

From this perspective, one can speak of divine permission, but only in a very precise sense: the divine will can be called "permissive" relatively speaking, in so far as it conforms to the ideality of things and to the most perfect.[151] *Permissive* becomes synonymous with *relative:* the divine will is permission only in so far as it follows the judgment of the understanding. This serves to moderate the notion of a positive will to evil: "God hates sins, not in the sense that he cannot bear the sight of them as we cannot bear the sight of things we detest—otherwise he would eliminate them—but in the sense that he punishes them."[152] God in his omnipotence allows sin, because it concords harmoniously with punishment. Thus, "sins are good, that is, harmonious, taken along with their punishment or expiation. For there is no harmony except through contraries."[153] Although sins, as such, inspire horror, they are good *relatively* speaking, because they are indispensable to the harmony that arises out of contraries. Thus, the Augustinian thesis of evil as nonbeing, although severely criticized, can be rehabilitated:

> Therefore nothing is to be considered absolutely evil; otherwise God would not be supremely wise in grasping it or supremely powerful in eliminating it.[154]

However, the rehabilitation is only apparent, since it presupposes a reinterpretation of Augustine. Evil is nothing in itself, but only because nothing is an absolute evil. There is only *relative* evil and this only for the one who suffers it and for its author who will be punished for it. For there is no evil with regard to the world considered in its totality and with regard to God. Sin does not alter the perfection of the world, nor does it affect God. Otherwise, God, who is omnipotent and who necessarily wills the best, would necessarily have eliminated it. On the contrary, when considered together with its punishment, sin is a good because it conforms to harmony.

Thus, the thesis that Leibniz here defends is not properly speaking a *metaphysical* thesis concerning the nature of evil and according to which evil is a nonbeing. Rather, it is a *teleological* thesis according to which evil only exists with respect to an end that is extrinsic to it, namely harmony. As Leibniz's notes on Bisterfeld (probably written between 1663 and 1666) already suggest, evil is possible only insofar as it is "can be ordered" (*ordinabile*) to the good and only exists insofar as it is in fact "ordered" (*ordinatum*) to the good of the thing itself. Therefore, "it clearly follows that no evil, large or small, exists nor can exist unbeknownst to or in spite of the sovereign good."[155]

Leibniz's first meditations on evil and justice reveal a position influenced by Luther, but undoubtedly by Hobbes as well. However, they also point up notable disagreements with these authors as well as a number of original positions. In considering the divine will to be necessitated to the best, Leibniz finds himself confronted with a problem that was foreign to both Luther and Hobbes. For the latter, who associates voluntarism with necessitarianism, to make God the cause of sin raises no difficulty. As the source of all motion and of all actions, including sin, God is always justified, no matter what he does, since his right, which expresses his omnipotence, takes precedence over any other justice:

> the *power* of God alone without other helps is sufficient *justification* of any action he doth. . . . That which he does, is made just by his doing it; just, I say, in him, though not always just in us.[156]

Therefore, God cannot sin, since merely by virtue of doing something he renders it just, and because he is not subject to the law of any more powerful being. To accuse God is to subject him to our justice and is, in this sense, a kind of blasphemy.[157] The case is otherwise with Leibniz. His rejection of the voluntarist thesis and of the equivocity of the notions of justice, good, and evil make justification of God necessary. In a sense, Leibniz's position is more difficult to maintain, since he must reconcile necessitarianism with the notion of a will governed by consideration of the best, which this will did not establish and which seems incompatible with the existence of evil in the world. Hence the appeal—partial, to be sure—of the doctrine of permission, the aesthetic metaphor of harmony, and the reappearance of the Augustinian thesis that had earlier been rejected in *On the Omnipotence of God*.

However, God's physical and moral concurrence with sin remain problematic. God is the ultimate reason of sin, and sin, which belongs to the most perfect harmony, which God cannot change and which he cannot fail to choose, becomes absolutely necessary. This necessity would not have been shocking to either Luther[158] or Hobbes. However, Leibniz (who, at the end of his letter, asks Wedderkopf not to reveal its contents) perceives the danger of affirming incautiously and unreservedly that sins are not only necessary but also good (when considered together with their punishment), and that consequently they are willed by God. Later Leibniz would add in the margins of the letter, "I later corrected this, for it is one thing for sins to happen infallibly, another for them to happen necessarily."[159] The *Confession of a Philosopher* would be an attempt to overcome these difficulties and to correct the excessiveness of these theses by proposing the first truly complete Leibnizian synthesis concerning the problem of evil and God's justice.

## NOTES

1. T Preface; GP VI, 43; Huggard, 67.
2. T Preface; GP VI, 43; Huggard, 67. See also Grua, 497.
3. FC (NL), *Leibniz's Life*, 386: "before the age of seventeen I undertook a discussion of certain controversies in a more serious manner. Indeed, I perceived that the task was easy for an exact and diligent man. I was extraordinarily taken with Luther's *On the Bondage of the Will* and Valla's *Dialogues* on freedom." In the *Dialogue on Human Freedom and the Origin of Evil* (Grua, 369; AG 117), Leibniz expresses admiration for "the excellent work of Luther on servitude of the will, which is extremely good, in my opinion, as long as one tones down some extravagant expressions, and which has seemed to me, from my childhood, to be the finest and most solid book he left us."

4. T §405; GP VI, 357; Huggard, 365.
5. T §277; GP VI, 282; Huggard, 297.
6. Cf. Grua, 375 and 378; T pd §50.
7. Leibniz to Morell (December 17, 1699), Grua, 145.
8. Ibid. (my emphasis). Leibniz adds: "The gentleness and moderation of Kempis, Böhme and Mons. Spener are much more to my liking and strike me as much more apt to bear fruit."
9. Cf. my introduction, p. 1 and p. 3.
10. Luther compares the human will to a "beast of burden": "If God rides it, it wills and goes where God wills.... If Satan rides it, it wills and goes where Satan wills." (*On the Bondage of the Will*, Preface, 140 [WA, vol. 18, 635]); "in relation to God, or in matters pertaining to salvation or damnation, a man has no free choice, but is a captive, subject and slave either of the will of God or the will of Satan" (143 [WA, vol. 18, 638]).
11. Ibid., 141 [WA, vol. 18, 636]. See also: ibid., 205–206 [WA, vol. 18, 688].
12. Ibid., 232 [WA, vol. 18, 709].
13. Grua, 506.
14. *On the Bondage of the Will*, 232–239 [WA, vol. 18, 711]. Cf. Psalms 18, 26–27.
15. *Unvorgreiffliches Bedencken*, d., Grua 434.
16. Grua, 435.
17. T pd §12; GP VI, 57; Huggard, 81.
18. *On the Bondage of the Will*, 184 [WA, vol. 18, 673].
19. Ibid., 228–229 [WA, vol. 18, 706].
20. Ibid., 259–260 [WA, vol. 18, 731].
21. Ibid., 296 [WA, vol. 18, 759]. Passage inspired by Paul, I Corinthians 1, 23–25.
22. *On the Bondage of Will*, 329–330 [WA, vol. 18, 784]. Some, shocked by what their reason cannot grasp, "demand that God should act according to human justice, and do what seems right to them, or else cease to be God. The secrets of his majesty are no recommendation; let him give a reason why he is God, or why he wills or does what has no semblance of justice—much as you might summon a cobbler or girdle maker to appear in court"(258 [WA, vol. 18, 729])
23. Cf. Leibniz to Seckendorf (December 17, 1691), Grua, 200.
24. Cf. *Unvorgreiffliches Bedencken*, Grua, 442.
25. T §338; GP VI, 315; Huggard, 328.
26. T §79; GP VI, 145; Huggard, 165: "we must judge charitably that the most rigid predestinators have too much reason and too much piety to depart from this opinion."
27. *On the Bondage of the Will*, 332 [WA, vol. 18, 785].
28. Passage cited in T pd §45; GP VI, 75–76; Huggard, 99.
29. T §280; GP VI, 283; Huggard, 298. Luther does not avoid the term, but rather distinguishes "necessity of immutability" according to which we do evil from "necessity of compulsion" (*On the Bondage of the Will*, Preface, 139 [WA, vol. 18, 634]).
30. Cf. Grua, 227.
31. T §413; GP VI, 361; Huggard, 369: the "chief defect" of Valla's dialogue is "that it cuts the knot and seems to condemn providence under the name of Jupiter, nearly making him the author of sin." For Luther, see the comparison with the horseman cited earlier p. 19–20.
32. *On the Bondage of Will*, 236–237 [WA, vol. 18, 712].
33. Robinet, *G. W. Leibniz: le meilleur des mondes*, 3.
34. *Notes on Stahl* (1663–1664?), A VI, 1, 27.

35. Ibid.
36. *G. W. Leibniz: Le meilleur des mondes*, 9.
37. Ibid., 11.
38. Suarez, *Opera omnia*, vol. 5, *De legibus*, II, 2, 9; II, 6, 7. See also Pufendorf, *On the Duty of Man and Citizen*, I, 2, § 6; Christian Thomasius, in *Institutes of Divine Jurisprudence*, I, 1, § 85: "The right of man [*jus hominis*] must ultimately be deduced from the will of God and in general from the will of a superior."
39. Cf. Sève, *Leibniz et l'Ecole moderne du droit naturel*, 46–49.
40. Cf. *New Method of Learning and Teaching Jurisprudence* (1667), A VI, 1, 301, Part II, §15: "Deus est subjectum Juris summi in omnia, nullius vero obligationis." See also Grua, 496–497, *Causa Dei*, §§5–6.
41. A VI, 4-B, 1653.
42. *New Essays*, I, 1, A VI, 6, 73; RB 73. See also Leibniz to Pellisson-Fontanier (July 27/August 6, 1692), A I, 8, 158.
43. A VI, 1, 52.
44. A VI, 1, 52, note 53.
45. Robinet, *G. W. Leibniz: le meilleur des mondes*, 10.
46. See the references in Thomasius's texts given by Richard Bodéüs, in *Leibniz-Thomasius. Correspondance 1663–1672*, 37–38, note 8.
47. Leibniz to Thomasius (September 2, 1663), A II, 1, 5.
48. See Bodéüs, *Leibniz-Thomasius. Correspondance 1663–1672*, 38, note 12.
49. Leibniz to Thomasius (September 2, 1663), A II, 1, 5.
50. Ibid.
51. Bodéüs, *Leibniz-Thomasius. Correspondance 1663–1672*, 42.
52. Ibid., 43.
53. Plato, *Republic* I, 338c.
54. A VI, 1, 230.
55. The comparative in Latin has the sense of a relative superlative when it occurs in a comparison of two things.
56. Robinet, *G. W. Leibniz: le meilleur des mondes*, 11.
57. Cf. A VI, 1, 51, note 51.
58. A VI, 1, 73. Cf. *Digest* 1, 1, 10, § 2.
59. *On the Combinatorial Art*, A VI, 1, 190.
60. *New Method*, A VI, 1, 294, Part II, § 5.
61. *On the Combinatorial Art*, A VI, 1, 190–191 (see also *New Method*, A VI, 1, 294, Part II, § 5).
62. Robinet, *G. W. Leibniz: le meilleur des mondes*, 22.
63. See, for example, Grua, 241: "Theologia est divina quaedam jurisprudentia, nostrae cum Deo societatis jura explicans"; Grua, 377: "magna Theologiae pars nihil aliud est quam jurisprudentia quadam sacra"; Leibniz to Kestner (August 21, 1709), Dutens IV-3, 261.
64. "ad instar Theologiae" (*New Method*, A VI, 1, 293, Part II, §2).
65. *New Method*, A VI, 1, 294, §4.
66. *New Method*, A VI, 1, 294, §5.
67. See also *New Method*, A VI, 1, 287, Part I, §35: the just is "that which is useful to all."
68. *New Method*, A VI, 1, 300–301, Part II, §14.
69. The distinction of the three degrees of law is traditional: the first principle declares that we must harm no one (strict or pure law), the second that we render to each his due (equity), the third that we live honestly (cf. Justinian, *Institutes*, 1, 1, §3).

70. *New Method*, A VI, 1, 344, Part II, §75.
71. Op. cit., 23.
72. *New Method*, A VI, 1, 344, Part II, §75. My emphasis.
73. Ibid. Note that this extension of the law is not original, but conforms to the *Institutes* of Justinian (1.2): "Natural law is what is taught by nature to all animals. For this law is not limited to the human race, but is the law of all animals born in the sky, on earth and in the sea."
74. *New Method*, A VI, 1, 344–345, Part II, §75.
75. Ibid., 341, §70.
76. For this reason, it seems wrong to speak of the "Hobbesianism of the *Nova methodus*," as does René Sève in *Leibniz et l'École moderne du droit naturel*, 124.
77. Robinet, *G. W. Leibniz: le meilleur des monde*, 23.
78. *New Method*, A VI, 1, 345, Part II, §76.
79. Leibniz to Arnauld (November 1671), A II, 1, 279. At the time of that letter, Leibniz was councilor of the supreme court in the electorate of Mainz.
80. Leibniz to Hobbes (July 13/23, 1670), A II, 1, 91–92; L 164.
81. Cf. Leibniz to Arnauld (November 1671), A II, 1, 279; Leibniz to Conring (February 8, 1671), A II, 1, 130.
82. Leibniz to Hobbes (July 13/23, 1670), A II, 1, 92; L 164. See also, for example, Leibniz to Velthuysen (April 6/16, 1670), A II, 1, 63.
83. See the beginning of *On the Combinatorial Art*, A VI, 1, 169–170.
84. *Elements of Natural Law*, A VI, 1, 431. See also 437.
85. Leibniz to Conring (January 13/23, 1670), A II, 1, 47: "Ego suppono cum Carneade (et Hobbius consentit) Justitiam sine utilitate propria (sive praesente sive futura) summam esse stultitiam." "Ergo omne Justum debet esse privatim Utile."
86. *New Method*, A VI, 1, 345, Part I, §75.
87. A VI, 1, 492.
88. Ibid. See also Leibniz to Thomasius (September 26 /October 6, 1668), A II, 1, 19.
89. Once it has been established that that which is immediately sensed without conceiving parts is in fact without parts, the propositions form a logical sequence: lack of parts implies lack of motion, and so immateriality, and so incorruptibility, which is to say, immortality (*Confession of Nature Against Atheists*, A VI, 1, 492–493).
90. "Omnis motor est corpus" (Leibniz to Hobbes, July 13/23, 1670, A II, 1, 94).
91. A VI, 1, 494.
92. Leibniz to Thomasius (September 26/October 6, 1668), A II, 1, 19. Concerning the relation between the nature of motion and the demonstrations of the existence of God and the immortality of the soul, see also Leibniz to Conring (February 8, 1671), A II, 1, 131.
93. *Confession of Nature Against Atheists*, A VI, 1, 492: "ob rerum pulchritudinem sapiens."
94. Leibniz to Thomasius (April 20/30, 1669), A II, 1, 35.
95. Cf. Leibniz to Thomasius (December 19/29, 1670), A II, 1, 120.
96. Ibid., 119. Emphasis added.
97. Leibniz to Arnauld (November 1671), A II, 1, 278.
98. Leibniz to Conring (February 8, 1671), A II, 1, 131.
99. *Von der Allmacht und Allwissenheit Gottes und der Freiheit des Menschen* (1670–1671?), A VI, 1, 537–546.
100. On the senses of justice, see the introduction, p. 6.
101. Cf. *On the Omnipotence of God*, §2, A VI, 1, 537.

102. See supra p. 31.
103. *On the Omnipotence of God*, §3, A VI, 1, 537; Sleigh, 7.
104. *On the Omnipotence of God*, §3, A VI, 1, 537; Sleigh, 7.
105. "Jupiter therefore condemns in me his own crime; he alone is guilty." (T §411, GP VI, 360, Huggard, 368). See Valla, *Dialogue on Free Will*, 174.
106. Cf. Leibniz to Duke John Frederick (February 13, 1671), A II, 1, 137: "What has ever been more fervently defended by all *philosophical* traditions and all popular *religions* than the question of *predestination* and what is connected with it?"
107. *On the Omnipotence of God*, §4, A VI, 1, 537; Sleigh, 7.
108. *On the Omnipotence of God*, §6, A VI, 1, 538; Sleigh, 9.
109. *On the Omnipotence of God*, §7, A VI, 1, 538; Sleigh, 9. *Versehen* has, among other meanings, that of "to provide for." Grimm's Dictionary (*Deutsches Wörterbuch*) indicates the use of *Versehung* to designate *praedestinatio* in theological debates among Protestants. Conversely, *Vorsehung* (*vor* = before, *sehen* = to see) signifies *praescientia* or *praevisio*.
110. Cf. *On the Omnipotence of God*, §8, A VI, 1, 539.
111. Ibid. §15, A VI, 1, 543.
112. Cf. Cicero, *On Fate*, 28–29. In the *Theodicy* Leibniz refers to this same sophism as "Turkish Fate," or *fatum mahometanum*, "because a similar line of reasoning, so it is said, causes the Turks not to shun places ravaged by plague" (§55; GP VI, 132; Huggard, 153).
113. Cf. *On the Omnipotence of God*, §13, A VI, 1, 542; Sleigh, 17: "If God has foreseen the end, he has also foreseen the means; if he knows that I shall be saved, then he also knows that I live a God-fearing life; if I am foreseen to be damned, then I am foreseen to sin."
114. *On the Omnipotence of God*, §13, A VI, 1, 542; Sleigh, 17.
115. Cf. *On the Omnipotence of God*, §13, A VI, 1, 542.
116. Ibid.
117. It can, for example, be found in Hobbes: "A judge in judging whether it be sin or no, which is done against the law, looks at no higher cause of the action, than the will of the doer" (*Of Liberty and Necessity*, EW IV, 260).
118. As Leibniz would maintain in the *Theodicy*: "No justice need trouble itself over the origin of a scoundrel's wickedness when it is only a question of punishing him: it is quite another matter when it is a question of prevention. One knows well that disposition, upbringing, conversation, and often chance itself, have much share in that origin: is the man any the less deserving of punishment?" (§264; GP VI, 274; Huggard, 289). Cf. Hobbes: "To let pass, that not the *necessity*, but the *will* to break the *law*, maketh the action *unjust*, because the *law* regardeth the *will*, and no other precedent causes of action" (*Of Liberty and Necessity*, 252).
119. For example, *Confession of a Philosopher*, A VI, 3, 138; *Conversation with Steno on Freedom* (November 27/December 7, 1677), A VI, 4-B, 1378 and 1379.
120. *On the Omnipotence of God*, §16, A VI, 1, 543 .
121. Ibid., §17, A VI, 1, 544; Sleigh, 21.
122. *On the Omnipotence of God*, §18, A VI, 1, 544; Sleigh, 23.
123. Cf. *On the Omnipotence of God*, §18, A VI, 1, 544.
124. *On the Omnipotence of God*, §18, A VI, 1, 544; Sleigh, 23.
125. *On the Omnipotence of God*, §18, A VI, 1, 544; Sleigh, 23.
126. *On the Omnipotence of God*, §18, A VI, 1, 545; Sleigh, 23.
127. *Positions* (1685–1686), A VI, 4-C, 2351; T §§30–31.

128. *Dialogue on Human Freedom and the Origin of Evil* (1695), Grua, 364; AG 114. T §33; §153.
129. See section 6.2.1.
130. *On the Omnipotence of God*, §19, A VI, 1, 545–546.
131. Cf. Leibniz to Hobbes (July 13/23, 1670), A II, 1, 91.
132. *Of Liberty and Necessity*, 250. Instead of two garments, Leibniz uses the example of two paintings in *The Author of Sin*, A VI, 3, 151; Sleigh, 111.
133. *Of Liberty and Necessity*, 278.
134. Leibniz to Magnus Wedderkopf, A II, 1, 186.
135. *On the Omnipotence of God*, §19, A VI, 1, 545; Sleigh, 23.
136. Cf. *On the Omnipotence of God*, §19, A VI, 1, 545; Sleigh, 23–24: "the will arises from the apparent good and this, in turn, from other circumstances as an effect from its perfect cause."
137. See *Of Liberty and Necessity*, 240.
138. Ibid., 274–275.
139. Cf. ibid., 246: "*That* which I say *necessitateth and determinateth every action . . . is the sum of all things, which being now existent, conduce and concur to the production of that action hereafter, whereof if any one thing now were wanting, the effect could not be produced.*"
140. Cf. ibid., 240: "I acknowledge this *liberty*, that I *can* do if I *will*; but to say, I can *will* if I *will*, I take to be an absurd speech." See also *Human Nature*, XII, §5, EW IV, 69: "*Appetite, fear, hope*, and the rest of the passions are *not* called *voluntary*; for they proceed *not from*, but are the *will*; and the will is not voluntary; for, a man can no more say he will will, than he will will will, and so make an infinite repetition of the word [will]; which is absurd and insignificant." See Leibniz to Wedderkopf, A II, 1, 187. Hobbes and Leibniz are here in agreement with Luther, according to whom man "cannot by his own powers omit, restrain, or change, but he keeps on willing and being ready. . . . This is what we call the necessity of immutability: It means that the will cannot change itself and turn in a different direction, but is rather the more provoked into willing by being resisted, as its resentment shows. This would not happen if it were free or had free choice" (*On the Bondage of the Will*, Preface, 139 [WA, vol. 18, 634]).
141. Leibniz to Wedderkopf, A II, 1, 187 (L 227); Leibniz to Fabri (beginning of 1677), A II, 1, 463: "Unde alius mea sententia gravissimus et periculosissimus ejus error nascitur, quod Bonitas pendeat a libero Dei arbitrio, non a natura rei."
142. Leibniz to Wedderkopf, 186 (L, 226). The adjective *fatalis* is a juridical term: "The terms prescribed by the laws are known among lawyers as *fatalia*" (T §57; GP VI, 134; Huggard, 154).
143. Leibniz to Wedderkopf, 186 (L 227).
144. Ibid., 186–187.
145. See respectively, *On the Bondage of the Will*, 281 [WA, vol. 18, 747]: "Whether God permits or turns, neither the permitting nor the turning takes place without God's willing and working; for the will of the king [Solomon] cannot escape the action of Almighty God, because everyone's will, whether it is good or evil, is impelled by it to will and to do"; *Of Liberty and Necessity*, 250: "I find no difference between the *will* to have a thing done, and the *permission* to do it, when he that permitteth can hinder it, and knows that it will be done unless he hinder it."
146. Leibniz to Wedderkopf, 186 (L 227).
147. Ibid. See also Leibniz to Conring (February 8, 1671), A II, 1, 131.

148. Cf. *Plan of Catholic Demonstrations*, A VI, 1, 499, ch. 51: "*Deus* seu Mens Universali nihil aliud est quam rer. Harmonia, seu principium pulchritudinis in ipsis"; Leibniz to Arnauld (November 1671), A II, 1, 280.
149. Leibniz to Wedderkopf, 186 (L 227).
150. *Elements of Natural Law*, A VI, 1, 460; *On the Omnipotence of God*, §10, A VI, 1, 540.
151. Leibniz to Wedderkopf, 187 (L 228) .
152. Ibid.
153. Ibid. The same idea is developed in the letter to Duke John Frederick (October 1671), A II, 1, 265: "I can likewise demonstrate that an ultimate reason for things, or Universal Harmony, that is to say, God must exist; that the latter is not the cause of sin, and that nevertheless sins by punishing themselves and recompensing themselves by punishment, conform to the Universal Harmony, just as shadows and dissonance render paintings and melodies respectively more pleasant."
154. Leibniz to Wedderkopf, 187 (L 228).
155. A VI, 1, 156.
156. *Of Liberty and Necessity*, 249.
157. Ibid., 250–251.
158. Cf. *On the Bondage of the Will*, Preface, 139 [WA, vol. 18, 634]: "Now, by 'necessarily' [*necessario*] I do not mean 'compulsorily' [*coacte*] but by the necessity of immutability (as they say) and not of compulsion." This distinction allows Luther to affirm that man sins, not by compulsion and in spite of himself, but willingly, while at the same maintaining that it is absolutely impossible for him to change or eliminate his sinful volition.
159. Leibniz to Wedderkopf, 187 (L 565, note 127).

# CHAPTER 2

# The *Confession of a Philosopher*

## Divine Justice and the Necessity of Sin

## 2.1 GOD AS *GROUND*, BUT NOT *AUTHOR* OF EVIL

### 2.1.1 Justice as Universal Love

Our examination of the texts preceding the *Confession of a Philosopher* has shown that while the young Leibniz's thinking was marked by the influence of Luther and Hobbes, it is distinguished from them by three theses: (1) The will, whether divine or human, is always determined by consideration of the best; (2) The best is not freely established by God, but expresses an eternal and immutable order; (3) This eternal and uncreated order encompasses all essences, truths and rules of justice, whose concept is univocal. This allows for the possibility of a universal jurisprudence. In opposition to Hobbes's voluntarism, Leibniz defends the priority of the understanding, while agreeing with him as to the absolute necessity of all things: of God's action as well as that of his creatures. The most perfect liberty consists in being constrained to follow the best as represented by reason.[1] The *Confession of a Philosopher* will confirm this priority of the understanding—a priority that will exonerate God by showing that his will plays no part in sin. In other words, God is the *ground* of sin without thereby being its *author*. However, two considerations lead Leibniz first to moderate his necessitarianism, at least with regard to what might seem shocking in its formulation, and in later texts to abandon it altogether: on the one hand, the greater and greater role assigned to the concept of possibility, and on the other hand, the desire to block any justification of God that would render sin necessary.

The *Confession of a Philosopher* is a dialogue between a philosopher and a theologian, written in Latin, probably between the autumn of 1672 and the beginning of 1673 when Leibniz was in Paris. The text, which may have been sent to Arnauld, was submitted to Nicolas Steno, the vicar Apostolic in Hanover, in 1677. Steno's remarks, together with Leibniz's replies, can be seen in the margins of the manuscript. According to the editors of the Academy edition, these remarks and replies—along with a corrected version of the final part of the dialogue—can be dated to the end of 1677 or beginning of 1678. However, it would be wrong to think that all the theses of the dialogue accurately reflect Leibniz's thought up until 1678 and that Leibniz accepted them entirely and without reservation up to that time. As we shall see, the texts from the period of *De summa rerum* (1676) provide clear evidence of an evolution of Leibniz's theory relative to the dialogue.[2]

The *Confession of a Philosopher* is a direct descendent of the earlier texts and is based on them insofar as it presupposes that the existence of God and the immortality of the soul have been demonstrated.[3] The title recalls the *Confession of Nature Against Atheists* of which it is in some sense a companion piece and continuation.[4] For it is not enough to prove, as a physicist, the existence of God by nature. It must also be shown, as metaphysician and moralist, that this being that is the origin of all things governs the republic of spirits with wisdom and goodness, despite the existence of evil. The two "confessions" share the same goal; they aim to oppose the atheism and impiety abetted by those naturalists (*naturalistæ*),[5] who claim to explain all natural phenomena without reference to God and by those who criticize providence in light of the apparent disorder in the world. Leibniz's constant goal is to silence the atheist and skeptic, but also to move beyond theological antagonism toward religious unity.

In fact, the dialogue pursues the task that Leibniz had set for himself in the *Catholic Demonstrations*, namely, to lay the foundations of a philosophical theology (*Philosophi Theologia*[6]), that is, a rational theology that can be accepted by all independently of confessional differences. This theology of reason is the necessary precondition of the reunification of the churches. It is a properly (and perhaps the only truly) *catholic* theology—in the sense of being the most universal and, consequently, comprising what is most certain in these matters. It is for this reason that at the end of the dialogue the philosopher expresses the hope of witnessing the end of all controversies and affirms the continuity and agreement of faith with reason, while condemning the excesses of a science that would spurn religion and of a religion that would reject philosophy.[7]

However, before this theological and philosophical peace can be established, one must first deal with the "thorny topic of *the justice of God*." For as the theologian observes, "nothing is opposed to providence more frequently or speciously than the disorder of things."[8] The philosopher intends to show that God is just in accordance with the following definition: "He is *just* who loves everyone."[9] This definition of justice in terms of love—a universal love directed at all spirits—was developed by Leibniz as a result of his work on natural law during the years 1670–1671. As I have shown elsewhere,[10] Leibniz has moved from a concept inspired by Aristotle, according to which justice is the golden mean between self-interest and the good of others, to a conception of justice as charity in which the good of the other is integrated into and identified with one's own good. Whereas so-called mercenary justice consists in willing the good of another insofar as it serves our own, true justice consists, on the contrary, in willing the good of the other for its own sake, as an end and not as a means.[11] Leibniz's "discovery," as he termed it, was to have realized that this demand of justice (to seek the good of the other for its own sake) is the same as that required by true love. This reveals the fundamental nature of justice: it is a kind of love. For, to love is nothing other than to take pleasure in the good of another.[12] The demonstration is summarized as follows in the *Elements of Natural Law*:

> Since justice, therefore, demands that we seek the good of others in itself, and since to seek the good of others in itself is to love them, it follows that love is of the nature of justice. *Justice* will therefore be the habit of loving others (or of seeking the good of others in itself and of taking delight in the good of others), as long as this can be done prudently (or as long as this is not a cause of greater pain).[13]

It is clear that this love, which leads one to promote the good of all "as necessarily as a stone falls" is not performed blindly, without moderation, without considering the quality of the beloved and without preferring to aid some over others.[14] Reason must regulate and guide love in order for it to become justice. As it is neither possible, nor equitable, to satisfy everyone at the same time and in the same manner, the just man must be wise. That is, he must possess the knowledge that will enable him to make the best choice in order to obtain the greatest good overall. Thus, as Leibniz observed to Arnauld,

> If the benefits of several people interfere with each other, that person is to be preferred from whose help the greater good in the end follows. Hence in case of conflict, other things being equal, the better man, that is, the one who loves more generally [*publici amantiorem*], is to be preferred.[15]

In the case of competing loves, the rule is not to give equally to each but to favor the one who already has possessions, the one whose situation (social, financial[16]) is the most advantageous or the least disadvantageous, the one who is wisest (power and wealth being equal), or the one most favored by God (wisdom being equal). For in this way, the benefits for the whole will be that much greater and so will profit others in turn.[17] To do good means to multiply, not add (whereas to do evil, by contrast, is to divide), as shown by the mathematical example of two numbers, the one greater than the other. When multiplied by the same number, the result is greater in the case of the greater of the two numbers.[18]

In introducing a calculus into justice to regulate conflicts between benefit and harm to others, but also between my benefit and harm and that of others, Leibniz is not content to repeat the traditional image of the prudent man taken from Aristotle nor that of the good man (charged with the task of deciding in cases undefined or unforeseen by the law) taken from Roman jurisconsults. The "good or just" man as Leibniz envisages him is considered from a much larger perspective: for he is the one who knows [*pernoscens*], who possesses the "knowledge [*scientia*] of the good,"[19] which encompasses the whole universe. One cannot truly know an individual thing without knowing the whole of which it is a part.[20] Beyond the determination of such perplexing cases, and the better to resolve them, the calculus is motivated by the search for what is best for the whole at the global level. Justice is at once the love of everyone and the understanding of the universal harmony of which God is the principle. It is not simply a middle ground (the mean between two affects), nor the evaluation of a mean between two *maxima*, but a maximal striving for the good, exercised in accordance with a hierarchy based on the perfection of the object and what is best for the whole. It is properly speaking the *charity of the wise man*—even if the term would not appear until 1677[21]—who takes up the general point of view.

In the *Confession of a Philosopher* Leibniz builds on the results of his investigations into the essence of justice. The union of love and wisdom in justice allows us to understand the sense in which God is said to be just and can be justified with regard to the existence of evil. The demonstration can be summarized as follows: God is delighted by harmony (which is "similarity in variety, that is, diversity compensated by identity"[22]). To be delighted is nothing other than "experiencing" or "perceiving" harmony.[23] Therefore, the happiness ("the most agreeable state") of spirits is harmonious. God, who has knowledge of happiness (since he is omniscient), delights in it. Now, to love is to delight in the happiness of others. So God loves all spirits. Therefore, he is just. The biblical promise, that God wishes all to be saved, is therefore demonstrated.

So why then are some damned? Love extends to all, but it consists nonetheless of degrees in accordance with the nature and qualities of the creature considered, and the demands of universal harmony. In the *Elements of Natural Law* and his letter to Arnauld of November 1671, Leibniz had already made clear that love differs in quantity or intensity according to its object. He had also laid out the rules to be followed in case of conflict with regard to the assistance to be given to each one. These rules apply equally to God, even if we are ignorant of the particular reasons why he prefers one spirit to another, and accords his grace to one while refusing it to another. God loves all spirits, though some more than others. Thus, even the damned are beloved by God, though to a lesser degree than the elect. The universal love of God (who cannot, properly speaking, "hate" anyone, since hatred is an evil and a weakness) is therefore compatible with the damnation of some. For election is nothing other than a preference, or better, a greater love. Reprobation is a lesser, inferior love.[24]

However, the explanation would not be complete without showing why God cannot love all spirits equally. The explanation lies in the nature of universal harmony. The universe is like a beautiful painting in which the brilliancy of the colors results from the contrast with the shadows, or again, like beautiful music whose harmony is all the more pleasing for following upon dissonance. Such comparisons had been commonplaces for justifying the existence of evil since the time of the Stoics. However, Leibniz's use of them to prove God's universal love, and therefore his justice, is original. Clearly God could only love all spirits equally and to the same degree, if they were all equal in perfection. Now if that had been the case, the world would not have had the diversity and variety that render it harmonious; everything in it would have been identical and uniform. Therefore, there must be those who are damned. Harmony, which God contemplates in its totality and which is the source of his pleasure, requires the variety of goods and evils, the diversity of states and perfections, and so, justifies God's differentiated and unequal love. Here a second scriptural teaching finds its explanation in reason: many are called, but few are chosen.

## 2.1.2 Physical Concurrence with Sin: God as First Member of the Universal Series

In the first stage of the dialogue, the notion of justice under consideration is that of a *perfection*[25] that is, the attribute of supreme goodness, by which

God wills and brings about the good of his creatures—i.e., loves them. However, this divine love raises difficulties, if we now consider justice in the sense of *law*. Indeed, God's conduct appears unjust on three levels:

1. With regard to *predestination*. God appears partial, and therefore, inequitable in the distribution of his gifts and grace, since as the apostle Paul said, "from the same clay, he brings forth some vessels intended for honor, others intended for disgrace."[26]
2. By his *concurrence* with evil. God appears not only as the promoter of sin (*fautor peccati*), which he foresaw and yet did not prevent, but also as its author, since he did everything necessary to bring it about.
3. With regard to *retribution*, there is a twofold difficulty. God punishes in the sinner a sin, of which God himself is the author and rewards the just, who is just only by the gift of God's grace. On the other hand, if there is no free will, if everything is necessary, God punishes a sin that the sinner could not have failed to commit. As a result, the system of sanctions appears doubly unjust.

In sum, the responsibility of God, who is the ultimate reason of all things, is fully implicated at every level, from one end of the chain of causes to the other, since he creates those he destines for damnation, leads them to sin, and punishes them for crimes they could not have failed to commit.

Here we have precisely the same difficulties raised in 1671 in *On the Omnipotence of God* and left largely unresolved. It is true that Leibniz had shown that the necessity of an act does not render its punishment illegitimate (nor its reward, if the act was good). Likewise, the letter to Magnus Wedderkopf had shown the possibility of reconciling freedom with necessity. However, it arrived at the shocking conclusion that sins are necessary and *good* (taken together with their punishment, to be sure). As the theologian remarks, these difficulties concerning God's justice follow from the use of the Principle of Sufficient Reason. According to this principle:

> nothing ever exists unless it is possible (at least for one who is omniscient) to assign a sufficient reason why it exists rather than not, and why it is thus and not otherwise.[27]

Whatever does not contain within itself the reason of its own existence must receive it from something else, which must itself (if it does not contain its reason within itself) receive it from another, and so on. The ascent from reason to reason can end only with a being that exists of itself and possesses within itself its reason for being—an absolutely first cause. Such a being is God, without whom the whole series of causes simply could not exist. Hence the paradox: the same principle (the Principle of Sufficient Reason) that makes possible the demonstration of the existence of God can also be used to show that God is the source of evil, and so seems to destroy his justice. For in the explanation of sin, one must likewise ascend from cause to cause all the way up to God, as the example of Judas illustrates (and the case of Pilate had already made clear in the letter to Magnus Wedderkopf[28]).

> Sin comes from ability and will. Ability comes from God, will from opinion. Opinion comes at the same time from the temperament of the person with the opinion and the object of the opinion. Both of those come from God; therefore, all the requisites of sin come from God. The ultimate ground for sin, like everything else, and hence even for damnation, is God.[29]

The ultimate ground of the world contains all that is required for sin, that is, "that without which the thing cannot exist." For, the collection of all requisites of a given thing is its complete cause.[30]

It is certain that, for Leibniz, the validity of the Principle of Sufficient Reason is incontestable. Therefore, it must be allowed that God is the ultimate cause of sin. However, this does not mean that he *wills* sin. He is the *ground* of sin—as he is of everything created—in that he is the first member of the series of things that constitutes the world. However, he is not the *author* of sin by his will, which tends only to the good. The distinction between *ground* and *author* affords a solution to the difficulty, by giving rise to the following paradoxical justification: evil exists because God exists (and cannot be other than he is), and not because God wills it. In fact,

> if God is taken away, so is the entire series of things, and if God is posited, so is the entire series of things, including those created things that were and those that will be, the good and evil acts of creatures, and, accordingly, their sins. Nevertheless, I deny that sins arise from the divine will.[31]

The solution consists in distinguishing between two kinds of causality. A thing can be a cause by its will or by its being, that is, its nature. God is the cause of sin only by his being, because he is—or rather because his understanding is—the universal harmony. Now the laws of universal harmony, which require the existence of evil, do not depend on God's will, since he can in no way change them. Rather, like truths and essences, these laws are uncreated and eternal. Therefore, sin cannot be attributed to his will, but only to his understanding, or what amounts to the same thing, to his existence, since harmony exists only because God exists (and thinks it). Must we then conclude that God is not omnipotent since he cannot eradicate evil? He cannot eliminate or prevent it without changing the nature of things, that is to say, without changing his own essence and causing himself to be other than he is. But this is strictly impossible.

The Principle of Sufficient Reason, which seems at first glance to accuse God of evil, serves in the end to exonerate him. Sin exists because God exists, but God is innocent of sin, because its origin lies in his understanding and not in his will. For only the will (to evil) renders one culpable. As the theologian summarizes the point:

> Sins occur to bring forth a universal harmony of things, thus distinguishing the light by means of shadows. However, the universal harmony is a result not of the will of God but the intellect of God, or of the idea, that is, the nature of things. Therefore sins are to be ascribed to the same thing; accordingly, sins follow from the existence of God, not the will of God.[32]

In Scholastic terminology, God is the *physical* cause of sin but not the *moral* cause. He contributes everything to its occurrence, but not by his will. He produces the physical reality of the act, but not its malignity, of which the sinner alone is the author—that is, the voluntary cause. Judas sinned because he could—an ability that came from God—and because he so willed, "because he [Judas] judged it good."[33]

This justification of God calls for three remarks:

1. The use of Scholastic terminology should not mislead us. Leibniz is not now embracing what he rejected at the time of *On the Omnipotence of God*, namely the division of concurrence with sin. Leibniz makes clear that he is reinterpreting the Scholastic thesis and giving it an acceptable meaning. He maintains that those who affirmed that the substance of the act—but not its evil—exists by God failed to explain "how it is that the evil does not result from the act."[34] For Leibniz, the distinction between physical cause and moral cause is acceptable only on condition that it corresponds exactly with the distinction between ground and author. Otherwise, it leads to confusion, as Leibniz would also make clear in a contemporary text entitled *The Author of Sin*.[35]
2. Leibniz agrees with Hobbes, who also appeals to the distinction between author and cause, to show that God is not the author of sin in the sense that "*Author*, is he which owneth an action, or giveth a warrant to do it," but rather its *cause*, as indeed he is the cause "of all actions and motions."[36] However, Leibniz's agreement with the English philosopher

remains superficial, since the justification of God rests, for Leibniz, on his conception of universal harmony, the idea of which is not created by God and expresses what is in itself best.

3. Leibniz's justification of God is ingenious. However, it turns on ascribing the same status to sin (and to every event of the world) as to mathematical truths. As a result, any distinction between contingent truths and necessary truths is implicitly abolished. The whole line of argument consists in demonstrating that the existence of sin in the universal harmony is as necessary—and independent of the divine will—as the proposition "3 x 3 = 9" or "the diagonal of a square is incommensurable with its side." Evil is in the nature of things, and it is as impossible for God to eliminate it, as it is for him to make 3 x 3 = 10! Evil appears necessary for two reasons: on the one hand, insofar as its existence is absolutely required by the universal harmony, which presupposes the coexistence of contraries, and, on the other hand, insofar as its elimination would result in not only another world but also another God (which is contradictory).

> It is no more possible that from the same ground—and a ground sufficient and entire, such as God is with respect to the universe—there should result opposed consequences, that is, that diverse things should follow from the same thing, than it is possible that the same thing should be different from itself.[37]

The distinction between *ground* and *author* leads to locating God in the series of things and identifying him with its first member. It likewise results in positing a perfect solidarity and perfect dependence of these things *among themselves*—such that no one of them can be different from what it is without all the others being different as well—*and with the first member*, such that no member can be modified without the first member also being changed, and that the first member itself cannot be different from what it is without all others being different as well. If God is posited, this universe containing sin exists *to the exclusion of any other universe*. Otherwise, God would not be its sufficient and complete reason. Conversely, if this universe containing sin were to be altered, or the least of its events eliminated, God himself would be altered or eliminated. The relation is conceived as a logical relation on the model of *modus ponens* and *modus tollens*: God is to the world as the antecedent of a hypothetical proposition is to its consequent (*If A exists, then B exists*), so that by contraposition the negation of the consequent implies the negation of the antecedent (*If B does not exist, A does not exist*). Yvon Belaval correctly notes that the term "series" is used to designate the chain of things, in conformity with Stoic usage. However, the comparison he makes with the mathematical notion of a series is more questionable.[38] In this context the term "series" refers rather to the idea of a relation of order[39] in which no term can be substituted for another, since each one occupies a determinate position, as determined by the law that grounds the series. If even a single element were replaced or modified, the ground of the entire series would thereby be altered.

It is astonishing to consider—compared to what would be argued in the *Theodicy*—that at no point in his demonstration does Leibniz appeal to the divine will to explain the universe coming into existence. Nor does he mention other series of possible things. On this point, Steno raises the following objection: if God is posited, then the whole series of things is, of course, posited, but only insofar as it is possible, not insofar as it actually exists. Leibniz's reply emphasizes, on the contrary, God's necessary relation to the world:

> It is just as if he were to say that God is not the sufficient cause of things. Series of other things are possible in themselves, but they are not compatible with divine wisdom.[40]

Further on in the text, Steno objects that Leibniz's argument is logically faulty: it is not true that if A (God) exists, B (our world) also exists, except as possible and in the same manner as C or D (other possible series), and so forth. Thus, if A is posited, the whole series of things possible "in God's idea" is posited. However, "it does not follow necessarily that this series rather than that series is posited in reality outside of the ideas, or even that any is posited."[41] Pressed somewhat by the objection, Leibniz finally appeals to the divine will and the grounds of existence of *this* series of things:

> The series is not posited because God is posited, except for the fact that God, who is the most wise being, wills nothing but the best. All possible series are in the idea of God, but only one under the aspect of the best.[42]

These two responses by Leibniz, dated—let us remember—probably from the end of 1677 to the beginning of 1678, make the necessity by which God chooses the best series into an absolute necessity, in conformity with what is asserted in the letter to Wedderkopf. Everything that exists is necessary, was necessarily chosen by God, and is the best.

This "optimistic" necessitarianism is original with Leibniz on two counts. On the one hand, as we have seen, because it identifies that which is necessary with the best, conceived as what is best in itself and not best because it derives from the divine will and power. Leibnizian necessity is not identical with chance or blind fate, but is the necessity of the most beautiful and rational order. On the other hand, because this necessitarianism does not exclude the possible, nor identify it, as Hobbes had done following Diodorus, with what is actual.[43] For Leibniz the possible is that which can be clearly and distinctly conceived and defined without contradiction.[44] A thing may be possible without ever existing, just as numerical relations are real, even if no one were ever to think of them or perform the calculation. Thus, Leibniz does not maintain that nothing could or can occur other than what has and will occur. Rather, his view is that although there were many other series of things that were possible in themselves (that is, conceivable without contradiction), they were not compatible with God *such as he is*. Only one was so compatible, and it is precisely the one that exists.

It should be noted that consideration of these other possible universal series does not render the chain of causes and effects in the existing series any less necessary. Leibniz's conception of the possible at the time of the *Confession of a Philosopher* could be characterized as "weak," since it serves to designate *negatively* everything that was not and could not be chosen by God (being incompatible with his wisdom), rather than to show the contingency of the world (as will be the case with the conception of the possible we shall call "strong"[45]). Of course, this necessitarianism is compatible with freedom and in no way justifies the Lazy Sophism.[46] Nor does it call into question the legitimacy of punishments and rewards. Nevertheless, it does raise two major problems:

1. It tends to eliminate the role of the will. If God is posited, his will to choose this world is thereby posited. Or rather, this series of things, which contains evil, exists, not because God wills it, but because he *exists*. It is not so much a question of choice as of the necessary consequences of the being for itself, who by his very existence, causes this world to exist. As a corollary, the act of creation (in general) and the particular act of creating this series rather than any other, which are completely necessitated, are indistinguishable. Their distinction (as Steno points out[47]) would have made it possible to demonstrate the twofold contingency of the world: God might have created nothing and, in deciding to create a world, might have created some world other than ours. At the time of the *Confession of a Philosopher*, the divine will does not enter the picture as a positive faculty of choice between various possibilities—a faculty that (with the aid of the creative power) brings the possible into existence. Rather, it is the universal harmony

that plays this role, insofar as it is the "determiner (*determinatrix*) of the existence of things."[48] Defined as delight in the existence of each thing in particular and in the harmony of the whole,[49] the will appears as passive consent, an acquiescence in what is (and what necessarily follows from God's existence), rather than as that exertion that brings the world into being. It is as if, far from inspiring the creative act, the will comes after it, to approve and rejoice in it. Here again God appears more as the physical than moral cause of the world—a weakness that we have already seen in the notes on Stahl.[50] God is a *ground* rather than *author*, a prime mover and origin of all things, rather than creator.

2. This necessitarianism does not place God outside the series of things but, on the contrary, makes him its first member. As we have seen, this connection excludes the existence of any beings or events other than those that are or have been, in consideration of the principle that different effects cannot follow from the same cause. Nevertheless, it does not make God dependent on creation, since the causal priority remains (the series derives from the divine cause as an effect), but rather like Hobbes's God, the "first link" of an incalculable number of concatenations of causes,[51] or again to Spinoza's God, from whom all things follow necessarily. Such a view carries two dangerous consequences:

   a. It would seem that all things, and not merely sins, must be referred not to God's will, but to his nature—that is, to the universal harmony (as the theologian in the dialogue observes). This seems to license the characterization of God as lacking a will and to make of him a mere physical rather than moral cause. In that case, there would be nothing to prevent the identification of God and nature, or a pure power indifferent to good and evil, and to conclude that the universe is not governed by any intellect whom we must honor and to whom we should give thanks for the goods we receive.

   b. All sins are necessary, as are all things that follow from God's existence.

Examination of these two difficulties will open up a new frontier in the discussion of God's justice, by moving it into the domain of God's moral concurrence (by virtue of his will) with the actions of creatures and by inquiring whether such actions are free. It is in this context that Leibniz will reintroduce the notion of permission and the Scholastic distinction between two kinds of necessity (absolute and hypothetical).

## 2.2  PERMISSION OF EVIL AND THE DISTINCTION OF TWO KINDS OF NECESSITY: A LIMITED REHABILITATION

### 2.2.1  Moral Concurrence: Will and Permission

The notion of permission that Leibniz had explicitly rejected in *On the Omnipotence of God* was only partially rehabilitated in the letter to Wedderkopf. One has the sense that Leibniz was still very reluctant to make use of it in the *Confession of a Philosopher*. Indeed, he is much more willing to use synonyms such as "tolerate" (*tolerare*) and "admit" (*admittere*), and he at first employs the term "permit" only in negative constructions, to say that God does not *permit* the entire series of things but wills it.[52] However, Leibniz cannot entirely forgo the term in explaining the relation of God's will to evil and accounting for his moral concurrence with the sins of his creatures.

Given the primacy of the understanding, what role is played by the will? Leibniz is clearly seeking to avoid two extreme theological positions: the notion of a God whose will is arbitrary (Hobbes, Descartes) and determines itself independently of the understanding and any consideration of the best ("what leads someone to will is never his willing to will but rather his believing that the thing merits it"[53]); and, conversely, the notion of an indifferent God, whose will plays no role in the events of the world (Epicurus), or indeed of a God who lacks both reason and will and is identical with fate and the necessity of things (Spinoza). Once again, Leibniz's solution rests on the distinction between *ground* and *author*. God is the ground of all things, both good and bad, by his nature, but strictly speaking, he is the author (i.e., wills) only of goods. Good things exist because God exists and wills them (that is, he delights in their existence). Sins exist because God exists and permits them—that is, he neither wills in favor of nor against them, knowing as he does that they are part of the universal harmony.[54] In Scholastic terminology, God is the physical cause of goods and evils but the moral cause only of goods. He does not will sins considered in isolation and taken by themselves. In other words, he does not delight in their existence and would even delight in their nonexistence. However, he allows them insofar as they enter into the most perfect universal harmony as inevitable consequences and are compensated by greater goods:

> [T]herefore, he tolerates or admits them, although he would have eliminated them if only, absolutely speaking, it were possible to do so, that is, to choose another series of things that is better without those evils.[55]

Thus, God is indeed a being endowed with intelligence and will. He is not reducible to brute necessity. However, it must be recognized that his will remains fundamentally subordinate, determined (even perfectly necessitated), and passive. On the one hand, it does not will what it shall will (according to the principle that one cannot will to will[56]) but rather consents to what the understanding represents to it as best (which the will cannot change). On the other hand, the will is not that which chooses or brings things into existence in collaboration with divine power. Rather, it is the pleasure that results from considering the existence of the universal harmony.[57] As a kind of awareness and approval of the good, it consists in the perception of pleasure.[58] It is the experience of harmony (according to the very definition of "to be delighted"[59]) and ultimately is indistinguishable from love itself. To will is to delight in the existence of each individual being and in the best that resides in the whole; with regard to the good of spirits, it is to love.

How can this passivity of the will be reconciled with the definition of *author*, which is to be the ground of a thing "by one's will," which seems to imply an efficient cause? God is the author of the good, because he is its cause not only by virtue of his existence but also by virtue of his will, since he delights in it. The will, then, is a cause in the sense of a *final* cause. For God's happiness is the end of universal harmony. Realization of universal harmony is the efficient cause of the greatest pleasure, which is, in turn, its final cause. The will, which is identified with the pleasure itself, is the end and not the means. It is not the effort, the positive tendency toward the best. Rather, it is the effect and the sign in the perceiver of its realization. As Leibniz here characterizes it, the will is, in a sense, that which expresses God's judgment in the first chapter of Genesis when on the sixth day, upon seeing what he has made, God declares that it is "very good."

Thus, the will is reduced to a passive adherence to what exists, to the delight in contemplating the world as it exists and which, being necessary, it cannot alter. Although the will rejects sin, which considered in itself causes displeasure, it can in no way eradicate it, but must accept it as the inevitable correlate of the best in the whole. The Leibnizian doctrine of permission reinforces this rather restrictive conception of the role of the will.

In the theological tradition dating back to Augustine, the doctrine of permission seeks to resolve the following dilemma: God, owing to his goodness, cannot will sin in itself. However, it cannot be said that God wills against it absolutely, since it exists—unless we suppose that he cannot do what he wills, which would be to deny his omnipotence.[60] Therefore, he *permits* sin, but only insofar as it is the precondition of obtaining a greater good elsewhere.[61] Leibniz makes use of the word "permission" while making clear that it is one of those terms inherited from the Scholastics, which it would probably be better to forgo altogether, and which in any case must be used with caution and treated as superfluous and captious, since they frequently lead to error.[62] He retains the idea that evil cannot be willed as such, but is nevertheless allowed for an end extrinsic to it, namely universal harmony.[63] Nevertheless, Leibniz's conception of permission is original in that he conceives of it as knowledge in the understanding of rather than an act of will. To permit sin is neither to will it directly nor indirectly, whether absolutely or relatively. Nor is it to will against it. Permission is neither complicity (indirect participation in evil) nor a resigned acceptance of what cannot be avoided, which occurs in spite of oneself.[64] Rather, it is a form of suspension or neutralization of the will. It falls within the domain of knowledge, not will. Therefore, to permit sin is neither to delight in its existence nor to be pained by it (otherwise God would be imperfect), but to know that it pertains to the best series of things where it is counterbalanced by a greater good. This knowledge (which is just God's omniscience) moderates, so to speak, the repugnance that God naturally has for sin. His hatred of sin softens into permission. God ceases to will against it, without for all that willing it positively. His point of view "changes" by shifting from consideration of the part (the evil, which he does not will) to that of the whole (universal harmony, which he does will). Consideration of the whole wins out, since his pleasure comes from contemplation not of the parts considered in isolation (even if he delights in all individual goods), but of the whole, that is to say, the general harmony:

> because of this compensation, the dissonant in this mixture is made indifferent from what was displeasing, the permitted from what was rejected. Only the whole is pleasing, only the whole is harmonious, only the configuration, as it were, of the whole is a harmony.[65]

Is God in some sense indifferent, since he neither wills in favor nor wills against? The kind of indifference at issue here is not indifference of equilibrium, but a sort of *indifference of sentiment* that takes the form of a suspension of the will. God neither delights in nor is grieved by the existence of sin in the world. Owing to its occurrence in the universal harmony, evil becomes indifferent to God, who is in no way affected by it.

Once again, this justification of God consists in safeguarding his will by showing that it is not implicated in evil and by redirecting the "accusation" so that it falls on the nature of things and the demands of universal harmony. One attribute (the understanding, which contains the essences of things) serves to excuse another (the will). Not only does God not will sin, but even in permitting it, his permission is not volition nor is it even related to the will. His permission does not fall within the realm of the will at all. It is merely the knowledge of universal harmony in which God sees in advance that some good will arise out of the evil.

As we have seen, this explanation of God's moral concurrence with evil comes at the cost of a highly reductive concept of the will. It also suffers from the problem of presupposing in God an indifference to evil correlative to its permission. This supposition is problematic for several reasons. First, it seems difficult to maintain within a theoretical framework, which generally excludes every kind of indifference as implying an impossibility that violates the Principle of Sufficient Reason.[66] Second, it contradicts other assertions by Leibniz that suggest that God is never indifferent with regard to evil. God hates evil as such and is indifferent neither to its punishment nor to the delightful contemplation of universal harmony in which evil appears corrected and compensated. Finally, there remains a certain ambiguity in the text: whereas permission seems to be abstention, the philosopher in the dialogue declares: "[God] must be said to will the entire series, not permit it, *and the same* for sins also insofar as they are not considered distinctly by themselves but are considered mixed in with the entire series."[67] This amounts to the claim that God wills them, at least *per accidens*, insofar as they are annexed to the best series of things. Thus, we see the extent to which the term "permission" must be read with caution when used by Leibniz. In this respect, it is significant that the definition of "permission" offered by Leibniz in the *Confession of a Philosopher* is not repeated in subsequent texts. Ultimately, this notion of suspension of the will could not satisfy him, insofar as it portrays God as an idle, even indifferent, spectator rather than a moral agent who governs the world by an efficacious and constant concurrence.

### 2.2.2. The Two Kinds of Necessity and the Restrictive Conception of the Possible

It remains to be shown that sin is not necessary, or rather, in what sense we are to understand its necessity, which is that of all things that follow from God's existence. By appealing once again to the distinction between *absolute* and *hypothetical* necessity, Leibniz hopes to avoid two dangers, which are more practical than theoretical. The first is the danger of causing a scandal by advancing a proposition that shocks common sense and is liable to be misunderstood. The other is the danger of giving comfort to fatalism by supporting the Lazy Sophism. Leibniz's goal was to moderate the strict necessitarianism set out, in private, in the letter to Wedderkopf, or rather to prevent drawing conclusions that could prove ruinous in the religious and moral spheres. The assertion that sin, like the damnation of Judas, was necessary, could seem unduly harsh and shocking to pious souls. Yet, for all that, the assertion is no less true, if the meaning of the term "necessity" is correctly understood. Here again, one must avoid the ambiguities that can result from abuse of those terms inherited from the Scholastics: necessary, possible, impossible, contingent, and so forth. When invited by the theologian to make use of these terms, the philosopher agrees to do so, but he emphasizes that they are superfluous and subject to caution. This reluctance shows that Leibniz does not fully embrace the traditional distinction between what is necessary in itself and what is necessary *ex hypothesi*.[68] For Leibniz, this distinction is merely a way of expressing what he had already established without it. Rather than offering a complete rehabilitation, Leibniz merely expresses in Scholastic terms—suitably redefined—a thesis that had already been independently established.

Leibniz defines the necessary as "the opposite of which implies a contradiction or cannot be clearly conceived." He then provides the following example:

> Thus, it is necessary that three threes are nine, but it is not necessary that I speak or sin. For I can be conceived to be *myself* even if I am not conceived as *speaking*, but three threes which are conceived not to be nine are three threes which are not three threes, which implies a contradiction.[69]

Inconceivability or unintelligibility implies a contradiction and impossibility, just as a clear conception or intelligibility implies possibility. Like possibility and impossibility, necessity is a modality derived from the thing considered in itself. It is derived from the contemplation of its idea and not inferred extrinsically from consideration of the series of causes.[70] Therefore, it would be wrong to claim that everything that follows from the necessarily self-existent being (God) is, by that very fact, also necessary in itself (the series of things that constitutes the world). The absolute necessity of the cause does not imply the absolute necessity of the effect. A thing is necessary *absolutely* speaking, as in the case of God or geometrical truths, if and only if its necessity follows from its essence and it possesses within itself the ground of its existence or truth. It is the mark of created things that the ground of their existence lies precisely in something else, so that nothing prevents us from imagining that it might not have existed or might have been different than it is. It is only accidentally necessary—*ex hypothesi* or conditionally—that is, on condition that its cause is posited. It is made necessary by its cause but is not necessary in itself. As for things that are possible in themselves (that is, conceivable and non-contradictory), yet do not exist, they are only impossible *per accidens*, because the cause that would allow them to be produced is lacking, or because they are incompatible with the universal harmony and the existence of God.

Thus, the necessity of sin, and indeed of everything that exists in the world, must be understood as hypothetical and not absolute:

> On this basis it is established that it is not impossible, i.e., a contradiction in terms, that Judas be saved, even if it is true, certain, foreseen, necessary *per accidens*, i.e., follows from the harmony of things, that he never will be saved.[71]

In no way does this necessity breathe new life into the Lazy Sophism (the second practical consequence to be avoided, which is the result of a logical fallacy consisting in the omission of the condition in ordinary language[72]), since it implies a causal relation: the effect will not occur without its cause, and thus it is not true that it will occur "*whatever you do or don't do.*"[73] On the contrary, the effect is only necessary insofar as its cause is given. If an event were to occur out of absolute necessity, it would have to have been produced per se—that is, without a cause, which is absurd.

Does this distinction between two kinds of necessity suffice to establish the contingency of the world and of our acts? There is ample room for doubt. The distinction comes down to the difference between that which exists per se and that which exists *by a cause*. Here the contingency of a thing (either a being or an event) simply means its causal dependence. It follows from the fact that the thing requires a cause to exist and that this cause may be lacking, that the thing could fail to exist. Contingency is not demonstrated on the basis of other series of possible things that God could have chosen to create. In any case, the crux of Leibniz's reasoning does not rest on this argument. On the contrary, having posited the series of existing things as following from God's existence, it would seem that only one world is possible *ex hypothesi*—that is, *effectively* possible. To be sure Leibniz allows for other possible objects, insofar as they are clearly conceivable fictions that are not contradictory in themselves but are nevertheless contrary to existing things, to harmony, and to the existence of God. Such possible objects are comparable to the inventions of poets, such as Barclay's *Argenis*, who is "clearly and distinctly imaginable, even if it is quite certain that she never lived, nor do I believe that she will ever live."[74] This conception of the possible, which assimilates it to the merely fictional and denies it any reality, is not yet the one that will later prevail when Leibniz affirms that possible objects are "realized"[75] in God and endowed with a claim (*praetensio*) to existence. Despite its inadequacies, this "weak" conception of the possible allows Leibniz to distance himself from those who, following Hobbes, "call impossible (absolutely, i.e., per se) whatever neither was nor is nor will be"[76] or who, following the "heresy" defended by Descartes,[77] maintain that all possible things will eventually occur in some part of the universe.

Finally, and perhaps especially, it is not certain that the distinction between the two kinds of necessity is pertinent within the theological framework set out in the *Confession of a Philosopher*. According to this distinction and the corresponding distinction between two types of impossibility, the existence of a series of things different from ours is not impossible in itself, but only *ex hypothesi*, "by position" or "*per accidens*,"[78] because it is inconsistent with the existence of God. However, one might well question whether the existence of God is an accident. On the contrary, it is absolutely necessary. Must we then say that this possible thing could exist if God were other than he is or did not exist? Clearly not, for without God, all things would be impossible,[79] and God cannot fail to exist (since he is the *necessary being*) nor be other than he is. It would seem, then, that contradiction on the existential level (with the existence of God) entails an *essential* contradiction. Once the relation of God to the world is conceived as that of the first member to the series whose order it determines, and no series other than the best can be chosen without God being either nonexistent or other than he is (both of which are impossible), the inexistence of possible things is no longer contingent and accidental but absolutely necessary. This effectively destroys the very notion of the possible, which proves to be nothing but a pure chimera.

To avoid this consequence, which renders the distinction between that which is impossible *by essence* and that which is impossible *by existence* purely artificial,[80] if not pointless, and to provide a more solid foundation for the contingency of the world, God must be placed outside of the series and no longer be considered its first member. In that case, not only would other worlds be conceivable, but it will also be the case that God could create any one of them without thereby ceasing to be what he is. This major conceptual shift would require a reworking of the concept of the possible and a redefinition of the role of the will, to make it a real faculty of choice. Likewise, it would require deepening the distinction between the two kinds of necessity,[81] whose meaning and implications had been limited heretofore by the theology of the *Confession of a Philosopher*.

### 2.2.3 Human Freedom and the Predestination of Souls

The doctrine of permission attempts to show that God gives no moral concurrence to sin, since he neither wills for it nor wills against it, while the
distinction between two kinds of necessity seeks to establish that sin is not
necessary in itself but only *ex hypothesi* or *per accidens*. It follows from these
that God's concurrence with evil is only physical and that evil is contingent,
since it might not have occurred. But then, if God is not the author of sin,
who is? The devil and man, apparently—unless the arguments by which
God was exonerated will also serve to excuse sinful creatures. Such is the
risk that every attempted Theodicy must run: namely, that what works for
God works equally well for the sinner. Leibniz had already noted this risk in
*On the Omnipotence of God*.[82] To be sure, the devil and human beings do not
merely permit sin, but will it—that is, delight in it.[83] Thus, they are indeed
the authors of sin. But from where do they get their power and will? These
have external sources. They come from the present state of things, which
itself follows from previous states of the entire series of things, which in
turn follows from the universal harmony and the eternal ideas in the divine
understanding. If the ultimate ground of the will lies outside of the one
who wills, and if the will is not under the control of the will, is man responsible for what he wills and therefore for what he does? Is "his" will really
his and imputable to him? "No one voluntarily makes himself evil, otherwise he would already be evil before he made himself evil."[84] "No one is the
voluntary cause of his own will, for what someone wills to will, he already
wills, just as, according to the rule of law, 'he who is able to bring it about
that he is able, is already able.'"[85]

It would seem that the human will can be exonerated in exactly the
same way as the divine will, by referring the cause of evil to the nature of
things such as they were already contained as ideas in the divine understanding. What, then, becomes of human freedom "if we depend on external things, if they are what causes us to will, if a certain fatal connection
guides our thoughts no less than the turnings and collisions of atoms?"[86]
Man is no longer free; his will is the result of necessary causes that follow
strictly one from the other. Like God, man, though further down the
causal series, appears to be the physical cause of sin—its *ground*—but
not its moral cause—its true *author*. Not that he does not will sin or that
he merely permits it when he sins, but because he cannot fail to will it.
Therefore, the sinner is not guilty. Like an atom that is determined to act
by collisions originating from outside it, man is the plaything of fate, which
determines him.

Thus, the question of divine justice leads to that of human justice and to the problem of human freedom. The legitimacy of retributive justice and the general system of sanctions is here called into question. It must be shown that those who are punished are justly punished, because they are guilty—that is, because they are the authors of sin and not merely its ground. To carry out this task, Leibniz will appeal to the same definition of the will used in the discussion of divine justice, since he considers concepts and truths to be univocal—however, with this difference, that in man the will is directed to what *appears* good and harmonious, whereas in God it tends toward the true good and harmony. The will is dependent with regard to both its *end* and the *means*:

1. The will does not give itself its object. It cannot be *causa sui*. Otherwise it would be a *will to will* (whose ground would have to be sought in another will, and so on to infinity) and would presuppose freedom of indifference—that is, the ability to act or not act without reason or in spite of every reason.[87] But such a power is a pure chimera. Not only is it theoretically and practically impossible, it is not even desirable.[88] As Yvon Belaval correctly notes, for Leibniz, "the will is defined, not as a bare power of free choice, but as this same power in its subordinate relation to the understanding."[89] Every volition is a volition for something good or apparently good. Its object is always provided by the understanding (in the case of man, the apparent good "depends on the disposition of the percipient, the object, and the medium"[90]), such that it would be absolutely contradictory to conceive of a will to evil considered as such or that tends to the non-harmonious as non-harmonious.

2. The will is also determined with regard to the means, which actuate it:

> But having posited that we believe something good, it is not possible that we do not will it; having posited that we will it and at the same time that we know that the external aids are available, it is not possible that we do not act.[91]

From the judgment to the will and from knowledge of the means to action, the causal chain is necessary, in the sense of hypothetical necessity. Neither opinion nor belief, any more than the will itself, are under the control of the will. Once again Leibniz is in agreement with Hobbes, who bases the freedom—or more exactly, the independence—of individual conscience on this principle.[92] However, Leibniz maintains that the mind possesses a kind of indirect power over itself. For although we can neither will nor believe what we will, we can make use of our reason "to investigate [*indagare*] by the most ample use of reason what things are to be considered good"[93] and to use reflection and attention to avoid being deceived and sinning.[94]

However, will in man, as in God, is conceived as a passive consent rather than an act. It does not decide between good and evil. It is the faculty that *senses* (*sentire*) them, experiences them. It approves the good, in which it delights, and rejects evil, which it suffers. Here again, it does not initiate action, but follows it. For action in rational creatures is the result of freedom and not, properly speaking, of will.

Freedom, as distinct from both the understanding and the will, is still defined by its submission to reason, as at the time of the letter to Wedderkopf. It consists in the power to act in the light of knowledge. Leibniz explicitly borrows from Aristotle two fundamental characteristics: *spontaneity*, in the sense that the principle of action is in the agent rather than anything external, and *knowledge*. As Leibniz tells Steno, freedom is a particular kind of spontaneity: "rational spontaneity."[95] The mind is more free to the extent that (1) it is more spontaneous—that is, its acts follow from its nature and are affected as little as possible by external causes, and that (2) it is more capable of choice—that is, has more understanding.[96] It follows that freedom admits of degrees, on the one hand, because the spontaneity of individual minds (other than God) cannot be complete and is a function of the power of each one (*qua* physical cause); on the other hand, because it is relative to our knowledge and resides in the right use of reason—the "true root of freedom."[97] This makes us moral causes. For freedom to be perfect is for

> the intellect to be constrained by things to recognize true goods, and for the will to be constrained by the intellect to embrace them—to be unable to resist the truth, to receive pure rays from objects, not refracted or discolored by a cloud of passion.[98]

The view that freedom consists in right use of the understanding and will is wholly traditional. Less so is the conception of freedom as not only compatible with necessity, but when considered in its full perfection, as identical with it. As Leibniz would maintain in his discussion with Steno, "the greater the necessity, the greater the perfection."[99] Necessity serves as the model for conceiving freedom and, by contrast, revealing its defects. We would be more free to the extent that we acted like an absolutely necessary cause—that is, on the physical level, with the greatest possible *spontaneity* as that which exists per se possesses in itself its own ground and is determined by no external cause, and on the moral level, following that most extensive possible knowledge, such that the understanding never failed to recognize the true nor the will to follow the good. The more enlightened the understanding, the stronger the moral constraint placed upon the will, or rather, the less this constraint will be felt, since there will be less and less resistance (to truth or to the good) to overcome. The practice of virtue would become in some sense natural. Thus, among the elect and the blessed angels, "when they have become infallible,"[100] sin becomes almost impossible. In God it is absolutely contradictory. Freedom in its highest degree is absolute necessity itself.

This conception of freedom is still marked by a necessitarianism that the distinction between the two kinds of necessity has not fundamentally altered. Moreover, it appears insufficient to render the creature truly culpable for the sins it commits, since the ultimate reason for the evil volition always escapes the agent. Beyond his will lie the circumstances, temperament, education, company, misfortune, and so forth, all of which are the result of universal harmony. Thus, we are led back to God and the eternal ideas of things. Is not the sinner innocent of the crimes with which he is charged? This conclusion, which to this point had been formulated by the theologian only as a question, becomes a complaint in the mouth of the damned.[101] They accuse God of having caused them to be born and to live in a time and place and circumstance such that they could not avoid succumbing to sin and without any help to deliver them from it. Juridical terminology runs throughout the text. The terms *querimonia* and *querela* signify the complaint brought before the judge by those who believe they have been wronged and demand reparations. This recourse to justice is legally admissible by virtue of the Leibnizian thesis of univocity. Notice that this charge against God before the tribunal of reason brings us to a new stage in the argument. For the damned reproach God not only with being responsible for what they have willed and what they have done; they also hold him culpable for *what they are*, for having been born with an evil nature by which they were destined to sin. The accusation shifts from the act to their very being and takes us from the problem of freedom to the problem of predestination, which appears perfectly arbitrary. For God seems to have chosen by pure caprice to save some and condemn others to eternal death.

From a juridical point of view, the accusation is twofold: (i) God did not give a more perfect nature to the damned, did not prevent him from sinning, and denied him the grace that would have saved him despite having had the power to do so. In legal terms, God lacked what is called the Principle of Innocent Use and is even guilty of a "harm of omission" scarcely different from a "harm of commission."[102] (ii) God punishes the sinner for a crime of which he is the victim rather than the instigator. The true culprit is not who we thought. God is like a father "who procreated badly, who provided the worst education, who ought to be punished himself [yet] actually wishes to punish."[103]

The philosopher responds by appealing to the argument already set out in *On the Omnipotence of God*: in punishing, the judge (whether human, as in a trial, or divine, as in the Last Judgment) only considers the will of the sinner and takes no account of the infinity of causes that may have determined this will.[104] For his judgment concerns the sin and its immediate cause and not the whole series of things to which they belong. The chain connecting each act with the universal harmony cannot be used to excuse the sinner. Otherwise all responsibility would disappear and justice would be destroyed.

As *On the Omnipotence of God* had already shown, this reference to juridical practice is valid on the juridical and moral level, but does not apply on the metaphysical level. For it is not enough to prove to the sinner that he can avoid damnation, *if he so chooses*, and that even the damned could put an end to their punishment if they ceased to hate God. Some response must be made to the complaint of the damned who push their inquiry into the cause of sin beyond the sinner's volition to the very nature of things. Their complaint transcends the strictly juridical and moral question and raises a fundamental metaphysical problem—if not *the* fundamental metaphysical problem—namely, why are things as they are? Or in Leibnizian terms, why is there something rather than nothing and why is this something as it is and not otherwise? Undoubtedly, it is for this reason that the justification of God, which will also be the goal of the *Theodicy*, is of such crucial importance to Leibniz. For underlying this demand for justification, which becomes a cry for justice in the mouths of the damned, is a demand of *reason*. God and reason are summoned to give account for *the way things are*.

By giving voice to the damned, who accuse God and the universal harmony of being the source of their misfortune, Leibniz shows the limits of a rational investigation into the cause of evil—that is, the limits of the use of the Principle of Sufficient Reason. For, there is something excessive and foolish, even absurd, in their complaint. The damned, having read their Leibniz, have understood that God's will is not at issue, since everything follows necessarily from his existence. Therefore, they do not accuse God of being unjust. They know that he could not have done otherwise, yet they curse the existence of God from which follows this series of things that includes their damnation. Implicitly, their complaint poses the following question: Why are God and the universal harmony such as they are and not otherwise? The damned abuse the Principle of Sufficient Reason by demanding a reason beyond God himself, beyond the ground of all things, beyond harmony, when in fact there is no such reason (which had already been indicated in the letter to Wedderkopf).[105] Their error is to refuse to call a halt to the demand for reasons (and justification) when that demand has already been satisfied. The question had already received a definitive answer: the nature of things is immutable and uncreated; it depends neither on our will nor on God's. Rather than accept this reply, the damned rebel. They contest this nature and are outraged by it, which amounts to wishing that God were not God, that truth were not truth, and that justice were not justice. It is here that the damned abandon rationality and succumb to folly. For they renounce reason by wishing it to be *irrational* (other than it is) and abandon justice by declaring it unjust (because it is not what they would have wanted it to be). They are like an insane man in his delirium, a furious man raging against what cannot be changed, a dog angry with a stone, or a gambler angry with fortune. In fact, their anger is

> as foolish as that of someone who computed badly and, realizing that the answers
> did not correspond with his operation, became indignant at arithmetic rather
> than himself and vainly took offense that three threes are not ten instead of
> nine (for the harmony of things is also based on such necessary proportions).[106]

Damnation is nothing other than the sorrowful experience of contradiction with the order of things in one who wishes that things were other than they are and that justice (which punishes him) were not what it is, while complaining in its name!

As the analogy drawn from mathematics illustrates, the nature of things and everything that follows, including damnation, are as necessary as mathematical truths. Therefore, it is just as absurd to complain of destiny or to bemoan the existence of the damned as to regret that three times three is nine. Such a conclusion once again diminishes the import of the distinction between the two kinds of necessity. The universal harmony, which presupposes both unity and diversity, requires that some be damned, just as the laws of music require that dissonance be introduced into a melody to make it more beautiful.[107] The world surpasses the limited understanding of man, who gleans only a few scattered notes of the general song and, discerning some particular disorders, presumes to judge the whole by its part. This raises the following question: If there *must be* some who are damned, why this soul rather than that one? What are the reasons for predestination?

The refutation of the Lazy Sophism offered a practical, though not a theoretical, solution to the problem of predestination. Once it has been shown that the end cannot be posited without the means, it is not necessary to await the outcome of the "entire debate concerning foreknowledge, fate, predestination, the end of life" prior to acting.[108] It is present action that determines our future and so will decide our salvation or damnation. The complaint of the damned requires that the question now be taken up in its theoretical aspect. This question is directly related to that of individuation. For to ask, with the damned man, why he was not created better is all the same as to ask why he is *this person* and not *that one*, and why he is not other than he is. As we have seen, the complaint is now posed at the ontological level. Nevertheless, the moral and juridical question is still present since the damned denounce the injustice of the unhappy fate that destiny has allotted them while others have been treated more favorably. The problem can be formulated in these terms: among souls that are by nature identical, or at least very similar, and differ only in number initially, why has this soul rather than that one been placed in this location and time and exposed to circumstances that will render it evil and ultimately miserable?[109]

At the time of the *Confession of a Philosopher*, Leibniz held that things are individuated, generally speaking, by time and place, and for beings other than spirits, by the relation these things have with a spirit that perceives them in a determinate time and place—as illustrated by the example of the two eggs.[110] Thus, a thing is individuated and distinct from others by extrinsic features, and not, as Leibniz would maintain some years later,[111] by solely intrinsic features. Despite its inadequacies, this doctrine permits Leibniz to draw out two important implications for ethics: it is the spirit that constitutes the identity of a thing, and the spirit is memory (it preserves past states). On the metaphysical level, it shows that the essence of an individual is inseparable from the particular series of things to which it belongs—a thesis to which Leibniz would constantly adhere.

Insofar as they are the same kind of being, all spirits can be considered in their pure nature as identical, not only metaphysically but also morally speaking (the elect are not fundamentally more worthy than the dammed). They are distinguished—that is, they become this one or that one—by time and place. As a result,

> to ask why this soul rather than another is subjected from the beginning to these circumstances of time and place (from which the entire series of life, death, salvation, or damnation arises), and why, consequently, it passes from one set of circumstances to others—the series of things external to itself bringing things forth in this manner—is to ask why this soul is this soul.[112]

This soul is this soul, precisely because it occupies those temporal and spatial circumstances that distinguish it from all others. In response to the question of the damned, why am I who I am, and not some other possessed of a better character, the response must be, because you are you, because you are this one (*hic*) existing at this place and time. God could have created you different, good and virtuous, but that would not have been *you*, but some other. The peasant who complains of not being the king's son is indignant for no reason, since "everything would come about in the same way, and he himself as the son of a king would not have dreamed of himself as the son of a peasant."[113] To be another would change nothing, because *I* would be this *other* and not me. The complaint is absurd, since it involves a contradictory desire: the desire to be at once *me* and *another*, two terms that exclude one another (since to be *I* supposes that I retain my nature, while to be *other* supposes it to be altered). Imagine my soul were that of the king I desire to be and who now exists. This soul that I call *mine* would not be mine but precisely some other, namely that of the king. The other can never be me without ceasing to be other, just as I can never be another without ceasing to be me. As Leibniz would say in a later text, at a time when he held that souls differ from one another in themselves "by their primitive nature":

> You will stress that you can ask why God has not given you greater strength. I reply: if he had done so, you would not exist, since the creature he would have produced would have been another and not you.[114]

Here we see the solution to two theological difficulties left unresolved in *On the Omnipotence of God*: Why did God maintain Adam and Eve in the world after the original sin (instead of replacing them with a better couple), and why did he permit the fault to be propagated to all their descendants?[115] The response has already been given, at least in its essentials, a few pages earlier in the dialogue: if sin had been eliminated, the whole series of things would have been altered, and God himself would have been other than he is. Consideration of the Principle of Individuation affords a more precise formulation of the thesis: without sin, the series would be completely different, and we ourselves would not exist, because different times and places and circumstances would lead to different individuals. A soul, considered in different spatial and temporal circumstances from those in which it exists would no longer be precisely *this* soul, but some other. Thus, God could not have created me differently—nether better nor worse—without bringing it about that *I* do not exist and without creating a different world composed of other individuals. The interdependence of all things belonging to the same series implies that an alteration in one would entail the disappearance of all the others (which would no longer be themselves)—in short, the existence of another world altogether. In other words, "without sin, we ourselves would not exist. There would be other creatures."[116]

Since the least alteration to the series of existing things would bring about a change to its first cause, it must be realized that I am such and not otherwise, because God *exists* and that if I were otherwise, or (what comes to the same thing) if I did not exist, God would be otherwise or would not exist, which is impossible. The theological consequences derived from the Principle of Individuation lead back to the universal harmony, which once again limits the investigation into the cause of evil. Those who criticize God for having permitted sin are fools

> since they must rather credit their own existence to God's tolerance of those very sins . . . as though someone of half-noble birth were irritated with his father . . . not thinking that if his father had married someone else, not he, but some other man, would have come into the world.[117]

The transition from the question of God's justice to that of human freedom and then to that of predestination and individuation does not fundamentally alter Leibniz's response to the problem of the cause of sin. Its ultimate source lies in the universal harmony. This harmony is the reason for the permission of sin and for predestination, which signifies nothing other than the conformity of each spirit with its own essence. This does not make the sinner any less guilty or punishable from a juridical and moral point of view, even if his will does not depend on him and his sin is necessary. Thus, the damned is "dismissed" as is said in the court. His complaint is no longer admissible, since it has been shown to be based on an abuse of the Principle of Sufficient Reason and ultimately to involve a denial of the Principle of Identity (namely, that harmony is such as it is, that God is God, that *this thing* is *this thing*, etc.). Salvation consists in a joyful acquiescence in the order of things, acknowledged to be rational and beautiful, and in the love of its source: God. This *Amor Dei* is an *Amor Fati* (love of fate), which undermines the Lazy Sophism and legitimates our action in the world. At the same time, this love is based on a freedom, both human and divine, that is subject to that necessity, which the wise man understands to be the necessity of the best.

Is the *Confession of a Philosopher*, as some commentators have maintained, a "first theodicy" or a "youthful theodicy"?[118] If "theodicy" is used as a generic term to designate any attempt to justify God by refuting arguments against his goodness, wisdom, and power based on the existence of evil, then it certainly is. However, it is undoubtedly not a theodicy if we compare the 1673 text with the *Essays of Theodicy* of 1710 and we understand the term according to its specific meaning, that is, with reference to the theses defended in this latter work. For, while it is true that there are—or appear to be— a certain number of positions common to the two texts, what is especially striking are the profound differences especially on the theological and metaphysical levels. In particular, the two texts differ with regard to three main points: (1) God's relation to the world and his physical and moral concurrence with evil, together with the abandonment of the distinction between *author* and *ground* in the *Theodicy*; (2) the conception of the will and freedom; (3) the definition of the possible and the two kinds of necessity, and the role played by the doctrine of possible worlds as the foundation of contingency.

Because of these differences, it is difficult to see the *Confession of a Philosopher* as the dialogue communicated to Arnauld in 1673, to which Leibniz twice refers in the *Theodicy*. According to Leibniz, this dialogue had already shown that God "having chosen the most perfect of all possible worlds, had been prompted by his wisdom to permit the evil which was bound up with it, but which still did not prevent this world from being, all things considered, the best that could be chosen."[119] As we have seen, the *Confession of a Philosopher* does not defend this thesis as such, at least not in those terms. Moreover, the concepts of the best, the possible, and permission have a different sense in the *Confession* than they would come to have after 1673, particularly in the *Theodicy*. Thus, either Leibniz is referring to a different text, though one from the same period as the *Confession of a Philosopher* that treats the same subject and is nevertheless based on different metaphysical principles, or—what is much more probable—the reference is indeed to the *Confession of a Philosopher* (or to a lost text that advances the same theses), and Leibniz is rewriting history and eliding differences to establish an artificial continuity in his intellectual biography. And this in spite of the fact that, as we shall see, his philosophy underwent important revisions and conceptual shifts in the intervening years.

## NOTES

1. Cf. Leibniz to Wedderkopf, A II, 1, 186.
2. See section 3.1.
3. CP, A VI, 3, 116; Sleigh, 27: "Recently we discussed more than adequately the immortality of the mind and the necessity of there being someone who governs the world."

4. That does not mean that the dialogue on the immortality of the soul and the existence of God to which the theologian alludes at the beginning of the text is the *Confession of Nature Against Atheists*. For this latter work is not in the form of a dialogue, nor are any of the surviving works written on this topic prior to 1673. The hypothesis of a lost dialogue, although rejected by Yvon Belaval (cf. *Confessio Philosophi*, 114, note 1), cannot be entirely ruled out.
5. Cf. *Confession of Nature Against Atheists*, A VI, 1, 490.
6. CP, A VI, 3, 149.
7. Ibid.
8. CP, A VI, 3, 116; Sleigh, 27.
9. CP, A VI, 3, 116; Sleigh, 28.
10. See Rateau, *La question du mal chez Leibniz*, 82–92.
11. "Est in Iustitia respectus aliquis boni alieni, est et nostri, non is tamen ut alterum alteri finis sit" (*Elements of Natural Law*, 1670–1671?, A VI, 1, 463).
12. *Specimen demonstrationum politicarum pro eligendo rege Polonarum* (*Specimen of Political Demonstrations for the Election of a King of Poland*, 1669), A IV, 1, 34 (prop. XXXVII).
13. *Elements of Natural Law*, A VI, 1, 465; L, 137.
14. Leibniz to Arnauld (November 1671), A II, 1, 280.
15. Ibid.; L 233.
16. Cf. Leibniz to Arnauld (November 1671), A II, 1, 280: "Imo in homogeneis, qui centena aureorum nummum millia habet, ditior est, quam sunt centum, quorum quisque habet mille. Nam unio usum facit; ipse lucrabitur etiam quiescendo; illi perdent etiam laborando."
17. Conversely, in the case of a shared harm, compensation must first be made by the most wicked and afterward by the less guilty. See also *Elements of Natural Law*, A VI, 1, 479–480, 482.
18. Cf. Leibniz to Arnauld (November 1671), A II, 1, 280.
19. Cf. *Elements of Natural Law*, A VI, 1,453: "*Sapientia* est Scientia boni"; and 466: "*Bonum* est quicquid appetitur à pernoscente."
20. Cf. ibid., 466.
21. Cf. *For Duke John Frederick*, (May 1677), A I, 2, 23: "Demonstrationes de jurisprudentia naturali ex hoc solo principio: quod justitia sit caritas sapientis."
22. CP, A VI, 3, 116; Sleigh, 29. Cf. *Elements of Natural Law*, A VI, 1, 479: "Major harmonia est cum diversitas major est, et reducitur tamen ad identitatem. (Nam non in identitate, sed varietate gradus esse possunt)." See also 484–485.
23. CP, A VI, 3, 116; Sleigh, 29; and *Elements of Natural Law*, A VI, 1, 484: "Delectatio seu *voluptas* est perceptio harmoniæ."
24. See CP, A VI, 3, 117.
25. Cf. Introduction, p. 6.
26. CP, A VI, 3, 117; Sleigh, 33. Cf. Paul: Romans 9:20–23.
27. CP, A VI, 3, 118; Sleigh, 33.
28. Cf. A II, 1, 186.
29. CP, A VI, 3, 120; Sleigh, 39.
30. (December 1676?), A VI, 3, 587.
31. CP, A VI, 3, 121; Sleigh, 41.
32. CP, A VI, 3, 122; Sleigh, 45.
33. CP, A VI, 3, 120; Sleigh, 37.
34. CP, A VI, 3, 121; Sleigh, 41.
35. See A VI, 3, 150.

36. *The Questions Concerning Liberty, Necessity, and Chance*, EW V, 214–215.
37. CP, A VI, 3, 123; Sleigh, 45.
38. Belaval, *Confessio Philosophi*, 119, note 38.
39. Cf. NE II, 25, §6; A VI, 6, 227; RB 227: the relation of order expresses "the position and the connection of all the terms or members [of a set of things to one another]." This real connection of all things rules out any denomination purely extrinsic to the subjects (NE II, 25, §5).
40. CP , A VI, 3, 121, note 7; Sleigh, 41.
41. CP, A VI, 3, 123, note 11; Sleigh, 47. Moreover, when Leibniz asserts that "God having been posited, sins and the punishments for sins exist" (CP, A VI, 3, 126; Sleigh, 53), Steno again amends this to read "can exist" (note 12).
42. CP, A VI, 3, 123, note 11; Sleigh, 47.
43. The thesis that only the real is possible is a consequence of the so-called "Master argument" of Diodorus Cronus, as reported by Cicero in *On Fate* IX, 17 and Epictetus in the *Discourses* II, 19.
44. *Elements of Natural Law*, A VI, 1, 460; *On the Omnipotence of God*, §10, A VI, 1, 540; CP, A VI, 3, 127.
45. See section 3.1.2.
46. Refuted once again in CP, A VI, 3, 129–130.
47. CP, A VI, 3, 123, note 11.
48. CP, A VI, 3, 137; Sleigh, 77.
49. See the definition of "willing" given at CP, A VI, 3, 127.
50. However, the conclusion is not the same: in the *Confession of a Philosopher*, God is not the moral cause of sin, on the grounds that no law binds him, but rather because by virtue of his existence, he is the reason that sin exists, without being its author by virtue of his will.
51. *Of Liberty and Necessity*, EW IV, 246–247.
52. CP, A VI, 3, 124.
53. CP, A VI, 3, 124; Sleigh, 49.
54. According to the definition of "permit" given at CP, A VI, 3, 127; Sleigh, 55: "To permit is neither to will in favor nor to will against, and nevertheless to know."
55. CP, A VI, 3, 124; Sleigh, 49.
56. Cf. Leibniz to Wedderkopf, A II, 1, 187.
57. CP, A VI, 3, 132; Sleigh, 67: "What is it *to will something*?" asks the philosopher. "To be delighted by its existence . . . whether we actually experience its existence or we imagine the existence of what does not actually exist," replies the theologian.
58. Similarly, to will against something consists in the perception of pain (cf. CP, A VI, 3, 127, note 14). The same passivity occurs in the definition of willing against: "to will against [*nolle*] something is to be sad at its existence or to be delighted at its nonexistence" (CP, A VI, 3, 127; Sleigh, 55).
59. See CP, A VI, 3, 116; Sleigh, 29.
60. Formulation of the problem (the existence of evil is incompatible with the goodness and omnipotence of God) traces back to Epicurus, if Lactantius is to be believed (*On the Anger of God*, 13, 20–21). See also Sextus Empiricus, *Outlines of Pyrrhonism*, III, 3, 10–11.
61. Cf. Augustine, *Enchiridion*, 3, 11. Thomas Aquinas invokes the same thesis in ST, Ia, q. 2, a. 3. ad. 1.
62. CP, A VI, 3, 125 and 126.
63. "Therefore, since sins are not pleasing because of their own harmony, they are permitted by the divine will solely because of a harmony foreign to them, i.e.

the universal harmony, which cannot be realized otherwise" (CP, A VI, 3, 131; Sleigh, 65).

64. Cf. *Conversation with Steno Concerning Freedom* (November 27/December 7, 1677), A VI, 4-B, 1383; Sleigh, 129: "Thus God tolerates and permits sins, *not reluctantly* [*non invitus quidem*]" (emphasis added). If evil occurred in spite of God, God would lack power.

65. CP, A VI, 3, 130; Sleigh, 63.

66. Indifference of equilibrium is rejected in *On the Omnipotence of God*, §19, A VI, 1, 545.

67. CP, A VI, 3, 124; Sleigh, 49. My emphasis.

68. This distinction can be traced back to Aristotle (*Metaphysics*, V, 5). Boethius distinguished *necessitas simplex* from *necessitas conditionis*, in the *Consolation of Philosophy*, V, Prose 6, 27. See also, for example, Thomas Aquinas's distinction between *necessarium absolute* and *necessarium ex suppositione* (ST, Ia, qu. 19, a. 3).

69. CP, A VI, 3, 126–127; Sleigh, 53–55.

70. Cf. CP, A VI, 3, 128, Sleigh, 57: "the necessity and impossibility of things are to be sought in the ideas of those very things themselves, not outside those things. It is to be sought by examining whether they can be conceived or whether instead they imply a contradiction."

71. CP, A VI, 3, 129; Sleigh, 59.

72. On this point see CP, A VI, 3, 128; Sleigh, 57: "whatever exists, it is necessary that *if it exists,* then it exists, or (substituting for *necessity* its definition) whatever is about to exist, it cannot be conceived that *if it is about to exist,* then it will not exist. But if the reduplication is omitted, then the proposition is false. For something that will be nevertheless can be conceived not to be such that it will be. And what was not nevertheless can be conceived to have been." Cf. also *On the Omnipotence of God*, § 11, A VI, 1, 541. Leibniz is drawing here on Aristotle, cf. *De interpretatione*, IX, 19a 23–30.

73. CP, A VI, 3, 129; Sleigh, 59.

74. CP, A VI, 3, 128; Sleigh, 59.

75. Cf. *On the Ultimate Origination of Things* (November 23, 1697), GP VII, 304–305.

76. CP, A VI, 3, 128; Sleigh, 57.

77. When Descartes asserts that matter takes on successively every form of which it is capable, in *Principles of Philosophy* III, § 47, AT, VIII, 1, 103.

78. Cf. (March 18, 1676), A VI, 3, 391.

79. See CP, A VI, 3, 122.

80. See (December 1675), A VI, 3, 463: "The notion of impossibility is twofold: that which lacks an essence, that which lacks existence, that is, which did not exist, does not exist and will not exist, that which is incompatible with God, or with existence or with the reason that makes things exist rather than do not exist."

81. Cf. chapter 3, p. 102.

82. Cf. A VI, 1, §18, 544–545.

83. CP, A VI, 3, 131. This pleasure is not without difficulties, given that "to take pleasure in" (*delectari*) is nothing other than to perceive harmony. How can we conceive of a harmony of evil, if evil is fundamentally dissonance?

84. CP, A VI, 3, 136; Sleigh, 77. See also *Conversation with Steno Concerning Freedom*, A VI, 4-B, 1379: "No one voluntarily [*se volens*] makes himself evil, for otherwise he would be evil before he made himself evil."

85. CP, A VI, 3, 137–138; Sleigh, 81. Cf. Digest 50, 17, Rule 174.

86. CP, A VI, 3, 132; Sleigh, 65–67.

87. It is that alleged "power that can act and not act, all the requisites for acting having been posited and, moreover, everything both outside the agent and inside the agent being equal" (CP, A VI, 3, 132; Sleigh, 67). The same refutation can be found in Hobbes: "Lastly, that ordinary *definition* of a *free agent*, namely, *that a* free agent *is that, which, when all things are present which are needful to produce the* effect, *can nevertheless not produce it*, implies a contradiction, and is nonsense; being as much as to say, the cause may be *sufficient*, that is to say, *necessary*, and yet the *effect* shall not follow" (*Of Liberty and Necessity*, EW IV, 275).

88. See CP, A VI, 3, 133. See also *Conversation with Steno Concerning Freedom*, A VI, 4-B, 1380.

89. Belaval, *Confessio Philosophi*, 122, note 54.

90. CP, A VI, 3, 132; Sleigh, 67.

91. CP, A VI, 3, 133; Sleigh, 69.

92. For Hobbes, no temporal authority can force conscience, since "to obey is one thing, to believe is another; . . . To obey is to do or forbear as one is commanded, and depends on the will; but to believe, depends not on the will, but on the providence and guidance of our hearts that are in the hands of God Almighty. Laws only require obedience; belief requires teachers and arguments drawn either from reason, or from some thing already believed" (*An Answer to a book published by Dr. Bramhall, Late Bishop of Derry; called the "Catching of the Leviathan,"* EW IV, 339).

93. CP, A VI, 3, 133; Sleigh, 69.

94. CP, A VI, 3, 135–136.

95. *Conversation with Steno Concerning Freedom* A VI, 4-B, 1380; Sleigh, 123. Cf. Aristotle, *Nicomachean Ethics*, III, 3–4, 1111a 22–1112a 17.

96. CP, A VI, 3, 133.

97. CP, A VI, 3, 135; Sleigh, 73.

98. CP, A VI, 3, 135; Sleigh, 73.

99. *Conversation with Steno Concerning Freedom,* A VI, 4-B, 1380; Sleigh, 125. Leibniz refers to Julius Caesar Scaliger, *De causis linguae latinae libri XIII*, Lyon, 1540, lib. 11, c. 166. In fact, Scaliger merely appeals to the distinction between *absolute* necessity and necessity *dependent* on another thing, arguing that the former belongs only to divine perfection, whereas the latter—which constitutes contingency—results from imperfection.

100. CP, A VI, 3, 135; Sleigh, 75.

101. CP, A VI, 3, 136–137.

102. Concerning *innoxia utilitas, dolus in omittendo/in committendo*, and *culpa omissionis*, see the *Elements of Natural Law*, A VI, 1, 462 (4) and Grua, 815–816. See also the definition of *innocent use* given by Emer de Vattel: "We call *innocent use* or *innocent utility* that which may be derived from a thing without causing either loss or inconvenience to the proprietor and the *right of innocent use* is the right we have to that use which may be drawn from things belonging to another without causing him either loss or inconvenience" (*The Law of Nations*, B. II, Ch. IX, §127).

103. CP, A VI, 3, 137; Sleigh, 77. See also *On the Omnipotence of God*, §14, A VI, 1, 542–543.

104. CP, A VI, 3, 138. Cf. *On the Omnipotence of God* §13, A VI, 1, 542; *Conversation with Steno Concerning Freedom*, A VI, 4-B, 1378.

105. A II, 1, 186.

106. CP, A VI, 3, 138; Sleigh, 81.

107. CP, A VI, 3, 146–147.
108. CP, A VI, 3, 130; Sleigh, 61. See also *On the Omnipotence of God*, §13, A VI, 1, 542.
109. See CP, A VI, 3, 147. Leibniz returns to a question asked by the theologian at the beginning of the dialogue: If God is just, why does he form from the same clay, "some vessels intended for honor, others intended for disgrace"? (CP, A VI, 3, 117; Sleigh, 33).
110. CP, A VI, 3, 147.
111. See *Meditation on the Principle of the Individual* (April 1676), A VI, 3, 491; *Middle Knowledge* (November 1677), A VI, 4-B, 1374; DM §9.
112. CP, A VI, 3, 148; Sleigh, 105.
113. CP, A VI, 3, 148; Sleigh, 107.
114. (March 1689 to March 1690?), A VI, 4-B, 1639. This shows that modification of the principle of individuation would not alter his response to the problem. See also DM §30; L 496, "how does it come that this man will certainly commit this sin? The reply is easy; it is that otherwise he would not be this man." In the *Specimen of Discoveries of the Admirable Secrets of Nature in General* (1688?), Leibniz refers to Hugh of Saint Victor's response to one who would ask why God loved Jacob and not Esau: "because Jacob is not Esau" (A VI, 4-B, 1619).
115. Cf. *On the Omnipotence of God*, §14, A VI, 1, 543.
116. *Critical Remarks on Bayle's* Dictionary, in FC (L) 180.
117. CP, A VI, 3, 148; Sleigh, 107.
118. Gaston Grua, in Grua, "Avertissement," vii; Yvon Belaval, *Confessio Philosophi*, introduction, 25–26; Robert Sleigh, "Leibniz's First Theodicy," *Noûs*, 30 (Supplement), 1996, 481–499.
119. Cf. Preface; GP VI, 43; Huggard, 67. See also §211.

# CHAPTER 3

✧

# Theoretical Changes After the *Confession of a Philosopher*

## *Toward a New Conception of God, the Possible, and Divine Concurrence with Evil*

The *Confession of a Philosopher* constitutes an important stage in Leibniz's thinking about evil and divine justice. However, it also involves difficulties that will lead him to revise several of his theological and metaphysical positions. Three major theoretical changes can be found after the dialogue of 1673:

1. Leibniz steers his theology toward a more personal God, especially in reevaluating the role of the divine will. He develops a new conception of the possible, which he takes to be real, and to which he attributes a striving for (*Pretention*) existence. These two theoretical developments allow him to reconsider the relation between God's understanding and will, interpreting them as two expressions of one and the same effort (*conatus*) from which the existence of the best combination of possibles follows (3.1).

2. Leibniz develops an original explanation of God's physical concurrence with evil based on the notion of the natural limitation or original imperfection of creatures. The development of this notion allows him to maintain both that God concurs completely with all of our acts on the physical level and yet that sin is imputable only to the sinner (3.2).

3. Leibniz reconceives God's moral concurrence with evil, by locating the permission of evil within a more general will regarding the world as a whole. The appeal to a unique and universal divine decree leads, in turn, to a reconsideration of the relation of part to whole, and more specifically, of the place of created things in the universe (3.3).

## 3.1 A REVISED THEOLOGY AND METAPHYSICS

### 3.1.1 The End of the Logical Model of Modus Ponens

By the end of the *Confession of a Philosopher* God stands justified, his will exempt from reproach. However, God's willing is no more than a passive and necessary consent to what exists, and sin is necessary. The Leibnizian conception of God and his relation to the world, dominated as it is by the hypothetical logical model (if A, then B), leads to a strict necessitarianism that the distinction between two kinds of necessity (absolute and hypothetical) does not, in truth, allow him to avoid. In certain texts Leibniz refers to this necessitarian period of his intellectual biography, a time in which he felt close to Hobbes and Spinoza.[1] Leibniz admits to having leaned to the side of absolute necessity and of those who are content to define freedom as lack of constraint and to subject it to necessity.[2] However, Leibniz also indicates that even during this period and prior to the discovery of the "reasons of contingency," he was not altogether satisfied with the arguments of Hobbes and Spinoza. What was it that prevented him from fully embracing them? There were, in my view, three main reasons. The first two are theoretical:

1. The thesis according to which God is the first member of the series of things that unfold necessarily and constitute the world leads to a theology that tends to assimilate God to pure necessity, destiny, or nature. Leibniz cannot allow this assimilation, which destroys any notion of providence and runs counter to the orthodox Christian conception of a personal God endowed with understanding and will.
2. Leibniz does not believe that the possible is reducible to what exists, has existed, or will exist. To be sure, his conception of the possible remains, as I have said, "weak" since it cannot serve as the basis of a true contingency and since it assimilates the possible to a fiction or to an imagination that contains no contradiction.[3] However, Leibniz's recognition of the possibility of a series of things other than our own (which

is nevertheless incompatible with God's existence) constitutes a major difference with Hobbes and Spinoza. It sets Leibniz on a path that will lead to the "strong" conception of the possible, according to which the possible will be not merely that which can be imagined or conceived without contradiction, but a reality endowed with a striving for existence (*pretensio ad existendum*) and existing in the divine understanding, even if it will never be created.

3. The third reason is practical. Leibniz considers the thesis that sins are necessary to be shocking and a source of misunderstanding, even when the necessity involved is merely hypothetical, since the distinction between the two kinds of necessity appears artificial in the *Confession of a Philosopher*. The thesis can be disheartening to the common man, who is liable to draw, albeit incorrectly, bad consequences from it (such as the Lazy Sophism). It is to avoid such effects that Leibniz will come to reconsider and sharpen the distinction between absolute and hypothetical necessity.

These three reasons explain, in my view, the revisions to the necessitarianism and to the theology and metaphysics it presupposes that Leibniz made subsequent to the *Confession of a Philosopher*. It is worth noting that, in general, Leibniz never makes a sudden shift from one conceptual framework or from one philosophical hypothesis to another. Rather, having become aware of the limitations and defects of his attempted solutions to a given problem, Leibniz reconsiders and corrects them, refining the relevant concepts and distinctions and, in this way, progressively develops new theories.

It is evident that the doctrine of God's justice, insofar as it concerns one of the divine attributes in particular, is directly dependent on theology, that is, on the manner in which God is conceived. Thus, it is to be expected that modifications to one's theological views will result in changes to one's manner of justifying God's conduct. In the texts that follow the *Confession of a Philosopher*, the relation of God to the world is no longer conceived as a necessary and reciprocal dependence among the elements of a unique series in which no element can be changed without affecting the whole, including the first term. Henceforth, the reason for the existence of things is explicitly located outside the series, that is, beyond the world:

> the entire series does not contain a sufficient reason for existing, because the entire series can be imagined or conceived to be different, which is why the reason it is as it is must be given outside of it.[4]

It is not surprising that this statement should occur precisely in the remarks on Spinoza. Leibniz is here attempting to distance himself from the Dutch philosopher, whom he met in 1676 and with whose metaphysical positions he was increasingly familiar (these positions would ultimately be included in the *Ethics*, which was not published until 1677).[5] However, what Leibniz rejects in Spinoza is, in fact, a consequence that can be drawn from Leibniz's own theology as set forth in the *Confession of a Philosopher*—namely, a God from whom all things follow necessarily and who is scarcely distinguishable from nature. In other words, Leibniz works to distance himself from Spinoza, in my view, because Spinoza explicitly defends a theology that Leibniz considers unacceptable but that can be correctly deduced from the principles that he himself set out in the *Confession of a Philosopher*. In reading the Jewish philosopher, did Leibniz discover himself to be something of a Spinozist *malgré lui*? I would prefer to say that in opposing Spinoza, Leibniz is struggling against a tendency and inclination inherent in his own philosophy.

The argument that Leibniz offers here for locating the reason of the world outside the world itself is original. It differs from the traditional argument, originating with Aristotle, that involves ascending the series of causes in search of an absolutely first cause (that is not itself the effect of a higher cause). The series of things is taken in its totality, which constitutes the world and is considered not to contain within itself the reason of its existence. Why? Because the series could have been other than it is without logical contradiction. Therefore, there must be a reason why it is thus and not otherwise—a reason which it does not contain within itself, and which therefore must be outside of it. Thus, God cannot be confused with the series, or with its first member, since God exists per se. He is the absolutely necessary being, who cannot not exist or be other than he is.

In sum, whatever can be conceived to be otherwise does not contain its reason within itself but depends on a cause distinct from itself. Such is the actual series of things, which therefore is contingent—that is, conceivable alongside other possible series. In this way, the notion of the series is freed from the logical model of modus ponens and designates only a chain of *possible* things, of which God is not the first term but the *external* reason for existing. Likewise, in removing God from the series of things, Leibniz avoids "pantheism" and the doctrine of necessary emanation (Spinoza), as well as necessitarianism according to which all things follow from the irresistible power of God (Hobbes). For the possibility in itself of other series implies that there has been a choice. From this, it follows that this external reason, which is the foundation of the world, is endowed with the intelligence for conceiving these possible series and the will for choosing that which exists. Against Spinoza, the idea of a personal and spiritual God endowed with understanding and will must be defended:

> God is not as some represent him—something metaphysical, imaginary, incapable of thought, will or action, so that it would be the same as if you were to say that God is nature, fate, fortune, necessity, the world. Rather, God is a certain substance, a person, a mind. . . . It must be shown that God is a person, i.e., an intelligent substance. It must be demonstrated rigorously that he senses his own action on himself, for nothing is more admirable than for the same being to sense and to be affected by itself.[6]

A God who produces everything, both good and evil, indifferently, who has neither understanding nor will, is merely blind fate by another name. This conception, which Leibniz certainly would not have accepted in such terms, but which could be deduced from the theology of God as "first term" is henceforth definitively rejected. Leibniz reestablishes the role of the will, which is no longer considered as purely passive, a mere delight in the existence of harmony, but as active by virtue of the choice it makes of the most perfect series.

Might God, nevertheless, have chosen some series other than the most perfect? The contingency of the world is based on the existence of other series of things that are possible *in themselves* and not on the contingency of the divine choice of this series rather than some other. Leibniz's revised theology—and, as we shall see, his new conception of the possible—provides the means of avoiding Spinozism, though at the cost of a displacement. The relation of necessity is no longer between God and the world, which are included in the same series, but within God himself, between his understanding which represents the best, and his will which cannot fail to embrace it. Thus, Leibniz can accept the Spinozistic thesis that all things follow from the necessity of the divine nature but only on condition of reinterpreting it:

> This must be explained as follows. The world could not be produced otherwise, because God cannot fail to act in the most perfect manner. Because he is very wise, he chooses the best. However, it must not be thought that all things follow from God's nature *without any intervention of his will*.[7]

Although the world is contingent (not all possibles exist, nor can they), the creation of this world rather than some other is necessary, because it follows from a will necessitated to choose the best:

[A]ll things are in God in the same manner that the effect is contained in its complete cause, and the property of a certain subject in the essence of that same subject. It is certain that the existence of things is a consequence of God's nature, which made it the case that only the most perfect things could be chosen.[8]

The role of the will is reconceived to avoid the assimilation of God to fate or to a mechanistic God (*Deus mechanicus*).[9] The inclination presupposed by the will is given even greater emphasis by Leibniz especially beginning in the years 1677–1678. It is defined as "practical thought, or thought accompanied by the effort to act" with regard to good and evil.[10] The peculiar characteristic of this practical thought (*sententia*) relative to simple thought, imagination, or representation lies in its relation to an effort to act in conformity with the thought.[11] A person who wills is disposed to act, unlike the person who merely deliberates.

However, there are two restrictions that limit this revaluation of the role of the will. The first is common to any "intellectualist" doctrine (that is, any view that maintains the primacy of the understanding over the will). Motivated by consideration of the good and never without reason, the will is always subordinate to the understanding because it relies on it. Thought precedes the inclination and effort so that the latter appears to be more a *reaction* and a consequence than an action and an initiative.[12] In this sense, the will still retains a passive dimension. The second restriction is owing to the fact that the transition from the divine understanding to the existence of the world seems to bypass the will, as illustrated by this famous note by Leibniz: "When God calculates and exercises his thought, the world is made (*fit*)."[13] The *fiat* of creation is, above all, the act of a thought that calculates. In my view, the omission of the will cannot be put down to a simple oversight. It shows that the role of the will is secondary, given that "Divine will follows the necessity of things,"[14] and its perfection consists in willing only the true good. In a sense only the best is possible or "feasible," given that "it is impossible that God not prefer it to other things."[15] The necessity of choosing the best is imperative for the sage as is the necessity of producing an equilateral triangle given just three points and no other particular determination. Furthermore, this necessity in no way detracts from freedom, which on the contrary, is greater the more it is determined—that is, inspired by just and well-founded reasons: "If the necessity of choosing the best in the sage were destructive of freedom, it would follow that God does not act freely when he chooses the best from among several things."[16]

Thus, the choice of the best appears at once as that which imposes itself independently of every other determination, according to an almost mechanical necessity (which renders all reference to the will, so to speak, superfluous), and as the result of the most perfect intelligence, which calculates and compares different possibles. This is a fundamental difference between Leibniz and Spinoza: although God's action is entirely necessitated, he is no less endowed with intelligence and will, and he always acts with a view to an end.[17] Henceforth, necessity is no longer in the world, but in God. While other series are possible in themselves, God cannot create anything but the best without contravening his perfection, that is, his essence (that which constitutes his divinity).

As is now apparent, a new theology and a new metaphysics are put in place following the *Confession of a Philosopher*. The evolution of Leibniz's thought is directly tied to the redefinition of the possible. Its characteristics are no longer purely logical (conceivability, non-contradiction) but metaphysical and, so to speak, dynamic, insofar as Leibniz now attributes to the possible a true reality, independent of our thought, together with a tendency and striving for existence. The divine understanding becomes the place where all possibles are in competition with one another, and from this conflict the best series of things results.

### 3.1.2 The "Strong" Conception of the Possible: Its Reality and Striving for Existence

In his letter to Simon Foucher of 1675, Leibniz shows that possibility, impossibility, and necessity are independent of us in two different senses. On the one hand, these notions are not chimeras that we arbitrarily construct. On the contrary, they are imposed on us, as soon as we consider them, "since all that we do consists merely in recognizing them, in spite of ourselves and in a constant manner."[18] It is impossible for us, for example, to conceive of a circle except as having the properties that necessarily belong to it. On the other hand, these notions continue to subsist outside of us when we are not actually thinking of them. Therefore, they have an autonomous existence, such that any mind can comprehend them in the same manner (whence their universality):

> Thus the nature of a circle with its properties is something which exists and is eternal, that is, there is some constant cause outside of us which makes everyone who thinks carefully about a circle discover the same thing.[19]

A possible thing and a necessary truth (a mathematical truth, for example) have this in common: they are realities existing outside of us and are permanent (eternal) and independent of our will. It is for this reason that possibles deserve to be called essences or natures, and necessary truths to be called eternal truths. These essences and truths precede the order of existing things (the possible and the necessary are prior to the actual) and are independent of it, since there are possibles that will never be realized in the world and since truths do not cease to be true just because no one has thought of them or continues to think of them. However, this independence does not imply that essences and truths could exist per se outside of all thought; they reside in God's understanding.

To be sure, in his letter to Wedderkopf,[20] Leibniz had already claimed that the possibility of beings does not depend on God's will but coincides with God himself. In the *Confession of a Philosopher*, he similarly claims that ideas of things subsist in God's understanding.[21] What then is new here? The possible is no longer defined solely in terms of its property of non-contradiction and conceivability. Its nature has changed, so to speak, both *formally* and *objectively*. *Formally*, the possible can no longer be identified with a simple imagination, a fiction, or pure supposition that we forge in the manner of poetic creations. It has become a reality independent of both our thought and the actual existence of things. For, a possible is no less something *real* even if it does not exist in the world or will never come into existence. This transformation of the possible into a being (its "ontologization" so to speak) constitutes a major change for Leibniz. In making the possible something more than a mere logical modality or manner of being, that is, in referring it to a real essence, he provides a metaphysical foundation for contingency and so for freedom, both divine and human.

*Objectively*, one possible is distinguished from another by the quantity of essence or reality—that is, of perfection—it includes. It is upon this objective difference among possibles that God's choice to create some rather than others is based. In addition to the degree of perfection that belongs to each possible, its realization in existence is determined by its simplicity and compatibility[22] with the greatest number of other possibles:

> The reason why the most perfect possibles should exist in the first instance is evident: for since they are both simple and perfect, i.e., include the most, they leave room for the greatest number of other possibles. Therefore one perfect being is to be preferred to many imperfect beings which are equal in power to it, for the latter impede the existence of others, whilst they occupy place and time.[23]

Both the plurality and diversity of possibles allow for the exercise of choice. Moreover, for the first time, so far as I am aware, there appears in

Leibniz's writings the idea of a divine creation based on the relation between the simplicity of ways—that is, of means (the possibles)—and the
maximum of essence or perfection realized by them:

> The necessary being acts by the simplest ways. For, among the infinite number
> of possibles, certain ones are the simplest, but the simplest are those that pre-
> vail by far. The reason for this is that there is no reason that determines the rest
> [the other possibles]. Harmony is precisely that: a certain simplicity in a multi-
> tude. It is in this that beauty and pleasure consist.[24]

The conception of harmony is modified or, at least, acquires a more metaphysical signification. Its definition, which at the time of the *Elements of
Natural Law* as well as of the *Confession of a Philosopher*,[25] was "similarity in
variety" and "diversity compensated by identity," becomes "simplicity in a
multitude." Harmony no longer refers only to agreement among contraries,
which produces beauty and thus pleasure in the spectator, in conformity
with the musical and pictorial models already present in the philosophical tradition. It now signifies the best combination of possibles, that is,
that combination in which the simplicity of means is conjoined with the
maximal compatibility of things. In later texts, this will be referred to as
"variety, opulence, and abundance . . . in regard to the ends or results."[26]

Possibles are realities and differ one from another by their respective
degrees of perfection, simplicity and compatibility. Thus, the conditions for
a genuine choice by God are realized (even if this choice is necessary). An
additional step is taken in the years 1677–1678 when Leibniz, in drawing
out the consequences of his new doctrine of possibles, grants them a
"striving for existence" in proportion to their degree of reality or quantity
of essence. If a possible is something real, and not something that is pure
potentiality, it must, like any being, be endowed with its own tendency,
with an inclination that is the more "powerful," the more perfection the
possible contains.

The idea of an inclination to exist inherent in the possible appears for
the first time in the *Elements of True Piety*. What explains this new account
of the possible? Given that the series of things that constitutes our world
is but one possible series among an infinity of others (which are no less
realities for being nonexistent), the question is no longer simply to determine why this series is brought into existence rather than some other
equally possible series, but more radically, why possibles exist, when there
might have been nothing at all. The contingency of the world is, in a sense,
doubled, for not only is there the possibility that there exists something
other than what actually does (that which might have been otherwise is

contingent) but also the possibility of there being nothing (that which might not have existed is contingent). The response to the first question (which comes to this: *Why are things thus and not otherwise?*) has already been given by Leibniz. Since all possibles cannot coexist, the series that exists is that which is most perfect from both a metaphysical and moral viewpoint (the simplest, in which a maximum of mutually compatible things is produced). It is precisely in response to the second question (which comes to this: *Why is there something rather than nothing?*) that the idea of *propension* is introduced:

> [S]*ince something exists rather than nothing*, it is necessary that something is contained in the essence itself, or the possibility from which actual existence follows, and hence reality or possibility possesses a certain propensity [*propensio*] to exist. . . . Because certain possibles exist, when they were equally able not to exist, it follows that "possibility" is a certain disposition to exist rather than not to exist.[27]

The two questions are related, and the response to the second (which in fact is first according to the order of reasons) applies equally to the first.[28] There exists something rather than nothing, because even prior to the will and creative power of God there is a tendency to exist in the essence of every possible. That this thesis is fundamental for Leibniz is confirmed by his subsequent elevation of the proposition "every possible demands [*exigit*] to exist" to the rank of absolutely first truth among truths of fact.[29]

It should be emphasized that Leibniz deliberately chooses the terms *propensity* and *disposition* rather than "virtue" or "force." Indeed, examination of the manuscript of *Elements of True Piety* reveals that after having written "virtue of existing" (*virtus existendi*) and "force of existing" (*existendi vis*), Leibniz scored them out and replaced them with "propensity to exist" (*ad existendum propensio*).[30] The correction is significant. One the one hand, it is a way for Leibniz to further distinguish himself from Spinoza, whose posthumous works Leibniz annotated in 1678 where he encountered the expression force of existing (*existendi vis*) defined as "power to act" (*agendi potentia*).[31] On the other hand, it shows that Leibniz has no wish to endow the possible with a true force. It is easy to understand why. For, that would amount to granting the possible an actuality that it cannot have precisely because of its nature, since it can forever remain inexistent. The choice of the terms *propensity* and *disposition* underscores the intermediate status of the possible's inclination to realization, which falls between power and act. The possible is not a mere possibility of existing (a "bare" possibility). *Negatively*, it is that from which existence follows, if nothing prevents or impedes it.[32] *Positively*, beginning with the *Dialogue Between Theophile and Polidore* (perhaps written toward the middle of 1679), it is a *"pretension . . . to exist,"*[33] lacking only the power "to bring itself into existence, and to come to light ahead of others." It is here that the term "combat"[34] makes its appearance to describe the opposition between different and incompatible possibles, all similarly striving for existence.

This pretension or claim to exist (*exigentia existentiae*),[35] which is proportional to the quantity of essence or degree of perfection in the possible, expresses the idea of a positive tendency to exist, whereas "propensity" or "disposition" might suggest a mere aptitude for existence, which would be insufficiently distinguished from potential being.[36] Proof of the reality of this pretension is always a posteriori, based on the actual existence of something rather than nothing: "If there were not, in the very nature of essence, a certain inclination to exist, nothing would exist."[37] The determinate (the actual) can never follow from the indeterminate (pure potentiality). The determinate exists. Therefore, there must be a determination (a virtuality) at the very heart of the possible.

The evolution of Leibniz's terminology continues with his appeal to the notion of effort (*conatus*) beginning in the years 1683–1685. The term "pretension" continues to be used, but Leibniz insists more and more on the analogy between the tendency internal to the possible and the motion of bodies. The possible is thus conceived as an *effort*, that is, as a "beginning of action,"[38] in accordance with the physical model of weights acting on a balance:

> [E]very essence or reality demands existence just as every effort demands motion or its effect, provided of course that nothing prevents it. And every possible includes not only possibility, but also the *effort* to actually exist, not that things that do not exist possess an effort, but because this is demanded [*postulant*] by the ideas of essences that actually exist in God. . . . In this way, just as the weights in a scale exert themselves on the arm as a function of their weight and demand its descent, if nothing prevents it, and the heaviest wins out, so too each thing aspires to existence as a function of its perfection and the most perfect obtains it.[39]

This definition of the *conatus* of the possible is unquestionably reminiscent of that of active force.[40] The comparison with dynamics, the new science of force developed by Leibniz based on his reform of Cartesian mechanics,[41] seems clear. According to André Robinet, from 1680 on dynamics becomes, in effect, the model that "supplants the mechanistic models in every domain."[42] Is the comparison between the *conatus* of possibles and the force of bodies an illustration of this? The *conatus* of possibles, opposing one another and combining together in the divine understanding, are like the motions of bodies that encounter one another in the physical world. If the object of dynamics is the interplay of real forces, the "divine *Mathesis*, or metaphysical mechanism"[43] would be nothing more than the exposition of a "dynamic" of possibles that gives rise to the world.

However, the reference to the dynamical model is not, in my view, satisfactory and, indeed, is a source of error. To begin with, we must recognize that the laws of the "divine *Mathesis*" admit of only a superficial comparison with the laws that govern the world of bodies. The former are ethical and metaphysical laws, which aim at the realization of the best (metaphysically and morally speaking), not of a mere (purely quantitative[44]) maximum. Furthermore, as we have seen, Leibniz never uses the term "force" (*vis*) to designate the pretension of possibles for existence. Indeed, the sole occurrence of the term *existendi vis*, in the *Elements of True Piety*, is scored out. Thus, there cannot be a force for existing in possibles. They have no power of bringing themselves into existence, since otherwise they would already exist (and the possible would reduce to the existent).

> Thus the essences of things clearly depend on the divine nature, and existences on the divine will. For, *it is not by their own force [propria vi]*, but by God's decree that they can obtain existence.[45]

The pretension, which includes a *conatus*, cannot be assimilated to a force, since by definition a force requires no impulsion from an external cause in order to act. The effort of possibles is real, but ideal, and cannot do without an external power (God), who seconds and *existentifies* it.[46] In the physical world, effort is inherent in the existing, spontaneous substance, which is self-sufficient and produces its effect immediately if nothing prevents it. The notion of a force preceding existence is contradictory, since there is no force that does not belong to an actually existing substance. Force is actual; essence is potential.

Pretension is neither force, nor a particular species of force, nor an inferior degree of it. Thus, the challenge is to conceive of *conatus* without power. A *conatus* that is not physical and actually existing, but mental without being a fiction, and real insofar as possibles are "realized" (*realisentur*) in the divine understanding.[47] Leibniz must maintain the gap between the possible and the existent in conformity with the biblical doctrine of creation if he is to avoid the threat of Spinozism. Creation is more than the mere actualization of that which is in potentiality and capable of being brought about, so to speak, naturally. For this reason, it is a miracle that requires the power of God. However, at the same time, Leibniz defends the notion of a *real* tendency existing in the possible. How are we to understand an effort that is real yet completely lacking in power?

Martine de Gaudemar suggests that we interpret the effort of possibles as the expression of "their objective value for existence in the eyes of a God who weighs the respective merits of the various possible universes." Lacking in themselves the power to exist, possibles have no real force other than "what they borrow from him [God] in his understanding" and which "is—in so far as there is no creative decision—the mere echo of God's power, expressed in his act of intelligence."[48] On this reading, pretension is merely the thought of a borrowed force, the reflection of one attribute (power) in another (understanding). As a result, the pretension to existence would become the expression of a possible decree, in conformity with the Leibnizian thesis that God's knowledge embraces his will qua possible.[49]

Against this reading it can be argued that the thought of an effort is not an effort, just as imagining that I am running is not running. The effort of possibles—if we are to take it literally, and not as mere metaphor—is not reducible to a mere representation in the understanding of what power is capable of, that is, of its capacity to realize the content of these possibles. The juridical connotation of the term *pretension* suggests a different interpretation of this exigency[50] of possibles, which "tend toward existence *with equal right* [*pari jure*] in proportion to the quantity of essence or reality."[51] *Pretension* signifies at once the *tension* (that is, the aspiration) of possibles for existence and their *demand* in the sense of a claim or assertion of a right. Possibles stake a claim to their rights in the divine understanding. Indeed, it is in these quasi-juridical terms that the ideal influence of one substance on another is sometimes described:

> This can have its effect only by the intervention of God, insofar as one monad may with reason *demand*, in the ideas of God, that God should have a concern for it in regulating the rest from the beginning of things.[52]

In the state of a mere possible, the monad is the expression of a well-founded claim, which demands to be taken into consideration and so calls out for God's intervention. Its pretension is not only to exist but also to govern all other substances and to subject them to its own law. It demands in some sense to be the referent by which all others must be regulated and according to which the entire universe must be ordered. It is in recognizing the rights of certain monads over others that God forms the world in which each one imposes its law on all others, while being subjected, in turn, to theirs.

This juridical interpretation offers two distinct advantages over the comparison to the physical:

1. It helps to explain how a *conatus* can be real and yet powerless, in the dynamical sense, and in need of an external power to be realized. The *conatus* is a right, which the jurist Leibniz knows can enter into conflict with others, exactly as in a juridical case with opposing parties, claims, and titles. In this way physical and efficient causality (which is difficult to reconcile with this purely ideal conflict) is then replaced by moral and final causality.

2. The identification of pretension with right alone is of a piece with the distinction, which Leibniz defends against Hobbes, between right and power. It is not the "strongest" possible that prevails (like the heaviest weight in a balance), since otherwise might would make right. Rather, it is the possible that best stakes its claim, by showing that it deserves to be satisfied—that is, deserves to exist because it contains the most perfection. However, it prevails only on condition of being seconded by an external power, which assists it and brings it into existence. For, despite its claim and the legitimacy of its reasons, and no matter how much better it may be, it must solicit God's power to be brought into existence. Pretension is not a kind of force, but an *appeal* to force. Were it otherwise, right would merely be another name for force, as Hobbes had maintained, and the ideal combat between possibles would resemble weights on a scale that lacks intelligence,[53] rather than "a conflict of reasons in the most perfect understanding."[54] Possibles are *reasons*, which God does not merely count, but weighs in his understanding.

Thus, the effort that possibles contain is not merely the reflection in God's understanding of that which his omnipotence is capable. It is the expression of a legitimate, well-founded reason, which presents itself to the divine understanding and without which nothing would exist (in accordance with the Principle of Sufficient Reason). This effort is of a moral rather than physical nature. It is similar to the inclination that leads us to recognize the legitimacy of a demand in a juridical argument or the truth of a proposition in light of its proofs in a logical argument. As for the combat of possibles, it is merely mental or ideal. It is similar to what occurs in the mind of one who considers several possible solutions to a problem and, after reflection and comparison, adopts the best (the simplest and most economical). On this "strong" conception of the possible, the assimilation of pretension to right has one final advantage: it prevents the implications of metaphysical mechanism, which tends to undermine the role of the will and suggest the, so to speak, automatic creation of the best possible. The consideration of right presupposes an intelligence that understands and evaluates and a will that prefers and chooses.

### 3.1.3 Pretension of Possibles and Inclinations of the Will: Two Expressions of a Single *Conatus*

This new conception of the possible has two consequences. (1) It has as a corollary a new conception of necessity and contingency. (2) In attributing an effort to the possible, it alters the traditionally established relation between God's understanding and will.

(1) At the time of the *Confession of a Philosopher*, the distinction between absolute and hypothetical necessity is of limited extent, since it consisted principally in the difference between possessing in oneself the reason for one's existence and truth (necessity per se) and drawing one's existence from an external cause (the necessity that follows having posited a cause).[55] Leibniz again invokes this distinction in the conversation with Steno (November 27, 1677) but develops a second feature. That thing is absolutely necessary, which, considered in itself, cannot be conceived as other than it is, whereas that thing is hypothetically necessary, which considered in itself, could be otherwise (or, in other words, is a possible) but is as it is for reasons external to itself. In the latter case, the necessity of the thing is not owing to itself but to its connection or relation to other things, which is the result of God's foreknowledge and consideration of the best.[56] Hypothetical necessity is *accidental*, whereas absolute necessity is *essential*. The explicit appeal to other series of possible things as the principal argument in favor of the contingency of the actual world is new. The world is *hypothetically* necessary, because on the one hand, there is no contradiction in its having been otherwise or having not existed at all, and on the other hand, it is brought into existence only with the positing of God's foreknowledge and will to create the best.

Thus, hypothetical necessity does not apply solely to that which exists *by another thing* (i.e., has a cause) but also to that which could have failed to exist or been otherwise. As a consequence, Leibniz will henceforth make systematic use of the terms *certain, infallible*, and *inevitable* to designate what is necessary *ex hypothesi* in opposition to what is absolutely necessary (and absolutely certain). Judas could have not sinned, though his act of betrayal was certain and infallible. Thus, it is no longer shocking to declare, following the gospel, that scandals must occur, since the necessity of sin is understood only hypothetically or accidentally.[57]

(2) By including a pretension to existence in the very heart of the possible, Leibniz renders the relation between God's understanding and will more complex. In classic intellectualist systems, the two faculties and their respective functions are clearly distinguished: the understanding represents ideas or essences (which are inert in themselves), and the will is then inclined to them according to their degree of perfection or intrinsic goodness. The will intervenes, followed by power, to give reality and efficacy to what lacks them in itself. The relation among these faculties in Leibniz's thought is novel, insofar as will and power are not simply "juxtaposed" with the understanding. God's choice and creative act correspond to a "preexisting" effort of the possible itself. The will encounters an inclination in thought. The collaboration between understanding and will is not purely extrinsic: it is founded on the union of two efforts.

In fact, this collaboration is only possible because there is already, so to speak, volition in the understanding, just as there is thought in volition. The pretension and effort attributed to the possible are clearly conceived on the analogy of the will. Obviously, it would be absurd to say that the possible *wills* to exist. Nevertheless, for Leibniz, possible, idea, truth, and volition all have this in common: they are all particular kinds of effort, inclination, or disposition.[58] For its part, volition is defined in intellectual terms, or at least, in terms that are clearly related to the exercise of thought: it is the thought (*sententia*) of good and evil, a thought directly associated with an effort to act.[59] It is "the ultimate thought" (that which immediately precedes action)[60] or again "the effort of the thinking thing."[61] This manner of defining one faculty in terms of another, while still maintaining their distinction, invites us to reconsider their relation. Understanding and will appear as the expression of one and the same *conatus*, which translates into thought as a right and an end, and into volition as an inclination.

In my view, Leibniz's contemporaneous use of the notion of *conatus* in his theory of the mind confirms this interpretation. The terms used to define the will are exactly parallel to those used to explain the pretension to existence of the possible:

> The will is an effort that one makes to act, because one has found it good. From which it follows that one never fails to act when one wills to and when one is able to at the same time. For when one makes the effort, the action itself follows necessarily from it, assuming there is nothing preventing it, that is to say, when one is able. It is therefore an axiom of the firmest and most certain kind that from the will and the power the action never fails to follow.[62]

As in the case of possibles, from which existence follows if nothing prevents it (and if power is joined), the *conatus* associated with the will, in the absence of any obstacle, obtains its effect and the potential becomes actual. For, effort is a kind of determination, which Leibniz defines in *On Affects* as "the state from which something follows, at least if nothing else prevents it."[63] Determinations (whether affects in the mind or impulses [*impetus*] in body) can associate and form a composite or, on the contrary, impede one another. Here again, as in the case of possibles, their respective weights are proportional to their degree of perfection: "determination to a series of thoughts is stronger as the rule of the series includes more reality."[64] In this way, one series of thoughts wins out over another, and "the mind is inclined to one thought rather than another, when the one includes more matter for thought than the other, at least for us."[65] Whence the "general law" that "what occurs [*fieri*] is always what includes more reality, that is to say, is more perfect."[66]

Here, two remarks are in order:

A. The generalized use of the axiom "from each thing follows the most perfect that can follow from that thing"[67] implies that we can ascribe to a *conatus* (i) the passage from one thing (a possible, a volition united to power, or a force) to its realization in existence, or to a greater perfection, and (ii) the realization of the effect that the thing carries within it, if nothing prevents it and nothing is lacking to it. Effort is nothing other than that which tends to bring about the best; that is, actual being (for that which is only in a state of possibility), metaphysical, physical, or moral perfection (for that which already exists).

B. Volition presupposes consideration of the good. It is an effort to act "*because it has been found to be good.*" As we have seen, there can be neither willing without the prerequisites for willing (in keeping with the Principle of Sufficient Reason), nor a will to will.[68] Volition is a determination to a good end, pleasure, or the avoidance of evil and pain. It is mixed with passion insofar as it is sensitive to good and evil. It "pursues the greatest good" and "flees the greatest evil, *of which it is sensible.*"[69] This sensibility places the volition on the side of affect and tends to assimilate its *conatus* to a reaction rather than an action (which, properly speaking, it is not, since it is a *tendency* to action), which follows the representation of a good or evil.[70] This reestablishes the primacy of the understanding over the will.

It is only with the *New Essays on Human Understanding* that the nature of the *conatus* of the volition is really clarified. In that text, Leibniz draws all the consequences, with regard to the will, of his psychology, which extends the soul's perception to the entire universe. Corresponding to this infinite perception of the universe is a will enriched with all the movements, impulses, and sensible and insensible solicitations of the universe (which ensure that it is never in a state of indifference). The "volitional" *conatus* is nothing but the result of this innumerable variety of unperceived motions that incline the soul. Leibniz uses the term "appetition" rather than "volition" to refer to these "efforts, arising from insensible perceptions, which we are not aware of," since "one describes as 'voluntary' only actions one can be aware of and can reflect upon when they arise from some consideration of good and bad."[71] Volition is the *conscious* effort that follows consideration of good and evil, whereas appetition is unconscious. Its action on the soul is real, although we are unaware of it.

The will, then, is marked by a kind of complexity (it is not a simple notion) and by the variety of things it includes, even beyond the realm of apperception and consciousness:

> Various perceptions and inclinations combine to produce a complete volition: it is the result of the conflict amongst them. There are some, imperceptible in themselves, which add up to a disquiet which impels us without our seeing why. There are some which join forces to carry us towards or away from some object, in which case there is desire or fear, also accompanied by a disquiet but not always one amounting to pleasure or displeasure.[72]

In addition, there are "impulses which are accompanied by actual pleasure or suffering," "new sensations or the lingering images of past ones (whether or not accompanied by memory)" that renew former impulses. "The eventual result of all these impulses is the prevailing effort, which makes a full volition."[73] The volition expresses a relation between concurrent and opposing forces of various kinds. It results from the composition of inclinations and impulses that differ as much by their origin, nature, and degree of distinction, as by their end—since all these inclinations do not "will" or rather do not tend to the same object.

Volition is not only the union of a great variety of elements but also a preference. It is both the effort resulting from all these impulses, which come together in unity (accord) or opposition (conflict), and the total inclination that wins out over all the others. As in a deliberative assembly, where the dominant party can be thwarted by smaller ones aligned together in opposition, it is not necessarily the strongest inclination that prevails, if the other tendencies join together to oppose it. It is always the case that "the final result is determined by how things weigh against one another" and in the "combat" between different inclinations

> everything which then impinges on us weighs in the balance and contributes to
> determining a *resultant direction*, almost as in mechanics; so that without some
> prompt diversion we will be unable to stop it.[74]

The comparison with the physical case and the reference to conflict between tendencies are obviously reminiscent of the composition of possibles into mutually incompatible worlds and of their contrary pretensions to existence. In both cases, Leibniz rejects the idea of a composition whose result is "automatic." Just as the best series of things prevails of itself, without excluding the possibility of other series in themselves, the final determination (the volition, properly speaking) that wins out inclines the mind without rendering any other choice impossible.

Owing to the univocity of notions,[75] the exact parallel between understanding and will holds in the case of both man and God. This parallel is not the result of a mere analogy between "intellectual" *conatus* and "volitional" *conatus*. The soul is characterized by a permanent state of change. It is constantly animated with efforts: the tendency of one thought for another or the inclination toward a greater good. In the understanding, this effort

> involves a composite tendency, that is to say, a multitude of present thoughts,
> each of which tends to a particular change according to what it involves and
> what is found in it at the time by virtue of its essential relationship to all the
> other things in the world.[76]

In the will, effort is the synthesis of an infinite number of movements, impulses, and all manner of solicitations: sensed and unsensed, present and past, divergent and concurrent. In fact, it is the *same* effort as that which constitutes the essence of the substance. The understanding and will express one and the same *conatus*, which is nothing but the limited force of created substances and the omnipotence of God. For, understanding and will are based on power. Power is their common subject, their source, their basis, and the essence from which they are derived.[77] Thus, it is the same power that is exercised through them, whether in the form of a possible in the divine understanding (a perception or idea in the creature) or in the form of a volition striving to realize the possible (an inclination, appetition, or volition in created substance).

In contrast to the classical intellectualist schema, Leibniz reconceives the relation between understanding and will. The will is conceived as the immediate and parallel translation of the idea into inclination and of the possible into effort, rather than as that which follows the judgment of the understanding to which it submits and of which it passively approves. A possible that tends to existence is *at the same time* an object that is willed in proportion to its perfection.

The tension previously observed between a purely intellectual meta-physical mechanism (from which the best necessarily follows) and the exercise of a will that freely chooses the best from among all possibles is thereby resolved. For, to explain things in terms of the understanding or the will ultimately amounts to the same thing. Both describe the ac-tivity of the same power. The quasi-mathematical approach in terms of an interplay of possibles tending toward existence, whose mechanical out-come is the most perfect combination, can be reconciled with the more "moral" approach in terms of a free choice of the will that inclines to the best. The former describes the calculations of a God-mathematician and concerns the efficient cause of the world. The latter takes into account the proposed end of a God, who is not only a builder but also a wise mon-arch, namely the glory he derives from a universe that unites the greatest variety with the most beautiful order while providing happiness for the greatest number of creatures. Thus, the point of view of the under-standing accords with that of the will, just as in nature the realm of power and efficient causes accords with the realm of wisdom and final causes. Both describe, in their own way, the reasons for creation. This agreement ensures that these two realms "interpenetrate without confusing or in-terfering with each other"[78] and—in conformity with Leibniz's theory of point of view, according to which each is true considered in itself—that each can be considered independently of the other without either being sufficient unto itself.

It is worth noting, however, that the parallel between understanding and will will only be perfectly realized once the distinction between *an-tecedent* and *consequent* will has been fully generalized. This distinction, which at first was limited to the question of salvation (especially at the time of the irenic negotiations between late 1698 and early 1699),[79] would only be fully exploited with regard to metaphysics and extended to all vo-lition during the composition of the *Theodicy* or a little before.[80] The rela-tion is the following: corresponding to the set of possibles, which equally strive for existence, and whose composition forms the best world in the divine understanding, is the composition of antecedent wills concerning every particular good and from which results the consequent and final willing of the best in general. In both cases there is the same conflict be-tween incompatibles, such that certain possibles are ruled out and certain particular wills (such as the will that all men be saved) prevented from being realized.

## 3.2 THE ORIGIN OF EVIL AND GOD'S PHYSICAL CONCURRENCE

### 3.2.1 The Notion of Original Imperfection

The *Confession of a Philosopher* does not afford a satisfactory response to the question of God's physical concurrence with sin. In affirming that God is the reason for sin without being its author (who is the sinner), Leibniz revives the Scholastic distinction between *physical* and *moral* causes: "the ultimate physical cause of sins, as of all creatures, is in God; the moral cause is in the sinner."[81] However, this distinction is explicitly criticized in *The Author of Sin*, an opuscule contemporary with the *Confession of a Philosopher*. Leibniz's complaint is not that the distinction is bad in itself, but that it is subject to abuse[82] and, consequently, a source of error. Indeed, it lends support to two theses that Leibniz firmly rejects beginning with *On the Omnipotence and Omniscience of God*: (1) the possibility of separating the physical reality of sin from its sinful nature, attributing the former to God and the latter to the sinner, and (2) the reduction of evil to a pure privation or nothingness.

Leibniz's rejection of these two theses leads him to cast doubt on the two main explanations of God's physical concurrence with evil that had been proposed by philosophers and theologians. According to the defenders of partial or mediate concurrence, God cooperates only partially[83] or indirectly (by his general concurrence[84]) with the actions of a creature, by giving it being and supplying it with a power, which it can subsequently misuse. For Leibniz, this explanation has two shortcomings.

On the one hand, it limits God's power and influence by maintaining that his action ends with the creation of the world and the beings that inhabit it. However, the dependence of created things on the creator continues beyond the act of creation itself. This dependence implies that the world and all it contains endure only insofar as they are maintained in existence by the divine power. As a result, conservation is only continuous creation, because it requires as much power to create the world on the first day as to preserve it in existence from one moment to the next.

On the other hand, the idea of a partial concurrence amounts to dividing the action into two and attributing one part to man and the other to God. Now, even if this division could be established with precision, how are we to conceive of the human contribution, if not as an act—an act with which, like all acts, God would have to concur, that is, to produce in part. Because this division would continue to infinity (with the part attributed to man diminishing with each iteration), the complete act would ultimately be attributed to God alone.[85]

As for those, such as Thomas Aquinas,[86] who maintain that God's concurrence with the actions of creatures is complete, they do not divide sin with regard to its "matter" (as do the defenders of partial concurrence). Instead, they separate the *moral* from the *physical*, by distinguishing the act, which is entirely produced by God, from its moral character—that is, from its illicit nature—for which the sinner alone is responsible. The act, with regard to what is real and positive (the action, for example, of striking someone), proceeds from God, who is the ultimate physical cause of all things. However, that which is morally blameworthy in the act (murder is forbidden) comes from man, its moral cause.

On this solution the act in itself, in its matter, is completely indifferent or morally neutral. Whether the act is good or bad, its physical nature remains the same. Here we must recall what was established by the example of the bad musician in *On the Omnipotence and Omniscience of God*.[87] The violinist cannot be the author of the motion of his bow without also being the author of the resulting dissonances. In other words, it is impossible to abstract the evil of a sin from the act, without separating, in some sense, the sin from itself. A good action does not differ from a bad one merely in that the former conforms to virtue and the latter is contrary to it—that is, only by a purely extrinsic denomination (its relation to the law). They also differ in their physical reality, insofar as the former contains more perfection than the latter.

Leibniz opposes those who, following Augustine, abstract evil from its ontological basis in order to reduce it to a pure negation without any reality. The theoretical appeal of such a reduction is obvious. If evil is nothing at the physical level, if God is the author of all that is real and positive in things—but not of their flaws and lacks—then he has no relation to sin and is immediately rendered innocent. Besides that it implies an inadmissible separation between the physical and the moral, this view suffers from the following inconvenience: it serves equally well to disculpate the sinner. For, as had already been emphasized in *On the Omnipotence and Omniscience of God*, what is true for God is likewise true for man:

> I am amazed that these people did not go further and try to persuade us that man himself is not the author of sin, since he is only the author of the physical or real aspect, the privation being something for which there is no author.[88]

If evil is lacking in reality, it has no need of a cause. It is nothing, and so is produced by nothing and by no one. Ultimately, no one, neither God nor man, is guilty of it. As a result, all justice is destroyed. Like matter and form, the physical and the moral are inseparable. Consequently, it must be conceded that evil is indeed *a thing*: it is the bad act considered as an indivisible whole. Sin is not nothing. It is, Leibniz maintains, a "creature" produced by God.[89] Sin can be called *nothing* only in a relative sense, namely, insofar as it cannot impede God's omnipotence and glory nor the perfection of universal harmony.[90]

Thus, God produces sin in its entirety, together with the volition and circumstances that lead to it. He creates man in the act of sinning and afterward conserves him in his sinful state. How then can we reconcile the reality of evil (which does not exist apart but is indistinguishable from the being of the evil thing) with God's complete physical concurrence, without calling into question divine justice or human culpability? The Leibnizian solution is to be found in the notion of the "original imperfection" of the creature.

The first occurrence in Leibniz's writings of the phrase "original defect of the creature," as an explanation of creaturely fallibility, occurs in his reading notes on Bellarmine taken between 1680 and 1684.[91] The idea of a limitation intrinsic to creatures, which prevents them from receiving more perfection, is put forward in the context of a discussion of election and damnation:

> God wills [*intendit*] the perfection of all, and so favors it as much as the nature of the creature will allow. However, he permits certain ones to fall short of perfection because of the nature of the creature. Whence it follows that he also permits certain ones to be miserable.[92]

Ontologically, this divine will ensures that God gives creatures all the perfection it is possible to give them. In theological terms, it means that he wills the salvation of all spirits. Here a crucial transformation has occurred. Divine concurrence is still conceived as complete and productive of everything that is real and positive in the creature. However, the reason for the incomplete development of the creature and of its privation of eternal happiness resides in its essence, which is incapable of receiving all the metaphysical and moral perfection that would render the creature better and happy. The inseparability of the being from its defect is maintained, since this defect does not come from an external obstacle but is owing to an internal lack of capacity or receptivity. It is the creature, and it alone, that limits the perfection it receives from God. This makes it possible to affirm that the cause of evil is distinct from God, while recognizing that this cause cannot (and ought not) be separated from the reality it limits. God is the sole author of creatures and of everything their essence contains. He produces creatures *with* their limits and imperfections. Nevertheless, he does not cause the resulting sins, which are imputable to the creature alone.

Obviously, Leibniz is not the first to attribute the cause of evil to the deficiency of creatures themselves. Augustine had already argued that because the creature is drawn out of nothing, it is by its very nature "imperfect, defective and corruptible."[93] In this he was followed by the majority of authors in the philosophical tradition, from Thomas Aquinas to Descartes. Nevertheless, the notion of "original imperfection"[94]—also referred to as natural or "congenital" limitation, "weakness" prior to original sin, or "privative imperfection"[95]—has in Leibniz's thought a signification and consequences that are unprecedented. For Leibniz, original imperfection must be understood in the dual sense of first cause ("original" refers to the origin) and principle of individuation ("original" also connotes originality and singularity). Lastly, and above all, it is tied to the notion of *capacity* or *receptivity*.

The nature of a thing determines its aptitude for receiving a certain quantity of being or perfection. It is both that which defines the thing (what it is and what it is capable of), that which *positively* constitutes it as an individual ("original") being, and *negatively*, that which marks its limits (what it is not, what it lacks, what exceeds its abilities) and limits its receptivity by preventing the acquisition of further perfection (its *non plus ultra*). The original imperfection of a creature is similar to the circumference of a circle, which circumscribes a certain reality in space and, at the same time, restricts it by excluding everything that is not part of this reality.[96]

### 3.2.2 The Ambiguity of Capacity

The notion of the capacity or receptivity of a creature and of the world itself—what the world can contain, the reality it can "welcome" given the constraints of space and time and the nature of things[97]—appears deeply ambivalent. Capacity, of which original imperfection is the negative side, is at once (1) that by which a certain perfection is realized according to a particular mode of development (a progression within the essential limits of the thing), and (2) an impediment to further perfection, the flip side of the possible's tendency to existence. In accordance with the analogy to inertia, this impediment can be assimilated to a kind of contrary effort or anti-*conatus*.

(1) As the previously cited notes on Bellarmine make clear, creatures receive as much reality as their nature allows, but certain creatures do not achieve further development because of their nature. Does this mean that certain creatures fail to attain the perfection of which they would otherwise have been capable had they not been prevented from doing so by their essential imperfection? On this showing, the limitation of creatures would in a sense be twofold: first delimiting their capacity and second constraining them again by leaving them with less than what they could (or ought to) have been. Imperfection would involve both a *negation* (the absence of perfection) and a *privation* (the absence of due perfection), although it is true that Leibniz usually does not draw this distinction.

However, there is another possible interpretation. Perhaps creaturely imperfection is not to be considered in relation to the creature itself (to its nature), but in relation to other, more perfect creatures, either existing or possible. Indeed, there is no reason to think that a creature cannot receive more perfection than it has—e.g., that it have more intelligence or good will, or that it be saved rather than damned. This creature so endowed with greater capacity, while not impossible in itself, would belong to another possible world, and would therefore be a completely different being than the existing creature originally considered. In this way, a creature can be considered as conforming to its nature (and in this sense "perfect") while at the same time judged imperfect with regard to what it might have been or less perfect than another possible being endowed with greater perfections.

These two interpretations are not incompatible. A creature can be said to be imperfect both from an extrinsic point of view (with regard to other creatures, either real or possible, endowed with a greater receptivity) and from an intrinsic point of view (with regard to its own nature), since its perfection is, of necessity, acquired little by little and by means of moral and physical evil:

> The cause of evil results from the original imperfection of things, that is, from the limitation of creatures, which is such that the perfection of which things are capable could only be obtained by means of faults and punishments, just as certain results can be obtained only by appeal to incommensurable lines and motions.[98]

Rather than a redoubling of limitation, original imperfection implies a certain kind of development both of the creature and of the world itself: a process of improvement by retreats and detours, forward leaps and backtracking, a progress that precludes obtaining perfection directly, completely, and definitively. Neither the individual creature nor the world as a whole is able to receive all its perfection at once, since sometimes things must *draw back to make a better jump*:

> As for the afflictions, especially of good men, however, we may take it as certain that these lead to their greater good and that this is true not only theologically but also naturally. So a seed sown in the earth suffers before it bears fruit. In general, one may say that, though afflictions are temporary evils, they are good in effect, for they are short cuts to greater perfection.[99]

Imperfection (not merely original imperfection, but imperfection in general) is as much a limitation of perfection as a particular manner of acquiring perfection, namely mediately. Like the seed that must rot in the soil in order to engender a plant, or the caterpillar that must be wrapped in its cocoon to become a butterfly, each creature can attain its perfection only in stages. In this sense, the creature always conforms to its own nature (which it realizes throughout the whole of its existence) while perpetually seeking higher perfection (so that it is always beneath its full potential), since Leibniz suggests that substances, or at any rate, spirits, are capable of infinite progress.[100]

(2) Capacity or receptivity is nothing but the power to be affected.[101] Its intrinsic limitation restricts the perfection coming from God. Beginning in the years 1685–1686, this limitation is compared to the retardation or inertia observed in bodies:

> I say in the first place that all perfection or reality in things is continually produced by God, but that limitation or imperfection comes from creatures, just as the force communicated to a body by an agent receives a limitation on account of the matter or mass of the body as well as the natural retardation of bodies, and all else being equal, a lesser motion is produced, if the body is greater.[102]

In Leibniz's dynamics, antitypy and inertia (as defined by Kepler and Descartes) are the two properties of primitive passive power inherent in matter. The former is the resistance to penetration, and the latter resistance or repugnance to motion, without which a small body could, without losing its force, set a larger body at rest into motion. By virtue of its impenetrability, one body yields to another that strikes it, rather than allow itself to be penetrated. However, it "does not yield without difficulty or without diminishing the total motion of the one that pushes it."[103] Inertia is a resistance that manifests itself negatively as a diminution of received motion, and "positively" as an *effort* of the struck body "to persevere in its prior state such that not only does it not abandon this state by its own initiative, but resists [*repugnet*] the one that changes it."[104]At issue here is that resistance,

> or what Kepler calls the natural inertia of bodies, and which Descartes, too, acknowledged somewhere in his Letters, in recognizing that bodies only receive new motion by force and even resist what pushes them and destroys their force.[105]

A parallel can be drawn between active and passive power. Just as active power is more than a simple faculty, because it includes an effort, so passive power is not simply the capacity to be moved, but also the effective resistance to received motion (impenetrability and inertia),[106] which resistance must be understood as a kind of contrary effort, or anti-*conatus*. Thus, passive force is not the negation (or absence) of active force, but its opposite. Inertia is not the privation of all tendency. On the contrary, it is an opposing, albeit negative, tendency.[107]

Reference to the inertia of bodies becomes a recurrent feature of Leibniz's explication of the origin of evil. It is first presented in the form of an analogy: the essential limitation of creatures acts as a curb on received perfection, just as the greater a body's mass, the more its speed is reduced,[108] or as a feather diminishes the force that is impressed upon it,[109] or as the larger a boat is, the more slowly it advances.[110] Beginning with the *Theodicy*, it will no longer be a mere analogy, since physical inertia will be explicitly made an illustration of "metaphysical" inertia.[111]

Thus, original imperfection is not a simple limit, a lack of being or a mere privation (belonging to everything that is not God), but also a curb on additional being, reality, or perfection, and an effort to remain in its present state. This curb and this effort can be interpreted as that which both guarantees the integrity of the creature and maintains it within the limits of its nature (beyond which it would cease to be what it is), and following the model of inertia, as a deep repugnance to any increase in perfection. Leibniz writes to Schulenburg (April 8, 1698): "Without doubt boundaries or limits are of the essence of creatures, but limits are something privative and consist in the negation of further progress."[112] As resistance to perfection, imperfection appears as the negative counterpart to the tendency to exist that constitutes every possible. For this reason, imperfection cannot be assimilated, at the psychological level, to the mere possibility or faculty of sinning. Rather, it is a disposition,[113] or even an inclination, to sin as well as the explanation for a sin once it has occurred:

I had said that every creature is essentially limited, and I called this limitation or negation a privative imperfection, and I had added that this latter was the source of evil, not only of peccability, but also of sin itself. For, if creatures had had the entire degree of perfection [required], they would not have fallen.[114]

This does not mean that sin is absolutely necessary. It is committed freely, though certainly, since original imperfection together with particular circumstances has led certain creatures (bad angels, the first human couple) to *actually* fall. That is why "it must always be borne in mind that this origin of evil is only inclining and not necessitating."[115] This origin is a real determination that inclines toward evil, without necessitating. It is a determination prior to original sin, but one which this latter renders habitual and irresistible without grace. Inclination then becomes a penchant. Leibniz writes:

The state of the creature, both before and after the fall, was an *inclination* to sin arising out of the very nature of the creature, if the creature was not held back by divine grace. As a result of the fall, this inclination became ordinary and perpetual. Now, this state is voluntary; and although inclined to sin, it is not yet peccaminous. Nevertheless, there is a non-voluntary first state, at least in the beginning, when the creature first begins to exist.[116]

Original imperfection appears here as an inclination such that without God's grace all spirits (not just the bad angels and first humans) would fall. On this point, the Academy edition presents an interesting variant for *Discourse on Metaphysics*, §30 (I put the variant in italics and Leibniz's deletions in square brackets): "there was an original limitation or imperfection connatural to all creatures, *which [inclined some] inclines them to sin and perhaps without God's [special] grace [they would all have sinned] all spirits would have fallen.*"[117] Such is the force of this inclination to evil that it would seem that creatures can escape it only by means of grace: grace given to spirits even before the fall, so that not all succumb as they otherwise would, and grace subsequently given to the sinner (after the sin of the first parents) by the sacrifice of Christ the Redeemer. Good appears as grace, in a world that is essentially imperfect (metaphysically speaking) and even originally given to sin.

Original imperfection is strengthened and consolidated by Adam's sin. It becomes an obstacle to perfection, a resistance to good and to grace, a positive effort toward sin. Here evil is not merely the absence or privation of good, but a *conatus* opposed to the good impetus coming from God.

### 3.2.3 Physical Concurrence and Moral Imputation

The cause of evil resides in original imperfection, a phrase Leibniz uses synonymously with natural limitation, privation, nothingness, and nonbeing.[118] This wavering with regard to vocabulary (in contrast to the Scholastics, who carefully distinguished privation from negation) engenders a certain confusion, which was perhaps intended by Leibniz. By assimilating original imperfection and nothingness, Leibniz is able to give the impression that he is adopting the Augustinian thesis according to which evil is nothingness and so claim the authority of this church father. In fact Leibniz understands this "nothingness" to be something other than a pure negation. As we have seen, imperfection implies a real resistance to perfection and even a certain inclination to evil. It cannot be defined as a nonbeing, except in a derivative sense, insofar as it is the mark of a deficiency or lack (of being or perfection).

Nothingness, understood as an absolute nothing lacking all attributes, is unthinkable as such. It is a word without a referent[119] and a pure abstraction. Therefore, it is neither an evil, nor even the direct cause of evil, which in fact is original imperfection, but rather the cause of its cause. As indicated in the *Dialogue on Human Freedom and the Origin of Evil* (January 1695), it is only at a higher level of analysis, when we search for the "origin of origins" that original imperfection can be related to Nothingness as its ultimate cause, or rather as its principle. For, Nothingness cannot be the cause of anything whatsoever. The infinite Nothingness, which like God is eternal, is the principle with which God must be combined to produce limited beings.[120]. However, to posit such a principle is not to reestablish some form of Manichaeism, since Nothingness is precisely Nothing. It is not a positive principle opposed to God, but rather a non-principle that cannot constitute a god to rival the supreme being. God is unique.

While it is necessary to refer to Nothingness when one wishes to pursue the investigation of evil beyond original imperfection and identify an even more original principle, the manner in which Nothingness combines with Being (that is, God) to form things remains problematic. The account found in certain texts of the origin of things out of God and Nothingness[121] constitutes, in my view, a theoretical construction that is both artificial and ultimately unsatisfactory. For not only is Nothingness, considered absolutely, a pure abstraction, but when joined to Being, it neither contributes nor modifies anything! "Whether *Nothing* is posited or not is of no consequence, that is, A + Nothing = A."[122] In the composition of things, the role assigned to Nothingness is to be that which subtracts, limits, and removes. It is the subtraction operator whose result is original imperfection.

However, subtraction presupposes there is something to subtract, some being to be limited. Thus, Nothingness cannot be a pure principle conceivable separately and per se, except in a purely theoretical way for the purposes of explanation and to satisfy the Principle of Sufficient Reason. For, by definition, Nothingness is always relative to being.

There is one final reason why there could be no pure Nothingness. For, even before the creation, there are possibles, which are real and tend toward existence. Does this thesis contradict the biblical dogma of creation ex nihilo? Rather, it implies that the dogma must be given a philosophical interpretation in two respects. On the one hand, creation ex nihilo underscores the perpetual dependence of the created on the creator. Nothing comes into being or continues to exist, except by the power of God. On the other hand, creation ex nihilo emphasizes that the creature is and remains by its very nature finite, limited, and "lacking in countless respects," as Descartes had already maintained.[123] Every created thing is imperfect and so participates in Nothingness. In this sense, evil arises from nonbeing. However, it is not absolutely speaking nothing, since it is not ontologically separable from the being of which it is the limit, corruption, or vice.

This explanation of the origin of evil has direct consequences for the doctrine of God's physical concurrence. For, it makes it possible to conceive at once the unity of the evil act and the distinction between perfection, which comes from God, and imperfection, which follows from the creature. It provides the key to rendering two apparently irreconcilable propositions consistent: (1) "because God is just, he is not the cause of evil," and (2) "because both creatures and their operations [good and bad acts] depend on God, there is no reality in things that does not exist—that is, is not produced—continuously by God."[124]

Leibniz offers an original account of God's physical concurrence. It receives a particularly clear formulation around 1686–1687 in a text that has been given the title *On Freedom, Fate and God's Grace* by the Academy editors. Leibniz maintains that no act, motion, thought or accident can be reduced to a mere modality or relation, but that each of these constitutes a new positive reality (*nova realitas*) that can only come from God given the dependence which all things have upon him.[125] Divine concurrence is not only general, but immediate, proximate, and continuous—unless the world is conceived as independent and having always existed (a doctrine, which according to Leibniz, leads to atheism or Epicureanism). In this context the Scholastic distinction between the *matter* of sin and its *form* is admissible only if it is redefined. According to this new conception, matter is not to be contrasted with form, as physical to moral, as if the physical were independent of the moral—that is, considered as a neutral reality that can be equally associated with a good or bad act. Rather, the distinction must be drawn at the physical level itself. *Matter* designates the being and perfection received from God, whereas *form* refers to their limitation—that is, the diminution or restriction effected by the creature, according to its capacity or degree of receptivity. The form is properly speaking that which informs— one might even be tempted to say *deforms*— "matter," which is the reality and perfections given by God. Form is also that which makes matter a particular, limited being (limitation being the negative side of individuation).

Thus, the sinner is guilty not only because he consents by his will—that is, morally—to the evil inclination (sin consisting in nothing but the adherence of the will to that which is contrary to the law). He is also guilty because he really (physically) restricts and resists the being received from God. Thus, there is an *ontological* difference between the vicious man and the virtuous man and between bad and good actions. They do not differ by an extrinsic moral quality with no corresponding trace in being. Contrary to Suarez, for example, who holds that from a physical point of view, God concurs with good and evil in exactly the same manner, Leibniz maintains that God communicates more perfection in a good act. For Leibniz, the bad act results from the lack of perfection that "arises out of the nature of the creature, or nothingness or limitation,"[126] as in the case of the projectile whose mass and weight reduce the impressed speed, and as the previously mentioned examples of the feather and boat illustrate.

The notion of original imperfection makes it possible to posit human physical concurrence, which makes the creature the sole author of evil, without calling into question the complete, immediate, and special concurrence of God. Existing within being as an ontological diminution or alteration, sin is not reducible to a mere non-conformity to the law (*anomia*[127]) but is imputable to the sinner *even in its physical reality* (which allows for an exact correspondence between the physical and moral levels). In this way, Leibniz is able to secure the innocence of God, who causes only what is good, perfect, and positive in the bad act. Likewise, he is able to blame the creature, who is the deficient cause by virtue of its limitations and defects (its ignorance, lack of attention, laziness, and weakness of will). Moreover, he accomplishes these things without separating, from a metaphysical or physical point of view, the creature from its essential imperfection, or the act from its sinful nature.

Imperfection and individuation are always connected. Being, although it is a gift from God, only becomes *a* being (that is, an individual creature or act) by passing through the filter of limitation. That which constitutes the being is, at the same time, that which limits it, while that which makes it *physically* an imperfect creature or action is, at the same time, that which makes it *morally* a sinner or sin.

The invention of original imperfection is a crucial stage in the evolution of Leibniz's doctrine of evil. It allows him, on the one hand, to tie together and explain a host of diverse properties, attributes, and phenomena: the limitation of essence, capacity, and receptivity; passivity; resistance to perfection; inertia; obscure and confused ideas in the understanding; ignorance; laziness; error; irresolution and weakness of the will and uneasiness. All of these are expressions of the same fundamental deficiency, which is more than merely negative; it is a source of obstacles and contrary *conatus*. The generic and unifying function of the notion of imperfection, which soon will come to be called "metaphysical evil," in terms of which the various different kinds of evil are conceived, is already present.

> Every perfection in creatures flows immediately from God [such as being, force, reality, magnitude, knowledge, will]. The [imperfections] defects that they possess flow from the creatures themselves and from their limits or *non plus ultra*, which entails the [finitude] limitation [such as limits of being, resistance to force, passion in reality, limitations of magnitude, obscurity in knowledge, irresolution in the will].[128]

On the other hand, by locating evil in the form rather than the matter (contrary to Plotinus), Leibniz offers a novel justification of God. God is innocent of sin because he is the author of matter—that is, of all positive reality ("that which is good in evil"[129])—and not of the forms or ideas of possibles, which are uncreated and are the sole reason of evil. The argument that makes the divine understanding the "location" of evil is not new, since it can already be found in the letter to Wedderkopf. However, its signification has changed. God is not the cause of sin. However, this is not because sin follows necessarily from the universal harmony, and so his will is not responsible for it. Rather, it is because creatures by their nature constrain the perfection they receive from God. Whence the possibility of evil.

## 3.3 GOD'S MORAL CONCURRENCE WITH EVIL AND THE RELATION OF PART TO WHOLE

### 3.3.1 Permission as Limitation of the Will and the Unity of the Divine Decree

The notion of original imperfection makes it possible to envisage both a complete divine concurrence, on the physical level, and a real participation of the sinner in the production of evil acts by virtue of the limits and re-sistance he opposes to the being and perfection received from God. Thus, sin cannot be imputed to God on the grounds that the sinner draws its existence and power from God, or that sin itself, considered with regard to its positive being, is, like all things, produced by him. Yet, what about the moral level? Is not God the accomplice of evil? Indeed, does he not will evil given that he foresees it and does not prevent it? Just as it was necessary in the physical order to reconcile God's causality with the causality of the sinner, so it is necessary, in the moral order, to reconcile the idea of a divine will that is wholly good with the existence of a world in which there is evil. It is here that the doctrine of *permission* comes into play.

The redefinition of the nature and role of the will following the *Confession of a Philosopher* leads Leibniz to abandon his conception of permission as knowledge without willing[130] together with the distinction between reason and author (which he had already criticized in *The Author of Sin*). In his conversation with Steno (1677), Leibniz treats permission as a kind of vo-lition: a volition that is conditioned. Like the musician who does not will dissonances in themselves, but only by accident, insofar as they make the melody more perfect, "God does not want sins, except under the condi-tion of punishment that corrects, and per accidens only, as a requirement for completing the perfection of the series."[131] To permit sin is to *will it by accident*—that is, not for its own sake (the will being unable to choose evil qua evil), but for a different reason, namely, that when compensated and punished, it is part of the best series of things. On this showing, God is no longer simply the reason for sin. He is the author of sin, since he wills it ac-cidentally: "It can be said in a certain way that God is the author of sin per accidens, i.e., God wills sins per accidens, as a musician wills dissonance."[132]

In the *Confession of a Philosopher*, justification of God consisted in eliminating the role of the will, by making the understanding alone con-cerned in permission. In 1677 the perspective changes radically. The so-lution lies not in the exclusion of the will, which would risk falling into Spinozism, but involves an appeal to different degrees (willing admits of more or less[133]) and kinds (willing *absolutely* or *accidentally*) of willing. The idea now is not so much to remove the imputation of evil from God as to make evil the object of his will, though only as a means. God is obliged to create evil, if he is to will the most perfect series of things.

It is now clear that the solution to the problem of God's moral concur-rence with sin must rest on an adequate account of the will. This is con-firmed by the *Theodicy* itself (§22). However, the doctrine of permission defended in 1677 is not yet satisfactory, insofar as it threatens to make God the author of sin, even if only by accident. This conclusion remains shocking and seems seriously to call into question God's goodness, which is difficult to reconcile with the positive, albeit conditioned, willing of evil. Thus, beginning in the years 1680–1684 Leibniz is led to revisit his explanation of God's moral concurrence.

Although he abandons the idea of volition by accident following the *Conversation with Steno*, Leibniz retains the idea that evil, even if it is not willed in itself, can be admitted as a condition, on account of other things or in view of something else (a greater good or the best whole). Permission takes the form of a limit imposed on the divine will (which tends only to the good), by the essence of things (the capacity peculiar to every creature) and the consideration of the best (the universal harmony). As indicated in the notes on Bellarmine (cited earlier), God wills the perfection of all creatures and favors it, but "he *permits* certain ones to fall short of perfection, because of the nature of the creature. Whence it follows that he also *permits* certain ones to be miserable."[134]

In permitting evil, God does no more than allow things to be as they must on account of their nature. That is, he allows their existence to conform to their essence, with all of the defects, limitations, and negative effects that this essence involves. Permission is neither a positive volition nor mere knowledge without willing. Rather, it is the result of a limiting constraint grounded in the uncreated nature of things and which is imposed on the divine will. Permission is the counterpart, on the moral level, to the limitation that follows, on the physical level, from the original imperfection of creatures, which diminishes the being and perfection received from God.

In this sense the essential imperfection of creatures affords an explanation of divine concurrence as much from the physical as from the moral point of view. This imperfection is both that which reduces and limits the positive that comes from God and the reason why the divine will to good is restricted (though not eliminated). Just as God dispenses all perfection and being, which every creature limits by its imperfection, so he wills that all spirits be virtuous, happy, and saved, while permitting certain ones, in conformity with their nature and freedom, to be evil, miserable, and damned. The notion of creature's capacity, insofar as it implies a constraint imposed on the creative power of God, occurs once again in the form of a limitation on his good will.

Of course, things do not exist in isolation but as part of a series that constitutes a world. To the individual limit inherent in every creature is added a second more general one, namely, that of the harmony of the world considered in its totality. This more general limit likewise imposes certain restrictions on the development of its constitutive elements for the greater perfection of the whole. Permission is the expression of this double restriction owing both to the nature of things considered in themselves and to universal harmony, which must take into account all things together:

> God does not will [Adam's] sin, that is, he wills to prevent it, *to the extent allowed by the harmony of things*. The depths of Paul are the harmony of things, which surpasses the human mind's ability to understand, although our mind knows that this harmony exists.[135]

Permission is the sign of a shift of the will with regard to the good of an individual thing (the part) upon consideration of the universal point of view (the whole). God wills the good; he does not will evil and even wills to suppress it *to the extent that* universal harmony allows. Are we to understand this change of the will as an effort toward the good that remains a mere velleity, a rejection of sin insufficient to prevent it, or even a lack of power? By no means. Rather, it is a case of the will *restricting itself* insofar as it does not tend only to the good of each individual but also to what is best for the whole. The divine will, which is wholly good, is not hindered or suppressed by a contrary will on God's part. It modifies itself upon adopting a more general view—that of the whole of things—of the world considered as a totality, instead of considering only the particular. Thus, there is neither contradiction nor velleity in God, but progression from a positive volition to prevent sin (considered in itself) to a "negative" volition not to prevent sin (considered now with regard to its consequences, together with the rest of things). The volition is *negative*, because it allows to occur what it does not cause but could, of course, prevent: "*to permit* is to be able to prevent and knowingly not prevent."[136]

Permission is the effect, for the part, of a choice that takes as its object the entire universe. It can be explained and justified only within the universal context. Consequently, to ask why God did not prevent such and such a crime from being committed or why he did not give Adam the grace to resist temptation to avoid the fall, amounts, in light of the connection between all beings, to asking why he did not choose a world other than ours—and, correlatively, why he created this one. Not being the author of essences,

> God does not decide whether Adam must sin, but whether this series of things that contains Adam, whose perfect individual notion includes sin, must nevertheless be preferred to all others. . . . It is that the perfect notion of an individual substance considered by God in the mere state of possibility, prior to any actual decree of existence, already contains everything that will occur if it exists, and even the entire series of things of which it is part. That is why we do not ask

whether Adam will sin, but whether Adam, who will sin, should be allowed to exist.[137]

The question is no longer, as at the time of the *Confession of a Philosopher*, "why did Adam sin?" (to which the answer was, because he is Adam and because his idea is contained in the divine understanding, the seat of universal harmony). Nor is the question, "why create Adam knowing that he will sin?" Rather, the question becomes, "why choose this world, which contains Adam's sin?" The answer is that Adam is part of the best possible world and it is on these grounds that his sin is permitted by God. Permission of Adam's sin is contained in a "more general and comprehensive" divine will[138] whose object is not Adam alone but the world to which he belongs. For God does not arrange things by parts or "disjointedly" (*à bâtons rompus*)[139] determining the fate of one creature without at the same time considering all the rest. God takes the global view; he cannot have detached and isolated—that is, *particular*—wills. His will takes as its object the entire universe, considered as a whole, and not such and such a being or such and such an act considered apart. Corresponding to the unity of the world—that is, the interlocking chain of all existing things—is the unity of the decree by which God chooses that world and brings it into existence.

Thus, at the moral level, the justification of God rests on two arguments. First, God decides nothing concerning human actions, the distribution of grace, or the details of things included in the best possible series (which he finds "ready-made" in his understanding and does no more than create).[140] Second, his choice to bring this series into existence does not imply that he wills *absolutely* and *expressly* everything it contains, especially sin. God wills the best possible universe and the good it contains, but he merely permits the evil it includes:

> If the action is good in itself, we can say that God wishes it and sometimes commands it, even though it does not take place. But if the action is evil in itself, and becomes good only by accident because the course of events, particularly punishment and satisfaction, corrects its malignity and repays the evil with interest in such a way that more perfection is found in the whole sequence than if the evil had not occurred—then we must say that God permits it but not that he wills it.[141]

Consideration of the unity and generality of the decree from which the world results resolves the question of moral concurrence, by causing all reference to a particular will to disappear. God cannot be suspected of complicity in sin, since his will does not terminate with the part, nor does it ever concern one single being in isolation; its object is the universe in its totality. Any "particular" decree, relating to a single creature, can be so only in a relative sense. Such a decree is only the universal decree considered from a certain point of view or is contained within it virtually.[142] For, in reality, any such "particular" decree concerns not just one individual creature but all others as well:

> But we should consider that God, while acting with perfect wisdom, does not form any decree without keeping in mind all the causes and all the effects in the whole universe, because of the connection of all things. Therefore it would be best to say that God only forms a single decree, which is the one to choose this universe from among the other possible universes, and in this decree everything is included, without there being need to look for order among the particular decrees, as if one were independent of the others.[143]

Evil is the result not of an express and positive divine will, but of that will that considers the whole and is merely permissive with regard to sin. The thesis of the global choice of the best possible world ultimately finds the reason for this permission in "a detail which involves infinite considerations"[144] that God alone can comprehend. To fully explain the least act or event in the world, it would be necessary to have "knowledge [*scientia*] of all things, that is, infinite knowledge."[145] Although, the ultimate reason for the permission of sin is beyond us, at least in this life, although it is impossible for us to explain why *this* evil has been permitted, we still have good reason to affirm in general that it had to be because it results in a greater good for the whole. As Saint Augustine observed, "God would not permit evil, if he did not draw some good out of evil."[146] Thus we cannot *comprehend* the specific reason for the permission of evil, but we should *know* in general that God has allowed it, because he has foreseen that it will be the occasion of a greater good that could not have been obtained without it.

Christian Revelation teaches us that Adam's sin permitted the incarnation and that Judas's betrayal made possible Christ's passion and with it the redemption of the entire human race. However, we must not conclude that God can will sin, even as a means of achieving a greater good. For, it is equally forbidden to God to do evil in order to obtain some good.[147] The existence of evil in the best combination of things cannot transform permission into a positive volition. For this reason, sin can never be a *means* willed by God, even accidentally (as Leibniz held it to be at the time of the conversation with Steno). It is only a *condition* of obtaining the best: "[God] wills the greatest perfection, he permits evils without which this perfection could not be obtained. Evils are not means, but conditions."[148]

Whereas the term "means" positively designates an instrument, the object of a volition tending to a certain end, a condition is conceived negatively, and that in a twofold sense. On the one hand, as a condition sine qua non, a condition is defined as that which cannot be willed as such (e.g., the fall of Adam), but whose absence would prevent the desired end from being achieved, and, consequently, that which God must resolve to accept in order to bring about the most perfect world. On the other hand, a condition is a kind of *necessary accident*, a prerequisite tied to and concomitant with the good, without which the latter could not be obtained. It is not the cause of the good, something productive in and of itself, but that which must be posited as precondition, a circumstance and constraint that is indispensable, not so much for what its presence makes possible, but for what its absence would prevent.[149] The difference between *condition* and *cause* is the difference between the body composed of bones and nerves, and the intelligence that acts:

> It is true that one who asserts that I couldn't do all of this without bones and nerves would be correct. However, there is a difference between the true cause and that which is only a condition without which the cause could not be a cause.[150]

Reflection on the permission of evil ultimately leads to the following paradox: the permitted is that which God could not avoid, given that his aim was to achieve the best. Moreover, the permitted is that which he could not eliminate, without himself erring—that is, without doing wrong and failing in what he owes to himself. If we once grant that God always chooses the best, given that he is absolutely perfect, then we are forced to acknowledge that it must be better to permit sin than to exclude it, since sin actually occurs in the world.[151] The fact of sin even licenses the conclusion that it would have been worse to prevent sin than to allow it (this thesis is explicitly defended, as we shall see, in the *Theodicy*). Permission is the other, negative, side of the moral necessity that moves God to choose the best. Finding sin and other evils included in the idea of the best possible universe, the creator could not exclude them without choosing a different universe—that is, without renouncing the best itself. In a sense, the existence of evil is a lesser evil. For, true evil would be the creation of a world inferior in overall perfection to the most perfect possible world, by a God who could have done better.

### 3.3.2  From the *Discourse on Metaphysics* to the *Theodicy*: Toward the Primacy of a Cosmic Point of View?

The inseparability of the divine decrees (and among them the one to permit sin), which in reality are reducible to a single general will, implies that there is neither logical nor temporal priority between them: "such is the connection among them that no one is considered *separately* from the others; and in this sense *the dispute concerning the order of decrees ceases*: namely, when the decree has the entire series as its object."[152]

The theory of a unique universal decree seems inevitably to diminish the importance of the part, and in particular of human beings in creation, with regard to the perfection and good of the whole. On this score, some commentators have detected an important evolution between the *Discourse on Metaphysics* and the *Theodicy*. In the *Discourse* Leibniz insisted on the preeminence and infinite value of spirits relative to other creatures and to the world itself. Leibniz even goes so far to declare that "a spirit is worth an entire world."[153] In the *Theodicy*, while still acknowledging the excellence of their nature (God certainly values a human being more than a lion), Leibniz relativizes it ("No substance is absolutely contemptible or absolutely precious before God") and emphasizes that the rest of creatures cannot be treated as negligible (it is not certain that God prefers a single human being to the entire race of lions). For, even if God valued a single human over all lions taken together, "it would by no means follow that the interest of a certain number of men would prevail over the consideration of a general disorder diffused through an infinite number of creatures. This opinion would be a remnant of the old and somewhat discredited maxim, that all is made solely for man."[154] In comparing these two texts, it can be seen, as Jean Baruzi has written, that "appeal is increasingly made to the cosmic point of view, which gradually overshadows the manner in which Leibniz understood the preeminence of spirits around 1685."[155]

This evolution is said to involve three major changes: (1) the revalorization of the natural realm, which, while still serving the realm of grace, is that to which the latter must likewise accommodate itself (*Theodicy* §118); (2) the happiness of spirits becomes one of God's ends, though not his exclusive, nor even principal, end (*Theodicy* §119); (3) the emphasis on the possible existence in the universe of forms beyond those known and even of other, more intelligent, creatures (*Theodicy* §19). This universalizing, aestheticizing, and naturalizing development, which has also been defended by Michel Fichant,[156] has as a corollary a somber, even pessimistic, vision of the human condition. Human beings are only a small part of the universe, whose global perfection may require the sacrifice of their individual good.[157]

There can be no doubt that between the *Discourse on Metaphysics* and the *Theodicy* the relation between part and whole is altered. However, it is not clear that this change involves relegating spirits to a secondary rank or that it provides comfort to the tragic vision of the world, which Baruzi describes. In the first place, it must be remembered that the "cosmic point of view" is already present in the *Discourse on Metaphysics* via the notion of expression. Indeed, this cosmic view lies at the heart of the concept of individual substance, one of whose fundamental characteristics is to express the entire universe. This has led Michel Fichant to speak of substance as a "universal individuality."[158] It is also worth emphasizing that although Leibniz affirms that the happiness of spirits is "God's principal end" (DM §5), "principal" does not mean unique, since God has not made the world solely for us (§19). Nor does "principal end" mean unconditioned end, one that must take absolute precedence over every other consideration. For, as Leibniz makes clear, God wants to bring about the happiness of each one "in so far as the general harmony permits" (§5; see also §36), which presupposes that harmony can prevent it. God's end is, above all, his own glory.

What is clear, in my view, is that in moving from one text to the other there is an inversion of the relation between universal and particular. In the *Discourse on Metaphysics* the world is conceived—one might even say constituted—on the basis of the individual substance. Whereas in subsequent texts (once the thesis of the unique universal decree has made its appearance), it is on the basis of the world, or rather *a* determinate world considered as possible, that individual substances are conceived (insofar as they are part of that world).

The *Discourse on Metaphysics* does not present the perfection of our world as the result of a divine choice from among an infinity of other possible worlds.[159] Our world is said to be the most perfect in itself, absolutely speaking, and not best in the relative superlative sense, that is, in relation to all others. It is significant that the possibility of other series of things is really only contemplated on the basis of "an infinity of other equally possible *persons*."[160] Our world could have been otherwise, not because there was an infinity of other possible worlds (strictly speaking, Leibniz speaks only of one world, namely the "general system of phenomena" discussed at §14), but because there was an infinity of other possible persons instantiating other possible points of view on this "general system of phenomena." The priority accorded to persons does not imply that God acts by particular and detached volitions, but that his choice bears on persons, who together make up a world, rather than on a world made up of persons.

According to the order Leibniz follows in the *Discourse on Metaphysics*, it is by the individual substance, or beginning with it—insofar as its complete notion includes not only all its predicates but also everything that has and will occur in the universe, given the connection of things (§8)—that the world is posited and, in some sense, "deduced." Individual substance is that by which the world is given but also that by which it becomes *this* particular, unique, and most perfect world. Given that individual substances are so many different points of view on the general system of phenomena (§14), God's choice to create some of them rather than others establishes the singularity and perfection of the chosen world—a world that contains both that which is represented or expressed (phenomena) and that which represents or expresses (substances).

Now it is precisely the constitution of the world by individual substances—assimilated to persons in the examples Leibniz provides (Alexander, Cesar, Judas, etc.)—that subsequent texts will correct. Henceforth, every particular decree concerning an individual substance will be explicitly referred to the general decree concerning the entire world to which the substance belongs. At the same time, reference to possible persons will gradually disappear in favor of consideration of "possible worlds," a term which likely appears for the first time in Leibniz's writings in 1686.[161] A double generalization—and correlatively a double relativization of the place of the particular—is effected. On the one hand, the individual cannot be considered alone but must be relocated in the entire series to which it belongs and whose global perfection God evaluates. On the other hand, this series itself must be considered as one among an infinity of other equally possible ones, relative to which it is judged more or less perfect.

If the part is subordinated to the whole and the particular good must yield to the universal best, must we conclude that creatures and the evils that befall them ultimately count for little relative to universal harmony? Must it likewise be said that the details matter little to God, who aims only at the perfection of the whole? On the contrary, Leibniz maintains that God neglects nothing and that he shows concern for each creature in particular.[162] Leibniz rejects the view of those who, observing the defects found among the parts, judge the whole to be bad and consider the world badly made.[163] However, he likewise criticizes those who, taking the opposite point of view (that of the whole), would conclude from the existence of those same defects that the part must count for nothing:

[A]s if there is no reason for the parts or as if it were enough for the world to be perfect as a whole, even though the human race should be wretched and there should be no concern in the universe for justice and no account taken of us, as is held by some who have not made sound judgments about the totality of things.[164]

The two inferences (from the part to the whole and from the whole to the part) are equally erroneous. The expressive nature of substance and the integration of particular goods into the general good exclude both the one and the other. However, the following three theses, each defended by Leibniz, must be made consistent:

1. Nothing can be detrimental to the part without also affecting the whole and vice versa, since the part expresses the whole, and the good of the part helps constitute the good of the whole.
2. The perfection of the whole implies that of its parts, such that perfection cannot be merely global, but must extend to all the parts in every detail: "Now, if the human race or even the least thing were not well governed, neither would be the universe, for the whole is made up of its parts."[165]
3. Universal perfection sometimes requires imperfection in the parts, since a particular evil may be the condition sine qua non or even a means of realizing the best in the whole.

The difficulty, in my view, arises from the existence of three concurrent models:

a. A *mathematical* (or quantitative) model according to which the whole is the sum of its parts. In this case, perfection is understood in an "absolute" sense.
b. An *aesthetic* (or qualitative[166]) model according to which the perfection of the whole is not reducible to the mere sum of the perfection of each of the parts, as the universal harmony even implies certain particular defects (the parts of a beautiful painting are not necessarily themselves beautiful). In this case, perfection is said to be "respective."[167]
c. An *expressive* model according to which the part is itself a whole (in-dividual substance as a "world apart") that represents the great whole and whose perfection lies in the more or less distinct manner in which it reflects the universe. Here the relation is between microcosm and macrocosm.

Reconciliation of these theses occurs at two levels:

i. It appears that the expressive model can be considered as the synthesis of the other two, for it allows the part to be envisaged as both a constitutive element and as a whole. In so far as spirits are representations and concentrations of the entire universe and will endure as long as the universe itself does "it can be said that [they] are *total-parts*."[168] The perfection of the universe is constituted by the perfection of the substance-mirrors (according to model a) while at the same time including more than their sum (model b), since these substances are worlds that are not the entire world; they are particular complete representations, which enrich the world by virtue of the variety they introduce into it. The universe contains all the perfections of the parts that compose it, that is, of all the distinct expressions that multiply its beauty *and* of all their imperfections, that is, of all the obscure, imperfect expressions that constitute its diversity. Thus, the expressive model combines the notion of a sum of perfections (according to quantitative model (a) with that of a gain obtained by the presence of imperfections (according to qualitative model (b)), while holding onto the idea of a substance that, whatever its degree of perfection, expresses the entire universe.

ii. The relation between the whole and its parts is regulated by justice in such a way that the creature who is miserable could not have been so without having merited it or without its misery contributing in some way to its perfection (and not merely to the perfection of the whole). This effectively rules out the possibility that its suffering is unjust or is considered a negligible quantity. The "law of justice" dictates that "each one shall take part in the perfection of the universe and his own happiness according to the measure of his own virtue and the degree to which his will is moved toward the common good."[169] The total quantity of perfection in the world is a good that is common to all parts, shared and distributed among them according to their merit.

However, this distribution raises its own questions insofar as it seems to do no more than to confirm a prior distribution—that of the perfections, qualities, merits, and grace accorded to some rather than others. God loves each spirit according to its perfection. However, it was God himself who distributed perfection, so that he crowns with recompense what are his own gifts and punishes with suffering those whom he has already abandoned. In response to such worries, Leibniz argues that to ask why God gave more perfection to this spirit than to that one is one of those vain questions, as if one had asked whether the foot is too large or the shoe that pinches it too small. And that is a mystery, ignorance of which has rendered obscure the whole doctrine of predestination and God's justice.[170]

Far from dismissing the legitimacy of the question, Leibniz expands the issue of divine justice to include consideration of the universal order in which relations are determined by a certain congruency. At issue is not to determine whether such and such a creature is more or less perfect than some other (whether the shoe is too large or too small), but what is its place (which foot the shoe fits), or rather, how does it enter into the plan of the most perfect world. Of course, we are ignorant of the reasons for a distribution (of being, perfection, or grace) that goes beyond the framework of retributive justice. However, we must believe that this distribution is rational and non-arbitrary under an infinitely good and wise God. In this way, justice has been given a larger extension. It is understood here not only as the law according to which God governs the republic of spirits, rewarding, and punishing[171] but also as the Principle of Fitness according to which God creates and orders the universe with a view to producing the most excellent harmony in which creatures will receive as many goods as possible and will have the fewest evils to suffer.[172]

Here Leibniz posits a distribution whose general principle is not "to give each his own" as his *due*, but rather to give each what he *ought* to receive in conformity with the universal economy from which the most perfect harmony of the whole results. However, it is still the same "law of justice," which must be understood as both *metaphysical* law and *juridical* law. For, it can be said that each receives his portion of perfection and happiness in conformity with the Principle of Fitness (or of the Best) *and* that each one shares in this happiness in proportion to his virtue and merit. Perfection is thus, according to the point of view one takes, a grace that is given or a merit that is earned—that is, a gift or a desert. In the former case, perfection follows from an initial distribution, while in the latter, it is owing to a subsequent contribution on the part of the human being.

Distributive justice (in the judicial sense), which God observes in his judgments, by punishing or rewarding a free being deserving of praise or blame, actually follows and confirms a prior ontological distribution that coincides with the act of creating *this* universe. This ontological distribution consists in a second distributive justice (in the metaphysical sense), which in fact is logically prior, since it results from the divine choice from among an infinity of possible universes. This original distribution is not arbitrary, since God's choice is dictated by justice taken in its most general signification: *goodness in conformity to wisdom*, that is, the will determined by the understanding and rendered effective, in God, by omnipotence, which converts right into fact and the virtual into actual.[173]

In this way, creation becomes the work of justice as the juridical interpretation I have offered of the striving of possibles has already suggested. Justice is the law of divine action (of creation and conservation), of providence, and of the government of the world. It is the love of God for his creatures, but a love that is regulated in accordance with a rational distribution, whose general principle we can know, though we lack a detailed understanding of his reasons, which involve infinite considerations. The question of whether God created solely for his glory by manifesting his perfections or whether instead he had spirits and their happiness in view no longer arises.[174] Not only does the end require the means, but the means are also an end. The whole of creation is at once the *instrument* and *subject* of glory. God is both architect and monarch. Moved by benevolent love, as a father loves his children, God wills the good of spirits as he does his own—that is, for itself and not on account of something else. Their good is his good, and, by the love they offer him in return, his good becomes theirs. As "parts" we are not subordinated to a higher end. Our happiness, taken as an end, merges with God's own end (his glory). To those who would insist that what is good for God may not be good for us, it can be answered that God would lack perfection if he did not also seek the good of his creatures: "otherwise they [things] could not be good for Him, or what is the same thing, they would not be sufficiently so. For what would also be good for [his works] would be better absolutely speaking."[175]

Particular evils (defects, imperfections, suffering) are still evils, even in relation to the supposed good of the whole: "what for me would be an evil would not cease to be such because it would be my master's good, unless this good redounded to me."[176] Consideration of the fate of the part does not disappear in favor of a grandiose vision of the harmony of the world. For the part is in fact a "total part." It is never, qua spirit, merely a means but always an end in itself. Furthermore, it can be an instrument of God only on condition of freely willing to be so,[177] by sincerely working for the general good. Thus, far from hiding a pessimism that is indifferent to the complaints of the wretched behind the affirmation of the beauty of the harmony of the world considered as a whole, Leibniz's philosophy places "cosmic splendor"[178] at the heart of substance (via expression) and makes a universal end of our individual good. For, "if we had true knowledge of the order of providence, we would find that it is capable of satisfying and even surpassing our desires, and that there is nothing more desirable or more satisfying, not even for us *in particular*."[179] Conversely,

Leibniz makes the universal good our concern, since true love of God demands complete satisfaction with regard to the past and a serious effort to bring about the best possible future.[180]

## NOTES

1. Cf. Leibniz to Jablonski (January 23, 1700), GP VI, 3.
2. Cf. A VI, 4-B, 1653; NE I, 1; A VI, 6, 73.
3. Cf. *On the Omnipotence and Omniscience of God*, §11, A VI, 1, 540.
4. *Communicata ex literis Domini Schulleri* (February 1676?), A VI, 3, 282. See also the different line of argument: *Conversation with Steno Concerning Freedom* (December 7, 1677?), A VI, 4-B, 1375; Sleigh, 113: "The series of things could have been otherwise, absolutely speaking (i.e., its being otherwise does not imply a contradiction). For this reason, even if one cause is resolved into another to infinity . . . nevertheless, however far we proceed a new question always remains, and a sufficient reason cannot be found in the series. Hence, it must be outside the series."
5. Cf. A VI, 3, 384–385.
6. *De arcanis sublimium vel de summa rerum* (February 11, 1676), A VI, 3, 474–475; Pk, 27.
7. *Notes on Three Letters of Spinoza to Oldenburg* (second half of October 1676?), A VI, 3, 364 (emphasis added).
8. Ibid., 370.
9. Cf. A VI, 4-B, 1376. In emphasizing the notion of a thinking, volitional divine agent, the theological revision is of a piece with the rehabilitation of final causes in physics (see, for example, between 1677 and 1678: A VI, 4-B, 1367; between Summer 1678 and 1680: A VI, 4-C, 1976 and 1994).
10. Cf. *Elements of True Piety* (early 1677–early 1678?), A VI, 4-B, 1360: "*Voluntas est sententia de bono et malo*" and p. 1361: "*Sententia est cogitatio practica, seu cogitatio cum agendi conatu.*"
11. Ibid., 1361: ". . . is qui aliquam sententiam habet paratus est ad agendum modo aliquo qui sit huic sententiae conformis." Substituting the definition for the defined term, it is clear that "voluntatem esse cogitationem de bono et malo cum agendi conatu conjunctam."
12. Cf. Notes on the Letter of Eckhard (May 1677), A II, 1, 533–534: "Voluntas est quaedam consequentia intellectus. Vult enim Deus quicquid perfectissimum esse intelligit." In *On Affects* (April 20–22, 1679), Leibniz first describes the will as an "action of the mind" (*actio mentis*) (A VI, 4-B, 1411), then as a "reaction of the mind" that follows practical thought (*sententia*) (1412).
13. *Dialogue* (August 1677), A VI, 4-A, 22.
14. Cf. Notes on the Letter of Eckhard (May 1677), A II, 1, 529: "Perfectio voluntatis in eo consistit, ut quis non nisi ea velit, quae vere bona sunt" and p. 531 "Voluntas divina sequitur ex rerum necessitate, quia et existentia Dei ex rerum necessitate consequitur, seu ex Dei essentia. Nam Dei essentia congruit cum rerum necessitate."
15. Cf. Notes on the *Ethics* of Spinoza (1678?), A VI, 4-B, 1708: "Quae sola certo quodam loquendi modo impossibilia sunt, quatenus impossibile est ea aliis a Deo

non praeferri." See also A VI, 4-B, 1776 concerning Proposition 33 of Part I of the *Ethics*.

16. A VI, 4-B, 1352. See also *Conversation with Steno Concerning Freedom* (December 7, 1677?), A VI, 4-B, 1383.

17. In the Preface to Part IV of the *Ethics*, Spinoza had written "this eternal and infinite being, which we call God or Nature, acts by the same necessity [*necessitate agit*] as that whereby it exists." Leibniz corrects the passage as follows: "it can act necessarily [*potest . . . necessario agere*] for an end" (A VI, 4-B, 1736, note 57).

18. Leibniz to Foucher (1675), A II, 1, 387–388; L, 236.

19. Ibid., 388; L, 236.

20. Cf. A II, 1, 186.

21. Cf. CP; A VI, 3, 122; Sleigh, 43.

22. The question of the compatibility of possibles is directly linked to the question (which Leibniz treats in the same period) of the existence of the *Ens perfectissimum*, the being comprising all perfections. See *Quod ens perfectissimum sit possibile, Ens perfectissimum existit, Quod ens perfectissimum existit* (November, 1676?), A VI, 3, 571–579. Although these three criteria (degree of perfection, simplicity, and compatibility) are closely connected, compatibility seems to prevail over the other two in determining what will exist. On this point, see A VI, 3, 582, *Elements of True Piety*, A VI, 4-B, 1362–1364. *General Investigations in the Analysis of Notions and Truths* (1686), A VI, 4-A, 763: "the existent is the being that is compatible with the greatest number of beings, that is, the being that is possible to the highest degree."

23. *De arcanis sublimium vel de summa rerum* (February 11, 1676), A VI, 3, 472; Pk, 21–23 (trans. modified).

24. A VI, 3, 587–588.

25. Cf. A VI, 1, 479, 484–485 and CP; A VI, 3, 116; Sleigh, 29.

26. DM §5; L, 469.

27. *Elements of True Piety* (early 1677–early 1678?), A VI, 4-B, 1363, SLT, 195 (emphasis added).

28. Cf. A VI, 4-B, 1634–1635: "Any reason which makes it that these things exist rather than any others also makes it that something exists rather than nothing; for if a reason is given why these things exist, one will also be given why some things exist. This reason consists in the prevalence of reasons for existing over reasons for not existing, or, as I would say in a word, in the tendency-to-exist [*Existiturientia*] of essences, so that the things which will exist are those which are not impeded. For if there were nothing that tended-to-exist [*existituriret*], there would be no reason for existing. Moreover, a reason cannot be given why one possible rather than another should tend-to-exist" (translated by Donald Rutherford). If all possibles were not endowed with a "Pretension" to exist in God's understanding, "it would be impossible to give a reason why things have gone as they have rather than otherwise" (PNG §10, L, 1039).

29. In a text dating from the second half of 1680, A VI, 4-B, 1442.

30. A VI, 4-B, 1363, line 12 and in note; line 11.

31. Cf. Leibniz's notes on the *Ethics* (1678?), A VI, 4-B, 1735 and 1771.

32. *On Affects*, A VI, 4-B, 1434: "Existence follows from every possibility, if nothing prevents it."

33. A VI, 4-C, 2232 (emphasis added).

34. Ibid.

35. Cf. A VI, 4-A, 631; A VI, 4-B, 1446; *On the Ultimate Origination of Things* (November 23, 1697), GP VII, 303.
36. This does not prevent persistent use of the term *propensio*. See for example A VI, 4-B, 1617.
37. A VI, 4-B, 1443. See also *On the Ultimate Origination of Things*, GP VII, 303.
38. *On Affects*, A VI, 4-B, 1412: "*Conatus* est initium actionis." *Conatus* is even defined as action ("from which motion follows if nothing prevents it") in C 481.
39. *Notationes Generales* (1683–1685), A VI, 4-A, 557. See also *On the Ultimate Origination of Things*, GP VII, 304.
40. See for example *On the Correction of Metaphysics and the Concept of Substance* (1694), GP IV, 469, L, 709: "Active force, in contrast, contains a certain action or *entelechy* and is thus midway between the faculty of acting and the action itself and involves a *conatus*. It is thus carried into action by itself and needs no help but only the removal of an impediment" (emphasis added).
41. Beginning in 1678. On this point, see M. Fichant, *La réforme de la dynamique*.
42. Robinet, *G. W. Leibniz: le meilleur des mondes par la balance de l'Europe*, 79.
43. Leibniz uses this term in *On the Ultimate Origination of Things*, GP VII, 304; L 792.
44. See section 5.1.3.
45. *Notationes Generales* (1683–1685), A VI, 4-A, 557 (emphasis added).
46. The tendency-to-exist (*existituriential*) in possibles requires, in order for them to actually exist, a cause that produces existence (*existentificans*), namely God (cf. GP VII, 289).
47. Leibniz uses the term in *On the Ultimate Origination of Things*, GP VII, 305.
48. Gaudemar, *Leibniz. De la puissance au sujet*, 47.
49. God already knows what he will choose, for "the free decrees of the divine will must be the object of the divine understanding before he conceives of them as having been executed. For God does nothing that he does not already know he will do" (text from late-1685 to mid-1686? A VI, 4-B, 1523). Cf. Grua, JUT, 294.
50. The term *exigentia* derives from *exigo*, which refers both to the action of pushing (out) or expelling, and of demanding, claiming. The verb *postulare* (used in *Notationes generales*, A VI, 4-A, 557, cited above) also has a juridical connotation and can mean to request, or even to take to court.
51. *On the Ultimate Origination of Things*, GP VII, 304; L, 791 (emphasis added). See also *Monadology*, §54, L, 1053: "each possible one having a right to claim existence in the measure of perfection which it enfolds."
52. *Monadology*, §51, L, 1052 (emphasis added).
53. In which case, Clarke's criticism would be valid (cf. his Fourth Reply, GP VII, 381).
54. T §201; GP VI, 236; Huggard, 253.
55. Cf. CP; A VI, 3, 128 and 129.
56. Cf. A VI, 4-B, 1377.
57. Ibid., 1380. Cf. Matthew 18:7.
58. Cf. NE, Preface; A VI, 6, 52; RB, 52: "This is how ideas and truths are innate in us—as inclinations, dispositions, tendencies, or natural potentialities, and not as actions; although these potentialities are always accompanied by certain actions, often insensible ones, which correspond to them." With regard to the will, see T §22.
59. Cf. A VI, 4-B, 1360 and 1361.
60. A VI, 4-A, 396.

61. Cf. *Elements of Natural Law*, A VI, 1, 457 and 482. Already in the *New Method for Learning and Teaching Jurisprudence* (1667), we read "to will is nothing other than to think on the goodness of a thing" (A VI, 1, 284).

62. *On Free Will* (Summer 1678 to Winter 1680–1681?), A VI, 4-B, 1407, SLT, 92. See also A VI, 4-B, 1444; NE II, 21, §5; A VI, 6, 172.

63. A VI, 4-B, 1426. He adds: "It is for this reason that determination establishes a presumption for the future, until such time as there is a proof of some imped-iment." The comparison with falling bodies is explicitly drawn (p. 1430). The same principle is used in dynamics: force is that "from which action follows when nothing prevents it: effort, *conatus*" (Leibniz to Pellison, July 1691, A I, 6, 226).

64. A VI, 4-B, 1427.

65. Ibid., 1424. See also, 1434–1435.

66. Ibid., 1428.

67. Ibid., 1429.

68. In addition to the references provided above (A II, 1, 187; CP, A VI, 3, 124 and 137–138), see *On Free Will*, A VI, 4-B, 1408; *Conversation About Freedom and Fate* (1699–1703?), Grua, 482; NE II, 21, §§22–23; A VI, 6, 182.

69. NE II, 21, §§31–35, 185; RB 185 (emphasis added).

70. Cf. *On Affects*, A VI, 4-B, 1411: "*volition* is an effort to act with regard to external things arising from thought." It is a "reaction of the mind," "the effort that follows the opinion of a present good or evil in the one who makes the effort (*conante*)" (p. 1412). See also A VI, 4-A, 396 and A VI, 4-C, 2768.

71. NE II, 21, §5; A VI, 6, 173; RB, 173. Leibniz makes clear, however, that there are also "apperceptible appetitions."

72. NE II, 21, §39, A VI, 6, 192; RB, 192.

73. Ibid.

74. Ibid., §40, A VI, 6, 193; RB, 193.

75. To be sure, the analysis of the will that Leibniz offers in the *New Essays* is based primarily on an investigation of human will. However, the difference between created and uncreated spirits is owing to their different degrees of perfection (so that there can be neither insensible perceptions nor movements without aware-ness in God), and not to the very nature of these faculties.

76. *Reply to the Thoughts on the System of Pre-Established harmony contained in the Second Edition of Mr. Bayle's* Critical Dictionary, *Article Rorarius* (1702), GP IV, 562; L, 942.

77. Cf. *Examination of the Christian Religion (Theological System)* (April–October, 1686?), A VI, 4-C, 2365: "For, from the force [*virtute*] or power of the divine es-sence flow the ideas of things or the truths that his wisdom comprehends, and from there they become the objects of his will in proportion to the perfection of each one, which also reflects the order of the divine persons." See also, Baruzi, *Leibniz*, 304; Leibniz to Morell (September 29, 1698), Grua, 139; T §149 and *Monadology*, §48.

78. *Tentamen anagogicum*, GP VII, 273; L 780.

79. The distinction is implicit in *Unvorgreiffliches Bedencken*, Grua, especially, p. 445. The distinction is explicit in Leibniz to Spanheim (February 20, 1699), Grua 449.

80. To my knowledge, the distinction first appears, outside the strictly theological context, in 1705–early 1706 (Grua, 468 and 474).

81. CP; A VI, 3, 121; Sleigh, 41.

82. *The Author of Sin* (1673?), A VI, 3, 150.

83. Like Ockham, *In Sententiarum* II, q. 4–5 and IV, q. 8–9; Erasmus, *De libero arbitrio*, III, ch. 4, ch. 6, ch. 12, IV, 8; Molina, *Concordia*, disp. XXVI; or Suarez, *De gratia* III, ch. 46, 18.

84. Such as Durandus of Saint-Pourçain (*In Sententias Theologicas* II, dist. 37, q. 1). Leibniz will mention other authors in T §27 and §381.

85. Thus Leibniz writes, "he who produces half the thing, and in turn half of the remaining half, and in turn half of the remaining half of the half—to infinity— produces the whole. This takes place in any act whatsoever, according to God's manner of operation. For let us suppose that God and a person concur in some action; it is necessary that God concur with this very concurrence of the person, and either it will proceed to infinity (nevertheless it will not any the less reduce to the same thing) or it will suffice to say right from the start that God actually produces the action, even if it is the person who acts" (*Conversation with Steno Concerning Freedom*, A VI, 4-B, 1382; Sleigh, 127).

86. ST, Ia, Part IIae 79, 2.

87. See also the example of the two paintings, of which one is larger than the other, in *The Author of Sin* (A VI, 3, 151).

88. *The Author of Sin* (1673?), A VI, 3, 151; Sleigh, 113.

89. This assertion appears in the *Conversation with Steno*, A VI, 4-B, 1382, Sleigh, 127: "Sin is a created thing; every created thing is continuously created by God. Therefore, the same thing holds even for sin."

90. Cf. Letter to Wedderkopf, A II, 1, 187; *Conversation with Steno*, A VI, 4-B, 1382: "Nothing is to be considered absolutely evil, nor can anything occur that is disagreeable to God. Otherwise, God would not be omnipotent."

91. A VI, 4-C, 2577: "homo *ex defectu originali creaturae* cujuscunque falli potest" (emphasis added).

92. Ibid., 2572.

93. As summarized by Leibniz at T §284; Huggard, 300. See Augustine, *Against the Epistle of Manichaeus called Fundamental*, c.35 and c.36.

94. This expression likely appears for the first time in the *Notationes generales* (1683–1685), A VI, 4-A, 557.

95. See A VI, 4-C, 2322; DM §30; A VI, 4-C, 2358; Leibniz to Molanus (February 2, 1698?), Grua, 412.

96. The non plus ultra of the circle is the limit described by the opening of the compass. Cf. *Dialogue on Human Freedom and the Origin of Evil* (January 25, 1695), Grua, 364; *Unvorgreiffliches Bedencken*, Grua, 436.

97. Cf. *On the Ultimate Origination of Things*, GP VII, 303.

98. *Notationes Generales*, A VI, 4-A, 557.

99. *On the Ultimate Origination of Things*, GP VII, 307; L, 797. See also Leibniz to Hartsoeker (February 6, 1711), GP III, 521.

100. Cf. *On the Ultimate Origination of Things*, GP VII, 308. On this point, see Rateau "Theoretical Foundations," Part II, 103–174.

101. The two kinds of power are active power, or "faculty," and passive power, "capacity or receptivity" (Cf. NE II, 21, §1; A VI, 6, 169).

102. A VI, 4-B, 1521.

103. Leibniz to Thomas Burnett (1699–1700?), GP III, 260.

104. Cf. GP IV (May 1702), 395. On this double aspect of resistance, both active and passive, see Leibniz to Alberti (October 1689?), GP VII, 444: the nature of body "requires a resistance or reaction that includes an action and a passion, *antitypian*."

105. GP IV (May 1702), 395. As Michel Fichant notes (*L'invention métaphysique*, 482, note 36), Leibniz uses the term "inertia" "in the already archaic sense of matter's natural *repugnance* or *resistance* to motion (whereas for Newton inertia is matter's *indifference* to both motion and rest). It is, in fact, the sense in which Kepler used the term." Fichant emphasizes the differences with Descartes's use of the term.

106. Cf. NE II, 21 §1; A VI, 6, 169–170.

107. As Leibniz explains to De Volder (April 3, 1699, GP II, 170; L, 839), a thing possesses a force (*vis*) "for remaining in its state," which force does not differ from the thing's essence. It is one thing to conserve a state until it is changed, and another "to have a force and an inclination, as it were, to retain its state and so to resist motion." This force excludes all indifference to received motion.

108. Cf. (late 1685–mid-1686?), A VI, 4-B, 1521; *Specimen of Discoveries* (1688?), A VI, 4-B, 1619-1620; Grua (around 1695), 355.

109. *On Freedom, Fate and God's Grace*, A VI, 4-B, 1605.

110. *Unvorgreiffliches Bedencken*, Grua 447 (the image is also invoked, though without reference to evil, in GP VII, 283, around 1690); Grua, 473; GP III, 34.

111. T §30 and §335; *Causa Dei*, §71. See section 6.2.1.

112. A II, 3, 426. See also Leibniz to Morell (May 14, 1698), Grua, 126.

113. DM §30, L, 497: before original sin, there is "an original limitation or imperfection connatural to all creatures, which makes them capable of sin or failure."

114. Letter to Molanus (February 2, 1698?), Grua, 412. See also A VI, 4-C, 2312: "the cause of sin is to be found not in God's will, but in the will of the creature, who by the nature of things, if it is not restrained by experience or the grace of God, is inclined [*prona*] to judge things that it does not sufficiently understand."

115. Leibniz to Molanus (February 22, 1698), Grua 413; GP III, 37.

116. A VI, 4-B, 1593-1594 (emphasis added).

117. A VI, 4-B, 1577.

118. See, for example, DM §30; A VI, 4-C, 2322 and 2358.

119. A VI, 2, 487.

120. Grua, 364.

121. Leibniz to Morell (May 14, 1698), Grua, 126; Grua, 371.

122. A VI, 4-A, 819.

123. *Fourth Meditation*, AT IX, 43; CSM II, 38.

124. Cf. A VI, 4-B, 1590 and 1591. See also *On Freedom, Fate and God's Grace*, A VI, 4-B, 1597.

125. Cf. A VI, 4-B, 1604.

126. Grua, 355. In opposition to Louis de Dole, see A VI, 4-B, 1459: "Utique fatendum videtur etiam ab his qui negant concursum Dei proximum immediatumque ad omnes actus, Deum alio modo concurrere ad actum amoris quam ad actum odii. Et tamen hoc videtur oblique negare P. Ludovicus de Dola pag. 107."

127. Cf. *The Author of Sin*, A VI, 3, 150 and *On Freedom, Fate and God's Grace*, A VI, 4-B, 1605.

128. *On the True* Theologia Mystica (1694–1697?), Grua, 147 (I put Leibniz's deletions in square brackets).

129. Leibniz to Naudé, Grua, 503. Cf. *Causa Dei*, §§68–69.

130. Cf. CP, A VI, 3, 131.

131. *Conversation with Steno*, A VI, 4-B, 1378, Sleigh 119.

132. *Conversation with Steno*, A VI, 4-B, 1382, Sleigh 129.

133. Cf. *Conversation with Steno*, A VI, 4-B, 1376; Sleigh 115: "There are gradations of willing, for we will one thing more than another. And we will more strongly that which appears better. Therefore, the more equality, the less we will one thing rather than another, and when the equality is at a maximum, we will nothing."
134. A VI, 4-C, 2572 (emphasis added).
135. A VI, 4-B, 1451 (text dating from between Summer 1680 and Summer 1684; emphasis added). See also DM §5; L, 469: "there can be no doubt that the happiness of spirits is the principal end of God and that he puts this principle into practice as far as the general harmony permits."
136. A VI, 4-A, 941(text dating from between August 1688 and January 1689?).
137. *Specimen of Discoveries* (1688?), A VI, 4-B, 1619.
138. Leibniz to Landgraf Ernst von Hessen-Rheinfels (April 12, 1686), A II, 2, 18.
139. Leibniz to Coste (December 19, 1707), GP III, 400.
140. Cf. Grua, 342–343: "We must not think that God chooses things particularly, if he inspires a man with an inclination to evil actions, but rather that He chose the universal series in which the existence and actions of this man are also contained. Before He had decided whether this man would exist, it had already been established that this man would sin. Thus, God decided nothing with regard to Peter's sin and repentance, Judas' sin and despair, the greater assistance to be given to Peter and the lesser assistance to be given to Judas. However, because this universe, considered as possible, already contained a certain amount of aid for each one, I mean, Peter having to sin, Peter deprived of certain assistance at the time of his sin, Peter favored once again and uplifted by the aid of grace; Judas having to sin, Judas having to be deprived of sufficient aid, Judas having to fall into despair. For this reason, we must not think that God forms any particular decrees with regard to the aid to be given to Peter or Judas. Rather, He wills to allow this possible Peter and this possible Judas to exist together with the whole series of assistances [of grace] and the circumstances already included in their complete concept."
141. DM §7; L 471.
142. Cf. Leibniz to Landgraf Ernst von Hessen-Rheinfels (April 12, 1686), A II, 2, 18 and 19. See also Grua, 345.
143. *Conversation About Freedom and Fate*, Grua, 482, SLT, 99.
144. DM §30; L, 497.
145. Grua, 350.
146. *On Freedom, Fate and God's Grace*, A VI, 4-B, 1602. Cf. Augustine, *Enchiridion*, ch. 11.
147. Cf. Paul, Romans, 3:8.
148. Grua, 342 (text dating from between 1691 and 1695).
149. As Fernand Brunner summarizes the distinction, "a means is something that one uses; a condition is something that one must accept." The condition is not willed, but permitted ("L'optimisme Leibnizien," in *Leibniz (1646–1716)*, 244 and 245).
150. *Opinions of Socrates Against the New Stoics and Epicureans* (1678-1680?), A VI, 4-B, 1388.
151. Cf. *Conversation on Freedom and Fate*, Grua, 485.
152. Grua 467. See also *Conversation on Freedom and Fate*, Grua, 482.
153. DM §36.
154. T §118, GP VI, 169, Huggard, 188–189.

155. "Du *Discours de métaphysique* à la *Théodicée*," 404. See also Blumenfeld, "Perfection and Happiness in the Best Possible World" in *The Cambridge Companion to Leibniz*, especially 404–405 and 410, note 41.

156. Fichant shows that with the invention of the concept of the monad, "the notions of *life, living* and *organism* come to occupy center stage in [Leibniz's] metaphysics" (*L'invention métaphysique*, 114). The theological influence that marks the *Discourse on Metaphysics* is replaced by "a kind of naturalization of metaphysics" in the *Monadology* (p. 135). See also "La constitution du concept de monade" in *Les Cahiers philosophiques de Strasbourg*, vol. 18, 29–56.

157. Cf. Baruzi, "Du *Discours de métaphysique* à la *Théodicée*," 407.

158. Cf. Fichant, "Leibniz et l'universel," in *Science et métaphysique dans Descartes et Leibniz*, especially 123 and 134 and "De l'individuation à l'individualité universelle," 143–162.

159. Cf. §§2–3. It is only specified (§30) that the series of things that exists is the most perfect "among all other possible kinds," which obviously does not amount to the same thing.

160. The phrase appears in §31; L, 498 (emphasis added).

161. Cf. *On Freedom, Fate and God's Grace*, A VI, 4-B, 1612; *Remarks on the Letter of M. Arnauld* (June, 1686), A II, 2, 47.

162. Cf. DM §37; T Preface; GP VI, 30–31.

163. Cf. CP, A VI, 3, 146; "as the jurisconsults say, it is truly unjust to render a judgment without having studied the whole law" (*On the Ultimate Origination of Things*, GP VII, 306; L, 795). See *Digest* 1, 3, 24.

164. *On the Ultimate Origination of Things*, GP VII, 307; L, 796. Cf. *Meditation on the Common Concept of Justice*, "There are people who imagine that we are too small a thing in the sight of an infinite God, for him to be concerned with us; it is conceived that we are to God that which worms, which we crush without thinking, are in relation to us. But this is to imagine that God is like a man, and cannot think of everything" (R, 51).

165. *Meditation on the Common Concept of Justice*, R, 50.

166. Cf. T §§212–214.

167. For the difference between absolute and respective perfection, see Leibniz to Wolf (February 21, 1705), GB, 19–20.

168. *On the Ultimate Origination of Things*, GP VII, 307; L, 797 (emphasis added).

169. *On the Ultimate Origination of Things*, GP VII; L, 796.

170. A VI, 4-C, 2804.

171. Cf. GP VII, 290 (20): "justice is also observed in the universe, since *justice* is nothing but order or perfection with regard to spirits."

172. See *Unvorgreiffliches Bedencken*, Grua, 431–432 and Grua, 675.

173. *Meditation on the Common Concept of Justice*, Mollat, 48.

174. Cf. T §78.

175. A VI, 4-B, 1514.

176. T §217; GP VI, 248; Huggard, 263.

177. Cf. A VI, 4-C, 2722: "Thus, we are not born for ourselves, but for the good of society, as are parts for the whole, and we must only consider ourselves as instruments of God, albeit living and free instruments that are capable of contributing to that good by our own choice."

178. In the words of Baruzi, "Du *Discours de métaphysique* à la *Théodicée*," 407.

179. Leibniz to Sophie (August 1696?) Grua, 379. See also T§217; GP VI, 248; Huggard 263: "One good thing among others in the universe is that the general good becomes in reality the individual good of those who love the Author of all good."
180. See chapter 7, p. 330–335.

# CHAPTER 4

∞

# The Genesis of Theodicy

## Its Scientific and Apologetic Aims

The conceptual evolution that followed the *Confession of a Philosopher* brought about important changes on the theological and metaphysical levels. It led to the development of an original account of the nature and origin of evil, and of God's concourse with sin. Within this new theoretical framework, Leibniz invented—perhaps as early as 1695—a neologism that was to have a brilliant future: *Theodicy*. The term was not explicitly defined but served during the years 1695–1697 as the title of a vast philosophical project, under the aegis of theology and jurisprudence, but whose precise limits are difficult to define. Thus, the project, although still programmatic at the time, was not initially tied to the writings of Pierre Bayle and the polemic to which they gave rise concerning the relation of faith and reason and the problem of evil. However, the project took on a new appearance and became more definite as a result of these polemical disputes, which Leibniz closely followed, but in which he did not participate (section 4.1). No one who took it upon himself to justify God and to account for the existence of evil in the world could ignore Bayle's objections. Leibniz was obliged to respond. To do so, however, required as a preliminary that the rules governing philosophical disputes be clearly established (section 4.1.3). It is on the basis of these rules that the defensive and refutational wing of the *Theodicy* is constructed. This component includes two further wings: on the one hand, what I shall call the "negative" defense or defense in the strict sense, and on the other the hand, "positive" or supererogatory defense of God's justice (section 4.2).

## 4.1 FROM THE PROJECT OF "THEODICIES" TO THE COMPOSITION OF THE *ESSAYS OF THEODICY*: SYSTEMATIC NECESSITY AND OCCASIONAL CAUSE

### 4.1.1. The Project of 1695–1697

The neologism "Theodicy" appears in its Latin form *Theodicaea* in the title of an unpublished fragment, which Grua dates to the years 1695–1697.[1] To my knowledge the term first appears in its French form in a letter to Étienne Chauvin of June 8, 1696. Far from emphasizing his terminological invention, Leibniz does not pause over it, nor does he take the trouble to explain it to his correspondent, as if it were a common noun or a readily understood term. Even more surprisingly, he uses the term in the plural:

> Someday I could discuss with you certain reflections that I have kept and examined for a long time, both by myself and by others, for inclusion in my Theodicies [*Théodicées*] on the source of evil and the difference between the necessary and contingent, in which I believe I have also discovered that those who do not seek the ultimate reason for the decrees favorable to us in our good qualities are not as mistaken as many believe them to be. I flatter myself that these Meditations drawn from natural Theology and Jurisprudence and based on certain philosophical demonstrations reserved for my universal Specious could help to establish the greatest truths more undeniably and in a manner as informal as a dialogue and as exact as a Geometrical argument.[2]

Leibniz speaks here of a work in progress, as yet unpublished, but which contains what are already his considered and long-standing views. He even claims to another correspondent to have had at hand the "Elements" of this "Theodicy" for some time.[3] Leibniz had already mentioned to Foucher the idea of publishing his thoughts on fate and contingency (*de fato et contingentia*) in the event that the *New System* (published in June 1695) should be favorably received by the public.[4] For Leibniz, the two publications were necessarily linked, since he believed that his new hypothesis—his concept of substance and the system of pre-established harmony—is precisely the one that best supports human freedom.[5] The project was very dear to him, if we are to believe another, probably contemporaneous (around 1695), declaration:

> I believe I will be doing something important, if I free the human race from the controversies surrounding fate, free will, divine justice, the cause of evil, [and] predestination.[6]

His reflections on these topics had already been committed to paper in part—they have been discussed in previous chapters—and some had been communicated to scholars (including Steno, Arnauld, and Thomas Burnett[7]). However, Leibniz now seems to have been planning to include these thoughts in a larger work that he called, still somewhat enigmatically, his "Theodicies." What precisely did he mean by this term? Was it the title of a projected book, as Grua seems to suggest?[8] It should be noted that in the letter to Chauvin the word "Theodicies" is written neither in spaced letters nor in capitals (except the first letter, but this is also the case with "Meditations," "Theology," "Jurisprudence," "Specious," "Geometrical"), as is customary when referring to the title of a work. Nothing serves to distinguish the word typographically nor to indicate a particular emphasis on the part of the author.

It is clear that the plural is explained by the reference to the "Meditations" in the final sentence of the cited passage. These "Theodicies" would appear then to be the name or the general title (in the sense of a collective designation and not necessarily the projected title of a particular work) given to a collection of thoughts at the intersection of theology and law focusing on evil, the distinction between necessity and contingency (and so freedom), predestination and its reasons (as indicated by the reference to "good qualities"). However, the characterization remains rather vague, in that the unity and limits of the object of these meditations are not further specified. To be sure, an attentive reader who is familiar with Greek could identify the subject of these reflections as relating to the general theme of the justice (*diké*) of God (*théos*). However, it should be emphasized that this theme is not explicitly mentioned in the letter.

Although drawn from different disciplines, these subjects must be treated with all necessary scientific rigor. Leibniz promises theologico-juridical demonstrations, as exactly constructed as those of mathematics, though expounded in a more familiar or exoteric manner. Thus, although the subject and status of these "Theodicies" are rather poorly defined, the text is more explicit as to the projected method and form. The plan is to develop arguments carried out *more geometrico*, even if the tone must be agreeable and the language accessible when treating a subject that is not "to the general taste."[9]

The scientific ambition of the project, like the diversity of its object of study, can be found in other programmatic texts from the same period. Beyond the themes already mentioned (contingency, fate, freedom, predestination, and the origin of evil), Leibniz promises reflections on the composition of things out of perfection and limitation (God and Nothingness), the connection of things, the unity of the divine decrees,[10] a "Vindication of divine justice and human freedom based on consideration of the complete idea God has of a thing capable of being created,"[11] examination of whether the misfortunes that occur are attributable to human wickedness,[12] reflections on the divine law, and the relation of man to God and of God to man in light of the universal harmony.[13]

Although the singular form of the term comes to dominate in the texts ("Theodicy" and no longer "Theodicies"), the multiplicity and disparity of the questions to be treated remain striking. To be sure, these subjects, whose number varies over time, are not unrelated. Nevertheless, they are drawn from different theoretical fields (natural theology, metaphysics, psychology,[14] ethics, and law) and make use of different kinds of arguments: a priori and a posteriori arguments, points of law and practical issues (like the interpretation of actual evils), and mathematical demonstrations and probabilities. In fact, the coherence of the project owes more to the two principal sources (natural theology and jurisprudence) from which the Theodicy is meant to draw its theses and to the end (apologetic) at which it aims. This can be seen in the title of the previously cited fragment as published by Grua:

> By William Pacidius. THEODICY or [*seu*] Catholic demonstrations on behalf of [*pro*] divine justice, established in accordance with the certainty and form of mathematics, drawn from natural Theology and Jurisprudence, by which humankind may be freed of its doubts concerning contingency and fate, freedom and predestination.[15]

The equivalence posited between "Theodicy" and "Catholic demonstrations on behalf of divine justice" (the "or" could be either alternative or ampliative) offers interesting hints with regard to the project of Theodicy, as it was conceived during the years 1695–1697.

1. In the first place, the term "Theodicy" does not at this stage designate a doctrine or science—not even a derivative one. Rather, it refers to nothing more than an ad hoc gathering together of a group of demonstrations, which should serve, directly or indirectly, to defend God's justice. Theodicy in itself does not establish or prove anything. It is the title under which various theses, drawn from other sciences and established within them, are gathered together on behalf of divine justice. Therefore, it is nothing more than a mere manner of exposition or presentation of these arguments and conclusions, whose function is above all defensive (hence the use of the term *vindicatio*)[16] and apologetic. It was for this reason no doubt that the neologism required no further explanation, since the unity of the proposed

end compensated in some sense for the lack of unity in the object of analysis.

As a manner of arranging truths to a certain end, Theodicy involves a method closely related to what Leibniz, in the *New Essays on Human Understanding*, calls the "analytical and practical" order. In the *New Essays*, Leibniz criticizes the traditional division of the sciences, inherited from ancient philosophy, into physics, morals, and logic, in which "each of the branches appears to engulf the others" and where "a single truth can usually be put in different places."[17] According to Leibniz, the distinction should be drawn not between rigidly bounded sciences, but between different ways of presenting and arranging the *same* truths. If we wish to follow the "order of proofs," that is to say, the order by which truths are discovered, we must arrange them "as the mathematicians do." By this method we advance from proposition to proposition, each one derived from the preceding propositions on which it depends, according to the *synthetic* and *theoretical* method. If, on the contrary, we wish to begin with a specific problem to be solved, or if we propose an end to be achieved (happiness, for example), we must follow the *analytic* and *practical* order. In the former case, this consists in breaking down the problem until we arrive at first truths and principles. In the latter, it involves seeking out the certain means of achieving the proposed end.[18]

These two kinds of ordering, to which we must add the order "according to terms" (which consists in compiling a systematic or alphabetical repertory of truths), should not be considered "as distinct sciences but rather as different ways in which one can organize the same truths, if one sees fit to express them more than once."[19] The distinction is not based on delimiting separate theoretical fields, but on a particular arrangement of truths, according to the proposed end—that is, according to whether we consider their foundation and mode of production, their practical application, or the manner of arranging them in a rational and useful order (systematic order, according to concepts, or alphabetical order, according to the chosen language). On this way of conceiving the sciences, Theodicy does not correspond to a distinct discipline, but rather to a particular ordering of truths with regard to a certain practical use, in this case apologetic. As such, the question of its boundaries and relations to other sciences does not arise.

Hence, the phrase "the certainty and form of mathematics" does not refer to the synthetic method used by mathematicians, but is meant, I believe, to emphasize the solidity and rigor of the theses presented in the future Theodicy. The choice of the analytic order in no way diminishes Leibniz's intention to provide demonstrations. Rather, it merely indicates the manner in which the demonstration will be carried out: that is, not from first principles, but as in the opuscule, *On Freedom, Fate and God's Grace,* by "taking up the conclusions that religion and practical philosophy command us to hold, and then reconciling them with each other and with the principles of speculative philosophy." This method is less "sublime" than the synthetic one, insofar as it is "easier and also safer owing to our weakness."[20] The goal, which is essentially practical, is not strictly speaking to demonstrate the truth of the theses at issue (a task that belongs to other sciences, namely theology and jurisprudence), but to take them up as problems, attempting to reconcile their conclusions—should they appear contradictory—and to defend them against objections. Such a process may lead us to analyze them and to trace them back to their first principles.[21] The procedure is analytic, since analysis, which is more useful in practice, considers only "the cause of the given problem and mounts up to principles, as if nothing had ever been discovered by us or by others."[22]

2. The association of Theodicy with "Catholic demonstrations" also sheds interesting light on the aforementioned fragment. It is, to my knowledge, the only text in which Leibniz associates the two. Obviously, the use of the term "Catholic demonstrations" alludes to the project developed under the aegis of the Baron Boineburg, undertaken in the years 1668–1671, renewed in 1679, and probably again in 1685, as evidenced by a number of opuscules and apologetic essays published in the Academy edition.[23] Was the Theodicy intended to be the continuation of this project or in some way its successor? Careful comparison of the two works reveals that they differ as much in their content as in their form and method.[24] However, they do share two characteristics, which undoubtedly explain why Leibniz linked them: a clearly apologetic aim, and the claim to genuine universality.

The demonstrations presented under the title "Theodicy" merit the appellation "catholic" insofar as they are universal, since they are drawn from the natural light and so are able to be accepted by every person of whatever religious confession. It is for this reason that the demonstrations might serve as the basis for the reunion of the churches, a prospect that Leibniz always kept in view. The choice of the pseudonym, William Pacidius, derived from the Latin *pax,*[25] is suggestive of this irenical aim and of the desire to calm the controversies. Indeed, it was Leibniz's hope that the "elements" of this planned Theodicy "could, in large part, be approved by theologians of every party and would perhaps contribute in some way to minimizing disputes."[26]

The reference to "Catholic demonstrations" and its subsequent disappearance from later texts (and in particular the *Essays of Theodicy*) suggest that the years 1695–1697 were a transitional period during which Theodicy, which was initially linked to these demonstrations or even conceived in terms of them, came to be disassociated from them so as to become a "new," specific, and autonomous project. Leibniz's youthful project, even as subsequently revised and corrected, was doubtless too ambitious. It mixed questions of philosophy and natural theology with questions of revealed theology and even ecclesiology and politics. With the Theodicy, the program seems to have narrowed (even if, as we have seen, the number of topics to be addressed remains large), since it is limited to a discussion of theology and natural law and reorients the issue toward the central question of God's justice.

This reorientation is all the more natural, insofar as the two sources of Theodicy can be seen to be but one, if we recall that for Leibniz theology is nothing more than a branch of jurisprudence, namely that "divine jurisprudence that explains the rights of our society vis-à-vis God."[27] It is for this reason that at times Leibniz speaks of only a single foundation for Theodicy: the notion of justice, defined as the charity of the wise, from which is derived universal jurisprudence, which itself includes divine law[28] by the relation of genus to species. Thus, justice appears as the central notion; the key concept around which all other questions (evil, freedom, contingency, predestination, etc.) will naturally be organized. The draft preface of the *Theodicy*, which can be roughly dated to the beginning of 1707, confirms this point: "I employ the title *Theodicy* because God's justice is the principal subject of the work, in which the questions of his goodness and holiness naturally arise."[29] It should be noted, however, that justice occupies this central place only because its scope has been greatly expanded, as shown in the previous chapter. It has not only a moral and juridical sense but also a metaphysical one. It is not merely the law that governs this world, and in particular the city of spirits, by means of reward and punishment, but also the law that governed the divine choice to create this world rather than some other equally possible one.

### 4.1.2. The Context of the Composition of the *Essays of Theodicy*

It is important to recall the circumstances that led to, indeed favored—but also delayed—the writing of the *Essays of Theodicy*. Two facts in particular seem worthy of attention: (1) the negotiations concerning the reunion of the Protestant churches (1697–1706); and (2) the controversies arising out of John Toland's *Christianity Not Mysterious* (which Leibniz had read and annotated as early as 1701) and the works of Pierre Bayle, notably his *Historical and Critical Dictionary* (the subject of conversations at the court in Berlin in the summer of 1702), on the topic of faith and reason. According to Leibniz, the *Theodicy*, although a long-standing project, was prompted by the writings of Bayle, who was, so to speak, its occasional cause.

1. The political events that led to the Treaty of Ryswick (September 1697) put pressure on the Protestants to unite. Leibniz put reflection into action by contributing to the negotiations between the Lutheran court of Hanover and the Calvinist court of Brandenburg.[30] Although composition of the Theodicy was thereby deferred, the project was neither abandoned nor even interrupted.[31] For not only was Theodicy explicitly connected to the hope of reconciliation, but Leibniz's correspondence with Molanus and Jablonski (1698–1701) takes up the issues of divine justice, human freedom and predestination in conjunction with the controversy surrounding God's absolute decree.

2. With regard to the gestation of the Theodicy, a second circumstance must be taken into account in light of its decisive influence on both the composition of the *Essays* and the decision to include the *Preliminary Discourse*: the controversy surrounding the conformity of faith and reason. This conformity had been called into question, on the one hand, by the excessive rationalism of Toland,[32] who had expunged all mystery from religious truth, and on the other by the equally excessive "fideism" of Bayle,[33] who, after having given full voice to reason, claimed to silence it in the name of the primacy of divine revelation over our natural light. Both thinkers rejected the traditional distinction between that which is *contrary* to reason and that which is *above* reason. Both end up insisting on the irreconcilability of faith and reason, though for opposite reasons. For Toland, who advocated a Christianity without mysteries, "true Religion must necessarily be reasonable and intelligible."[34] Bayle maintained that although Christian dogmas agree with the "supreme and universal" (that is, divine) Reason, human reason can have no knowledge of this agreement. However, for Leibniz those who would exalt reason are as misguided as those who would denigrate it.[35]

The controversy that began between Bayle and Isaac Jaquelot,[36] and was later taken up by Jean Le Clerc, was of great interest to Leibniz. Although he took no public part in the debate, Leibniz followed it from the beginning,[37] and gave his opinion to Jaquelot (who, prior to its publication, had sent a copy of his *Conformity of Faith with Reason* to Leibniz in September 1704) and to Basnage, who (perhaps at Bayle's instigation) seemed to solicit Leibniz's direct intervention.[38] Leibniz preferred to avoid the risk of confrontation, which he believed would prove prejudicial to religion, because it would provoke Bayle to "put his objections in an even clearer light, if that is possible."[39] Leibniz counsels moderation and even a kind of ruse[40] when dealing with an author "who can render so many services to letters and even, if he will so apply himself, to religion, that it is appropriate to treat him with caution."[41] It would be wrong to consider this an evasion, since Leibniz's *Discourse on the Conformity of Faith with Reason* was already in preparation at the time (1706). However, by intentionally remaining on the sidelines, Leibniz, who was not in the habit of precipitance, was in all likelihood awaiting a calmer atmosphere and more propitious circumstances in which to publish his *Discourse*.

My hypothesis is that Leibniz deferred publication for a different and more fundamental reason, which concerns the close relation he came to see between what is at issue in the controversy surrounding the conformity of faith and reason and in the project of Theodicy on which he was working. The importance of the controversy was that it pointed out, from a theoretical and systematic point of view, the question by which it made sense to begin, since a large part of the difficulties concerning evil and God's justice are based on the alleged conflict between revelation and the natural light. The *Discourse on the Conformity of Faith with Reason* will play the role in the *Essays* of a Preliminary Discourse, because it treats a difficulty whose successful resolution is a precondition of the very possibility of Theodicy. Bayle's merit was to have put his finger on one of the central issues by focusing attention on a question that Leibniz had not planned to discuss (judging by the programmatic texts dating from the years 1695 to 1697). Leibniz came to see that the issue was closely linked to his topic. Consequently, the controversy provoked by the *Historical and Critical Dictionary* played a decisive role in the very conception of Theodicy, both as doctrine and defense. For, it caused Leibniz to reconsider both the content, by including a question (the conformity of faith and reason) that was not initially among those to be discussed, and the form, by aligning necessary demonstrations with probable arguments.

Leibniz refused to enter directly into the polemic, so that he might respond in a more complete fashion to the problem Bayle raises. The problem is indeed complex. In fact, it is twofold. It concerns, on the one hand, the general relation between faith and reason (or "the use of philosophy in theology"[42]) and, on the other hand, the specific difficulties that Bayle deduces from their apparent disagreement with regard to the question of evil and its origin. Indeed, Bayle had explicitly cited the question of evil as the issue on which faith and reason are most at odds. Consideration of these two aspects of the problem would naturally have led Leibniz to avoid premature intervention, since, by itself, a demonstration of the conformity of religious truth with rational truth is insufficient to put an end to the debate over the existence of evil and divine justice. The *Discourse on the Conformity of Faith with Reason* is the path by which we enter into Theodicy. However, a complete solution to the problem requires us to go further, since it involves a discussion of the doctrine of freedom and predestination. This appears to be Leibniz's response to those of his correspondents who pressed him to stake out a position publicly. Leibniz refers to his long-standing plans and to his meditations on fate, freedom, and predestination (subjects he had pondered since his adolescence), which he desired the leisure to "suitably organize."[43]

Thus, there appears a sort of convergence between a long-standing, highly developed project and the circumstances that favored its realization, though not without forcing certain adjustments to the content and mode of exposition. Whereas in the earlier projects, Theodicy was limited to the domains of *natural* theology and jurisprudence—that is, to those domains insofar as they depend solely on reason—the discussion of the relation between faith and reason led him to broaden the field to include questions pertaining to revealed theology.[44] In fact, the preface to the *Essays* observes that "some astute persons, who are pleased to make difficulties" (notably Bayle) having sought "to increase our perplexity by conjoining the controversies aroused by Christian theology with the disputes of philosophy" have linked "questions concerning necessity, freedom and the origin of evil" with "those concerning original sin, grace and predestination."[45] As a result, Theodicy also aspires to eliminate the difficulties[46] arising from dogmas of faith.

In recounting the circumstances under which the *Essays* were composed, which he describes as "particular and weighty reasons inducing him to take pen in hand for discussion of this subject,"[47] Leibniz chose to situate his work within this polemical context in which philosophy and theology are implicated:

> The greater part of this work was written by scraps while I was at the court of the late Queen of Prussia, where these matters were often discussed in conjunction with the *Dictionary* and other works of M. Bayle, who was widely read. During these conversations it was my habit to respond to the objections of M. Bayle and to show the Queen that they were not as strong as certain people, who were scarcely favorable to religion, would have us believe. Rather frequently Her Majesty ordered me to put my replies into writing so that they could be carefully considered. After the death of this great Princess, I collected together and expanded those pieces at the insistence of my friends who knew of them. Out of them I composed the work of which I have just spoken.[48]

Grua rightly downplays the role of these conversations at the court of Queen Sophia Charlotte in Berlin during the summer of 1702. He argues that the majority of Bayle's texts commented on in the *Essays* are subsequent to the Queen's death in February 1705. According to Grua, "the *Dictionary* is of secondary importance, often appearing in citations and references found in the *Reply [to the Questions of a Provincial]*."[49] Thus, if it is reasonable to harbor some doubts concerning Leibniz's declarations ("the greater part of this work . . . "), how are we to understand the factual reconstruction Leibniz felt obliged to produce and willingly repeated to his correspondents?[50] In my view, Leibniz's account remains an important source of information concerning the *theoretical* and *practical* aspects of the book.

(a) Leibniz invokes the conversations at the royal court in order to identify Bayle as his principal adversary. His disagreement with Bayle concerning the relation of reason and faith is not an isolated one, but it reveals a more fundamental disagreement. Bayle represents a philosophical and theological position exactly opposite of Leibniz. In affirming the radical impotence of reason to establish any definitive truth and its inevitable divorce from faith, Bayle's skepticism is destructive of all natural theology and thus of any attempt at Theodicy.[51] The (external) contradiction of reason and faith is coupled with the (internal) contradiction of reason with itself. Reason is the very instrument of doubt, a "principle of destruction and not of edification," fit only "for raising doubts, and for turning things on all sides in order to make disputes endless," capable only of "making man aware of his own blindness and weakness, and the necessity for another revelation."[52]

Although Bayle allows that the natural light can be made to agree with revelation with regard to the unity and perfection of God, he insists that the compatibility of both moral and physical evil with the supremely good and perfect Being surpasses "our philosophical lights." As a result

> explanations of the permission of sin, other than those drawn from the mysteries revealed in Scripture have this defect: that no matter how good they are, they can be opposed by other reasons that are at once more convincing and more in conformity with our ideas of order.[53]

Consequently, the Manichean hypothesis of an evil principle involves a fundamental paradox: though false and contradictory in theory (a priori), it nevertheless appears true from the point of view of experience (a posteriori).[54] The problem of the origin of evil, the great stumbling block of rational reflection, is like "a hydra from which a head cannot be severed without causing it to grow others." For, "when you think you have walled off one objection, you find you have opened the door to several other difficulties."[55]

The implications of Bayle's objections go far beyond the simple formulation of difficulties or even aporias. They aim to show that every attempt at rational justification of evil is, in principle, doomed to failure because of the natural inability of reason to establish anything solid or certain, in addition to its unavoidable conflict with the teaching of scripture. However, far from ensuring the triumph of "the cause of God," the affirmation of the supremacy of revelation destroys all possibility of defense by introducing a gap between faith and reason. This, in turn, favors equivocity (of words and concepts) and rules out any kind of hearing in the court of reason. It is precisely the univocity of concepts that the *Essays* will attempt to reestablish by showing the conformity (that is, the similarity with regard to form) of faith and reason. What would be the value of a discourse concerning God and his nature and conduct whose principles and conclusions, drawn entirely from reason, might afterward be contradicted by revelation?

> I begin with the preliminary question of the *conformity of faith with reason*, and the use of philosophy in theology, because it greatly affects the main subject of my treatise, and because M. Bayle raises it everywhere.[56]

Leibniz opens the discussion with this question of the *conformity of faith with reason*, because it poses the problem of the unity of the truth and of the legitimacy of the use of reason—not only in the theological domain, but in general. The Theodicy is nothing but the product of reason having been reconciled with faith and with itself.

(b) Finally, the reference to the reception of Bayle's works reveals a practical concern, namely an awareness of the proliferation and success of theses that, in Leibniz's view, endanger true knowledge of God and the enlightened practice of piety. Written in French, both the *Dictionary* and the controversial works that followed its publication attained a wider audience than merely theologians and philosophers. What is needed is an antidote to the poison infused in the minds of readers by these objections to the teachings of faith and the coherence of truth.[57] Leibniz's account of the circumstances and motivations behind the *Essays* bears witness to this concern by presenting the book as arising out of an obligation, and even a kind of moral imperative. The moment had arrived for making public those thoughts, which were the result of a long and painstaking effort. It had become urgent to enter into the debate publicly, as the Queen of Prussia had already summoned Leibniz to do and his friends had similarly

urged him.[58] Leibniz perceived the publication of his *Theodicy* to be a significant *act* in light of the practical stakes. The choice of French, despite
being a second language, was forced on him "because others have recently
made use of that language in discussing the matter, and because it is more
widely read among those whom we seek to benefit with this small work."[59]
In this way, Leibniz could expect a wider circulation of the work among the
public at large[60] and so hope to make an impact comparable to that of the
*Dictionary* itself.

### 4.1.3. The Two Wings of Theodicy and the Theory of Disputation

Whereas the programmatic texts of 1695–1697 promised demonstrations
on the model of mathematics, Leibniz insists on the polemical and defensive dimension of Theodicy when he began to compose the work in ear-
nest (probably beginning in early 1707). The title given to the short draft
published by Grua bears this out:

> Theodicy, or Apology of our notions of the attributes of God on the occasion [of
> the recent debates between M. Bayle and several other able persons] of the latest
> works of M. Bayle.[61]

It would appear that at this stage Leibniz wished to prioritize the refutation of Bayle and the pleading on behalf of divine justice over a dogmatic
and demonstrative exposition. In this way, Theodicy becomes synonymous
with "Anti-Baylean dissertation" (*dissertatio Antibayliana*) or an "opuscule
against Bayle" (*opusculum contra Baylium*).[62] In the published text, reference to the author of the *Dictionary* will be more discrete than in the
draft. Ultimately, Leibniz decided to give his work a more general scope.
Nevertheless, the apologetic and defensive aspect will not entirely disappear, for as Leibniz observes in the preface, "it is the cause of God that is
being pleaded."[63]

These two aspects and two aims—refutational and defensive, on the
one hand, and demonstrative and scientific on the other—of Theodicy
are at the heart of its originality, but also explain the composite and dis-
concerting structure of the text. One cannot help but be struck by the
variety of arguments and proofs, and by their very unequal weight and
value. Sometimes Leibniz considers a priori reasons, particularly when he
speaks of the nature of God. However, in other passages he uses probable
arguments and even simple conjectures or reasons drawn from experience,

as for example when he discusses whether the quantity of good exceeds the quantity of evil in the universe as a whole (see 4.2.3). The value of a conjecture, a presumption, or a probability (which also has degrees) is obviously not the same as the value of an apodictic demonstration. Of course, philosophically, what is drawn from the a priori has greater significance than what comes from a posteriori considerations. According to some commentators, this use of different kinds of proofs, not all of which are strictly demonstrative, reveals a lack of rigor. It shows that the *Essays* is not really a scientific book and that Leibniz was more concerned to persuade than to provide valid arguments.[64]

I believe, on the contrary, that the appeal to probable arguments, and not just those that are absolutely demonstrative, is justified provided that they are considered within the relevant framework: namely, within the framework of a defense, even if these same arguments can appear insufficient and inconclusive when considered within the framework of a properly doctrinal exposition. In my view, Theodicy must be seen as a kind of diptych, composed of two panels: the one *defensive*, and the other *doctrinal*. Leibniz's rhetorical strategy presupposes that different forms of discourse are to be used depending on whether the aim is to refute Bayle's objections or to demonstrate positively the justice of God or even (if possible) the existence of the best possible world. In my view, it is a mistake to confuse these two wings and to fail to see the precise function of the various proofs Leibniz puts forward in the one and the other.

The *defensive* wing (which is developed in particular in the *Preliminary Discourse* and parts II and III of the *Theodicy*, where Leibniz offers a detailed examination of Bayle's objections) is composed of two kinds of defense: the one I call *negative* defense or defense in the strict sense. Its aim is simply to reply to the objection and to show its weakness. The other kind of defense I call *positive* and *supererogatory*. It aims to go further and to show that some a posteriori arguments speak in favor of divine providence. In this defensive wing, we find arguments founded on ignorance of detail, conjectures, presumptions, and various degrees of probability. These do not have real demonstrative value but are sufficient if we bear in mind their true aim.

The doctrinal wing (developed in particular in part I of the *Theodicy*) is likewise divided into two parts: (1) the theological component, which concerns "divine conduct" (God's moral and physical concourse with evil), showing that sin cannot be attributed to him, and establishing, though without absolutely demonstrating, the existence of the best possible world; (2) the *anthropological* component, which establishes the freedom of human beings and their responsibility with regard to evil and sets out the moral rules that govern their actions. As we shall see in chapter 5, this doctrinal wing, which claims to offer only a priori and demonstrative arguments, in fact includes arguments that provide moral or "infallible," but not absolute, certainty.

It is crucial to keep this twofold structure in mind, since it explains why Leibniz could give different answers to the same question, depending on whether he is adopting the defensive or the doctrinal perspective.[65] While these two wings must be carefully distinguished, they must each be seen as essential components of Leibnizian Theodicy. In particular, it would be a mistake to consider the defensive wing to be of secondary importance. This would amount to denying the relevance for Leibniz of any argument that is not absolutely conclusive and is founded only on probability. It would be to ignore his interest in a species of logic that would allow us to estimate the weight of proofs based on probability and plausibility in a field where no demonstration is, strictly speaking, possible (as is the case with everything that belongs to the realm of facts). This "science of proofs"[66] would be of great use when we are called upon to make decisions with regard to facts, as is the case in medicine, politics, jurisprudence, ethics, and theology. We must remember that evil is a matter of *fact*. Its explanation requires less an abstract theory of the best possible universe than an appropriate defense capable of proving both that objections against God's goodness are groundless or fallacious and that there is more empirical evidence in favor of divine perfection than against it. Although the defensive wing is weaker than the doctrinal at the theoretical level, it may, paradoxically, be more decisive and successful at the level of appearances and phenomena. Given that, for Bayle, the existence of evil undermines a priori arguments in favor of the perfection and goodness of God, only a posteriori considerations will carry any weight against him and allow Leibniz to claim ultimate victory.[67]

In this sense, defense and doctrine are complementary and even closely connected. Defense relies on the results of doctrine, which it constantly presupposes. On the other hand, doctrine is not sufficient without defense: it is vulnerable and open to criticism.

With regard to the development of the defense, the *Preliminary Discourse* plays a capital role. Discussion of the conformity of faith and reason provides Leibniz with the opportunity to set out the general rules to be followed in a philosophical or theological debate.[68] For Leibniz these rules must be observed if we are to avoid such endless controversies as the one that pitted Bayle against the "rational" theologians (as Jaquelot, Le Clerc and Bernard). The point is to determine the manner in which these debates must be carried out and the defense conducted, by defining the role and respective duties of each party to the debate, namely the *defender* or *respondent* (who supports the thesis or dogma) and the *opponent* (who attacks the thesis or dogma by offering objections).

The procedure to be followed is based on a conception of debates inspired by judicial procedure in which the goal is not to determine whether the respondent can demonstrate his right, that is, give an account of it, but whether he can defend it against objections. Bayle's mistake lay in his failure to distinguish these two tasks, that of *demonstrating* a thesis and that of *defending* it against objections. Whereas the first belongs to dogmatic exposition, the second belongs to the defense properly speaking. In fact,

> he who maintains a thesis (the *respondens*) is not bound to account for it, but he is bound to meet the objections of an opponent. In law, a defendant is not bound (as a general rule) to prove his right or to produce his title to possession; but he is obliged to reply to the arguments of the plaintiff.[69]

The dispute arises out of a contest in which the initiative belongs by definition to the opponent. The point is not to examine the relevant thesis in and of itself nor to establish it by positive arguments. Rather it is to judge its acceptability as well as the cogency of the arguments offered against it. Therefore, the objection is in fact the principal object of debate, as in the case of an accusation, where the issue is to determine whether it is well-founded or baseless. The defendant occupies the role of the accused, who is obliged to prove neither the legitimacy of his right nor his innocence, but who is required to respond to the demands and allegations of the one who has brought him to court.

Hence arises a strict delineation of responsibilities. The responsibility to prove falls squarely on the plaintiff (opponent). The defendant enjoys the presumption of truth and innocence insofar as he has not yet been convicted of falsity and found guilty. Indeed, since he is not obliged to offer proofs of the soundness of his thesis or of his right, he can even acknowledge that he has no truly conclusive proof, since what he defends does not admit of demonstration (such is the case with regard to the mysteries, which can be *explained* but not *understood*). Conversely, the opponent can prevail only if he offers arguments and contrary demonstrations that are absolutely decisive—that is, incontrovertible.[70] Thus, unlike the case of a dogmatic treatise, where the obligation to demonstrate falls on the one making positive affirmations, in the disputation, this obligation can be required only of the one who denies.

It is now possible to assign to each party to the dispute its respective tasks. The opponent must prove that the thesis is contradictory, whereas the defender must respond, by showing the weakness or fallacy in his opponent's arguments, without being obliged to enter into an examination of his own. This, too, Bayle failed to understand. He maintained that reason cannot resolve objections against the mysteries, unless these latter can be understood by it and reconciled to its principles. He failed to see that to explain or defend a thesis or dogma does not necessarily imply the ability to comprehend or prove it.[71] *To explain* a thing is to set out its meaning so that we understand what we are discussing. The Christian mystery of the incarnation is explained when we say that it is the dogma according to which the Son is united to human nature, while preserving his divine nature. How is this union to be understood? We can form a certain idea of it by analogy with the union of body and soul. However, our explication cannot go beyond this analogical understanding.[72] We cannot comprehend the mystery, since we cannot say *how* such a union can occur. *To comprehend* a thing is to grasp it and penetrate it perfectly and completely; it is to have a clear, distinct, and adequate idea of what it is and what it contains.[73]

Nor can we *prove* the mysteries—that is, demonstrate them by accounting for them a priori. Otherwise, we would be able to comprehend them. On the other hand, we are able to *defend* them against objections, by showing that they involve no contradiction and are not opposed to reason. Thus, it is possible to defend what we cannot comprehend. For, to defend a thesis or dogma does not consist in demonstrating it. Rather it involves showing that the objection raised against it does not hold and that the opponent declares contradictory what he does not understand and confuses that which goes against appearances with that which goes against reason.

Thus, Leibniz turns Bayle's argument on its head. It is not the defender who must demonstrate his thesis in order to reply to objections. It is the opponent who must make the antithesis appear reasonable to refute his adversary incontestably. Consequently, it is the opponent (and not the defender) who by entering into the realm of truths that are above reason, claims to attain to the mysteries and to subject them to rational principles. He ventures into a field where he cannot help but lose and into which the defender does not claim to enter, since he considers the mysteries as indemonstrable, though not contradictory.

The dispute is characterized by an asymmetry in the respective obligations of the two parties; an asymmetry that is unfavorable to the opponent, as Leibniz's military analogy makes clear.[74] The defender, like the besieged, is entrenched behind his fortifications and can remain within the protection of his walls awaiting attack, secure in the knowledge that it will have no effect on his defenses.[75] He can launch an offensive, engaging in "some sortie beyond what is necessary" with the goal of destroying the enemy guns (with the privilege, in case of failure, of retiring to his fort without being subject to censure[76]—that is, without anyone being able to consider him vanquished). The opponent, like the besieger, is out in the open. With no possibility of retreat, he must destroy all of his adversary's defenses to be declared the victor. He can only win "when all the premises and all the consequences [of the objection] are well proved,"[77] whereas the defender has satisfied his obligations once he has shown that the objection is not decisive. A simple examination of the form of the objection or the express demand that it be cast in logical form suffices without any further obligation to enter more deeply into the matter (which is normally the responsibility of the objector).

All the classical devices of refutation, as well as the traditional tropes of skeptical arguments can be fairly made use of by the defense, which has nothing to prove and can freely acknowledge its ignorance: "For the purpose of doubting only, I need not at all probe to the heart of the matter; on the contrary, the more ignorant I am the more shall I be justified in doubting."[78] Among the usual maneuvers are doubting the premises or consequences of the objection and demanding their demonstration;[79] calling for the explication of ambiguous terms, or even offering some distinction in order to reveal the equivocation concealed in the opponent's argument; denouncing every illegitimate generalization drawn, without other proof, from a particular proposition; contesting every faulty conclusion (based on experience or appearances), by underscoring its relativity and showing "the bare possibility" of the defendant's thesis.[80]

In a certain sense, skepticism goes over to the other side and places itself in the service of the thesis. The result is a paradoxical reversal: the dispute now concerns the refutation of the objection. The roles are thereby reversed: the defense appears as an objection to the objection—indeed, as an attack, which repels the charge of an opponent who has been put in the position of having to defend himself. The opponent is now called upon to establish the antithesis by entering into "the heart of the matter." However, with no possible retreat and his batteries neutralized, he is vanquished in the same way as those, on the side of the defense, "who claim that God's conduct with regard to sin and the consequences of sin contains nothing they cannot account for."[81] For, none of the arguments offered in favor of the thesis or the antithesis constitute a true demonstration, strictly speaking.

## 4.2 THEODICY AS DEFENSE: IGNORANCE OF DETAIL, PRESUMPTIONS, AND PROBABILITIES

### 4.2.1 The "Negative" Defense or Defense in the Strict Sense

In setting forth the general rules according to which a philosophical debate must be conducted, the *Preliminary Discourse* distinguishes the obligations of the defender (defense in the strict or "negative" sense) from the supplementary arguments, which he may choose to put forward in order to defeat his opponent by means of positive considerations on behalf of the defender's own thesis (the "positive" or supererogatory defense). What use does Leibniz make of these rules within the framework of his defense of the cause of God? Leibniz takes the position of the defender, supporting the thesis that God is good and just in spite of the evil he permits in the world and places Bayle in the position of the opponent. As early as 1706 Leibniz sketches an outline of the negative defense while examining the following argument from Bayle:

> The means of reconciling the moral and physical evil of man with all the attributes of this unique, infinitely perfect Principle of all things surpasses our philosophical lights, such that the Manichean objections raise difficulties that human reason cannot resolve.[82]

Leibniz concedes the first proposition, according to which the means of reconciling evil with divine perfection exceeds our lights but only with regard to the "details of the reasons that led God to permit these evils." However, he denies that it follows from this "that the objections made in this regard cannot be resolved,"[83] since, according to the rules of dispute, it is the responsibility of the opponent to demonstrate divine imperfection *positively*:

> For it is possible that God has such reasons [for permitting evil], although we cannot discover them. And anyone who would offer an objection that cannot be resolved must prove that it is impossible that God has these reasons. That is, he must produce an argument that infers God's imperfection from the permission of evil and is such that we cannot respond as required. That is, this argument must have a correct form and, as for the matter, all of the propositions must either be granted or proved by another argument of the same kind.[84]

Mere consideration of the *possibility* that such reasons exist, though unknown to us, is sufficient. It does not constitute, properly speaking, a proof, except provisionally. Nevertheless, it offers a *presumption* in favor of divine perfection, and this presumption holds good so long as it has not been demonstrated that there could not be valid reasons for permitting evil. The defender has no need to develop his response any further, since the mere presumption (which is more than a simple supposition or conjecture[85]) must be taken for true until such time as a proof, or rather *demonstration*, of the contrary is provided.

Leibniz employs a similar argument in the *Preliminary Discourse* (§§32–33), although in this case the presumption is on the side of the accusation. He invokes Bayle's objection that those who would justify God on the grounds that he merely permitted sin, but is not complicit in it (although he foresaw and even facilitated it), would fail to convince any judge hearing a similar case in a human tribunal. Imagine a father who attempted to exonerate himself of the crimes committed by a child, who is his legal charge and under his surveillance, on the grounds that he merely *permitted* the evil. The judge would surely take this "permission" to be complicity and declare the father guilty of a crime by omission.

Leibniz responds that to foresee an evil, to fail to prevent it when able to do so, and even to favor its occurrence does not *necessarily* imply that one is an accomplice to it. All of this amounts to a very strong presumption in favor of complicity. Ordinarily, such a presumption suffices for a guilty verdict in human courts, where it takes the place of truth. However, in the case of God, one cannot rest satisfied with presumptions, however powerful they may be. For, one must be absolutely certain that God did not have very good and overriding reasons to permit the evil.

This is not to claim that divine action is governed by a justice that is higher or of a different order. Nor is it a renunciation of the fundamental thesis of the univocity of notions and principles. It is simply an acknowledgment that God cannot be defended or judged in the same way that we defend or judge a human being. Our ignorance of all the circumstances of an event, of all the causes and consequences of an act, and the need to have recourse to the testimony of a third party make it the case that, often in our investigations and in our tribunals, we must rest content with judging on the basis of clues, probabilities, and presumptions rather than truths. Now, to render a guilty verdict against God, who is presumed good and wise in the absence of an express proof to the contrary, we must engage in "an exact consideration of the facts"[86] and prove beyond all doubt his culpability or at least the impossibility of finding any reason that would excuse him of having permitted evil.

It should be clear that presumption cannot be considered in the same manner when used by the defender as when used by the opponent. For the defender, presumption is a proof that, although insufficient on the theoretical level, acquires proportionally greater weight than what it would normally carry as a probable argument. For it cannot be destroyed by any contrary presumption or appearance—even a stronger one. Only a contrary demonstration can destroy it. Now, whereas presumption is a solid and sufficient argument on behalf of the defense, it becomes a weak and ineffective weapon in the hands of the opponent—even when it is objectively stronger in terms of *probability*. Thus, even though the presumption against God's goodness based on the permission of sin (which would suffice to condemn a human being in parallel circumstances) is indisputably stronger than the contrary presumption, which is based on the bare possibility of superior reasons that authorize the permission of evil,[87] within the framework of the dispute the latter presumption wins out, since it wins out over every objection that is not a formal demonstration of the contrary.

Notice that later in the text (§34) Leibniz refuses to rule out the possibility of a case, even among human beings, of a father, a tutor, or a friend who is led to permit the sin of his child, pupil, or young companion for valid and compelling reasons, and who therefore cannot be accused of complicity. Such a case would be extraordinary, but it is not *in itself* impossible. Indeed, a "skilled writer of fiction" could invent just such a case. Leibniz's appeal to such theoretical possibility, like the factual argument according to which God *must have had* such overriding reasons since evil does indeed exist (§35), does not strictly speaking belong to the negative defense but already anticipates the positive or supererogatory defense. Here the point is not simply to reply that God could have had reasons to permit evil, and that it is the burden of the opponent to prove positively that God could not have had such reasons, but rather to meet the opponent on his own terrain (that of appearances) and to show that a human being (under conditions that are, to be sure, very difficult to realize) could have such overriding motives that would excuse him.

Before looking at this second kind of defense, we must first examine the second principal argument of the negative defense, which consists in alleging the *ignorance* of the defender. In affirming the compatibility of the infinitely good and wise being with the existence of evil and the perfection of the world at the global level, Leibniz is not claiming to know in detail God's reasons for creation or the considerations he took into account in creating (the comparison of possible worlds, which are infinite in number) or the details of the universal harmony, which involves infinity. For Leibniz, it is as impossible to show a priori and in detail that "evil could have been avoided without losing some greater good" as to "show the connection of these evils with the greater goods,"[88] since both are beyond the capacity of human reason. The objection that it would have been easy for God to create this greater good directly while bypassing the associated evil or that this good is not always evident (not to say extremely doubtful) would be valid if the defender claimed to be capable of explaining every evil in particular and of identifying beyond a shadow of a doubt the good it makes possible. However, this is something the defender never claimed to be able to do.

This avowed ignorance is not a mere rhetorical expedient in order to guarantee the victory of the defender within the particular framework of the dispute. Rather, it defines, in my view, the limits of Theodicy both as *defense* and as *doctrine*, which neither can nor should, go beyond a certain level of generality in its explanation of evil. In fact,

> it appears that M. Bayle asks a little too much: he wishes for a detailed exposition of how evil is connected with the best possible scheme for the universe. That would be a complete explanation of the phenomena: but I do not undertake to give it; nor am I bound to do so, for there is no obligation to do that which is impossible for us in our present state. It is sufficient for me to point out that there is nothing to prevent the connexion of a certain individual evil with what is best on the whole. This incomplete explanation, which leaves something to be discovered in the life to come, is sufficient for answering objections, though not for a comprehension of the matter.[89]

According to the rules of a dispute, to defend a thesis against objections does not require that one understand it (or is able to understand it fully). We must rest content with the available explanation not only at the level of disputation but also at the doctrinal level. The *Discourse on Metaphysics* had already made this clear: although we are in a position to affirm *in general* (on the basis of a certain number of a priori considerations derived from the idea of God) that the created universe is the best and that the sin we find within it is compensated elsewhere at the global level, we cannot, at least in this life, penetrate "the admirable economy of this choice [of this universe]." Moreover, "it is enough to know it without understanding it" and to recognize with the Apostle Paul "the depth and the abyss, of the divine wisdom, without seeking a detail which involves infinite considerations."[90] The explanation can only be a priori and metaphysical and can offer nothing more than the general reasons for the existence of evil. It cannot be particular, explaining this or that evil as observed a posteriori in the world, nor can it establish with certainty the greater good each particular evil makes possible. It answers the question, "why does evil exist?" but not the question, "why does *this* evil exist?"

The originality of Theodicy, relative to other attempts at a rational jus-tification of evil, is to posit and defend this distinction between a general explanation of the manner in which God acts and the perfection of the world considered as a whole, and the interpretation that can be offered of particular evils. On this point, Leibniz's project is markedly different from that of the Stoics, for example, who attempted to explain every evil in particular, even to the point of alleging benefits from harmful animals![91] Leibniz writes:

> [I]t seems that the reason for permitting evil rests in the eternal possibilities, in accordance with which this kind of universe which allows evil and has admitted it to actual existence is found to be more perfect, considering the whole, than all other possible kinds. But we go astray in trying to show in detail the value of evil in revealing the good, as the Stoics do—a value which St. Augustine has well recognized in general, and according to which we step back, so to speak, in order to leap forward better. For can we enter into the infinite particulars of the universal harmony?[92]

In affirming that the details are beyond our grasp, Leibniz refuses to show how such and such an evil finds room in the best divine plan. He rejects as improper every particular application of the general thesis ac-cording to which God permits evil with an eye to a greater good, since such applications inevitably pave the way for reckless speculation concerning the good. Thus, Leibniz has nothing in common with the character Pangloss created by Voltaire in *Candide* in which the ridiculousness lies precisely in the inappropriate application of the general to the particular. Leibniz would have been the first to reject such applications. It is rather prudence and reserve that are called for:

> It is in some sense by physical necessity that God does everything for the best (although no creature is able to apply this universal proposition to individual cases or to infer certain consequences relative to free divine actions).[93]

Notice however that the interpretation of facts differs depending on whether it is a good or an evil at issue. Whereas a particular evil, which is the object of a divine permission, ought not give rise to any conjecture concerning the greater good of which it is the condition, every good, on the contrary, ought to be considered as expressly willed by God.[94] The appeal to final causes must be made cautiously in the case of evils but boldly and un-reservedly in the case of goods. One cannot, as it were, carry "finalism" too far by attributing too many good intentions to the creator. Our recognition of his blessings will always fall short of the intentions of an infinite wisdom and supremely good will.[95]

Thus, Leibniz's Theodicy in both its defensive and (as we shall see) doctrinal aspects marks the limits of the justification of God. This theoretical limitation is not without implications at the level of dispute, since it renders vain all objections based on the experience of evil and the disorders of the world. No fact, no event however catastrophic and terrifying it may be or appear can contradict a thesis that pertains only to the universal and does not pretend to explain the reason for each individual thing, nor God's ultimate ends. The defender is immune to all criticism based on the appearances of injustice and imperfection observable in this tiny corner of the universe we inhabit. For he can always appeal to that universal harmony that we cannot comprehend but which we have good reason to believe most perfect.

Thus, the dispute is a clash of two kinds of ignorance. The first is, so to speak, "learned" and "wise." It is the ignorance of the defender, who acknowledges his inability to explain the details of the universal harmony, but who remains certain of the perfection of the whole (since an "infallible" certitude is established by doctrine). The second is a pretended knowledge, that is, in fact, an ignorance that is ignorant of itself. It is the ignorance of the zealous, but blundering, apologist who hopes to justify God even with regard to particulars, or conversely, the ignorance of those who despise the order of the world, and who, by a faulty generalization, judge the whole on the basis of the part and criticize the author of things on the basis of this partial knowledge.

> God's object has in it something infinite, his cares embrace the universe: what we know thereof is almost nothing, and we desire to gauge his wisdom and his goodness by our knowledge. What temerity, or rather what absurdity! The objections are on false assumptions; it is senseless to pass judgment on the point of law when one does not know the matter of fact. To say with St. Paul, *O altitudo divitiarum et sapientiae,* is not renouncing reason, it is rather employing the reasons that we know, for they teach us that immensity of God whereof the Apostle speaks. But therein we confess our ignorance of the facts, and we acknowledge, moreover, before we see it, that God does all the best possible, in accordance with the infinite wisdom which guides his actions.[96]

Within the negative defense, appeal to the argument from possibility and the argument from ignorance allows the defender always to remain outside the subject under discussion and to avoid taking up the heart of the matter by declaring himself incapable of discussing it. By refusing to commit himself with regard to the details of universal harmony and God's reasons and ends, the defender does not enter the terrain upon which the opponent seeks to lure him. As a result, the latter, if he hopes to triumph, is obliged to *demonstrate* that God could not permit evil for any good reason and that such and such a defect or sin disfigures the world to such an extent and renders it so imperfect that no wise man who considers it in its entirety would judge it to be the best. But it is impossible to make good on this obligation, since to do so would require nothing less than that omniscience which belongs to God alone. At this stage the defender has discharged all his duties and can legitimately take leave of the dispute in victory.

### 4.2.2 The "Positive" or Supererogatory Defense (1): Evidence Drawn from the Experience of a Universal Order

The "negative" defense suffices to put an end to the controversy. Consequently, all the arguments that the defender can now add on behalf of the perfection and order of the world and of the goodness, wisdom, and justice of God should be considered supererogatory—that is, over and above what is strictly required. Not content to have shown the emptiness of the objection and repelled the attack, the defendant may choose to go further and defeat the opponent on his own ground, where he had believed himself most secure: at the level of experience and appearances. In offering a response beyond what is strictly required, the defender runs no risk. The victory achieved through the negative part of the defense cannot be contested. As in a military siege when the besieged, convinced of his strength, seizes the initiative and launches a counter-attack beyond the walls of the citadel, it is always within his power to retreat. Any "battle" waged on the field of phenomena that might turn against the defender could neither result in his defeat nor weaken his position. Such a defeat can only be achieved by a demonstration on the part of the opponent.

These arguments of the defender, which are meant to be more convincing than those of his opponent (even if they are not demonstrations), belong to what I call the "positive" defense. This second kind of defense consists in responding to objections drawn from appearances, not as in the case of the negative defense, by showing their inadequacy, but by offering counterexamples, contrary appearances or stronger presumptions in favor of divine justice. In addition, the positive defense seeks to take advantage of the a posteriori marks and evidence that nature provides of the harmony of the world, as well as the reasons for believing that the totality of good exceeds that of evil in the universe as a whole.

Although theoretically insufficient and inferior to doctrine, this super-erogatory part of Leibnizian Theodicy paradoxically appears more decisive and more able to land telling blows against a philosopher such as Bayle, who maintains that in this matter only a posteriori considerations (i.e., those based on experience) are truly conclusive. The appeal of taking up the struggle on the field of phenomena is clear: if the defender (Leibniz) can show that his position is not only safe from any attempted refutation and logically immune according to the rules of dispute but moreover that it is more consistent with appearances, the most plausible, and therefore the most convincing,[97] his victory will be complete and the "siege" definitively broken. Not only will he have proved that the objections are inconclusive, he will have destroyed the fundamental thesis on which they are based, namely, that from the point of view of experience, certain facts are wholly incompatible with the existence of a unique, infinitely good and perfect principle (God).

The positive defense is the field of application par excellence of this logic of probability whose rigorous development Leibniz had called for (whereas ordinary logic suffices for the negative defense). In the realm of facts and appearances, where probabilities are opposed to other probabilities, it would be very useful to have a scale by which we could determine the respective weights of different kinds of proof, presumptions, and evidence and determine which side should be preferred and which position adopted. The example of the father or tutor who under certain conditions can be excused for the sin of his child or pupil provided an occasion to cite several of the arguments used to justify God and show that the appearances (which at first glance appeared unfavorable) support the defender. Besides the theoretical possibility of such a case of licit permission among humans, our knowledge of divine perfection and holiness strongly suggests that God had indispensable reasons for allowing evil and that he can in no way be an accomplice to its occurrence.[98] Once again the goal is not to provide absolutely conclusive arguments but rather to oppose one set of appearances to another and one set of probabilities to even stronger presumptions in order to blunt the objection and win assent.

The philosophical interest of this defense should not be overlooked. Its most positive, if not most important, results are to be found (1) in the appeal to obvious marks of a universal order established by a wise and superior being, (2) in the evidence this defense provides of the prevalence of good over evil in the world in general (4.2.3).

Leibniz does not believe that the phenomena have nothing to teach us concerning the essence of reality. To be sure, for Leibniz, only substances are truly real. Phenomena or "appearances" merely exist within the substances that perceive them. These appearances are always partial and truncated and so subject to caution. Any judgment that makes unreserved use of them is subject to error. This critique is not new; it is commonplace in the history of philosophy. However, it is given a particular twist by Leibniz, who maintains that appearances are never completely unrelated to the truth and so are not to be entirely rejected. Although that which is perceived of a thing is not to be confused with the thing itself, there must necessarily be some affinity between them, since the phenomena always stand in a relation of expression to the substances that produce them. Although we must never judge the whole of the universe on the basis of the tiny part we observe, nevertheless it must be the case that this small portion reflects, partially and in its own way, the order and perfection of the whole, given the connection of all things and the analogy between microcosm and macrocosm.

In other words, our experience, however limited and fragmentary it may be, must provide us with evidence of an intelligence at work in nature. Two considerations underwrite this *teleological* reading: the first is the rule of interpretation already mentioned, according to which every good end and every perfection must be credited to God.[99] The second is a consequence of the principle of univocity of notions and principles. If creation is good and beautiful, not simply because God is its author but intrinsically and in itself, then the work must make evident a posteriori, by sensible and recognizable marks, the perfection of its maker. The spectacle of the beauty of the world speaks much more in favor of an ordering wisdom than of lawless, blind chance as Epicurus believed.[100] Does it not suffice to examine a plant, an animal, a human being, or the structure of any complete being to infer the action of a divine architect? To be sure, Epicurus's argument— namely, that among the infinity of worlds assembled at random there must be some that are well made and well ordered, including the one in which we have been placed by chance!—is not an "absolutely impossible" fiction— that is, a logical contradiction. However, this fiction is "as scarcely plausible as to suppose that an entire library was formed one day by the chance encounter of atoms."[101] Therefore, we are justified in attributing the origin of the world to a supreme intelligence, for the appearances speak more in its favor, although it is only a strong probability rather than a demonstration, a "moral belief" rather than "certain knowledge [*certa scientia*]."[102]

We remain in the realm of defense, since teleology based on observation of the anatomy of creatures and the admirable organization of their organs cannot by itself provide a sufficient argument against the Epicurean hypothesis of a perfectly regulated universe that is nevertheless the product of chance. For Leibniz, the argument, which following Kant, is commonly referred to as the "physico-theological" proof of the existence of God, based on the order and perfection observed in nature, cannot amount to a genuine *proof*. In fact, its true function is different: not to demonstrate the existence of God, nor even to provide us with an idea of him, but to elicit the notion we already had of him. By pointing out the evidence of a divine intelligence, who is the author of the universe and the beings that inhabit it, the study of the natural sciences provides the occasion for the soul to look inward and to *apperceive* an idea that it innately possesses and so is not acquired by means of experience. These signs and indications do not prove anything. Rather, they confirm a posteriori what we know by other means, namely, the idea of God that we have in ourselves and everything that reflection on this idea allows us to discover a priori (God's perfections, and in particular his greatness, wisdom, and goodness, which are studied in the doctrinal part of Theodicy).[103]

However, in the *Essays of Theodicy* Leibniz goes further. He attempts to make this presumption based on physical teleology pass for almost a complete proof by appealing to a new argument. According to this new argument, examination of the laws of nature (such as the laws of motion) shows that they cannot be reduced to the absolute necessity of efficient causes, and that in order to explain them we must have recourse to final causes and the Principle of Fitness. Thus, experience reveals more than simply order and beauty. The laws that are verified by experience, because they do not admit of a complete demonstration (as is the case, for example, with geometrical propositions) and are neither absolutely necessary nor arbitrary, inevitably refer us back to an original choice of an intelligence. Thus, even the strictest mechanism leads to God:

> I can demonstrate these laws in various ways, but must always assume something that is not of an absolutely geometrical necessity. Thus these admirable laws are wonderful evidence of an intelligent and free being, as opposed to the system of absolute and brute necessity, advocated by Strato or Spinoza.[104]

Doubtless Leibniz considers the contingency and fitness of natural laws to be a novel proof drawn from his own "system," a proof that provides considerable support to the physico-theological argument. It should be noted, however, that this proof still amounts to only a strong presumption in favor of the existence of a divine creator and cannot take the place of a demonstration. The findings of the natural sciences together with a body of corroborating empirical observations are not sufficient. What more can they do than confirm, rather than prove, those theses established a priori at the doctrinal level (such as the existence of God, his wisdom, and his free choice of the best)? It is not the data of sense, our collected experiences and the laws discovered by natural philosophy that serve as the foundation of doctrine. On the contrary, it is doctrine that, so to speak, serves as their foundation by supplying the theoretical framework within which they must be interpreted. Nonetheless, to call attention to these indications and ends to which physics itself attests, and so to make of science the greatest ally of religion, is particularly useful in an apologetic context. It serves to counter the skeptical or atheistic opponent and "to convince the profane."[105]

### 4.2.3 The "Positive" or Supererogatory Defense (2): Prevalence of Good over Evil at the Universal Level

The arguments employed in the "positive" defense are inseparable from the metaphysical and theological positions developed in the doctrinal part of Theodicy (which will be examined in subsequent chapters). The asser- tion that the sum total of goods in the universe exceeds that of evils is no exception, since it is a consequence of the thesis that God chooses the best of all possible worlds. Within the context of the defense, Leibniz does not attempt an empirical proof of this preponderance of goods. Rather, he attempts to show that the objections leveled against it, insofar as they are based on partial experience and subjective human testimony, fail to take into account either the whole extent of the world or the partiality of the witnesses, who are generally more attentive to evil than good. In fact, there is every reason to believe that an accurate examination at the uni- versal level will find in favor of good rather than evil. As in the case of the empirical evidence for the order of the world, the goal here is to show that the appearances can and indeed must—in one way or another when judged appropriately—corroborate metaphysical truth (although they do not pro- vide a foundation for it).

The first argument put forward by Leibniz is *physical* and *theological* in nature. The spatial extension of the physical universe, unknown to the ancients, but which modern science has discovered, suggests that the spiritual city is of similar extent. Thus, even if evils did outnumber goods here on earth and the number of damned were greater than those who are saved, such evil would still be miniscule in comparison with the innu- merable other suns and planets where rational, albeit nonhuman, creatures may be happy. Therefore, it may well be the case that there is on the whole among spirits more virtue than vice, more happiness than misery, and a far greater number of elect. Leibniz considers the hypothesis of a vast space beyond even the stars that is filled with happiness and glory (similar to the

Empyrean Heaven of which theologians speak), like a vast ocean "whither flow the rivers of all blessed creatures, when they shall have reached their perfection in the system of the stars."[106] In comparison with this great immensity bathed in divine light, what are the earth and its inhabitants? Nothing or very little; "something incomparably less than a physical point."

> Thus since the proportion of that part of the universe which we know almost disappears into nothingness in comparison with that which is unknown, and which we yet have reason to assume, and since all the evils that may be raised in objection before us are in this near nothingness, it may be that all evils are almost nothingness in comparison with the good things which are in the universe.[107]

To be sure, the argument is merely an extrapolation from astronomical observations. Still, the presumption stemming from its mere possibility suffices[108] to consider it admissible and even to render it unassailable, since according to the rules of dispute it falls to the opponent to demonstrate that it cannot be the case that good surpasses evil at the global level. Such a demonstration is impossible for a finite mind, which cannot comprehend the world and all its parts.

At this point, the critique remains external, insofar as it consists in nothing more than relativizing our particular experience by relating it to the universe as a whole. The second argument, which is *psychological* in nature, takes more direct aim at the objection by calling into question the validity of our subjective experience in light of our propensity to exaggerate the share of evil relative to the good. Belief in the predominance of evil, which is shared by a number of authors (including Homer, Pliny, and La Mothe-Le-Vayer[109]) and by common opinion, is the result of our natural relation to good and evil. The good is usually ignored; we only take notice of it when it is lost (as with health when we fall ill[110]). Evil, by contrast, is more frequently noticed; we are often led to magnify and exaggerate it.

Paradoxically, this inequality, owing to our lack of attention on the one hand and our extreme sensibility on the other hand, proves that good outweighs evil. Good goes unnoticed only because it is more habitual, whereas evil commands our attention only because it is rarer. In this way, subjective testimony is turned back against the objection that it was supposed to underwrite. Our very sense that evil outstrips the good shows on the contrary that it does not.[111] Moreover, our extreme sensitivity, which is the natural result of our general well-being, undermines the reliability of this sentiment as an exact measure of good and evil. As Lactantius said, "men are so squeamish that they complain of the slightest ill, as if it swallowed up all the goods they have enjoyed."[112] Present sentiment is a source of error, insofar as a single evil, even a weak one, is enough to make us forget all present and past goods and so tip the balance in favor of evil. The current and predominant state of the soul together with habit tend to affect our judgment. The effect is even more pronounced among those who are more accustomed to happiness, like the great, when they are suddenly struck by adversity.[113]

Consideration of the immensity of God's kingdom and the critique of judgment as it is compromised by our sensitivity (which varies from one person to another, according to differences of character, temperament, habit, passions, etc.) seriously weakens the objection, or at least, greatly limits its significance. To be sure, they are not by themselves a sufficient response to the objection. However, they serve as an indispensable first step insofar as they clear the way for a more positive and bolder argument in favor of the predominance of good in the universe as a whole.

This argument is based on a calculation that involves counting and weighing goods and evils to determine which outweighs the other on the whole. Obviously, the result will be no more than a general estimation. However, its degree of probability is not for all that less sufficient for the purposes of the defense. The evaluation is complex for a variety of reasons. On the one hand, it mixes empirical data with theoretical extrapolations, subjective experiences with probabilities. On the other hand, it is itself the result of several partial calculations based on types of good and evil (physical, moral, and metaphysical) and according to kinds of creatures (rational and/or non-rational) within which one can compare and contrast different classes (human/animal, humans/spirits and angels), while including or excluding consideration of the afterlife (the saved/the damned).

In accordance with the class of objects considered and the criteria adopted, the results can vary. Although there would appear to be more vice than virtue among human beings owing to original sin, the balance tips in favor of moral good when we take into account the totality of spirits (including genies, angels, and demons), even when we include the damned. With regard to human life during our time on earth, it must at least be acknowledged that "considered without prejudice," it is "ordinarily acceptable," that is, bearable and even agreeable. Here, too, then good outweighs evil in general, even if not by a great margin. The term "ordinarily" refers to the majority of cases. Thus, the judgment must be understood as general, expressing an estimated average, which is itself the average of an average (of goods and evils), the result of which, according to Leibniz, inclines toward the good. However, when we "add in the motives of religion, we shall be content with the order God has set therein."[114] If we would persist in maintaining that God does not sufficiently favor human beings and their happiness, we must remember that it is the perfection of the whole at which God aims. Although a human being is of greater worth than a lion, the general order will not allow non-rational creatures to count for nothing, as if all that mattered were the good of humans:

> [I]t can hardly be said with certainty that God prefers a single man in all respects to the whole of lion-kind. Even should that be so, it would by no means follow that the interest of a certain number of men would prevail over the consideration of a general disorder diffused through an infinite number of creatures.[115]

Human happiness is one of God's ends, but it is not the only one. Although it is part of God's plan to make human beings happy and to make them share in his glory (which is his principal aim), their moral and physical goods and evils are not of such a nature as to justify, in order to secure the one and prevent the other, a complete overturning of everything else, for they do not infinitely surpass metaphysical goods and evils, which consist in the perfection and imperfection of creatures.[116] God procures human happiness to the extent allowed by the universal harmony. There are other goods besides ours that must be taken into account, goods that also contribute to his glory.

Ultimately, what the argument shows is that if at any given level (the life of a particular human being; human life in general; the whole collection of human beings, living and dead; all spirits), it is not sufficiently obvious that the good predominates, we must expand our consideration to include the next higher level, until we reach the entirety of things considered as a whole, in all times and all places (that is, the world). Still, this method is not without difficulty. One may well object to comparing and weighing in such a way different kinds of good and evil, along with their various degrees of intensity and seriousness with regard to the beings themselves. How are we to compare creatures of different[117] levels of perfection to be assured that quantity (of non-rational creatures) can, given a sufficient amount (how much?), compensate for quality (the excellence of spirits), in such a way that the quantity of metaphysical good among animals, which are less perfect but incomparably greater in number, can counterbalance physical and moral evils of more perfect, yet less numerous, beings?

The problem is that such calculations involve quantities that are heterogeneous and apparently incommensurable, unless physical and moral good and evil can be reduced to metaphysical good and evil, as Leibniz suggests, on consideration of the metaphysical good and evil which is in all substances, whether endowed with or devoid of intelligence, and which taken in such scope would include physical good and moral good, one must say that the universe, such as it actually is, must be the best of all systems.[118]

It seems that the heterogeneity of goods and evils can be overcome by virtue of the fact that they can be reduced to degrees of ontological perfection, that is, to metaphysical goods and evils. A good is a certain quantity of perfection, whereas an evil is a lack of perfection. In this way, the calculation, being now between homogenous and commensurable entities, becomes possible. Is such a solution satisfactory? There is room for doubt. Mere consideration of goods and evils from an ontological point of view cannot form the basis of a just and accurate calculation, since it expressly rejects that which constitutes the specificity of vices and virtues, pains and pleasures. To be sure, physical and moral goods and evils are perfections and imperfections in or of being. However, these perfections and imperfections, owing to the spiritual, reflexive, and free nature of the subjects to which they belong, have an irreducibly moral and juridical signification, which any truly comprehensive evaluation must take into account. Vice is not merely a lack of being (like any other imperfection in the world) and the sign of this lack. It is also a positive violation of the law. Moreover, if pain is an indication of a lesser perfection, it is also the punishment of the sinner or a trial that the just man encounters on the road to excellence. It would seem then that the calculation can be correct—and the proposition that in general good outweighs evil in our universe shown to be true—only if a *separate* calculation is antecedently made for each type of good and evil.

However, there are still problems, since the goods and evils of different kinds of creatures must also be taken into account:

> But why might not the surplus of good in the non-intelligent creatures that fill the world compensate for and even exceed incomparably the surplus of evil in rational creatures? It is true that the value of the latter is greater; but by way of compensation the others are incomparably greater in number; and it may be that the proportion of number and quantity surpasses that of value and quality.[119]

In addition to the problem, which we have already considered, of comparing different kinds of good and evil (physical and moral good and evil on the one hand, and purely metaphysical good and evil on the other), the notion of a possible compensation between the superior quality of spirits and the greater quantity of less perfect creatures seems highly debatable. How could the metaphysical good of non-rational monads, worse still, of simple monads (even apart from the question of the number and "limit" beyond which the quantity could compensate for the quality) counterbalance the moral and physical evil of certain spirits? It is hard to see how damnation could be compensated by anything other than a good of the same kind, namely, the beatitude of the elect.

The argument seems hardly more convincing with regard to the comparison of the damned and the blessed, where this time the value must outweigh the number:

> [I]it is possible, and even a very reasonable thing, that the glory and perfection of the blessed may be incomparably greater than the misery and imperfection of the damned, and that here the excellence of the total good in the smaller number may exceed the total evil which is in the greater number. The blessed draw near to divinity through a divine Mediator, so far as can belong to these created beings, and make such progress in good as is impossible for the damned to make in evil, even though they should approach as nearly as may be the nature of demons. God is infinite, and the Devil is finite; good can and does go on ad infinitum, whereas evil has its bounds.[120]

Good predominates because the comparison here is between a good that never ceases to increase and an evil that is, by definition, limited. Thus, there is an ever increasing gap between the totality of good in paradise and the totality of evil in hell, such that the virtue and happiness of the elect (although fewer in number) must always surpass the vice and misery of the damned, who cannot go beyond a certain level of imperfection. The blessed perpetually approach God without ever reaching him, whereas the damned must arrive at the limit set by the demonic nature. Thus, proportionally, the former will enjoy greater beatitude than the latter will experience misery.

According to whether it is the quantity or quality that is infinite, number will outweigh intrinsic value (as in the case of non-rational creatures, which are "incomparably" more numerous than spirits) or, conversely, intrinsic value will outweigh number (as in the case of the blessed whose perfection eternally approaches God's, whereas the imperfection of the damned, although they are greater in number, is limited). Two observations are in order here:

(1) Leibniz's hypothesis of an infinite number of creatures is based on the infinite divisibility of the continuum and on the extent of the universe as established by recent cosmological discoveries. As a result, there is no basis for claiming that the number of intelligent creatures must be limited.

Leibniz even seems to suggest the contrary. After having declared that the non-rational creatures are "incomparably greater in number" than the others, Leibniz asserts later in the same text (!) that

> an opponent cannot prove that in the whole City of God, composed as much of spirits as of rational animals *without number and of endlessly different kinds*, the evil exceeds the good.[121]

(2) The intrinsic limitation of evil presupposes that there is no possible progression from the diabolic nature toward greater imperfection. However, this contradicts the thesis that "imperfections descend to infinity,"[122] a proposition illustrated in the fable of Sextus by the image of a pyramid with no base. In fact, there is no world inferior to the best that "does not also have less perfect worlds below it: that is why the pyramid goes on descending to infinity."[123] On this account, it is the best, represented by the apex, rather than the worst that would appear to be limited. One could maintain that the progression to infinity among the less perfect occurs only at the level of worlds. However, besides the fact that this restriction is not made clear, there would seem to be no reason why the damned cannot indefinitely approach the greatest imperfection (Nothingness) without ever reaching it, in the same way that the blessed approach the supreme perfection (God) without ever attaining it. Moreover, the perpetual progression of the one and the perpetual regression of the other were defended by Leibniz in certain texts.[124]

These difficulties, or rather, contradictions, show the limits of the positive defense, which ultimately struggles to provide conclusive arguments. Here again, however, the rules of dispute protect the defender from any possible defeat: "one is justified in assuming that a thing may be so as long as it has not been proved to be impossible."[125] The defense proves nothing, but it can allow itself certain presumptions. The assertion that good outweighs evil ultimately rests on a traditional thesis: the Scholastic theory of the convertibility of being and goodness. The good in general outweighs evil, because every creature, however imperfect and defective it may be, is and remains a being and so a good. So long as being subsists, there will always be more good than evil. The opposition between the infinity of God and the finitude of the devil prefigures this fundamental inequality between good and evil. There will always be less evil than good, since by definition evil cannot exceed the good it limits. There remains the problem of a global evaluation, one that is not exclusively arithmetical but which is able to take into account the specificity of physical and moral goods and evils. The inference from quantity to quality does not always hold. Doubtless, what is needed here is a scale like that which is sought in the logic of probability and by which goods and evils may not only be *counted* but also *weighed*.[126] By this means, the precision and reliability of the estimate would be improved, although it would never be more than probable. Hence, the positive defense would seem to be perfectible.

Thus, the defender has perfectly discharged his duty. Indeed, he has even gone beyond what is strictly necessary with regard to the supererogatory wing of the defense (whose imperfections and inadequacies in no way call into question the results of the "negative" part). His victory is indisputable. The debate is over, and yet the heart of the matter has not really been considered. None of the arguments put forward so far are truly decisive, nor do they aspire to be. Their role is completely different. However, analysis of these arguments shows that they ultimately refer us to the doctrine from which they take their rise. This doctrine must now be considered in its own right.

## NOTES

1. Grua, 370.
2. Leibniz to Chauvin (June 8, 1696), A I, 12, 625.
3. Leibniz to Magliabechi (September 30, 1697), A I, 14, 521.
4. Leibniz to Foucher (July 15, 1695), GP I, 423.
5. See for example the review of his discussion with Fardella in March 1690, in A VI, 4-B, 1667.
6. Grua, 347.
7. With whom Leibniz had had "discussions *de libertate et Fato*" (Leibniz to Burnett, November 22, 1695, GP III, 167).
8. Grua, 370, note 260.
9. Leibniz to Chauvin (June 8, 1696), A 1, 12, 625.
10. Cf. Grua, 370–371.
11. *Vindicatio justitiae divinae et libertatis humanae, sumta ex consideratione ideae integrae quam Deus de re creabili habeat* (Grua, 371).
12. *An eventus mali actionum improbarum improbitati sint imputandi?* (1696–1697?), Grua, 372. This question is said to pertain to Theodicy ("ad Theodicaea mea pertinet").
13. Leibniz to Magliabechi (September 30, 1697), A I, 14, 520.
14. The issue of freedom and the connection of substances is related to what Leibniz calls his "psychological meditations" on the union of soul and body as presented in the *New System* (cf. Leibniz to Chauvin, June 8, 1696, A I, 12, 624).
15. Grua, 370.
16. *Vindicatio justitiae divinae et libertatis humanae*, Grua, 371. The term appears in the form of the German verb *vindiciren* in Leibniz to Jablonski (January 23, 1700), GP VI, 3.
17. NE IV, 21, §§1–4; A VI, 6, 522–523; RB 522–523.
18. NE IV, 21, §§1–4; A VI, 6, 524.

19. NE IV, 21, §§1–4; A VI, 6, 525; RB 525.
20. A VI, 4-B, 1595. Leibniz goes on to mention the series of theses (*positiones*) that it is necessary, according to pious and wise men, "to defend and preserve as much as possible."
21. It is for this reason that the two methods ultimately amount to the same thing (cf. ibid.), or in any case, should be conjoined (NE IV, 21, §§1–4, 524).
22. *On Universal Synthesis and Analysis, or the Art of Discovery and Judgment* (Summer 1683–early 1685?), A VI, 4-A, 544. According to Leibniz, whereas synthesis discovers "the use or application of something, as, for example, given the magnetic needle, to think of its application in the compass," "analysis, on the contrary, is best suited for discovering the means when the thing to be discovered or the proposed end is given" (ibid., 545; L 358).
23. Cf. A VI, 4-C, 406 to 415. The equivalence between the "Catholic demonstrations" and an "Apology for faith by reason" is formulated in the title given in text number 410, 2323.
24. On this point, see Rateau, *La question du mal chez Leibniz*, 328–338.
25. Leibniz had already employed the name in 1676, at the time of the *De Summa rerum* (cf. A VI, 3, 526; A VI, 3, 529). It seems to have been formed from *pax* (peace) and *placidus* (calm, tranquil). It should be compared to Leibniz's given name, "Gottfried" which means "God's peace."
26. Leibniz to Magliabechi (September 30, 1697), A I, 14, 520–521. See also Leibniz to Jablonski (January 23, 1700), GP VI, 3: "However, this plan [to compose a Theodicy] would greatly benefit if one day God were to give me the grace to develop properly these thoughts (of which you have seen only small samples) in oral conversation with excellent persons, in order to win over minds and promote the union of Protestant churches."
27. Grua, 241. Cf. chapter 1, p. 29.
28. Leibniz to Magliabechi (September 30, 1697), A I, 14, 520.
29. Grua, 495.
30. For an excellent and thorough treatment of this issue, see Rösler, Negotium Irenicum.
31. See Leibniz to Jablonski (January 23, 1700), GP VI, 3; to the same (March 26, 1700), Guhrauer, II, 161.
32. The author of *Christianity not Mysterious; or a Treatise showing, that there is nothing in the Gospel contrary to Reason nor above it: and that no Christian Doctrine can be properly called a Mystery*, London, 1696. On the relations between Leibniz and Toland, see Dagron, *Leibniz et Toland*.
33. Bayle's *Historical and Critical Dictionary* was first published in 1696–1697 with a second edition appearing in 1702.
34. *Christianity not Mysterious*, Preface, xxvii; sect. 3, ch. II, 75: "And, first, I affirm, That nothing can be said to be a Mystery, because we have not an adequate Idea of it, or a distinct View of all its Properties at once; for then everything would be a Mystery."
35. See T pd §30; Huggard, 91–92.
36. The polemic was initiated by Jaquelot in his *Conformité de la foi avec la raison; ou Défense de la religion contre les principales difficultés répandues dans le* Dictionnaire historique et critique *de Mr. Bayle* (Amsterdam, 1705).
37. T Preface; GP VI, 39; Huggard, 63: "I followed their dispute, and was even on the point of entering into it."

38. Basnage to Leibniz (January 15, 1706), GP III, 142. Leibniz wrote to Jaquelot (early 1706?, GP III, 480) that Basnage "had challenged [him] on this occasion to respond to the objections that M. Bayle had raised and reinforced against the truths of religion on freedom and predestination. This seems to have come from M. Bayle himself."

39. Leibniz to Basnage (February 19, 1706), GP III, 144.

40. Ibid. "To refute Mons. Bayle usefully, I would propose the following strategy: I would like for someone to be set on challenging the arguments he offers from time to time in favor of religion. By this means, he would be obliged to defend them, and thus to make a thousand beautiful observations, which would be advantageous to religion and to himself"; Leibniz to Th. Burnett (May 26, 1706), GP III, 306.

41. Leibniz to Jaquelot (October 6, 1706), Grua 64.

42. Manuscript Preface of the *Theodicy* (early 1707?), Grua 495.

43. See Leibniz to Jaquelot (early 1706?), GP III, 481 and Leibniz to Basnage (February 19, 1706), GP III, 143.

44. See Leibniz to Jaquelot (early 1706?), GP III, 481: "and it seemed to me that one could give a sound treatment of those theological points that serve to exonerate God from the charge of evil and those of *revealed* religion that exempt us from having to grant an absolute damnation prior to any relation to sin" (my emphasis).

45. T Preface; GP VI, 35; Huggard, 59.

46. Cf. T Preface; GP VI, 38; Huggard, 62.

47. T Preface; GP VI, 39; Huggard, 62; Leibniz to Coste (May 30, 1712), GP III, 422: "My principal aim was to meet the objections of M. Bayle."

48. Leibniz to Thomas Burnett (October 30, 1710), GP III, 321; T Preface; GP VI, 39; Huggard, 62–63; Leibniz to Hugony (November 30, 1710), GP III, 680: "it is a patchwork of things I had previously said and written to the Queen of Prussia, who took pleasure in reading M. Bayle, and at whose residence we often spoke of the difficulties he raises in these matters."

49. Grua, 494, note 449.

50. Apart from the "hommage" rendered in the form of a "literary monument" ("ein literarisches Denkmal" as Gerhardt puts it in GP VI, 10) to a queen to whom Leibniz was very attached.

51. Whether this fideism is genuine or not is of no importance here, since, according to Bayle, it is the position to which all Christians are inevitably reduced when they draw out the consequences of the faith they embrace. On this point and on the issue of the relation between faith and reason in Bayle and Leibniz, see Rateau (2011).

52. *Historical and Critical Dictionary*, article "Manicheans," remark D; Popkin, *Selections* 151. *Reply to the Questions of a Provincial*, II, Preface, OD III-2, 632: "deference to divine authority is the true livery of a Christian." However, as Leibniz remarks, the tension between faith and reason does not prevent Bayle from maintaining that the revealed mysteries, though inaccessible to human reason, can be in conformity with the "supreme and universal Reason that is in the divine understanding, or to Reason in general" (T pd §61; Huggard, 107).

53. *Historical and Critical Dictionary*, article "Paulicians," remark E; Popkin, *Selections* 175.

54. *Historical and Critical Dictionary*, article "Paulicians," remark E; Popkin, *Selections* 173: "Who will not admire and deplore the fate of our reason? Behold that here

the Manicheans, with a completely absurd and contradictory hypothesis, explain experiences a hundred times better than do the orthodox, with their supposition so just, so necessary, and so very true of an infinitely good and all-powerful first principle."

55. *Reply to the Questions of a Provincial*, II, Preface, OD III-2, 631.
56. T pd §1; GP VI, 49; Huggard, 73.
57. See T pd §40; GP VI, 73; Huggard, 97.
58. See Leibniz to Hanschius (June 23, 1707), Dutens V, 162; T Preface; GP VI, 29 and 39; Huggard, 53 and 63.
59. T Preface; GP VI, 48; Huggard, 72.
60. See Leibniz to Hanschius (June 23, 1707), Dutens V, 162.
61. Grua, 495 (I put Leibniz's deletion in square brackets).
62. See respectively, Leibniz to Des Bosses (April 24, 1709), GP II, 371; Leibniz to Des Bosses (July 31, 1709), GP II, 379.
63. T Preface; GP VI, 38; Huggard, 62.
64. See for example Gerhardt (GP VI, 13); Russell (1900), 1–2; Schrecker *Leibniz. Opuscules philosophiques choisis*, 10.
65. For example, with regard to the question of God's permission of evil, it is interesting to compare what Leibniz says in the *Preliminary Discourse* (§33) with what he says in Part I, §23 and following.
66. See Leibniz to Burnett (February 11, 1697), GP III, 193–4; NE II, 21, §§66–67; A VI, 6, 205–207; NE IV, 2, §14; A VI, 6, 372–373.
67. On this point, see Mormino "Optimisme *a posteriori* et lois du mouvement dans les *Essais de Théodicée*," especially 847.
68. See T pd §58 and §72 to §79.
69. T pd §58; GP VI, 82; Huggard, 105.
70. See Leibniz to Jaquelot (October 6, 1706), Grua, 65–66: "What is a demonstration if not an invincible argument, that is, [an argument] whose form is correct and whose matter consists of propositions that are either evident or proved by similar arguments until one arrives at only evident propositions?"; T pd §25.
71. Concerning these four operations of the understanding, see T pd §5; Leibniz to Basnage (February 19, 1706), GP III, 144.
72. See T pd §§54–55.
73. See T pd §73.
74. See T pd §75. The reference to a military siege reappears at T §108.
75. This posture of withdrawing and waiting conforms to the order of dispute, according to which the opponent always preserves the initiative in principle. It exempts the defendant from the positive work of conceptual elucidation and demonstration: "when another brings up some philosophic maxims against us, it is not for us to prove clearly and distinctly that these maxims are consistent with our dogma, but it is for our opponent to prove that they are contrary thereto" (T pd §77; GP VI, 96; Huggard, 118). See also T pd §78; GP VI, 96; Huggard, 118: "But it is not for the defender (*soutenant*) to adduce reasons; it is enough for him to answer those of his opponent."
76. T pd §76; GP VI, 95; Huggard, 117.
77. T pd §75; GP VI, 94; Huggard, 116.
78. T pd §72; GP VI, 92; Huggard, 114.
79. Cf. T pd §73, §74, and §75.
80. Cf. T pd §72, §79. Notice however that the appeal to an "instance of a bare possibility" is already considered as supererogatory.

81. T pd §57; GP VI, 82; Huggard, 105.
82. Grua, 62.
83. Ibid., 63.
84. Ibid.
85. The presumption holds good so long as a definitive refutation has not been offered. It is in this way that a borrower is presumed to be obliged to pay, unless he can show he has already done so, or that the debt has ceased for some valid reason. "To *presume* something is not to accept it *before* it has been proved, which is never permissible, but to accept it *provisionally* but not groundlessly, while waiting for a proof to the contrary" (NE IV, 14 §§1–4; A VI, 6, 457; RB 457).
86. T pd §33; GP VI, 69; Huggard, 93.
87. Here I am considering only that presumption drawn from what is possible, and not probable arguments, which offered in the framework of the "positive" defense, will allow victory on the field of appearances and probabilities. See 4.2.2.
88. Leibniz to Jaquelot (October 6, 1706), Grua, 66.
89. T §145; GP VI, 196; Huggard 214.
90. Cf. DM §30; A VI, 4-B, 1576–1577; L 497. See also the *Dialogue on Human Freedom and the Origin of Evil*, Grua, 366; AG 115: "B.—Thus, we must believe that God would not have allowed sin nor would he have created things he knows will sin, if he could not derive from them a good incomparably greater than the resulting evil. A.—I would like to know what this great good is. B.—I can assure that it is, but I cannot explain it in detail. One would have to know the general harmony of the universe for that, whereas we know only a very small part. It is when speaking in rapture about the depths of divine wisdom, that is, when explaining this same matter, that Saint Paul exclaimed, 'Oh, depth of riches.'"
91. Plutarch reports that in the fifth book of *On Nature* Chrysippus asserts that "bugs profitably awaken us out of our sleep, that mice make us cautious not to lay up everything negligently, and that it is probable that Nature, rejoicing in variety, takes delight in the production of fair creatures" (*On Stoic self-contradictions*, 1044d).
92. GP IV, 567; L 948.
93. A VI, 4-B, 1520.
94. Cf. *Critical Thoughts on the General Part of the Principles of Descartes*, GP IV, 360–361; L 637 "In general, whenever we see that anything is particularly useful, we may safely assert that one, among others, of the ends which God has proposed to himself in creating this thing is precisely that it render these services, since he both knew and planned this use of it."
95. Cf. DM §19.
96. T §143; GP VI, 188; Huggard, 206–207.
97. It must not be forgotten that Leibniz's goal in the book is "edification," cf. T Preface; GP VI, 47.
98. For a fuller examination of these arguments, see Rateau, *La question du mal chez Leibniz*, 470–476.
99. Cf. above p. 164–165.
100. See the *Conversation du Marquis de Pianese et du Pere Emery Eremite*, A VI, 4-C, 2267–2268.
101. Ibid., 2268.
102. *On Freedom, Fate and God's Grace*, A VI, 4-B, 1605.
103. Cf. NE I, 1, §§2–4; A VI, 6, 76.
104. T §345; GP VI, 319; Huggard, 322. See also §§346–350; GP VI, 319–322.

105. Cf. Leibniz to Thomas Burnett (1701), GP III, 279.

106. T §19; GP VI, 114; Huggard, 135.

107. T §19; GP VI, 114; Huggard, 135.

108. As Leibniz points out in T s, II; GP VI, 379.

109. Cf. T §253 and §258.

110. Cf. T §251 and §259.

111. Conversely, we can imagine that if it were our sense that the good outweighs evil, we would have to conclude that the good is rarer, and so in reality it is evil that outweighs the good.

112. T §259; GP VI, 270; Huggard, 289.

113. T §261; GP VI, 271; Huggard, 286: "the constant experience of the fair aspect of their condition renders them unaware of good, but greatly aware of evil."

114. T §260; GP VI, 271; Huggard, 286.

115. T §118; GP VI, 169; Huggard, 188–189.

116. Cf. T §246; GP VI, 263–264; Huggard, 279: "God does not neglect inanimate things: they do not feel, but God feels for them. He does not neglect animals: they do not have intelligence, but God has it for them. He would reproach himself for the slightest actual defect there were in the universe, even though it were perceived by no one."

117. Not to mention that the degrees of perfection differ not only between classes, but among the individuals within a given class (among humans, among animals, among angels, etc.).

118. T §263; GP VI, 273; Huggard, 288.

119. T s, II; GP VI, 378; Huggard, 379.

120. T s, II; GP VI, 378; Huggard, 379.

121. T s, II; GP VI, 379; Huggard, 380. Emphasis added.

122. DM §3, A VI, 4-B, 1534.

123. T §416, GP VI, 364; Huggard, 372.

124. Cf. A VI, 1, Ch. 52, 499; CP; A VI, 3, 139.

125. T s, II; GP VI, 378 and 379; Huggard, 379–380.

126. See Leibniz to Th. Burnett (February 11, 1697), GP III, 194, where evaluating the weight of reasons is discussed.

# CHAPTER 5

✧

# The Best of All Possible Worlds and Divine Permission of Evil

L eibnizian Theodicy cannot rest on a mere presumption—however strong and well-supported—in favor of God's justice and the perfection of the world. At the polemical and defensive level, it is enough to neutralize objections and to lay out in opposition to the appearance of disorder and injustice in the world, the marks of divine wisdom and goodness. One can even marshal positive evidence in favor of a universal order and of the predominance of good over evil at the global level. However, at the theoretical level the "cause of God" requires more conclusive considerations or even a demonstrative argument. In this way any remaining doubts will be dispelled, and even the experience of evil in the world will not shake established certitudes:

> It is thus that, being made confident by demonstrations of the goodness and justice of God, we disregard the appearances of harshness and injustice which we see in this small portion of his Kingdom that is exposed to our gaze.[1]

With regard to the doctrinal wing of his Theodicy, Leibniz's ambition is to furnish a priori arguments, the only ones that are absolutely decisive:

> It will therefore sufficiently refute the objection to show that a world with evil may be better than a world without evil. But I have gone still further in the work, and have even *shown* that this universe must indeed be better than every other possible universe.[2]

As Leibniz writes to Thomas Burnett:

> There are also here and there [in the *Theodicy*] clarifications of my system of pre-
> established harmony, and of a number of topics from general philosophy and
> natural theology, in which I maintain that everything can be settled *demonstra-*
> *tively*, and for which I have provided the means.[3]

Does Leibniz entirely fulfill his promises? It is not clear that the theses
advanced in the doctrine can be considered *demonstrations*, strictly
speaking, given his exacting criteria for a well-ordered demonstration. The
first aim of this chapter is to show how the thesis of the existence of the
best of all possible worlds, which lies at the heart of the Theodicy, is established and to determine its precise meaning and significance (5.1). Next,
I shall determine whether God's choice of world is absolutely necessary and
hence demonstrable or whether it is contingent and, by that very fact, indemonstrable. This in turn will allow us to determine the precise nature of
the argument developed in the doctrinal wing of the Theodicy (5.2). Finally,
I shall examine how the best possible world, as represented in God's perfect
understanding, becomes the object of his will, and how as a result his moral
concurrence with evil is to be explained. This, in turn, will lead us to consider Leibniz's theory of permission in its "definitive" form (5.3).

## 5.1 THE THESIS OF THE BEST OF ALL POSSIBLE WORLDS

### 5.1.1 Divine Obligation and the Unicity of the Best

Having settled the "rights of faith and reason" in the *Preliminary Discourse*,
Leibniz announces in §1 of the first part of the *Essays of Theodicy* that he
will discuss God and man with regard to evil. He rehearses two series of
difficulties arising out of human freedom, on the one hand, and "God's
conduct" on the other hand. Thus, Leibniz's method does not follow the
*demonstrative* order of reasons, according to the "synthetic and theoretical" method of the mathematicians, but rather an order that might be
called *problematic and diaporematic* in the "analytic and practical"[4] manner.
The question here is not, as in other texts,[5] to begin with the notion of
God—that is, with the definition of his perfections—and to draw out its
consequences and implications. Rather, Leibniz begins with the following
two puzzles: How can God's holiness and justice be reconciled with the existence of evil with which he seems to concur both morally and physically?
How can human freedom—which seems to be required if man is to be

guilty and deserving of punishment—be reconciled with God's foreknowledge and predetermination of all things?

Leibniz's preference for this *problematic* or *diaporematic* presentation is explained by the manner in which he takes up the problem of evil, namely in terms of the question of *imputation*. The starting point of his analysis is not the traditional metaphysical examination of the origin of evil ("whence evil?"[6]) or of its essence ("what is evil?"), but rather a juridical or judiciary inquiry that may be summed up as follows: "To whom is evil to be imputed?" Is evil to be imputed to man, who freely commits it, or to God, who foresees it and contributes to its existence by his power? The whole of the doctrine is structured to provide an answer to this question and to resolve the difficulties to which the proposed solution gives rise. Leibniz begins by examining God's conduct. It is in this context that he is led to explain God's choice of this universe from among an infinity of equally possible worlds and to establish the thesis of the creation of the best of all possible worlds.

This latter thesis is established in paragraphs 7 and 8 of the *Theodicy* by an argument that combines a priori proof with a posteriori proof, or proof *ab effectu* (from the effect). It consists of two main stages. The first is *regressive* (§7): it begins with the empirical fact of the existence of the world, understood as "the whole assemblage of contingent things" and mounts up to its first, necessary, and eternal reason, which is God. The second stage, which proceeds in the opposite direction, is *deductive* (§8). It begins with the a priori consideration of the perfections of the supreme being (whose existence has been proved *ab effectu* from the contingent existence of the world) and returns back to the world to conclude that it must be the best possible. The argument in its entirety may be summarized as follows. (1) There exists a world, whose contingency requires a necessary being as its ultimate origin. (2) This necessary being, whom we call God, is such that he must possess an infinite understanding (comprehending all possible worlds), a wholly good will (which chooses one of these worlds), and unlimited power (which brings it into existence). (3) This necessary and wholly perfect being can produce only what is best (by a necessity that Leibniz will characterize as "moral" and not absolute). (4) Because our world is the one that exists—the one that was chosen—it must be the best possible world.

Obviously, the argument is not a strict demonstration, since otherwise the world would be a necessary emanation of God and God would not be free. The created universe is contingent for three reasons. The first is *metaphysical*: the world does not carry within itself the reason of its existence. The second is *logical*: there is an infinite number of other possible worlds. The third is *moral*: God's choice is free; he could have brought some other world into existence or even abstained from creating altogether. Though wisdom, goodness, and power are necessary attributes of the divinity (that is, they belong to his essence such that God would no longer be God were one of them lacking), no effect follows necessarily from their conjunction. As Leibniz puts the point, "this supreme wisdom, united to a goodness that is no less infinite, *could not have failed to choose* the best."[7] Notice that the obligation to choose the best is expressed in the form of a double negation, as a moral impossibility to do otherwise. In using the expression *could not have failed*, Leibniz emphasizes that the (internal) constraint to which God is subject is not logical but moral, and that it bears on his will and not on his understanding. The choice of the best is not absolutely or metaphysically necessary such that every other choice would imply a contradiction. Yet for all that, it is no less the result of an indispensable duty, which God cannot fail to fulfill on pain of sinning, since "there would be something to correct in the actions of God, if it were possible to do better."[8]

Here the obligation is presented negatively, as an imperative that God cannot flout without contravening his wisdom, and not, as in other passages, in its positive formulation, as that moral necessity, which Augustine characterizes as "happy" in that it infallibly leads the will to the good and, far from being contrary to freedom, renders the one who submits to it perfectly free.[9] Why does Leibniz present God's determination to the best in this negative form—that is, as the moral impossibility of doing the contrary? Doubtless, Leibniz makes use of this formulation because it provides him the means of clearly marking his opposition to those, like Malebranche, but also, in a sense, Thomas Aquinas, "who believe that God could have done better."[10]

Malebranche maintains that a better world could have been created, but that the additional perfection could not have been obtained without compromising the simplicity and uniformity of the laws.[11] Thus, the created universe is the most perfect possible *relative* to God's ways (which alone are best *absolutely* speaking). This position rests on a distinction, which Aquinas had already drawn, between the *object* upon which God exercises his power (the world) and God's *manner* of acting (his ways). On this view, the former could always be better, whereas the latter cannot be. Thus, it can be said, "the universe, the present creation being supposed, cannot be better, on account of the most beautiful order given to things by God; in which the good of the universe consists." However, it is equally true that "God could make other things, or add something to the present creation; and then there would be another and a better universe."[12]

Leibniz rejects any such distinction. For him, the term "best" refers inextricably to both God's way of acting (his mode of operation) *and* to the object of his choice (the result of that action)—that is, the universe understood as the best among all others. For God's ways form an integral part of the work. His means are themselves ends,[13] and the laws of a world cannot be separated from the world in which they obtain. If God could have made a world better than ours, he would have erred in creating this one. Now since he is infallible, it must be the case that he could not have done better. He could not have done better, because there was nothing better to be done, for there is nothing better than the best. However, this gives rise to the following objection: How is it possible to find perfection within the finite order? Is it not the case that nothing in creation is so perfect that it is impossible to conceive of something more perfect and so on to infinity?[14] The Thomistic view avoids the difficulty by acknowledging the possibility of an indefinite progression of ever more perfect worlds and reserving absolute perfection for God alone (that is, the absolute perfection of his being and mode of acting, whatever may be the degree of perfection of the created world). By rejecting this solution, Leibniz commits himself to proving that a thing, although it is finite or created, can be the most perfect in its genus, that there is an absolutely unique best world, and that to assert that the world is the best does not amount to identifying it with God nor making of it another god.

Here again Leibniz's argument mixes a priori reasons with a posteriori considerations. The claim is no longer simply that the actual world must be the best, since otherwise God, who cannot do wrong, could not have chosen it. Rather, it is that the actual world must be the best, because otherwise God could not have chosen at all, since any choice would have been impossible. We are necessarily led to the conclusion that the most perfect of possible universes exists if we are to avoid two contradictions: the *moral* contradiction of a God who has erred, and the *logico-metaphysical* contradiction of a God who cannot choose where there is no best, and so creates nothing. The a priori concept of God implies his possession of all the perfections in the highest degree. Consequently, it excludes all error or fault in him. The reality of our world (argument *ab effectu*) proves that a choice has indeed been made. Therefore, there must be a best among the infinite number of possible worlds.

> As in mathematics, when there is neither maximum nor minimum, in short nothing distinguished, everything is done equally, or when that is not possible nothing at all is done: so likewise it may be said in respect of perfect wisdom, which is no less orderly than mathematics, that if there were not a best (*optimum*) among all possible worlds, God would not have produced any.[15]

The existence of a unique best world is established by the joint application of a *reductio ad absurdum* and the Principle of Sufficient Reason. In fact, there are three possible hypotheses.[16] According to the first (A), all possible worlds are equal in perfection, such that no one of them can be declared the best (the infinity of worlds, superimposed one upon the other, could be represented as an infinite parallelepiped of only four sides). The second hypothesis (B) maintains that the possible worlds are all unequal in perfection, but that no one is the best, since it is always possible to conceive of others that are more perfect (the progression continues to infinity, in the form of a pyramid with neither summit nor base). The third (C) also affirms that they are all unequal in perfection but maintains that there is one alone that can be correctly called the best (the progression continues to infinity among the imperfect, but reaches a limit within the perfect; the pyramid has a summit, but no base[17]). Leibniz establishes (C) by showing that it would be contradictory to defend either (A) or (B), given God's perfect nature, the Principle of Sufficient Reason, and the fact that a world actually exists (namely, ours).

If (A) were true, that is, if there were other possible worlds equal to ours in perfection or if all were perfectly equal, God would have had no reason to create this world rather than some other. Being no more led to one than the other, in a state of perfect equilibrium and indifference, he would either have produced all of them (which is both *logically*[18] and *morally*[19] impossible) or none at all. The Principle of Sufficient Reason rules out any unmotivated or arbitrary choice. Furthermore, the existence of the world proves that choice has been made. Therefore, there must be a difference among the possible universes, one of which was the best.

Hypothesis (B), according to which there simply is no best world, but rather an infinite progression of ever more perfect worlds, is equally untenable for at least two reasons. On the one hand, it would follow that God, whatever he created, did wrong, given that "a lesser good is a kind of evil if it stands in the way of a greater good" (§8). For however perfect the world he creates may be, because a more perfect world would always be possible, he would always be, as it were, at fault—guilty of having done wrong by not having wanted to do better. Given that a world now exists, hypothesis (B) would prove that those who maintain that God could have done much better were correct. Such a position is incompatible with his perfection and glory. On the other hand, if there were no one world that is better than all the rest, and beyond which no better world is possible, then once again God would not have created "for he is incapable of acting without reason, and that would be even acting against reason."[20] His choice would have been impossible, not that he would have been in a state of indifference (as in the case of the equality of all worlds), but because he would have been incapable of willing anything at all. For any reason he might have had to create a given world would have been immediately outweighed by another reason, namely the reason he had to create some better world, and this latter reason by another, and so on to infinity. Nothing would have been produced, since his will would have been perpetually impeded. His will would have been suspended, not because it had no reason to choose, but paradoxically because it had too many! God would have willed nothing, because he would always have wanted better. He would have done nothing, because he could always have done better.

The very conditions for the possibility of choice demand hypothesis (C): "God or the perfect sage will always choose the best that they know of, and if one side were not better than the other, they would choose neither the one nor the other."[21] The alternative is simple: *either God creates nothing*, because no one world stands out among all the others as deserving to be chosen, or *God creates the best*, because there is a best and he cannot create something less good, without exposing himself to the reproach of having done wrong, that is of acting contrary to the dictates of wisdom. Now, because there actually is something rather than nothing, we can be assured (i) that there is a difference among all possible worlds, (ii) that there is some one world that is better than all the others, (iii) that this latter is unique, and thus we can conclude *ab effectu* (iv) that *our* world is that world.

However, the problem raised by the claim that there exists an absolute best outside of God in the order of creation still remains. If a unique best world is required for there to be a choice and so for there to be creation, some response is needed to the previously raised objection, according to which nothing is so perfect that there cannot be something yet more perfect.

As had already been indicated in §3 of the *Discourse on Metaphysics*, the objection rests on a mistake. It is true that the greatest number, the greatest figure, and the fastest motion imply a contradiction,[22] since it is always possible to conceive a greater number or figure, or a faster motion. However, the idea of the most perfect possible world does not involve any impossibility, since in this case there is no such infinite progression. The case of the best universe is like that of power and knowledge, which are true perfections in that they "admit of a highest degree,"[23] that is, they can be raised to a maximum without contradiction. The difference between that which is maximizable (admits of a maximum) and that which is not lies in the relation between the whole and its parts. There are two cases to be considered.

In the first case, the perfection of the whole is entirely derived from that of the parts of which it is composed. In this case, no whole can ever be said to be the most perfect, since another that includes a greater number of parts or more perfect parts will necessarily be superior (and, for the same reason, some other could be yet more perfect, and so on to infinity). In the second case, the fact that some whole is the best does not result from the perfection of its parts, but from what it is considered in and of itself. The whole is not the result of the parts but, on the contrary, is prior to it.[24] In this case it can be said to be the best, not merely with respect to others that are inferior, but absolutely speaking and for intrinsic reasons, because it cannot be surpassed in its genus. The examples to which Leibniz most often appeals are taken from geometry. The circle is the most perfect of regular plane figures, because it is the one with the most extensive (*capacissima*) circumference.[25] Similarly, the equilateral triangle is most perfect in its genus, since it is the three-sided figure that encompasses the greatest surface.[26] In this connection, we can also mention spirits, which are the most perfect of all created beings, because they "occupy the smallest volume, that is to say . . . least obstruct each other."[27]

These examples prove that there is an absolute best within the realm of the finite. It is possible to affirm both that the circle is the most perfect figure and that nevertheless there will never be any concrete figure (not even a circle, however large it may be) that cannot be surpassed in size by another. Likewise, it can be said that spirits are the most excellent of creatures and that nevertheless there is none in creation that is not always capable of increasing in perfection or of being surpassed by another that is more perfect. The distinction between *absolute* perfection and *relative* perfection (which can coexist in one and the same subject, namely in that which is most perfect in its genus while at the same time being perfectible in itself) together with the relation between the whole and its parts, or more exactly in the case of the world,[28] between a collection and its components, afford a reply to those who deny the possibility of producing the best on the grounds that something more perfect is always conceivable.

> I answer that what can be said of a creature or of a particular substance, which can always be surpassed by another, is not to be applied to the universe, which, since it must extend through all future eternity, is an infinity.[29]

The error lies in thinking that what is true of the part is true of the whole and that we can correctly infer from the finite to the infinite case. What is judged *best* is not a certain state, or moment or part of the world, but the universe itself considered as the totality of created things (*Universitas creaturarum*[30]) and events at every time and place. This collection or assemblage of all existents extends to infinity, not only in time but also in space, since "there is an infinite number of creatures in the smallest particle of matter, because of the actual division of the *continuum* to infinity."[31]

However, we must be careful here. It is not because the world is infinite that it is the best possible. Rather, it is because it is infinite that its perfection cannot be judged in the same way as that of a finite entity, which can always be surpassed by something more perfect. An infinite can only be compared to another infinite. To repeat, our world is not the most perfect because it is infinite, but because it is the best with regard to other infinites—that is, with regard to other equally possible worlds. Within the genus "universe" our world is the most perfect form, just as the circle is the most perfect in the genus "regular plane figure." However, there remains an important difference. In the case of the circle, although it is the best of its kind, it is always possible to find a greater because it is a *finite* shape (a circle with a greater diameter is always conceivable). In the case of our world, it is not only the most perfect of its kind, but it is also impossible to find another that exceeds it with regard to size or extent, since it is *infinite*.

In light of its infinity, the universe can be considered the best possible, not in a merely relative sense, *secundum quid* (with regard to all others which are inferior in perfection), but absolutely, *secundum se* (in itself), and without thereby making of it a god.[32]

### 5.1.2 The Best as the Most Determinate Form

Leibniz is evidently not satisfied with a *reductio ad absurdum* to establish the thesis of the best possible world and refute opposing views. If we remain at the theoretical and a priori level, and set aside the evidence of order and universal perfection drawn from experience, as well as the various arguments in favor of the prevalence of good over evil at the global level,[33] we find in the *Theodicy* if not positive proofs, at least a definition of the best world that allows us to identify certain fundamental characteristics.

As the comparisons drawn from architecture, gambling, geometry, and optics illustrate, the best must be understood as that which best corresponds to a given end in light of the prevailing conditions (land, matter, space, time). It results from combining means and end, such that the means are best employed and the end best realized. This appraisal of the relation between ways and effects is reminiscent of Malebranche, whose system Leibniz claims is reducible to his on just this point.[34] However, the assimilation is merely superficial and above all tactical, occurring as it does in the context of his polemic with Bayle, who sympathizes with Malebranche on this point. It is merely superficial not only because, as we have seen, Leibniz does not separate means from ends but also because for him the concept of best has a very distinctive signification. For Leibniz, the best must be understood in the sense of the method of optimal forms (*de Formis optimis*), the method he introduced in order to move beyond the *maxima and minima* method employed by mathematicians ever since Fermat. The best designates the most determinate (and thus the most determining for the divine will), which is the most intelligible, the most rational, and unique.

Indeed, it is no coincidence that the notion of *optimum* is introduced in §8, precisely in the context of a comparison with the calculus of *maxima and minima*. This calculus is used to determine the point or points at which the function of a variable x (where x belongs to the domain of real numbers) yields the largest or smallest possible value(s) with regard to its law of variation. The goal is to "find the maximum or minimum ordinates of a given curve, which is only a corollary of the ordinary Method of tangents." In the case of the determination of *optimal forms*, the problem is, in a sense, the reverse: "what is sought is the curve itself, which must *optimally* satisfy a given condition."[35] Here the goal is to find the curve that corresponds to certain given conditions (for example, an inclined plane, points to be connected, travel time between those points), rather than to determine the coordinates on the basis of a given curve. Thus, it is the curve itself that must exhibit a maximal property. The geometrical problems are of a completely different order from those treated by the calculus of *maxima and minima*, which are purely quantitative. The method developed by Leibniz allows one to move from quantity to quality (*maximum aut minimum praestantibus*) and so proves particularly useful "in applications from geometry to mechanics and to nature: in fact, it consists, in choosing from among all possible shapes, that which *best* satisfies a certain condition."[36]

The solution to the problem of the catenary, of the brachistochrone curve, as well as the calculation of optic paths demonstrates the fecundity of this method and illustrates the principle that the simplest and easiest path is not necessarily the shortest. Thus, light reflected by a concave mirror, takes the longest path. The *optimum* can be either a maximum or a minimum. In every case, it involves the *most determinate*, because, to repeat, the point of view is not quantitative (the shortest distance between two points is always a straight line) but qualitative (the fastest way of getting from one point to another may be the longest[37]).

What is meant here by the greatest determination? That thing is *determined* from which something follows in the absence of any obstacle,[38] that is, if no stronger determination prevents it. The most determinate path, which is unique,[39] is that which is distinguished from all others by its particular characteristics, because of what it permits, and for that very reason it prevails. However, this implies neither an absolute necessity nor the impossibility of other possible paths. The advantage the most determinate path offers, with respect to a certain end, relates to a choice or selection among other possibles and so to the aims of an intelligent being. The principle of the easiest path, that is, of the *best*, leads to the reintroduction of finality, which Descartes, together with the other great representatives of modern science, had banished from physics. This principle takes us from the "realm of power, according to which everything can be explained *mechanically* by efficient causes" to the "realm of wisdom, according to which everything can be explained *architectonically*, so to speak, or by final causes."[40]

Consideration of final causes (without which, in Leibniz's view, Snell would never have discovered the laws of refraction) has not only a *heuristic* use, which aims at facilitating discoveries,[41] but also an *epistemological* import, with regard to the modal status of the laws of nature. In addition, it has a *theological*, or even *apologetic*, import, in that it leads us to posit an intelligent being who is endowed with a will and is responsible for the origin of the world and to admire its wisdom. If nature were "brute," that is, completely governed by a geometrical or absolute necessity, nothing would guarantee that the easiest, or more generally, the best way prevails. The example of a triangle whose only specified condition is its size illustrates the principle that only a nature governed by "architectonic" considerations could produce an equilateral triangle (the most determinate figure). A nature governed solely by geometrical determinations would produce nothing in this case.[42] Like all laws of nature, the rules of catoptrics and dioptrics are arbitrary, if by that is meant that they are the result of a will (*arbitrium*), that is to say, a divine choice. But far from being indifferent, as Descartes maintained, "they originate in the wisdom of their Author or in the principle of greatest perfection, which has led to their choice."[43]

It is not enough to observe that the laws of nature are contingent, that they could have been otherwise, that they are not demonstrable in the strict sense, unlike geometrical truths whose negation is contradictory. We must also note that these laws cannot be entirely arbitrary, given their reasonableness and conformity with the most perfect and most beautiful order ("abstract or metaphysical"[44] considerations) and the precision with which they are adjusted to the world they govern, with regard to the nature of created things and to the produced effects. It is this lack of absolute necessity, together with an admirable fitness, that constitutes one of the most sensible proofs[45] of the existence of a wise and free author. These laws cannot be explained in a purely geometrical manner by efficient causes, because they do not depend on God's understanding alone, but also on his will, which aims at certain ends. These laws are established in conformity with a necessity of choice, or *moral* necessity (whose contrary implies imperfection),[46] and not an absolute necessity (whose contrary implies a contradiction).

It is this same principle of the best together with the same moral necessity to adhere to it (considered this time in its "positive" aspect) that are at work in God's choice of world. It is the same as regards the determination of the best universe as with the determination of the best possible form according to the method of *optimal forms*. Given certain ends (the glory of God, the satisfaction he will find in his work, the pleasure he takes in being loved by intelligent creatures) and certain conditions (things as they are, their essences that are uncreated and therefore independent of God's will, the inherent constraints of the spatio-temporal order), the "problem" is to find that unique combination of beings, events, and phenomena that is the most perfect. Here again, the question is not simply to calculate a *maximum*, the greatest "brute" quantity of reality or essence, nor even the greatest sum of particular goods, but rather to achieve a *best*—that is, a form that stands out and is distinct from all the others in that it best satisfies the aim and makes best use of the means for achieving it.

The *maximum* relates to power, the *best* relates to goodness.[47] Whereas the former can be achieved without appeal to other than geometrical considerations or to anything besides efficient causes, realization of the latter presupposes an understanding that conceives of various possibilities and a will that chooses in accordance with reasons that incline without necessitating. There is not, nor can there be, a best unless there is intelligence and choice, and therefore, contingency. Intelligence, choice, and contingency are the three prerequisites for freedom.[48] Therefore, the best requires freedom. It is an object of freedom and cannot arise without it.

The reduction of the "problem" of the best world to a particular instance of the method of *optimal forms* gives rise to an objection. If our universe is the best of its kind, as the brachistochrone curve is the best of its kind, it would seem to follow that each part of the universe must likewise be the best, since the portion (however small) between any two points of the trajectory of the most rapid descent is likewise the most rapid between these two points. As Leibniz makes clear in the *Tentamen Anagogicum*, the best form is not only in the whole but also in each of the parts as well, and were that not the case it would not be in the whole. From this Leibniz concludes, "it is in this way that the smallest parts of the universe are ruled in accordance with the order of greatest perfection; otherwise, the whole would not be so ruled."[49] Yet, does he not affirm precisely the opposite at *Theodicy* §212–213, where he argues that we cannot always infer from quantity to quality?

> The part of the shortest way between two extreme points is also the shortest way between the extreme points of this part; but the part of the best Whole is not of necessity the best that one could have made of this part. For the part of a beautiful thing is not always beautiful, since it can be extracted from the whole, or marked out within the whole, in an irregular manner.[50]

The objects of mathematics are homogenous and uniform (points on a plane, numerical quantities), that is to say, abstract and fictitious. As a result, what is true of the part is likewise true of the whole, since the whole is derived from the parts and so inherits their characteristics and properties. By contrast, the universe is composed of heterogeneous and concrete parts, in which no entity can be identical with another and in which we find various kinds and degrees of perfection. The perfection of the whole cannot be measured by that of its parts nor is it reducible to the mere sum of these partial perfections.

Are these texts contradictory? No. For we must consider that it is the method of *maxima and minima* and not of *optimal forms* (which applies to quality) that is under discussion at *Theodicy* §212–213. Furthermore, the *Tentamen Anagogicum* aims only to show that the principle of perfection applies not only in general but "descends also to the particulars of things and of phenomena," which are therefore also governed by the most perfect possible.[51] Now the assertion that, considered in itself, the part of a perfect whole (the universe) is not necessarily the most perfect *absolutely speaking* and that it can even seem very imperfect with respect to some other possible object (belonging to another possible world) does not imply that this part is neither well-ordered nor perfect, *relatively speaking*, insofar as it is connected with the best universe.

It is important to take note of this caution against the use of mathematical comparisons in metaphysics. One must always be prudent, given that mathematical entities are mere abstractions and fictions. As such, they cannot take the place of real beings. In emphasizing the difference between quality and quantity, Leibniz seeks to forestall any erroneous interpretation of his metaphysics and theology. Leibniz's God is not merely a God who calculates, a mathematician, who having found the best possible form brings it about, as it were, mechanically. "When God calculates and exercises his thought, the world is made."[52] The danger of this declaration is obvious: the derivation of the world from God's thought appears immediate

and necessary. The calculation takes no account of considerations of goodness, justice, or, more generally, final causes. Without a will that chooses
between the infinity of possible worlds, nothing would distinguish God
from brute necessity or Fate. The divine mathematics (*Mathesis Divina*) or
the metaphysical mechanism (*Mechanismus Metaphysicus*[53]) is therefore incomplete, or rather insufficient and even sterile, in the absence of a will
that freely chooses the best.

### 5.1.3  Relative Perfection and Universal Harmony

Leibniz has shown that God cannot fail to choose the best possible world,
that the actual world is that world, and that it is impossible to conceive of
one that is better. The best designates the form that is most determinate,
and hence the most determining with regard to the divine will. How then
can evil be reconciled with the thesis that the best possible world exists?
Here experience proves useful to fill out the thesis and clarify it. What in
fact does experience show? That the best is not identical to the good, that
what is good is not always best, nor what is evil always the worst. We must
recognize, *ab effectu*, that the most perfect world is not that which consists
of only the good or that which contains the greatest number of particular
goods (in absolute terms), nor that in which every part is the most perfect considered in itself. To be sure, a universe without sin or suffering was
possible, but as Leibniz observes, "I deny that in that case it would have
been *better*."[54] While it may be permissible to dream up utopias and imagine marvelous worlds in which virtue and happiness reign, yet we must
recognize that such worlds would be "very inferior to ours in goodness."[55]

The reason for this is, in the first instance, negative. It follows from a
factual argument we have already seen: we know these worlds without evil
would not have been better than ours, since they were not in fact chosen
by God (who can create nothing but the most perfect). To this Leibniz adds
two positive considerations. The first concerns the definition of a world.
The universe, like any other sequence of possible beings, is "all of a piece,"
like an ocean in which "the least movement extends its effect to any distance whatsoever, even though this effect become less perceptible in proportion to the distance."[56] The solidarity among all of its parts, and hence,
of all the divine decrees that concern them (which in reality make up but
one decree[57]), the connection between all substances and their phenomena
are such that nothing can be altered without affecting all the rest—that is,
without constituting a different world. Now, this other world would be inferior in perfection to ours, since once again, it is not the one that God has

chosen to create. To remove the least evil or the most insignificant event from the world would amount to conceiving of another, entirely different world: "it would no longer be this world; which, all things considered, was found to be the best by the Creator who chose it."[58]

The second consideration is related to the role that evil plays in realizing the best possible world. While neither willing nor approving evil as such, God makes use of it to achieve his ends. It is for this reason that he permits it, as a sine qua non of a superior good (in the case of sin), or even as a means of obtaining such good (in the case of pain and imperfection in general[59]). We know that when two evils are joined together, their bad effects may be annulled, and they may even have a beneficial effect, as when two poisons act as a remedy or some wrongdoing has beneficial consequences. Such is the case of the general, whose error leads unexpectedly to victory, or the fall of Adam which led to Christ's intercession.[60] It must be recognized that the "best course is not always that one which tends toward avoiding evil, since it is possible that the evil may be accompanied by a greater good."[61] To be sure, God *can* eliminate all evil from the world, but he does not *will* to do so by his consequent will, "because he would then banish good at the same time, and he would banish more good than evil."[62]

To remove evil from the world would in reality eliminate more good than evil. As a result, our assessment of the part, which at first blush appeared very imperfect, is altered. For were we able to consider the universe as a whole and compare it with all other possible worlds (as does Theodorus in the apologue of the *Theodicy*), we would see not only that it could not have been better made, but also that there is not even anything better to be desired in particular,[63] in regard to each of its parts, insofar as each in its own way contributes to the most perfect whole or, in any case, is indissolubly linked to it.

Paradoxically, the best is more than the good, because it includes evil. In moving from good to best, we move from part to whole and from quantity to quality. Unquestionably, a world without sin and pain, a world that contained nothing but an infinite number of spirits (the most perfect of creatures), who have been given all the virtue and happiness of which they are capable would include more good than ours. If perfection consisted in nothing more than the simple quantity of essence realized, such a world would be the most perfect possible. It would unite the greatest metaphysical perfection (the perfection of those creatures who are ontologically closest to the divinity) with the highest moral and physical perfection (beatitude). Yet, we must believe that such a world composed exclusively of goods would, by that very fact, be less good—that is, worse than ours (if it is indeed true that a lesser good is a kind of evil). There are two reasons for this. First, the accumulation of all these goods would not make possible those superior goods, which can be attained only by the mediation of evil, and of which we would be deprived by the elimination of evil. Second, and above all, the term "perfection" does not have the same meaning when applied to a homogenous whole as when applied to a collection of heterogeneous things.

In the first case, the whole is the result of its parts and is perfect only insofar as they are. This perfection, called *absolute*, is particular to quantities. In the second case, the whole is prior to its parts. It is perfect in itself, and its parts are perfect only *relatively* insofar as they contribute to the perfection of the whole. This perfection is qualitative.[64] In the case of quantity we consider parts that are identical and indiscernible, and whose location and arrangement are of no consequence. With regard to quality, we consider distinctive parts, whose nature, order, and disposition are determinative with regard to the whole. The relation is not so much that of element to composite, but of condition or means to end. Thus, the most perfect world is not the one that contains the greatest sum of goods, but the one that achieves the best combination or harmony of different and heterogeneous entities. With regard to the part, "perfect" designates that which is *compatible* with the greatest number of things, or negatively, that which prevents the fewest possible things. With regard to the whole, it designates the most *harmonious*.

At the universal level, perfection is the harmony of things. As Leibniz explains in a letter to Wolff of May 18, 1715,[65] its significance is at once *metaphysical* and *epistemological*. It is "agreement or identity in variety" (a phrase reminiscent of the famous definition of harmony in the *Confession of a Philosopher*[66]) and that which renders all things notable and worthy of consideration (*observabilitas universalium et gradum considerabilitatis*). From an ontological point of view, perfection involves a relation between contraries (unity/multiplicity, identity/difference). From an epistemological point of view, it involves a degree of intelligibility, since "order, regularity and harmony come to the same thing."[67] For a thing to be possible, it is enough that it be intelligible or conceivable, that is, that it include no contradiction. However, to be actualized, "there must be a prevalence of intelligibility or order; for there is *order* to the extent that there is much to be noticed in a multitude."[68] The best possible world is the one that is most rational, in which nothing is done in vain, nor left to chance. It is the world in which no being fails to play its role part in the divine plan, no event that does not contribute to this in some way, no time or place that is not utilized. In the best possible world, everything is subjected to order and corresponds to an end; everything is governed by simple and general laws. There is no need of permanent miracles to compensate for the inadequacies of creatures, since the best is drawn from the nature of things (from what they *are* and *are capable of* in themselves) and the conditions imposed by space and time.

At the metaphysical level, the letter to Wolff explains the sense in which our world incorporates the greatest quantity of reality or essence. For Leibniz, the essence or degree of perfection of a thing is measured by its "harmonic properties."[69] In other words, quantity of essence is equivalent to degree of harmony. Thus, the demand for a maximum of being or essence coincides with the demand for a maximum of harmony at the global level.[70] The world that allows the most possibility and the most reality to be brought into existence is not the one, for example, that contains the most individuals or particular goods. Rather, it is the one that includes the most "harmonic properties." Now, harmony is incompatible with a world in which there is only good. The excess of good would be an evil. It would result in a homogeneity and uniformity contrary to beauty. If there were only good, there would be less good. If only the greatest goods existed, excellence would lose its value:

> [I]t turns out that if there were only virtue, if there were only rational creatures, there would be less good. Midas proved to be less rich when he had only gold. And besides, wisdom must diversify. To multiply one and the same thing, however noble, would be superfluity, and poverty too. To have a thousand well-bound Vergils in one's library, always to sing the airs from the opera of Cadmus and Hermione, to break all the china in order only to have cups of gold, to have only diamond buttons, to eat nothing but partridges, to drink only Hungarian or Shiraz wine—would one call that reason?[71]

Richness consists both in plurality, that is to say quantity (a single virtue or a single species of creature, however noble, would be a defect) and in diversity, that is to say, in quality. It requires that there be various degrees of virtue and of relative perfection in substances (including within a single kind of substance, such as spirits[72]). Harmony requires heterogeneity and variety, not repetition of the same thing, not even of that thing that is most perfect in its genre.

The best possible world, if it is the most harmonious, represents a certain equilibrium point, which is also a limit point. It is a form that is unique, remarkable, most determinate, for it is that which involves the greatest possible diversity, beyond which identity itself would be threatened.[73] It is a compromise between the goal of maximal variety and richness among the effects and the demand for unity and similarity, as had already been indicated in the *Confession of a Philosopher*:

[F]or harmony is unity in multiplicity, and it is greatest in the case where it is a unity of the greatest number of things disordered in appearance and reduced, unexpectedly, by some wonderful ratio to the greatest symmetry [*concinnitas*].[74]

Beauty results from the resolution of this tension, at the threshold of universal disharmony, which could result either from an excess of diversity (deformity) or an excess of identity (uniformity). The greatest harmony is a limit (which explains its uniqueness). It presupposes the exacerbation of difference, the profusion of variety, the deployment of multiplicity up to the point beyond which unity and identity would be destroyed. At the same time, it is the demand for similarity and unity carried to the point beyond which all difference and diversity would be eliminated. The perfection of the world no longer refers merely to the brute quantity of being or produced essence, that is, to *ontological* perfection, but equally and perhaps especially, to a *qualitative* perfection, which is related to both an intelligible order and to pleasure—to the aesthetic pleasure of the omniscient spectator who contemplates it.

The most perfect universe is the one that best corresponds to God's end, namely his glory, to which every other end is subordinate. Thus, "it can be said that men are chosen and ranged not so much according to their excellence as according to their conformity with God's plan."[75] It is not what is best in itself that is chosen, but what is most appropriate to the determined end. God wills the happiness of spirits, *as far as possible*, for he takes into consideration the whole of things. The perfection of the whole is not reducible to the sum of particular perfections—that is, to the quantity of being and goodness actualized in the world. The global calculation must include that which does not strictly arise out of quantity but out of quality: the order, connection, and harmony of that great variety of things that compose the world. Our universe is the best both in a *relative* sense, in comparison with other possible worlds, and insofar as it expresses a relation between the means, the prevailing conditions and the ends, and in an *absolute* sense, in that it constitutes the most determinate, intelligible, and unique form.

## 5.2 THE MORAL NECESSITY OF THE DIVINE CHOICE

### 5.2.1 Is the Existence of the Best Possible World Demonstrable?

Before considering how the difficulties concerning God's moral concurrence with evil can be resolved, it is worth pausing to examine the status of the arguments that have been developed up until now as part of the doctrinal wing of Theodicy. Are we dealing here with demonstrations in the strict sense? Does Leibniz demonstrate, in the true sense of the term, that God created the best of all possible worlds? For Leibniz a demonstration is not a proof like any other. The criteria it must satisfy are particularly demanding. Not only must the form of the argument be logically correct, but also all of the premises must be fully proven—or, in other words, must themselves have been demonstrated.[76] Nothing must be granted that has not been demonstrated or is capable of being so. Demonstration consists in showing by analysis (*resolutio*) the inherence of the predicate in the subject.[77] What Leibniz refers to in certain texts as "absolute a priori demonstration" involves only definitions and previously demonstrated theorems. Because to demonstrate a theorem is to derive it from definitions, it follows that an "absolute a priori demonstration" is nothing but a chain of definitions.[78]

Only truths of reason are *demonstrable* in the strict sense, insofar as their analysis is carried out in a finite number of steps, either because they can be reduced to previously demonstrated truths, or because they are directly reducible to "first truths" (of the form A = A), such that the inherence of the predicate in the subject is made manifest. Such truths are necessary in that their negation implies a contradiction. They offer absolute certitude. Geometry, logic, and metaphysics are the three disciplines to which these truths belong. By contrast, truths of fact cannot be demonstrated but only *proven*, since their analysis is never complete but continues to infinity. It approaches the form of an identity tangentially without ever reaching it. To explain the least contingent thing, one must know not only its causes but also (in light of the relation that each thing has to all other things) the universe as a whole, as well as the reasons for which God chose to create this universe rather than another equally possible one. God alone is capable of such a priori knowledge, which does not amount to a demonstration for him either. For he does not see the final step of the analysis, of which there is none, but comprehends in a single intuition ("at a glance" as it were) the infinite series of reasons.[79] These truths are contingent, since their opposite is possible in itself, and their certainty is moral. The mathematical comparison with commensurable and incommensurable quantities provides an illustration of the difference between these two kinds of truths.[80]

Both the world and the creative act by which it comes into being are contingent. In declaring in §8 of the *Essays of Theodicy* that God *could not have failed* to choose the best, Leibniz does not mean that God could not have not chosen the best, but that he *was obliged* to choose it, and would have failed—that is, would have been at fault—if he had chosen other than he did. This obligation to do the best is, as I have said, a necessity that is internal to God. It is not absolute, since it does not render impossible every choice other than that of the best. Nor does it render what has not been chosen (other possible worlds) contradictory.

In its doctrinal part, Theodicy can demonstrate that God is just, because justice is among the perfections that make up the definition of the supreme being. However, strictly speaking, it can demonstrate neither that he always chooses the best nor *a fortiori* that the existing universe is the most perfect possible. This is not because Theodicy is somehow imperfect or deficient, but rather because such a demonstration is impossible, not only *in fact*, given the limits of our intelligence, but also *in principle*, even for God himself, owing to the nature of contingent propositions.[81]

In fact, we would be in a position to demonstrate a priori that God created the best possible world only if his choice were absolutely necessary, or in other words, if it were not free. As Leibniz writes in a text from the years 1680 to 1684:

> The first principle concerning existences is this proposition: *God wills to choose the most perfect [perfectissimum]*. This proposition cannot be demonstrated; it is the first of all propositions of fact—that is, the origin of all contingent existence. It is one and the same thing to say that *God is free* and that *this proposition is an indemonstrable principle*. For, if a reason could be given for this first divine decree, by that very fact, God would not have made it freely. Therefore, I maintain that this proposition can be compared to identity statements. For, just as the proposition *A is A* or *a thing is equal to itself*, so the proposition *God wills the most perfect* cannot be demonstrated. This proposition is the origin of the transition [*transitus*] from the possibility to the existence of creatures.[82]

Such a demonstration is impossible because God's will is only inclined but not necessitated by his understanding, which represents to him what is best. Only that which is logically or metaphysically necessary is demonstrable. Therefore, to affirm that God is free and the world contingent entails that a demonstration of the existence of the best possible world is unachievable.

Robert M. Adams has criticized Leibniz's arguments that aim to show that the proposition "God chooses the best" is a contingent truth.[83] If the contingency of our world is grounded in the existence of other possible worlds, the contingency of God's choice to create this world rather than some other seems, according to Adams, much more difficult to establish. For Leibniz, this choice is contingent because the decree "to always do what is most perfect" is a free decree of God.[84] The argument is problematic in that it presupposes that God can freely give himself the will to always do what is best and consequently that he can *will to will*.[85] To grant this will to will would lead to an infinite regress, since it implies that every will must be based on a prior one (that literally "wills" it), and that one on another, and so on. Elsewhere Leibniz explicitly rejects this idea, affirming that the will cannot be under the control of the will.[86] He offers two main reasons for this. First, one cannot will to will something without already willing it,[87] so that the redoubling of the will is useless and even absurd. Second, the regress to which one commits oneself in admitting this redoubling of the will to infinity violates the Principle of Sufficient Reason, since it would be impossible to arrive at an original will that is the reason of all the others.[88] As a result, one would never be able to will anything!

Beyond this initial difficulty, we must consider Leibniz's main argument for the claim that God's choice of the best is contingent, namely, that every other choice by God (that is, other than the best) remains in itself possible. That God does not choose the best does not imply a contradiction. Is this so obvious? Can the infinitely perfect and good being truly act contrary to the dictates of his wisdom, that is, act wrongly, if to act wrongly is to choose other than what one ought? God's nature excludes all imperfection, error, and sin. On this point, Leibniz draws a distinction between the good angels, who *can* sin (even if it is certain that they will not) and God himself, who is strictly incapable of sinning, since to do so would contradict his absolute perfection.[89] Adams writes, "thus Leibniz seems unable to escape the conclusion that it is demonstrable, and hence logically necessary, that God, as an absolutely perfect being, does what is best."[90]

In a previous book,[91] I arrived at the same conclusion by a different route while examining the implications of the moral necessity of the best for God. There I paid special attention to the texts in which Leibniz maintains that a choice other than the best is contradictory, since it would result in the destruction of God:

> If God were to choose what is not the best absolutely and on the whole, that would be a greater evil than all the individual evils which he could prevent by this means. This wrong choice would destroy his wisdom and goodness.[92]

A choice of something other than the best would be a bad choice, and hence, a sin. However, a sin on God's part would imply a negation of his divinity. For this reason, such a choice is absolutely (and not merely morally) impossible.

> In God, every fault would represent a sin; it would be even more than sin, for it would destroy Divinity. And it would be a great fault in him not to choose the

best. I have said this many times. Thus, he would be preventing sin by something worse than all sins.[93]

Here I would like to reconsider this conclusion, which I shared with Adams, since it tends to efface the distinction between moral necessity and logical (or metaphysical) necessity in God and to affirm that God simply cannot choose anything other than the best. It is difficult to believe that in the same text (the *Theodicy*) Leibniz could have defended two contradictory theses: (1) that God's choice of the best is contingent, and (2) that the choice of anything other than the best is absolutely impossible in that it is incompatible with his perfect nature. Could Leibniz have failed to notice this contradiction? Perhaps he did overlook it, since in fact it is only apparent. Might it not arise from an ambiguity in the meaning of *being possible* (*possible*) and *being able to* (*pouvoir*)? As Leibniz explains,

> God chose between different courses all of which were possible: thus, metaphysically speaking, he could [*pouvait*] have chosen or done what was not the best; but he could not morally speaking have done so.[94]

One must distinguish the question of possibility from that of actuality, just as one must distinguish power from the will.[95] When we consider a possible in itself (a substance, an event, or a world), its intelligibility and its presuppositions, we consider it independently of God's will and his actual choice. Every possible is represented in the divine understanding and can be the object of his power. Because his omnipotence extends to everything possible, it can be said that God *is able to* create a world that is less perfect than ours (which is the best). Thus, with respect to the attribute of omnipotence, God's choice of the best is contingent. If we now consider those things that actually exist, the question is different, since we must now take into account God's will, his holiness and his ends. Here, the choice of a world less perfect than ours is impossible, since that would imply an *imperfection* in God. With respect to the attributes of wisdom and goodness, it is necessary, *morally speaking*, that God choose and actualize the best. A world worse than ours must be considered as a possible object of his omnipotence, but not of his will.

Thus, between the possible and the actual—that is, the creation of a single world from among the infinite number of possible worlds—three levels must be distinguished:

1. God's omnipotence is limited by the possible, so much so that whatever is logically or metaphysically impossible is impossible for God. God

    cannot create a square circle, nor bring it about, for example, that a being is and is not at the same time.

2. God's omnipotence extends to all possibles and to their infinite combinations, which are called "possible worlds."

3. The infinite wisdom and perfect goodness joined to this omnipotence lead to the choice of a unique combination of possibles, the only world that God is *morally* able to create without sinning. By virtue of his omnipotence, God can do whatever is possible. However, his wisdom and goodness lead him to bring into existence what is best. This moral necessity, however strong and binding it may be in God, cannot alter the nature of the contingent (the divine choice of the best) and render it absolutely necessary.

Thus, it is possible to affirm at the same time—though in two different senses—that God *can* choose other than the best (in light of his omnipotence) and that he *cannot* choose other than the best (in light of his wisdom and goodness). The distinction between *proximate power* (*pouvoir prochain*) and *remote power* (*pouvoir éloigné*) can help shed light on this point, although it should not be taken as more than an analogy. Remote power concerns logical or metaphysical possibility, for example, the ability of the damned to make amends and be saved or of the elect to sin. However, this is rendered impossible *ex hypothesi* or accidentally by the proximate power, namely, the engrained habit of sinning in the damned and the habit of doing good in the elect. By way of illustration, Leibniz borrows the following comparison from Pierre Nicole:

> It is considered impossible that a wise and serious magistrate, who has not taken leave of his senses, should publicly commit some outrageous action, as for example, to run about the streets naked in order to make people laugh. It is the same, in a sense, with the blessed; they are even less capable of sinning, and the necessity that forbids them to sin is of the same kind.[96]

This remote power—which still remains—is the condition sine qua non of the freedom of rational agents. God's omnipotence, considered prior to creation as the power to create whatever is possible, can be viewed by analogy with this remote power, which is constantly enjoyed by created spirits. However, this same omnipotence can also be compared with their proximate power insofar as it is subordinate to the dictates of wisdom.

Therefore, God is not absolutely, but only morally, necessitated to choose the best. Consequently, the proposition "God always chooses the best" is not demonstrable in the strict sense of the term. Must we then conclude that the doctrinal part of Theodicy does not ultimately contain any decisive argument in favor of the existence of the best possible world, so that on this point we are left with nothing more than mere belief? Certainly not. The thesis that God created the best possible universe is a contingent truth, which given its nature, cannot be demonstrated. Nevertheless, it can be *proved*, since there are a priori reasons in its favor based on our knowledge of the divine perfections. The thesis is convincing, though not entirely conclusive, since the proof does not amount to a demonstration.

How then should we characterize the arguments that Leibniz develops with regard to the doctrinal part of his Theodicy? They are not mere presumptions, much less pure conjectures. However, as we have seen, they are not demonstrations in the strict sense of the term. To understand their particular status, we must return to Leibniz's conception of demonstration.

Leibniz distinguishes two kinds of demonstration: (1) what he calls "demonstrations of necessity,"[97] which concern truths of reason and are demonstrations in the strict sense, and (2) what he calls demonstrations of probability, or "moral" demonstrations. The goal of these latter is to assess the degree of verisimilitude and credibility of a thesis in areas where it is not possible to achieve absolute certainty by accurately weighing the reasons in its favor.[98] When the question at issue is of a practical nature (for example, a medical consultation, a war council, or a legal litigation), this involves gathering together all the available facts and evidence, to investigate the circumstances so that one may determine the most reasonable course of action, and thus to make the best choice. This second kind of demonstration involves bringing together various proofs of different kinds and weights (experience, appearances, presumptions, inductions based on particular facts, etc.), all of which converge on the same conclusion. The result is a demonstration that approaches the highest level of certainty, yet, is not entirely conclusive. For this reason it is considered an inferior form of demonstration. Nevertheless, it remains extremely useful and fecund on the practical level.

It would seem that the a priori argumentation that Leibniz employs in the doctrine on behalf of the thesis that God chooses the best possible world has an intermediary status between these two kinds of demonstration. Like demonstrations of probability, it concerns truths of fact. It belongs to the realm of the probable but in the highest possible degree, which Leibniz calls "infinite probability or moral certainty"[99] in contrast to metaphysical certainty, which is restricted to "demonstrations of necessity." The existence of the best possible world is not a mere supposition or hypothesis, nor simply a presumption to be admitted in the absence of a formal proof of the contrary. It is a *morally certain* thesis, that is "incomparably more probable than the opposite"[100] and of which we have "infallible" certainty. In fact, Leibniz prefers the adjective "infallible" to "moral," because this certainty is founded exclusively on a priori considerations, whereas "moral certainty" applies to inferences based on experience, authority, or testimony.[101] However, the arguments on which the thesis of the best possible world rests also have characteristics in common with demonstrations of necessity insofar as these arguments are a priori and based on a certain kind of necessity, namely moral necessity, which as we shall see (5.2.2), is a form of internal obligation.

We can now see why Leibniz defines Theodicy as a "quasi kind of science" in his correspondence with Des Bosses:[102] not only because of the existence of the defensive wing, but also because Theodicy contains no demonstrations of necessity in its doctrinal wing. The lack of demonstration is the counterpart of God's freedom and the contingency of the universe. The propositions "God always chooses the best" and "ours is the best possible world" are proved by reason and based in the a priori but are not demonstrable on account of their contingency. They are "infallibly" but, not absolutely, certain.

### 5.2.2 From Can to Ought: Moral Necessity

The concept of moral necessity allows Leibniz to maintain at once the freedom of God, the infallible certainty of his choice of the best, and the contingency of this world. The world is contingent not only because it does not contain within itself the reason of its existence, nor because other worlds are possible in themselves, but because it results from a free, though determined, choice. This concept belongs to the vocabulary of jurisprudence. Synonymous with obligation,[103] moral necessity is equated with the necessity of the "good man," who must always strive to do what ought to be done. Leibniz compares it to a precept of Papinian: "we ought to believe that we are incapable of any things that are contrary to good morals."[104] A *morally necessary* action is one from which we cannot be exempted and which we cannot forgo without fault. In his attempts to transcribe deontic modalities (obligatory, forbidden, permitted, indifferent) into classical modal logic (necessary, impossible, possible, contingent), Leibniz adds specifically moral modalities, which he defines as follows: "I call *morally impossible* what cannot be done without sinning." Similarly, "what is morally necessary" is called "what is owed (*debitum*)," and what is "morally possible" is called "licit."[105]

It is worth noting that the expression "moral necessity," which was first used in juridical and moral texts, seems not to have been applied to God's conduct prior to 1707.[106] Until that time, when talking of God's conduct Leibniz speaks of acting in the most perfect manner, of the necessity of choosing the best or of the necessity of the best,[107] of "happy" necessity,[108] of "physical" (that is, natural) necessity,[109] of "the great principle of the perfection of God's works,"[110] of "a necessity of choice whose contrary means imperfection,"[111] or even more simply of the certain and infallible choice of the best. How then shall we explain the introduction of moral necessity into theology? There would seem to be two reasons for this.

(1) There remains a certain indecision in Leibniz's texts prior to 1707 whether the proposition "God always chooses the best" is necessary, and whether it is absolutely impossible that he choose other than the best.[112] Without deciding the question definitively, Leibniz limits himself to making two points in his notes on Bayle (which Grua dates to approximately 1706). On the one hand, even if this proposition should prove to be necessary, it would not imply that whatever is chosen is necessary, because it cannot be demonstrated that what is chosen is the best. On the other hand, the proposition "it is necessary that God wills the best" is not strictly equivalent to "God necessarily wills the best," since it can also mean "it is necessary that God wills the best necessarily" and "it is necessary that God wills the best freely."[113] The necessity can be understood *de dicto* (that is, as applying to the entire proposition) or *de re* (that is, as applying to the object of the proposition, namely, God's will of the best). Here, Leibniz is clearly following Aristotle and his refutation of the master argument. However, at this stage, the question of whether God necessarily wills the best remains undecided.

In fact, Leibniz is confronted with the following difficulty. In order to avoid absolute necessity, he must maintain the idea of a God endowed with intelligence and will, who acts freely, rather than mechanically in the manner of blind fate or "brute" nature. However, to avoid pure indifference and arbitrariness, which are incompatible with supreme wisdom, Leibniz must posit in God some form of determination that is so powerful and "infallible" that nothing other than the best can be chosen, although every other choice remains possible in itself. It is in the juridical notion of moral necessity that Leibniz finds the means of simultaneously satisfying these two theoretical requirements.

Thus, the solution lies in the doctrine of justice. It consists in reformulating the problem in other terms by shifting from the logical point of view that had dominated up until now (God necessarily or freely wills the best) to a juridical or moral point of view (God *ought* to will the best), that is from consideration of the necessary (that whose contrary is logically impossible) to that of the permissible and the just (that whose contrary is illicit and morally impossible). This change of perspective and the resulting transformation of the problem allow Leibniz to identify, in the form of the highest obligation, a necessity that is as constraining on the moral level as is metaphysical necessity on the logical level, while still being compatible with freedom: moral necessity. To the logical constraint that limits divine power (God cannot do the impossible) is now added a juridical and moral constraint that limits his will: God can do nothing contrary to the laws of wisdom and justice. Thus, God always and infallibly does the best, not because he cannot do otherwise, but because he *ought* to do what is best, because he cannot do what is unworthy of his perfection or contrary to his justice. To create something other than the most perfect world possible was not *logically* but *morally* impossible. It would have implied not a contradiction but an imperfection.

The distinction between *can* and *ought* affords a response to those, who, following Bayle, appeal to divine omnipotence in objecting that God, had he wanted to, could have prevented Adam's sin or made all human beings happy:

> God (so they say) could have given happiness to all, he *could have* given it promptly and easily, and without causing himself any inconvenience, for he can do anything. But *ought* he? Since he does not do so, it is a sign that he had to act altogether differently.[114]

Consideration of this obligation leads to the second reason for applying moral necessity to God: justification of the permission of evil.

(2) The reference to moral necessity appears in an opuscule from 1707 in a specific context: in response to the problem of divine permission of evil. Invoking Augustine's maxim that God would not permit evil if he did not draw some greater good out of it, Leibniz warns against misinterpreting the maxim with regard to moral evil (or evil of guilt). Sin can never be a "permissible object of the will," even if it were to bring about some good, since it is a violation of the law and so an act of disobedience. As the Apostle Paul observed, "evil ought not to be done so that good may ensue."[115] Because sin cannot be a means, but only a condition sine qua non of good, its permission (unlike that of other evils) requires additional justification.

> Therefore, the only legitimate reason for permitting sin is this: sin is permitted whenever it cannot be prevented without failing to do one's duty, as in the case of one, who—especially in some time of danger—is stationed in a post that he

must not abandon without the express order of a commander or officer and hears that two other soldiers from among his friends wish to fight one another in a duel. It would not be permissible for him to fly to them in order to prevent the evil. Similarly, it might happen on some occasion that a prince cannot prevent the sin of one of his subjects without himself sinning, in which case permission of the other's sin would be necessary anyway. God, who is incapable of sin, is bound by the *moral necessity* of his wisdom and goodness to do and to choose the best, and his failure to do so would be worse than any creaturely sin, because it would be contrary to divine perfection. For a lesser good is the reason for evil. That is why the reason for which God permitted sin can be no other than the following: he could not fail to permit it, with his wisdom intact [*salva sapientia*], since he has certainly chosen from among innumerable possible worlds, that which is best, in which some moral evil was included, as we can judge to be the case *a posteriori*, that is, by the effect, or from the fact that he permitted it.[116]

Moral necessity is invoked in cases in which the evil cannot be reduced to a lesser good, to a subsidiary good or to a means—that is, in cases where its existence is most difficult to justify and can be allowed only on the basis of a superior motive of sufficient weight. This necessity takes four forms.

a. It first takes the form of a double negation, as a duty that the agent cannot not perform without fault. It is an imperative that admits of no exception, derogation, or dispensation.[117] Its constraint appears as the moral impossibility of not carrying it out or of doing the opposite of what it requires. God cannot do other than the best without contradicting his wisdom—that is, without renouncing his own essence.
b. Next, it takes the form of a superior obligation, by virtue of which one duty outranks another in case of conflict. A soldier's duty to carry out an order and to protect a city under threat outweighs his duty to prevent a particular crime (and to help his neighbor), just as the divine duty to abide by his own wisdom and to choose the universe that is best on the whole outweighs his duty to prevent moral evil in individual creatures.
c. More positively, moral necessity appears as the effect of wisdom and goodness[118] on the will, and, as a result, as the very expression of justice. For justice, which Leibniz defines as charity in conformity with wisdom, consists in the correct relationship between the faculties (the will subordinate to the understanding, which illuminates it) and constitutes the rule that governs both the divine choice and the order of the world ultimately chosen. If the possibles organized into worlds strive for existence in the divine understanding in accordance with the juridical model

I have identified,[119] the rule according to which God decides between them is the necessity by which he wills and does what is most worthy of his glory. This necessity, which is only a necessity by analogy with metaphysical necessity, and does not foreclose the possibility of the contrary, is called *moral*, "because for the wise what is necessary and what ought to be done [*dû*] are equivalent things"[120] and *happy*, because it always tends to the good[121] and because it constitutes the happiness of the one who abides by it.[122] Far from diminishing one's freedom, it provides "the true and most perfect freedom,"[123] since it allows us to make the best use of our freedom by infallibly accomplishing the best.

d. Lastly, the form of constraint associated with moral necessity is of a very specific kind. Moral necessity does not constrain so much as it *persuades* and makes itself be loved. In God, "the eternal truths, objects of his wisdom, are more inviolable than the Styx. These laws and this judge do not constrain: they are stronger, for they persuade."[124] The resulting determination is not the effect of an external force, of a *fate* to which God is subject and which he fears, as Jupiter feared the law of the Styx. These eternal truths, together with all possibles and their combinations, are in God himself.[125] They constitute his wisdom, which *convinces* him to abide by it by showing him what is best. This is also why moral necessity is happy and why it is the condition for exercising true freedom: because the sage submits to it only because he approves of it.

### 5.2.3 Duty, Circumstances, and Motives

This conception of moral necessity can seem paradoxical. For it combines the notion of an irresistible and almost absolute constraint ("a supreme necessity may constrain one to comply [*condescendre*] with evil") with an understanding of duties as conditional,[126] whose fulfillment depends on an awareness of circumstances and an evaluation of anticipated goods and evils. Indeed, the predominance of one duty over another depends on a host of circumstances: whether it is a question of public interest (the city over which the soldier must keep watch or the entire universe which is in God's care) or merely private (a quarrel among friends or the sin of individual creatures), the nature of the agent involved, whether it is created or uncreated, its rank (a prince in relation to his subjects, God in relation to his creatures), and finally the greater or lesser probability of the expected good or bad consequence[127] (the destruction of a city, the death of one or both men in a duel, or in the example of the queen that occurs at *Theodicy* §25, the crime of an individual and the welfare of the state).

The assessment of all these circumstances must make it possible for the rules of justice to be correctly applied, so that the conflict of duties is really only apparent. For the first precept of law, that which commands us to refrain from harming others and to aid those in need, does not require us to do so to our own detriment or at the expense of some greater general good (as is made clear by the qualifier "so far as possible"). Divine as well as human permission of sin is entirely justified by "strict law" (*jus strictum*). Neither God nor man ought to prevent evil, if in doing so he will fail in his duty to himself. In the name of self-interest, "it is indeed beyond question that we must refrain from preventing the sin of others when we cannot prevent their sin without sinning ourselves."[128]

In this way, the appeal to moral necessity leads to a kind of reversal: not only does justice render the permission of sin legitimate but also makes it an obligation. This obligation must not be understood "in a human sense [*humano more*] but θεοπρεπῶς (as it is proper to God), namely, that otherwise he would act contrary to his perfections."[129] It would be a sin on God's part not to permit evil—a sin against the principle of the best in choosing a world other than the most perfect (which includes the fall of man) and a sin against himself in acting in a manner unworthy of his perfection. In this way, the permission of evil is both the effect of God's goodness and the consequence of an essential obligation internal to God himself:

(i) the existence of evil, far from being an accusation against God, becomes paradoxically that which justifies him by exhibiting his goodness:

> Wisdom only shows God the best possible exercise of his goodness: after that, the evil that occurs is an inevitable result of the best. I will add something stronger: *To permit evil, as God permits it, is the greatest goodness.*[130]

To permit evil is, in effect, to permit the actualization of the best possible world.

(ii) Moral necessity in God is not some externally imposed constraint. It is nothing other than an internal law of his nature. God, who has no superior, is his own judge, and his supreme duty is that which he owes to himself. This means that he must act in accordance with his divine nature and on behalf of his glory. True evil, the greatest sin, could not be that of creatures, but of the creator who would wish to prevent evil, and for that reason, would choose a world other than the best. Such a choice would be a worse evil "than all the individual evils which he could prevent by this means."[131] It would be, in a sense, the supreme and absolute evil. In fact, it is an impossible choice, since it is contrary to God's nature. As we have seen, it would be *"even more than sin*, for it would destroy Divinity."[132]

No creaturely sin, nor even all the sins that occur in the world, could compare to this evil worse than any sin, namely God's denial of his own divinity. The choice is between an evil (creaturely evil) that is incomparably less than all the good in the universe[133] and a sin (God's sin) that is incomparably greater than all the evil in the universe. Leibniz turns the objection on its head: what would be evil would be that there was no evil in the world. For the absence of evil would indicate the imperfection of both the world and its creator. The paradox, simply stated, is that evil exists because God exists and is all-perfect.[134] Given the weight of human sin and the difficulty of justifying its permission by an absolutely good being, one must appeal to an infinitely greater sin, something "more than sin," and an irresistible obligation to do the best in God himself. However, although violation of this obligation would lead to something absolutely impossible—that God is not, or is no longer, God—it is an obligation whose necessity remains moral rather than metaphysical.

By way of conclusion, let us consider some possible criticisms of this interpretation of moral necessity. Some have challenged this interpretation, which they consider strictly "deontic." These commentators see Leibniz as having inherited the Jesuit conception of moral necessity or at least claim to discern a troubling similarity between the two views.[135] Against this, I would insist that it has yet to be established that Leibniz had sufficient knowledge of these Jesuit authors to speak of a genuine influence. Moreover, it would be astonishing if Leibniz, who was so quick to make a show of his erudition and so concerned to win the assent of various religious factions, should make no mention of this influence in the *Theodicy*. Des Bosses is supposed to have been the first to draw a connection between the Leibnizian conception of moral necessity and that of certain Jesuits such as Ruiz de Montoya, Antonio Pérez, and Sebastián Izquierdo. However, Leibniz's response substantially weakens the case for some real influence. Leibniz thanks Des Bosses for the references to Ruiz de Montoya and Perez on the subject of God's choice of the best (references of which he would seem then to have been unaware!) and shows great caution regarding their interpretation. He requests further explanation and observes rather laconically that on the whole (*in summa*) their views do not seem very far from his.[136] As for Sebastián Izquierdo,

Leibniz indicates his disagreement with some of the passages that Des Bosses cites, while acknowledging that at bottom "we seem to agree."[137] In short, the influence is debatable and the conceptual similarity appears doubtful even according to Leibniz himself.

Furthermore, it seems to me that the two main criticisms[138] that have been made of the interpretation of moral necessity as obligation are easily overcome. The first is that every obligation presupposes a superior, which obviously cannot be the case with God. In response, I would first point out that, as we have seen, the obligation at issue here is not to be understood in the human sense, but as "θεοπρεπῶς (as it applies to God),"[139] because God can do nothing that contradicts his perfections. Secondly, the absence of a superior does not destroy the obligation, since it is purely internal. God has no need of a superior in order to carry out his duty of his own accord. Thirdly, supreme wisdom—which is nothing other than universal Reason itself—acts as a "superior" in God with respect to his will and power. This subordination with regard to wisdom implies that God, even if he is not accountable for his acts before a superior external agent, must "justify himself to himself as a wise sovereign."[140] Thus, were it possible for him to be summoned before the tribunal of the wise—as was Mars before the Areopagus—he would be declared just by unanimous decision.[141]

The second criticism is that there is no pure obligation in Leibniz's ethics and that what "obligates" the good man is nothing other than the motive to act for the greatest good. No duty in and of itself can be a source of motivation, nor has it any effect on the will simply by virtue of its imperative form.[142] Against this, I would argue that to conceive of moral necessity as an obligation in no way implies a separation of duty from the motives that cause one to will—that is, to separate duty from consideration of good or best. Neither in God nor man is obligation ever a pure "you ought." Rather it is a "you ought" that is based on some good that is recognized and desired as such by the agent. God infallibly chooses the best not only because this choice is most worthy of his wisdom but also—and equally—because of the intrinsic quality of the object chosen (namely, the excellence of the world). In God, as in the wise, that which ought to be done is *at the same time* that which is most amiable to the will.

However, recognition of the agreement between motives and duty should not lead us to confuse two questions. On the one hand, there is the question of what motivates our choices (or God's choice), and more generally, the question of the determinants of the will (inclinations, passions) that explain the final choice. I shall return to this issue in the next section (5.3). On the other hand, there is the question of the rules to be followed in puzzling cases or cases where there is a conflict of duty, as in the example of the soldier on watch or the prince who outlaws dueling. Here the issue is not to determine whether there are motives or whether these motives are sufficient. Rather, it is to be in a position to determine how to act when these motives conflict. Here there occurs a consideration that goes beyond the merely motivational: the duty to act according to the best (and to prefer the general good to the particular good), the obligation to act in accordance with justice (the "strict law" commands us not to harm ourselves), and, for God, the obligation to make a choice that befits his divine nature. Of course, it could be said that this "deontic" consideration amounts to positing a superior motive, one which outweighs all others. This would return us once again to the level of motivations. However, I reply that this motive must be distinguished from obligation and that, even if it accompanies obligation, it is not the cause or foundation of it. Rather it is the effect of obligation or the counterpart in the will.

Thus, it strikes me as an oversimplification to reduce moral necessity to the modality of the connection between motives and the choice that follows from them.[143] This kind of "psychological" interpretation is not borne out by the texts since moral necessity is not mentioned in the analysis and description of the chain of motives that produce volition. Leibniz speaks rather of hypothetical necessity (and not moral necessity) in explaining the process that leads to the final and consequent will, whether in man or God. Motives and reasons *incline* without necessitating. However, moral necessity, understood on the psychological level as determination to the best, is not reducible to this inclination, that is, to its strictly motivational aspect. Moreover, it is not applicable to every kind of inclination. If it is true that moral necessity, in the form of a motive, inclines the will without necessitating it (since the will can always resist it), not every determination that "weighs" on the will and so inclines it can be considered *ipso facto* a moral necessity—otherwise we would be forced to abandon the idea of obligation that is clearly present in the texts. The inclination that results from prevailing motives is not in every case morally necessary, although it is always hypothetically necessary. Here again there are two questions which must not be confused. First, there is the modal question of the kind of determination that applies to the will (absolute or hypothetical necessity). Second, there is the question of the source or foundation of this same determination depending on whether it originates in the passions (a sensible motive) or reason (the representation of a duty). Only in this latter case (the representation of a duty) can the determination truly be called moral necessity.

## 5.3  GOD'S MORAL CONCURRENCE WITH EVIL: THE DOCTRINE OF PERMISSION

### 5.3.1  The Extension of the Concept of Will and Its Divisions

We have seen in what context the appeal to moral necessity is required. Only an invincible obligation could legitimately lead one to permit an evil as difficult to justify as sin. It remains now to explain how this permission can be reconciled with God's equally irrepressible hatred of sin, which not only prevents him from engaging in it but which should also lead him to positively will to prevent it. Leibniz's solution involves the distinction between *antecedent* and *consequent* will.

This distinction, drawn from John of Damascus and the Scholastics,[144] makes a late appearance in Leibniz's vocabulary. After being explicitly rejected in *On the Omnipotence and Omniscience of God*,[145] it appears in a discussion of election at the time of the irenic negotiations (begun after 1697) in response to the "particularists," who in accordance with the maxim "he who can and wills, does," maintained that God does not will salvation for all, since only a small number of men are saved.

> For if this term [will] is taken for an inclination so strong that it makes a person employ all his power to obtain the effect, as it is in the philosophers' axiom, "qui vult et potest, ille facit," it is certain that God does not will the salvation of all by such a will. But when the term is taken more generally for an inclination that tends towards the effect, provided that greater reasons do not prevent it, it can be said that it is in this way that God seriously wills the salvation of all. And we do not see anything which should prevent . . . using the distinction of John of Damascus and the Scholastics between the antecedent will, which always aims to produce good, and the consequent or resultant will, which arises out of the final clash [of all antecedent wills], and makes it so that the good willed antecedently is not always willed effectively and consequently, on account of stronger reasons that divert it.[146]

Later Leibniz would employ the distinction beyond the particular case of election, probably around the time he was annotating *An Exposition of the Thirty-Nine Articles of the Church of England* of Gilbert Burnet and preparing a preface to the Latin translation of that work (probably around 1705). The concurrence of inclinations of the will toward the good, from which the best results, is compared to the composition of tendencies of motion,[147] and God is said to will every good *antecedently* and the best *consequently* "by an entire will."[148] Henceforth, the theological question of election is placed within the framework of a global metaphysical explanation in which the salvation of all men is but one example among others of an antecedent will that does not realize its full effect.[149] This expanded use of the distinction between antecedent and consequent will seems only to have been fully embraced from 1707 onward.[150] Its importance is twofold:

1. The distinction between two kinds of will provides an explanation of God's *moral* concurrence with evil, by offering an explanatory model that is better able to reconcile the permission of evil with the positive and serious will to prevent it (5.3.1 and 5.3.2).
2. The composition of antecedent wills in a consequent and final will is the corollary of the competition of possibles striving for existence in the divine understanding. This in turn offers a means of reconciling, at least apparently, the explanation of the creation of the world by the purely intellectual "metaphysical mechanism" with the notion of a free choice of the will that is determined to the best under the influence of an infinite number of prior inclinations (5.3.3).

With the division of the divine will into antecedent and consequent, permission appears less the result of an opposition between reasons, which prevents certain particular goods from being actualized, as the effect of a concurrence by which all the particular wills must in some sense be realized in the final will.

We have seen that following the *Conversation with Steno* (1677), Leibniz ceases to equate permission with a conditional or accidental volition of evil and begins to speak instead of a bending of the will to prevent evil out of consideration for universal harmony. Because it is impossible to produce at the same time all particular goods and what is best for the whole (which must include certain evils), the permission of sin appeared as a necessary and legitimate derogation from the good in the divine will. God does not will evil. However, out of consideration for overriding reasons, he does not will to prevent it. The same holds true in the legal realm, where the exception made to one law is the effect of a superior law. The model Leibniz defended was that of a conflict in which the general will for the best had in the end to override the particular will for a good (that would go unrealized).

The model adopted beginning in 1707 and retained in the *Theodicy* is new in that it is based on an expanded definition of will. Will is no longer understood as merely the final *conatus* (effort) that results from an infinite number of movements, inclinations (and, in the human case, sensible and insensible impulses), but as all these movements and partial inclinations as well. The "will" signifies in general "the inclination to do something in proportion to the good it contains."[151] As a result, it comes to signify a unique kind that includes a great variety of tendencies that are specified not according to their nature or inclining force but are grouped under two headings, according to whether they are considered separately and in themselves, as "antecedent wills,"[152] or combined together to form the "consequent will."[153] This division, which is based not on a difference in kind, but on considering wills from two different points of view (taken in themselves or in combination with others), has two consequences:

a. What heretofore was considered as a simple tendency is elevated to the status of (antecedent) will. Inclination, which enters into the composition of the final will, is now a real and efficacious will in its own right. It is not a velleity or the inefficacious formulation of a wish.
b. Permission always relates to the will and not to mere knowledge (as was the case at the time of the *Confession of a Philosopher*), since it results from the transition from antecedent to consequent will (on this point see 5.3.2).

Taken in the broad sense, the will is defined in reference to two limits. The first is *internal*; it is nothing but the proportionality of the inclination to the degree of real or apparent perfection of the object sought or rejected (the *conatus* is more powerful as the good to be sought or the evil to be shunned appears greater). The second is an *external* limit, which is imposed by the other *conatus*. The actual carrying out of the will depends on the absence of contrary prevalent inclinations. If every good could be realized and every evil avoided in the same world, every will would be at once antecedent and consequent, or every antecedent will would be consequent. The two are distinct (antecedence in God does not refer to temporal priority, but only logical priority or "priority of nature") only because complete realization of the good and complete exclusion of evil are impossible, given that certain goods are mutually exclusive and/or cannot be obtained without the occurrence of evil.

What then can be said of those antecedent wills that are not "carried out"? They cannot be vain or amount to a kind of velleity. The task is to justify God's conduct while avoiding the following unpalatable alternative: a God lacking in will (that is, who does not truly will salvation for all, since many are damned) or a God lacking in power (that is, who wills universal salvation but cannot bring it about). The notion of antecedent will provides the means of avoiding two defects, both of which are incompatible with God's perfection: power without enough will and will without enough power. Antecedent will is characterized as "serious" because it is a real inclination toward the good—that is, a will in the true sense of the term (as fully a will as is consequent will), rather than a semi-will or a lesser and incomplete one. Considered in itself, it is as determinant and efficacious as consequent will:

> It may even be said that this will is efficacious *of itself (per se)*, that is, such that the effect would ensue if there were not some stronger reason that prevents it: for this will does not pass into final exercise (*ad summum conatum*), else it would never fail to produce its full effect, God being the master of all things.[154]

Antecedent will is a tendency in which nothing is intrinsically lacking to produce its effect. Thus, it is neither a "will expressed in the sign" (*voluntas signi*), revealed by God but contradicted by his "will expressive of the good pleasure" (*voluntas beneplaciti*), which alone occurs,[155] nor a conditional will[156] of which velleity is a "very imperfect kind."[157] In the case of velleity, "one would if one were able, and would wish to be able."[158] A velleity is not carried out because it lacks both the power to be fulfilled and the will to persevere in its willing. It is a "will" that one neither can nor truly wishes to execute. Of course, such impotence and imperfection cannot have place in God, whose antecedent will is not only sure and firm but also truly productive.

The point is worth emphasizing: the efficacy of each antecedent will is that of an inclination, which regardless of whether it is seconded or thwarted, always remains active in the consequent will. As the analogy with the composition of tendencies in motion makes clear, all antecedent wills contribute to the effect in the final will:

> Now this final and decisive consequent will results from the conflict of all antecedent wills, both those which tend towards good and those which reject evil. It is from the concurrence of all these particular wills that the complete will comes. As in mechanics where the compound movement results from all the tendencies that concur in one and the same moving body, and satisfies each one equally, in so far as it is possible to do all at one time. It is as if the moving body took equal account of these tendencies, as I once showed in one of the Paris journals (Sep. 7, 1693), when giving the general law of the compositions of movement. Likewise, it is in this sense that it may be said that the antecedent will is efficacious in a sense and even effective with success.[159]

The comparison to mechanics must be understood in the context of Leibniz's reform of physics. Antecedent wills are like forces, which are always conserved (unlike quantity of motion), although their *effect* can be counteracted or annulled by that of superior forces. Like solicitation in the moving body, inclination cannot be modified *in itself*—neither augmented nor diminished—once joined with other inclinations. It conserves its own force that depends on the degree of perfection or imperfection of the object that is willed or rejected. The *external* limit (the relation to other inclinations) does not alter the *internal* limit (the force of inclination relative to the nature of the object pursued or shunned). Just as no force can be annihilated by a contrary force—although its effect can be prevented—so too, no antecedent will is destroyed or even constrained in itself. Only its execution can be prevented.

The comparison to mechanics suggests the following interpretation of the transition from antecedent to consequent. That only a small number of men are actually saved does not indicate that the declared will of God to save all men has been suppressed or limited by reason of superior motives (represented by concurrent wills). For the *effort* (*conatus*) must not be confused with the *effect*, nor measured by it. Absence of effect—or its merely partial realization—does not imply absence (or even diminution) of effort. Considered in themselves, God's love of virtue and hatred of vice are infinite. However, they are applied in proportion to the nature of the intended object and "as the nature of things prompts it."[160] The will to good can thus be infinite in and of itself (as antecedent will) and at the same time limited in its exercise, when considered consequently. By contrast, the will to the best, as a consequent will, is infinite both in itself and in its exercise. God's love of virtue and hatred of vice "tend indefinitely to bring virtue into existence and to prevent the existence of vice," just as his will continues to tend to procure the happiness of all men and to avoid their misery.[161] God wills always and invariably the virtue and felicity of *all* human beings, even if it is necessary that evil occur and that some are damned. God's antecedent will remains intact, and its inclining force persists, even if its effect is impeded for some time, though perhaps not for all eternity.

One may object that ultimately it is only what results from God's consequent will (that is, what effectively happens) that matters. Yet the effort is no less *real* than the effect. Not only does it persevere indefinitely, whatever the final result, but it is executed, even if not fully.[162] Just as motion in a body "satisfies" all the tendencies from which it arises or, according to another comparison, just as all the parts of a glass container feel the pressure exerted by compressed air inside of it, the consequent will feels the effect of all of the antecedent wills and satisfies them so far as possible. The soul is like "a force which exerts itself [*fait effort*] on various sides simultaneously, but which acts only at the spot where action is easiest or there is least resistance."[163] The effort toward each side produces an inclination, and the "easiest" path, which ultimately wins out, is simply that which "touches the most." Antecedent wills are never in vain, since with regard to the concurrence, each one acts to the full extent of its force.[164] Furthermore, with regard to the final decree that each one helps to produce, even the will to save all men is not entirely without effect, since some men are in fact saved! Nor is the will to prevent sin without influence, since it assures that permission is never a positive volition for sin, not even a conditional or accidental one.

There is one final sense in which antecedent wills are satisfied in the final will: precisely insofar as they tend to the particular good only *in proportion to* its perfection.[165] A good is willed to the extent that it is worthwhile or merits it: "each particular act of antecedent will entering into the total result has its value and order, in proportion to the good to which this act inclines."[166] This proportionality of the inclination to the quality of the intended object means that there cannot be, strictly speaking, an absolute, unconditioned will for any good whatsoever (any more than there can be an absolute, unconditioned will to avoid a particular evil)—that is, such that it ought not yield to the will for a good recognized as superior. Thus, it is not that God does not will enough, but rather that he wills more. It is not that he does not will with a consequent volition the good he had willed antecedently, but rather that he prefers a greater. There is a preference and a choice, rather than a genuine conflict between wills.

This rule of proportionality does not render antecedent wills conditional, but makes it possible to abandon a lesser good (which becomes an evil relatively speaking) in favor of a greater good. This possibility allows us to conceive the passage from antecedent to consequent will without contradiction or discontinuity. For from the antecedent to the consequent, it is still fundamentally the same will, which considers first (according to a logical rather than temporal priority) each particular good in itself, then decides in favor of the combination that results in the greatest possible good and least possible evil as a whole. Thus, the antecedent will is neither suppressed nor even altered. As will, that is as a fundamental tendency toward the good, its end always subsists. It extends into the consequent will and is fully executed in it as will, moving by virtue of its nature beyond a particular good to the good in general—or rather, beyond the good to the *best*.

And it cannot be said that the felicity and perfection of God *qua* will is in any way diminished by the fact that not all his acts of will produce their full effects. For he wills what is good only according to the degree of goodness which is inherent in it, and his will is the more satisfied the better the result obtained.[167]

Were the antecedent will to prevent evil to achieve its effect, it would in fact fail to accomplish its end—which is always the good—since in that case a greater good would be prevented. Failure to carry out this will is, from a certain point of view, a way of realizing it. Thus, there is in God no opposition between his wills, no contrariety and no remorse.

### 5.3.2 Permission as the Effect of the Concurrence of Antecedent Wills

"God wills *antecedently* the good and *consequently* the best."[168] The transition from antecedent to consequent will is a transition from the particular to the general and from the good to the best. It is by means of this transition that evil is introduced, since evil is inextricably bound up with certain goods such that to will the latter entails allowing the former. Such is the case of reason, a good which men sometimes make bad use of.[169] Hence the following paradox: evil enters into the world because God wills the most good possible. "There must, indeed, be a reason for God to permit the evil rather than not to permit it; but no reason of the divine will can be determined by anything but the good."[170] As we have seen, the existence of evil is a proof of God's goodness. If God had excluded evil from the world, if he had willed consequently only certain goods, as for example the happiness of all human beings, he would have been lacking in goodness. For he would not have "satisfied" all his inclinations for the good (his antecedent wills). He would have rested content with some goods or with inferior goods, while rejecting those greater goods that certain evils (such as sin) would have allowed him to obtain. Evil exists because God cannot limit himself to willing a lesser good. He wills the best—the superior good chosen at the cost of evil.

However, choosing the best possible universe does not mean willing everything it contains equally or in the same manner. Otherwise, there would be no difference between the antecedent wills and the consequent will. Evil occurs "in concomitance,"[171] accidentally. It is never willed antecedently. However, its relation to God's consequent will differs depending on whether it is *moral, physical* or *metaphysical* evil:

(1). God can never will sin, whether antecedently or consequently, absolutely or even relatively speaking. Although sin may be the occasion of a great good, it can only be permitted as the result of an indispensable duty—in the name of a moral necessity—not as a means, but "as a *sine qua non* or hypothetical necessity which connects it with the best."[172] Permission is a kind of will. The *permissive will* consists in not preventing evil. It is defined by three characteristics:

(a). It concerns not the acts of the one who wills (as with *productive will*), but the acts of another.[173] It is, as we have seen, an omission without complicity, since it is motivated by a supreme interdiction (that of not sinning oneself). The permissive will is reducible to a productive will that is hindered in the sense that the will not to prevent another's sin follows from the will to refrain from sinning oneself.

(b). The object of the permissive will is not sin itself, but its permission. God does not will the evil committed by another, but wills only to permit it.[174] His relation to sin is doubly indirect, since he wills neither to commit a sin himself nor that sin be committed by another (as in the case of the prince who is complicit in the crimes that he carries out by means of his subordinates). However, God does not will to prevent sin from occurring through the fault of another. In the case of permission, sin is doubly removed from the divine will, which preserves all the more God's holiness.

(c). The reason for the permission of sin is at once moral and metaphysical. Sin must be permitted, because God would himself sin were he to prevent it and because sin cannot be separated from the world to which it belongs. Everything in this world is connected in such a way that no part of it can be changed without thereby making another world. In fact, the moral reason for permission of sin is based on the metaphysical reason: it is because God cannot exclude sin from the world without thereby renouncing this world to which sin ineradicably belongs—that is, without renouncing the best of all possible worlds—that he must permit it. Permission is *morally* necessary only because sin is *hypothetically* necessary.

This does not mean that the antecedent will that inclines God to reject sin is suppressed. Sin, which is admitted only as a concomitant event rather than as something willed for its own sake, does not constitute, strictly speaking, a cause of good or a positive means of obtaining it (although this good cannot be obtained without it). Rather, it is a condition sine qua non, a *prerequisite*[175]—that which it is impossible *ex hypothesi* to forgo if the best is to be realized. It is in this sense that Leibniz interprets the words of Christ, "it is necessary that offenses will come"[176] as well as the expression "O Happy Fault" (*O felix culpa*) of the Exsultet of the Roman liturgy, which sees in Adam's fall the condition (sine qua non) of the redemption of Christ.[177]

(2). God does not will "in an absolute manner" physical evil (pain), which he tends to eliminate antecedently just like other evils. However, at times he can and ought to will it consequently and not merely permit it. On these occasions, God's willing is, of course, relative: (a) in consideration of sin "as a punishment owed to guilt" and (b) in consideration of a good to be sought or an evil to be avoided, "as a means to an end, that is, to prevent greater evils or to obtain greater good."[178] In the first case, it is not evil as such that is willed, but the punishment inflicted on the sinner in accordance with the law of justice according to which every crime must be punished. In the second case, it is evil insofar as it serves the good—as an auxiliary and not a mere negative condition. It is a means by which to obtain a greater perfection (like the grain that must spoil in order to sprout[179]) or by which a greater evil is avoided. Notice that the first case is not completely reducible to the second. For, although punishment can equally serve as an instrument for good both by reforming the guilty and dissuading others from similar acts,[180] it is no less required even when no sinner is reformed and no one is dissuaded from sinning.[181]

Thus, physical evils can be assimilated to "subsidiary goods."[182] They are called "goods" relatively speaking on account of the good they make possible and, for this reason, become legitimate objects of consequent will. Although previously rejected by the antecedent will (because they cannot be willed in themselves), these evils appear as auxiliary goods when considered together with all goods and evils. Pain, which is an evil in itself, is considered good by extension and by reference to a greater good that it makes possible or a greater evil it prevents. Pain contributes to moral good (virtue) by purifying the sinner, affords greater appreciation of physical good (pleasure) by way of contrast, and contributes to metaphysical good by setting the just man on the path to superior perfection.[183]

(3). Metaphysical evil (or imperfection in general) may be willed by God insofar as it is reduced, as in the case of physical evil, to a "subsidiary" good.[184] Metaphysical evil is constitutive of created beings. It is the limitation inherent in that which is finite and does not draw its being from itself. To create is of necessity to create the imperfect and limited. The perfect, absolutely speaking, is uncreated: it is God. Thus, the imperfection of creatures is necessary. However, God is not properly speaking its author, since he produces only what is real and positive in the creature (by virtue of his physical concurrence).

Metaphysical evil is the condition sine qua non of creation. Yet in what sense can it be a relative good, a means of obtaining a greater good? Leibniz does not clarify this point. Nevertheless, it is possible to see metaphysical evil as the means of achieving the greatest possible variety in the universal harmony. It is that by virtue of which creatures differ from one another and are diversely limited. The great multitude of species of creatures whether spiritual, animal, or vegetable, even the existence of inanimate beings and the different degrees of perfection internal to each species, all of this makes up the beauty and excellence of the world. Uniformity, homogeneity, and identity would be a defect. Wisdom demands variety.[185] Moreover, the imperfection of creatures opens to them the possibility of progress. It is the condition of their elevation and merit:

> There are degrees among creatures: the general order requires it. And it appears quite consistent with the order of divine government that the great privilege of strengthening in the good should be granted more easily to those who had a good will when they were in a more imperfect state, in the state of struggle and of pilgrimage, *in Ecclesia militante, in statu viatorum.*[186]

Notice that Leibniz considers natural "disorders" (such as cataclysms, earthquakes, volcanic eruptions, deluges, and inundations) as metaphysical evils. These "disorders" prove to be useful and even beneficial by virtue of the changes and transformations they make possible on the surface of the globe and, in particular, the formation of metals and sediments. The history of the earth bears witness to these upheavals, which make possible human industry and agriculture.

> But who does not see that these disorders have served to bring things to the point where they now are, that we owe to them our riches and our comforts, and that through their agency this globe became fit for cultivation by us. These disorders passed into order.[187]

Ultimately, the existence of all three species of evil is justified by the good. The reduction of physical and metaphysical evils to "subsidiary" goods, which as such are suitable objects of a consequent will—not as ends (for that would be contrary to antecedent wills), but as the means of achieving good ends—restricts permission to moral evil. Sin is the sole evil that God cannot will in any way and that he can only *will to permit*, provided that it is a condition sine qua non of the best. Moral evil is never a good, not even a lesser or subsidiary one. It is an evil that God must resolve to allow once he wills the best possible world. Nevertheless the "happy fault," though bound up with the best, and even compensated and redeemed within the whole harmony, remains *always* and *absolutely* what it is: a criminal disobedience that can never become a good, not even a relative one.

The restriction of the term *permission* to sin does not preclude a broader use, as Leibniz often makes clear. In this more general sense, it is true of all three species of evil that they are only permitted by God. Is this to be understood as the effect of the enduring antecedent will that tends to reject all evil? Or is it perhaps the result of Leibniz's justificatory ambitions, which lead him to put as much distance as possible between the divine will and evil by insisting, for example, on the "automatic" character of punishment, which arises as a *natural* result of sin and so requires no particular intervention on God's part? It is true, particularly in this polemical context, that it is better to deny any relation to evil whatsoever—even an indirect one—which an opponent might take as a sign of God's complicity. Leibniz sometimes suggests that physical evil is permitted insofar as it is considered as a consequence of the permission of sin. God is the author of physical evil,

> when moral evil is assumed to be already in existence; but speaking generally, one might assert that God permitted physical evil by implication, in permitting moral evil which is its source.[188]

Although certain physical evils are considered to be "subsidiary" goods, it is difficult to allow that God can always will them, even as means. For this reason Leibniz makes clear that God can "sometimes" will them.[189] Thus, God must only permit the afflictions of the good man, either as a consequence of the sins of his persecutors or as a painful ordeal that can be imputed neither to the one who suffers nor to anyone else, but rather to the constitution of the body or to illness.[190] Therefore, physical evil is not always connected with a moral fault, and for this reason, it is not always merited.

### 5.3.3 The Composition of Wills and Combination of Possibles: Are the Two Models Compatible?

The parallel between will and understanding seems perfectly exact. The "volitional" model, according to which the final will of the best proceeds from wills that aim at each particular good accords with the "intellectualist" model (the "metaphysical mechanism"), according to which the best universe arises out of the interplay of possibles tending toward existence. The two models are complementary. More precisely, they are two versions of one and the same explanation of God's choice and creation of the best of all possible worlds. They describe the same divine *conatus* (effort) and the same divine act from the respective points of view of the understanding (taking into consideration all possibles as they strive for existence) and the will (taking into consideration all motives and inclinations). Understanding and will are two faculties rooted in the same infinite power, the same "common subject" and the same essence.

However, two difficulties appear in this connection. The first concerns the possibility of establishing an exact one-to-one correspondence between what occurs in the understanding and what occurs in the will. The second concerns an explanation of the will that mixes two contradictory perspectives: the "mechanical" perspective of the composition of wills, in which the final will is the result of the antecedent wills, and the "harmonic" perspective, in which the final will trumps the antecedent wills and the understanding appears at times as that which solely determines the best.

(1) The "volitional" model, which explains how the best is finally chosen by God, seems to be perfectly independent of the "intellectualist" one, since it does not refer to an idea of the world that would preexist in the divine understanding—and that the divine understanding would provide to his will. It is as if there were in operation a "volitional" or "moral" mechanism—similar to the purely intellectual "metaphysical mechanism"—by which necessarily arises (according to a hypothetical necessity, to be sure) the best possible world, understood as that combination that satisfies as much as possible the infinite number of antecedent wills. It is not clear that these two mechanisms can coincide, although Leibniz's introduction of a "middle" will, which serves as an intermediary between antecedent will (which he calls "primitive") and the consequent will can be taken as an argument in favor of their coincidence.[191] According to this new distinction, the transition is from the pure antecedent wills to the middle antecedent wills (which concern particular combinations of goods and evils) and then to the consequent will, which is the unique decree that brings the best total combination into existence. It would seem that a parallel can be drawn with what takes place in the understanding, where beginning with separate possibles (corresponding to pure antecedent wills), divine wisdom considers possibles arranged in a series[192] (corresponding to middle antecedent wills) and finally the best possible universe (the object of the consequent will).

If the analogy between separate possibles and pure antecedent wills holds, it presents a problem beginning at the second stage with the comparison between possibles combined into a series and middle antecedent wills. For middle wills concern *particular* collections of goods and evils and not, properly speaking, *universal* series—that is, complete possible worlds containing an infinite number of creatures. The analogy between the best possible world (considered as an idea) and consequent will is even less apt. In the understanding the best possible world is the one judged to be so in comparison with all other equally possible worlds. These other possible worlds, having been rejected and without influence on the chosen world, will not be brought into existence by God. By contrast, consequent will is not the one that prevails over all others. It is the unique result of the combination of all antecedent wills. No antecedent will is, strictly speaking, suppressed or set aside, since each has its effect and influences the final decretory will. According to the "intellectualist" model, the best is solely determined by the understanding, which examines and weighs all the possibles and their infinite combinations. It is then recognized as best by the will and chosen to the exclusion of all others. Now, according to the "volitional" model, the best is the result of the interplay of antecedent wills. Thus, *all of these wills*—without exception—contribute to the final will, even if all of them do not obtain their end.

(2) Furthermore, the distinction between antecedent and consequent seems difficult to reconcile with an account of the relation between understanding and will according to which the will ("the origin of existences") is considered as a secondary faculty that comes into play only at the end of the intellectual process in order to authorize what the understanding ("source of essences")[193] has already conceived, according to a logical priority. On this account, the best possible world does not result from the combination of all antecedent wills in the final will. Rather, it is a possible series represented ideally in the divine understanding together with an infinite number of others. This series, which is complete and fully determined right down to the smallest detail, is afterward proposed to the will for its approval. What then becomes of the "volitional mechanism" described above? While Leibniz does appeal to it, it can be integrated into the explanation only artificially and at the cost of considerably distorting its character:

> It follows that among the infinite number of possible series God has selected the best, and that consequently this best universe is that which actually exists. For all things in the universe are in mutual harmony and the truly wise will therefore never decide without having taken the whole into consideration, nor will his judgment bear on anything but the whole. With regard to the parts taken separately, the *divine will may have been antecedent*; with regard to the whole, *it must be understood as a decree.*[194]

While the antecedent will, insofar as it considers the good in itself, can be assimilated without difficulty to the *particular* will (which concerns an isolated part), a shift in meaning has certainly occurred with regard to the consequent will, which becomes synonymous with *general* will (whose object is the whole). Leibniz passes imperceptibly from the "physical" model of the composition of wills, in which out of the conflict of particular goods arises the greatest quantity of good in the whole (the whole is engendered by the parts)[195] to a "harmonic" model. According to this latter model, the whole preexists its parts, and the idea of the whole determines the choice and disposition of its constitutive elements as illustrated by a comparison drawn this time not from mechanics, but from art, and in particular architecture.[196] In this way, "it may happen that for a construction or a decoration one will not select the most beautiful or the most precious stone, but the one which fits best into the empty space."[197] The best is not so much the maximum of particular goods that can be realized, as the maximum effect and order obtained at the universal level with the minimum of means, materials and expense. The particular good becomes a "subordinate"[198] end with regard to the best, which is understood as the good of the whole and the ultimate end.

Still, might not the "volitional" mechanism be reconciled with the "harmonic" conception in the same way that the order of efficient causes accords with the order of final causes? The reconciliation remains difficult, since the meaning of "consequent" changes in moving from one model to the other. On the one hand, the consequent is conceived as the result of the antecedent (according to a relation of cause and effect), while on the other hand, it is conceived as a total decree to which all partial decrees are subordinate. In the latter case, the relation between antecedent and consequent runs in the opposite direction, since the generality of the design determines the elements it contains:

> As God can do nothing without reasons, even when he acts miraculously, it follows that he has no will about individual events but what is a *consequence* of some general truth or will.[199]

The general will is logically prior to the particular, so that it appears as it were "antecedent," whereas the particular will is the result of the general, so that it appears as it were "consequent." To be sure, the distinction between general and particular will is not based on the fact that the object of the will is the whole, or a thing considered separately, but rather corresponds to the distinction between rule and exception.[200] However, beyond the question of miracles at issue here (which can only be a violation of the laws of nature and not of the general order), the rejection of the possibility of "primitive particular volitions" in God has larger implications. For the point is not merely that God cannot violate the general order and will something in particular without reason. It is that he can will nothing particular, neither an event nor an individual, in isolation and without relation to an infinite number of other things. No particular decree can be conceived independently of a total decree that concerns the entire series to which the particular thing under consideration belongs. How then can we understand the idea of an antecedent will that considers each good individually and in isolation, if by definition, that good cannot be conceived by itself nor be separated from the universe with which it is connected? How can God will some particular being, action, or event without this will amounting to a general will or without being dependent upon such a will (in conformity with the thesis of the unique universal decree)?

Moreover, the appeal in certain texts to wisdom as an intermediary between antecedent and consequent contributes nothing by way of clarity or coherence. On the contrary, the understanding now seems to intervene directly in the volitional process, which until now had been considered independent:

> Nevertheless, when one says that *goodness* alone determined God to create this universe, it is well to add that his goodness prompted him *antecedently* to create and to produce all possible good; but that his wisdom made the choice [*le triage*] and caused him to select the best *consequently*; and finally that his power gave him the means to carry out *actually* the great design which he had formed.[201]

The distinction between antecedent and consequent is no longer internal and specific to the will but applied to the relation between God's faculties. The final will is no longer the "mechanical" result of the composition of antecedent wills nor even the effect of the combination of middle wills. Rather, it is that which follows from the mediation of wisdom, which selects from among the possibles, which are first the object of the antecedent will. This insertion of the understanding into the "volitional mechanism" engenders some confusion, since the need to proceed to a "triage" is contrary to the idea of a conflict of the *conatus*, which concur immanently and by themselves to form a unique final inclination (the consequent will).

In sum, four explanatory models of the creation of the best possible universe can be distinguished. Two of these adopt the point of view of God's understanding and will respectively. These are, on the one hand, the "metaphysical mechanism" and on the other hand, what I have called the "volitional mechanism," which cannot be to the will exactly what the former mechanism is to the understanding. The remaining two models consider understanding and will together in an attempt to link up the two "mechanisms." On the one hand, the "harmonic" model contrasts prior wills to the final will as parts to the whole (represented by the understanding) at the cost of altering the relation of antecedent to consequent. On the other hand, the "mixed" schema suggests a collaboration in which wisdom constitutes the *medium* by which one passes from the previously willed antecedent (the good) to the finally willed consequent (the best).

The problem is that these four explanations are not simply theoretical constructions developed ad hoc with an eye to resolving this or that particular difficulty. Leibniz appeals to them on a number of occasions and does not hesitate to juxtapose them or even to mix them together in the same text, as in the following passage:

> I shall say that God, by virtue of his supreme goodness, has in the beginning a serious inclination to produce, or to see and cause to be produced, all good and every laudable action, and to prevent, or to see and cause to fail, all evil and every bad action. But he is determined by this same goodness, united to an infinite wisdom, *and* by the very concurrence of all the previous and particular inclinations towards each good, and towards the preventing of each evil, to produce the best possible design of things. This is his final and decretory will. And this design of the best being of such a nature that the good therein must be enhanced, as light is enhanced by shade, by some evil which is incomparably less than this good, God could not have excluded this evil, nor introduced certain goods that were excluded from this plan, without wronging his supreme perfection. So for that reason one must say that he permitted the sins of others, because otherwise he would have himself performed an action worse than all the sin of creatures.[202]

Here, Leibniz lumps together by means of the conjunction "and" two distinct ways of interpreting antecedent and consequent will and of conceiving the transition from one to the other: by uniting goodness with wisdom *and* by the interplay of particular inclinations united together in the manner of physical motion (or according to the dynamic analogy). Then, in line with a third interpretation (whole/parts), he goes on to invoke the harmonic totality, whose perfection requires those particular defects that God does not will in themselves but cannot eliminate without himself being at fault. The simultaneous appeal to three different models merits two remarks. The first concerns Leibniz's way of doing philosophy; the second concerns the consistency of his doctrine.

(a). The multiplicity of models reveals great conceptual inventiveness and fecundity. At the same time, however, their imperfect correspondence, or even incompatibility, suggests a limit to the overall coherence of the (or a) "system." Recognition of this fact leads us to distinguish, within Leibniz's texts, specific explanatory systems, or "partial" systems or "microsystems," which coexist at different levels, sometimes in the same work—or even in the same paragraph! These variants show that there can be no unique and absolutely unequivocal explanation of God's choice of world—except perhaps at a very general level—and that Leibniz is led to complicate his model as he enters further into the description of the combination of possibles in the understanding and the combination of inclinations in the will. The differences among the models and arguments he employs are explained by the goal at which he aims: whereas the "metaphysical mechanism" aims to show that the best emerges as the most rational (while nevertheless preserving contingency), the "volitional mechanism" aims to guarantee God's goodness and justice by showing that he never wills sin but only permits it in the name of a superior good.

(b). This multiplicity of explanatory models and the difficulties to which it gives rise should not be allowed to obscure an undeniable convergence to which the previously cited text briefly alludes: whatever interpretation we choose of the transition from antecedent to consequent, it is always "this same goodness" that is exercised by God and that lies behind all his actions. There remains throughout the idea of a will in two "stages": first, a "pure" will which aims at every possible good, followed by a will that tends by itself (internally) to the best or is oriented to the best by a distinct faculty (wisdom) i.e., externally. This distinction within the will is of fundamental importance for the justification of God, since it shows that if it is always good to *will* the good, it is not always good to *produce* it. God is good because he wills all good, but he is just because he actualizes the good only when it is fitting to do so. The good is the object of goodness; the best is the object of justice insofar as it is goodness in conformity with wisdom. God is as much justified with regard to his antecedent will (he is not lacking in good will) as with regard to his consequent will, by which he does his duty (he is not lacking in power).

Ultimately, behind these different models lies the same conception of permission as the will not to prevent the sin of another in order to avoid sinning oneself. God would have sinned himself had he prevented the sin of his creatures, since this would have led him to reject the best universe, which contains it. This permission is conceived to make it possible to reconcile an infinite hatred of vice and an infinite love of virtue (an abiding inclination to eliminate evil and produce good) with the actual existence of sin.

## NOTES

1. T pd §82, GP VI, 98; Huggard, 120. See also T §6, GP VI, 106; Huggard, 127: "if there are plausible appearances against us there are proofs on our side."
2. T s, I; GP VI, 377; Huggard, 378. Emphasis added.

3. Leibniz to Thomas Burnett (October 30, 1710), GP III, 321. Emphasis added.
4. Cf. NE IV, 21, §§1–4, A VI, 6, 524, passage cited p. 146.
5. Cf. for example DM §1; GP III 29–38.
6. This question is not raised until §20.
7. T §8, GP VI, 107, Huggard, 128 (emphasis added; translation modified). See also §218, GP VI, 248.
8. T §8, GP VI, 107, Huggard, 128. On the meaning of this duty, see section 5.2.2.
9. See section 5.2.2.
10. See the title of DM §3.
11. *Treatise of Nature and Grace* I, I, §14.
12. *ST*, Ia, q. 25, a. 6, ad. 3.
13. Cf. T §208. Cf. Grua, 492: "I believe that the ways must be included in the work, for the means that God chooses are themselves ends as far as possible, so that the greatest amount of good possible is produced."
14. Cf. DM §3.
15. T §8, GP VI, 107, Huggard, 128.
16. Notice that all three presuppose that there are an infinite number of possible worlds, rather than the existence of a single possible world (the one that exists).
17. Following Leibniz's analogy at §416 of the *Theodicy*.
18. Here it must be remembered not only that not all the possibles are compatible among themselves (§201), but also that the created world is unique. Leibniz rejects the idea of simultaneous existence (in different places) or successive existence (at different times) of a plurality of worlds (cf. §8).
19. For among these worlds, there are some in which the just are damned and the wicked rewarded with eternal felicity. Such universes, which are contrary to justice, are incompatible with divine perfection (cf. Grua, 300; GP IV, 344).
20. T §196, GP VI, 232, Huggard, 249.
21. Leibniz to Coste (December 19, 1707), GP III, 401, AG 194.
22. Cf. A VI, 3, 463; DM §1.
23. DM §1.
24. Cf. A VI, 3, 520.
25. Cf. *Elements of True Piety*, A VI, 4-B, 1362; Leibniz to Molanus (April, 1677), A II, 1, 478–479.
26. Cf. *Tentamen Anagogicum*, GP VII, 278.
27. DM §5; L 469.
28. Which cannot constitute a whole properly speaking.
29. T §195, GP VI, 232, Huggard, 249.
30. According to the formulation in *Causa Dei* (§15).
31. T §195, GP VI, 232; Huggard, 249.
32. On this point, see Leibniz's refutation of the arguments of the theologian François Diroys at §§200 and 202.
33. Cf. above 4.2.3.
34. Cf. T §208.
35. GM V, 334.
36. *Response to the Accusations of M. Nicolas Fatio Duillier*, GM V, 347.
37. Thus, the brachistochrone is the curve (equivalent to the arc of a cycloid) which allows a heavy body to pass from one point to another in the least possible time.
38. Cf. *On Affects*, A VI, 4-B, 1426.

39. This uniqueness is represented by the reunion of twins (or, we might say, by the absence of a twin, that is of a symmetrical case) in the analysis of the reflection of light in a convex or concave mirror. Cf. *Tentamen Anagogicum*, GP VII, 275.
40. Ibid., 273; L 780.
41. Cf. DM §22.
42. Cf. *Tentamen Anagogicum*, GP VII, 279.
43. Ibid., 272; L 779. See also T pd §2.
44. These laws guarantee that the universe is the best ordered and most intelligible system, in which there are "the same quantity of total and absolute force or of action, also the same quantity of relative force or of reaction, and, finally, the same quantity of directive force," and in which the equivalence between the full cause and the entire effect is respected (PNG §11, L 1039; see also T §346).
45. Cf. PNG §11.
46. "a little like the saying in jurisprudence, *Quae contra bonos mores sunt, ea nec facere nos posse credendum est*" (*Tentamen Anagogicum*, 278; L 787).
47. T §227.
48. T §288.
49. *Tentamen Anagogicum*, 272–273; L 780.
50. T §213, GP VI, 245; Huggard, 261.
51. *Tentamen Anagogicum*, 272; L 780.
52. Recall that this occurs as a marginal note by Leibniz (*Dialogus*, A VI, 4-A, 22).
53. Cf. *On the Radical Origination of Things*, GP VII, 304.
54. T §9, GP VI, 107, Huggard, 128.
55. T §10, GP VI, 108, Huggard, 129.
56. T §9, GP VI, 107, Huggard, 128.
57. On the uniqueness of the universal decree, see T §84; GP III, 35; *Causa Dei*, §42; Leibniz to Coste (December 19, 1707), GP III, 400; and section 3.3.1 this chapter.
58. T §9, GP VI, 107, Huggard, 129.
59. On the distinction between a condition *sine qua non* and a means, see chapter 3, p. 125, T §158 and §230, and *Causa Dei* §36 and §39.
60. Cf. T §10.
61. T s, I, GP VI, 377, Huggard, 378.
62. T ob, §27, GP VI, 435, Huggard, 441. It is in this way that Leibniz's paradoxical declaration must be understood: "To permit evil, as God permits it, is the greatest goodness" (T §121, Huggard, 195).
63. Cf. T §125, GP VI, 180.
64. With regard to this distinction, see Leibniz to Wolff (February 21, 1705), GB, 19.
65. GB, 172: "*perfectio* est harmonia rerum . . . seu consensus vel identitas in varietate."
66. A VI, 3, 116: "Similitudo in varietate, seu diversitas identitate compensata."
67. GB, 172.
68. Leibniz to Bourguet, GP III, 558.
69. GB, 172.
70. Of particular interest on this point is Gregory Brown, "Leibniz's Theodicy and the Confluence of Worldly Goods" (1994) in *G. W. Leibniz: Critical Assessments*, edited by Roger S. Woolhouse, 466–467.
71. T §124, GP VI, 179, Huggard, 198.
72. Cf. T §120.
73. Cf. *Elements of Natural Law*, A VI, 1, 479.
74. CP, A VI, 3, 122; Sleigh, 45.
75. T §105, GP VI, 161, Huggard, 181.

76. T pd §25, GP VI, 65.
77. See, for example, A VI, 4-A, 135; A VI, 4-C, 2786.
78. Cf. A VI, 4-C, 2787. See also Leibniz to Conring (March 19/29, 1678), A II, 1, 599. A definition is the expression of the concept we have of a thing (the thing defined or the term). Contrary to Hobbes, definitions are not arbitrary. In order to be suitable for use in demonstrations, a definition must be *real*, that is, it must establish that its object is possible (i.e. does not imply a contradiction).
79. Cf. A VI, 4-B, 1658.
80. Cf. *Specimen of Discoveries* . . . , A VI, 4-B, 1616; A VI, 4-B, 1659-1663. As Herbert Knecht has correctly pointed out, the distinction between two kinds of truths does not rest simply on this formal property of analyticity. This logical property is rather the indication and the sign of the real and objective difference between them. See Knecht (1981), 216.
81. It must be borne in mind that "all contingent propositions have reasons for being as they are and not otherwise or, what amounts to the same thing, that they have a priori proofs of their *truth* which make them certain and which show that the relation between subject and predicate of these propositions has its basis in the nature of both. But we must consider too that these proofs are not demonstrations of *necessity*, since these reasons are based only on the principle of the contingency or of the existence of things, that is to say, on what is or appears to be the best among several equally possible things. Necessary truths, by contrast, are based on the principle of contradiction and on the possibility or impossibility of the essences themselves, without considering in this relation the free will of God or of the creatures." (DM §13, A VI, 4-B, 1549; L 478).
82. A VI, 4-B, 1454. See also A VI, 4-B, 1446: "it is necessary that God love himself, since this is demonstrable from the definition of God. But that God does what is most perfect cannot be demonstrated, for the contrary does not imply a contradiction, without which the contrary would not be possible, which is contrary to the hypothesis." Grua, 336; Grua, 351 and Grua, 493.
83. See Adams (1994), especially Chapters 1 and 2.
84. Cf. DM §13.
85. Cf. A VI, 4-B, 1454-1455.
86. As early as Leibniz to Wedderkopf (May, 1671), A II, 1, 187. See also CP, A, VI, 3, 132; NE II, 21, §23, A VI, 6, 182; T §51.
87. CP, A VI, 3, 137–138.
88. Cf. Adams (1994), 41.
89. Cf. Grua, 333 and 360.
90. Adams (1994), 40. See also, p. 42: "it is fair to say that the view that 'God chooses what is best' is contingent must not be regarded as a thesis of Leibniz's philosophy, much less as a basis of one of his principal solutions to the problem of contingency."
91. Rateau (2008), Chapter 7, 517–536.
92. T §129, GP VI, 182, Huggard, 201.
93. T §131, GP VI, 183, Huggard, 202. See also §158 and §159; *Causa Dei*, §67.
94. T §234, GP VI, 256, Huggard, 271–272.
95. Cf. T §235 and §171 (against Abelard).
96. T §282, GP VI, 284, Huggard, 299.
97. Cf. DM §13, cited note 81.
98. "Even when it is only probabilities at issue, one can always determine what is most likely *ex datis*. It is true that this part of useful logic does not yet exist.

However, it would be wonderfully useful in practice, with regard to presumptions, indications and conjectures, to know the degrees of probability, when there are a number of apparent reasons on both sides of some important question. Thus, when there are not enough conditions given to demonstrate certainty, with regard to a question that is merely probable, one can always at least give *demonstrations concerning probability* itself. I am not speaking here of the probability of casuists, which is based on the number and reputation of Doctors, but of that which is drawn from the nature of things in proportion to what is known of it and which can be called verisimilitude" (A VI, 4-A, 706–707; emphasis added). See also, Leibniz to Burnett (February 1/11, 1697), GP III, 193–194.

99. *Plan of Catholic Demonstrations*, A VI, 1, 494, Ch. 5.

100. "Anything that is confirmed by numerous signs that could scarcely occur together unless it is true, is morally certain—that is, incomparably more probable than the contrary" (A VI, 4-A, 530). See also A VI, 4-A, 136; NE, Preface, A VI, 6, 68.

101. For example, the proof of a divine intelligence based on the beauty and finality observable in nature (*Plan of Catholic Demonstrations*, A VI, 1, 494, Ch. 5; *Conversation du Marquis de Pianese et du Pere Emery eremite*, A VI, 4-C, 2268; *On Freedom, Fate and God's Grace*, A VI, 4-B, 1604-1605), proof of the reality of phenomena (A VI, 4-B, 1502), the "motives of credibility" in favor of the truth of the Christian religion (T pd §5, §29; A VI, 4-A, 470).

102. " . . . est enim Theodicaea quasi scientiae quoddam genus . . . " (Leibniz to Des Bosses, February 5, 1712, GP II, 437).

103. See for example, *New Method . . .*, II, §14, A VI, 1, 301: "necessitas moralis dicitur *Obligatio*"; *Elements of Natural Law*, A VI, 1, 465: "*Obligatio* necessitas viri boni"; A VI, 4-C, 2778, 2838; A VI, 4-C, 2850: "*Obligatio* autem est moralis necessitas, illi nimirum imposita, qui viri boni nomen tueri velit," 2855, 2863.

104. See A VI, 4-C, 2778; 2863: "Nam quae contra bonos mores sunt ea nec facere nos posse credendum est: atque eo sensu dici potest, *jus* quod habemus agendi aut non agendi potentiam quandam sive libertatem moralem esse, *obligationem* vero necessitate." Cf. Digest 28, 7, 15.

105. Respectively, *Question* (1675), A VI, 1, 471; A VI, 4-A, 407; *Causa Dei*, §66, GP VI, 448.

106. GP III, 32, 33. Grua had already made this observation in JUT, 234.

107. Leibniz to Wedderkopf (May, 1671), A II, 1, 186.

108. Cf. A VI, 4-B, 1447; Grua, 333. The expression is taken from Augustine (*Against the Second Reply of Julian*, Book I, 100).

109. Cf. A VI, 4-B, 1520: "It is in a way a matter of physical necessity that God does everything in the best possible way. . . It is also a matter of physical necessity that the angels or the blessed, who are confirmed in the good act in accordance with virtue . . . "

110. DM §32; L 499.

111. *Tentamen Anagogicum*, GP VII, 278; L 787.

112. Leibniz offers opposing responses in A VI, 4-B, 1452 and A VI, 4-B, 1652.

113. Cf. Grua, 493–494.

114. T §122, GP VI, 177, Huggard, 196 (emphasis added). Cf. *Causa Dei*, §38.

115. GP III, 32; *Causa Dei* §36; S 121. Cf. Romans, III, 8.

116. GP III, 32–33 (emphasis added). The same example of the soldier occurs at T §24; *Causa Dei*, §66. See also the similar example borrowed from Descartes at T §165.

117. It is an "indispensable duty" (T §24, GP VI, 117). In God, the law of the best "admits of no exception or dispensation" (T §25, GP VI, 117).
118. In T pd §2 (Huggard, 74), it is equated with the "the wise one's choice which is worthy of his wisdom." It is the "principle of wisdom and goodness" (T §174; see also §128).
119. Cf. section 3.1.2, p. 100–102.
120. T s, VIII, GP VI, 386; Huggard, 387.
121. Ibid.; T §175, GP VI, 219; T §374, GP VI, 338; T ref §3, GP VI, 390.
122. Cf. T s, VIII, GP VI, 386.
123. Ibid. See also the *Fifth Letter to Clarke* (August, 1716), §7, GP VII, 390, L 1134: "For when a wise being, and especially God who has supreme wisdom, chooses what is best, he is not the less free upon that account; on the contrary, it is the most perfect liberty not to be hindered from acting in the best manner. And when any other chooses according to the most apparent and the most strongly inclining good, he imitates therein the liberty of a truly wise being, in proportion to his disposition. Without this, the choice would be a blind chance."
124. T §121, GP VI, 175, Huggard, 194–195.
125. Cf. T §191, GP VI, 230.
126. On this conditionality, see the example of the entrusting of arms and the promise (T §121).
127. The consideration of probability does not apply to God, who is omniscient and for whom "nothing is doubtful" (T §25, GP VI, 117).
128. T §27, GP VI, 118, Huggard, 138.
129. *Causa Dei*, §66, GP VI, 449, S 128.
130. T §121, GP VI, 175, Huggard, 194–195 (emphasis added).
131. T §129, GP VI, 182, Huggard, 201.
132. T §131, GP VI, 183, Huggard, 202 (emphasis added).
133. Indeed, it must be remembered that, "this design of the best being of such a nature that the good therein must be enhanced, as light is enhanced by shade, by some evil which is incomparably less than this good, God could not have excluded this evil, nor introduced certain goods that were excluded from this plan, without wronging his supreme perfection. So for that reason one must say that he permitted the sins of others, because otherwise he would have himself performed an action worse than all the sin of creatures" (T ref §11, GP VI, 397–398, Huggard 402).
134. This position is reminiscent (though occurring in a very different metaphysical framework) of the one defended in *Confession of a Philosopher*. Cf. above chapter 2, p. 60–61.
135. Knebel (1991), Murray (1995 and 1996).
136. Leibniz to Des Bosses (February 5, 1712), GP II, 436–437.
137. Leibniz to Des Bosses (June 16, 1712), GP II, 450.
138. Cf. Anfray (2011), 64–65.
139. *Causa Dei* §66, GP VI, 449.
140. *Meditation on the Common Notion of Justice*, Mollat, 42; R 46.
141. *On Freedom, Fate and God's Grace*, A VI, 4-B, 1596.
142. Cf. Anfray (2011), 64–65.
143. Cf. ibid., 76.
144. John of Damascus, *An Exact Exposition of the Orthodox Faith*, II, 29; Thomas Aquinas, *ST*, Ia, 19, 6, ad 1; *On Truth*, question XXIII, 2; Duns Scotus, *Reportationes parisienses*, I, dist. 46, qu. XI.

145. Cf. §5, A VI, 1, 538.
146. Leibniz to Spanheim (February 20, 1699), Grua 448–449; trans. Strickland, http://www.leibniz-translations.com/spanheim.htm.
147. See Grua, 468.
148. *Synopsis* (December, 1705), Grua 474.
149. It is for this reason that the distinction between antecedent will and consequent will is introduced in the *Theodicy* in a discussion of the problem of permission (§22), well before the question of election is taken up (in §80).
150. Notably in GP III, 30, 31–32. See also Leibniz to Naudé (December 29, 1707), Grua 502.
151. T §22, GP VI, 115; Huggard, 136.
152. These are also referred to as "detached" or "particular" wills (T §22, GP VI, 115–116), "prior," "inclining" "less complete" and relative (*secundum quid*) wills (*Causa Dei*, §24, GP VI, 442). In the *Monadology* (§90), they will also be called "presumptive."
153. Also called "complete," "final and decisive" and "total" (T §22, GP VI, 116), "decretory" and "absolute" (*Causa Dei*, §24, GP VI, 442), "secret" (*Monadology* §90). Without altering the general explanatory schema, consideration of a "middle volition" (T §119, GP VI, 170) allows for the possibility of particular combinations of goods and evils that are intermediate between antecedent wills and consequent will. See below, p. 227.
154. T §22, GP VI, 116, Huggard, 136–137.
155. This distinction, which is of Scholastic origin, is criticized at Grua, 442–444. In Section §164 of the *Theodicy*, Leibniz explains in what sense it can be accepted, referring to the example of the sacrifice of Isaac commanded, but not willed in itself by God (who demands obedience, but not the act).
156. GP III, 31.
157. T §404, GP VI, 354, Huggard, 365.
158. *Causa Dei*, §25, GP VI, 442; S 119. See also NE II, 21, §30, A VI, 6, 183.
159. T §22, GP VI, 116, Huggard, 137 (emphasis added). Cf. *General Rule for the Composition of Movements* (September 1693), GM VI, 231–233; *Two Problems Constructed by G. W. Leibniz using his General Rule for the Composition of Movements*, GM VI, 234: "Problem II. Given a single moving body that is pushed simultaneously by an infinite number of solicitations, find its motion. I call 'sollicitations' the infinitely small efforts, or *conatus* by which the moving body is solicited or invited, so to speak, to move, as is the case for example with the action of gravity, or of the centrifugal tendency, of which an infinite number would be required to compose an ordinary movement."
160. T §117, GP VI, 250, Huggard, 187.
161. T §222, GP VI, 250, Huggard, 266.
162. *Causa Dei* §27, GP VI, 443, S 119: "Hence it is evident that even the antecedent wills are not altogether vain, but have their own kind of efficacy. For though they produce effects, these effects are not always full, but are restricted by the concurrence of other antecedent wills."
163. T §325, GP VI, 309, Huggard, 322.
164. Cf. GP III, 30.
165. See, for example, GP III, 31 and T §80.
166. T §84, GP VI, 148, Huggard, 168.
167. *Causa Dei*, §27, GP VI, 443, S 119–120. Nothing can offend, inconvenience or aggrieve God (T §114, GP VI, 166).

168. T §23, GP VI, 116, Huggard, 137. See also GP III, 31.
169. Cf. T §119.
170. *Causa Dei*, §36, GP VI, 444, S 121.
171. GP III, 32; T §119, GP VI, 170; §153, GP VI, 201; §209, GP VI, 242.
172. T §25, GP VI, 117; Huggard 138.
173. Cf. *Causa Dei*, §28 and §37.
174. Cf. *Causa Dei*, §28; T §158; T s, IV, GP VI, 382, Huggard, 383: " . . . one may say with the same reason, that God wills by his antecedent will that men sin not, and that by his consequent or final and decretory will (which is always followed by its effect) he wills to permit that they sin . . . "
175. In logic a condition *sine qua non* is that upon which a thing depends such that if it is absent or suppressed, so is the thing itself. Leibniz equates it with the prerequisite: "*Requisitum* est suspendens natura prius, <vulgo causa sine qua non>" (C 471). See also A VI, 3, 587.
176. *Causa Dei* §39, GP VI, 444; S 122. Cf. Matthew 18:7; Luke 17:1.
177. Cf. GP III, 35; T §10, GP VI, 108; T s, I, GP VI, 377.
178. T §23, GP VI, 116, Huggard, 137; *Causa Dei* §39, GP VI, 444.
179. Cf. John 12:24. Cf. *On the Ultimate Origination of Things*, GP VII, 307–308.
180. T §23.
181. In accordance with vindictive justice. On this point, see section 7.1.4.
182. Cf. Grua, 474; GP III, 32; *Causa Dei*, §35.
183. T §122, §241; *On the Ultimate Origination of Things*, GP VII, 307–308.
184. GP III, 32; *Causa Dei*, §35, GP VI, 444.
185. Cf. T §124, GP VI, 179 (cited above p. 199). See also T §200, GP VI, 235, Huggard, 251: "If each substance taken separately were perfect, all would be alike; which is neither fitting nor possible."
186. T §120, GP VI, 173, Huggard, 193.
187. T §245, GP VI, 263, Huggard, 278. Cf. Leibniz's writings on the formation and history of the earth, in particular *Protogaea*, edited and translated by Claudine Cohen and Andre Wakefield, University of Chicago Press, 2008.
188. T §378, GP VI, 340, Huggard, 352.
189. Cf. T §25.
190. Cf. T §342, GP VI, 318, Huggard, 330–331: "There are also many painful evils that it is not in our power to avoid. As a break in the continuity of our body is a consequence of many accidents that may happen to us, it was natural that this imperfection of the body should be represented by some sense of imperfection in the soul." The structure of the human body "involves susceptibility to pain" (T §343, GP VI, 318, Huggard, 331). See also Leibniz to Veyssière La Croze (December 2, 1706), Dutens V, 483: "Often good men are unhappy. Moreover, a difficult death accompanied by raging and moaning, being the effect of illness and the constitution, can happen to the best Christian in the world."
191. Cf. T §119.
192. Cf. T §225; *Causa Dei*, §15.
193. T §7, GP VI, 107.
194. *Causa Dei*, §41, GP VI, 445, S 122 (emphasis added).
195. Cf. GP III, 31: "fit ut ex conflictu omnium voluntatum antecedentium oriatur *Voluntas consequens* seu *decretoria*, sapientiae maxime conformis, per quam oritur, quantum maximum oriri potest."
196. Cf. T §78; §119; §200; §215.
197. *Causa Dei*, §137, GP VI, 459, S 143.

198. GP III, 32; *Causa Dei*, §39; §136, GP VI, 459, S 143: "But it is not always the supe-riority [*praestantia*] of the object, taken absolutely, which constitutes the reason for selection. Frequently the fitness of the object for a certain purpose, given a certain set of conditions, will bear a greater weight."
199. T §206, GP VI, 240, Huggard, 256 (emphasis added). See also T §337. "Consequent" appears here in a sense as "antecedent" and "antecedent" as "consequent."
200. On these two senses of the distinction, see DM §7.
201. T §116, GP VI, 167, Huggard, 187. Wisdom combines all possibles and "the re-sult of all these comparisons and deliberations is the choice of the best from among all these possible systems, which wisdom *makes in order to satisfy good-ness completely*; and such is precisely the plan of the universe as it is" (T §225, GP VI, 252, Huggard, 267–268; emphasis added). See also *Causa Dei*, §26.
202. T ref §11, GP VI, 397–398, Huggard, 402 (emphasis added).

# CHAPTER 6

⚘

# Evil in Being and in the Actions of Creatures

## *Reality or Appearance?*

## 6.1 GOD'S PHYSICAL CONCURRENCE, THE ORIGIN AND NATURE OF EVIL

### 6.1.1 A Complete, Continuous, Immediate, and Special Concurrence

The divine will stands at a double remove from sin, since God neither sins nor wills the sin of creatures. He merely permits sin as a condition sine qua non of the best possible universe. His moral concurrence with sin does not call into question his goodness, justice, or holiness. Still, is not God the author of sin by his power, given that he does not merely allow it to occur but also furnishes the sinner with both the force and occasion to commit it?[1] Indeed, "someone will perhaps object that it is God himself who acts and who produces all that is real in the sin of the creature."[2] All things depend on God. No being can persevere in existence or act unless God conserves it—that is, creates it anew each moment and confers the power to act upon it. Is it not the case, then, that God is an accomplice to every sin that is committed? Here the accusation shifts from God's will to his power, from his moral concurrence to his physical concurrence, by which created substances exist and carry out all of their actions. The solution to the difficulty rests in large part on the theoretical advances of the previous years, concerning the origin of evil in creatures (their original imperfection) and its privative nature, as illustrated by the analogy with the inertia of bodies.[3]

The actions of creatures require God's permanent physical concurrence on account of the state of dependence in which creatures find themselves with regard to God, who is the source of their being and the cause of all that is positive in them. In fact, the term "physical" carries two meanings here. On the one hand, it refers to an *ontological* reality: God's physical influence is nothing but the being he bestows on creatures, the perfection or quantity of reality or essence he gives them. On the other hand, it refers to the idea of *nature* and its laws: God's physical concurrence is his natural or ordinary concurrence (as opposed to his extraordinary concurrence, by which miracles are brought about). In this latter sense, it designates everything that occurs in creatures and by creatures by means of efficient causes, according to the order of nature (as opposed to the order of grace).

For Leibniz, the question of physical concurrence is indistinguishable from that of conservation and creation (since conservation is only a continuous creation), except that it concerns more specifically God's influence on the *actions* of creatures. In addition to the semantic ambiguity in the term "physical," there is also an ambiguity in the word "concurrence," which suggests the coming together of two or more causes that collaborate to produce the same act. This cooperation suggests that it would be possible to determine the contribution of each cause—in the case at hand, to distinguish within evil that which is owing to man and that which is owing to God. Now, very early on, from the time of *On the Omnipotence of God*, Leibniz had shown the impossibility of any form of partial concurrence on account of the absurdity of dividing the act into two parts (of which only the "sinful" part would be imputable to humans[4]) or of separating the act itself from its moral status as sin.[5] For Leibniz, then, concurrence is *complete* and *continuous* in conformity with the natural and perpetual dependence that the creature must have on its creator. This concurrence is likewise *immediate* and *special*. On this point, Leibniz opposes the defenders of a "general and mediate" concurrence, reducible to the conservation of created being and without any direct participation in its particular actions. At the same time, he distances himself from those, like Bayle and Malebranche, who "[carry] the cooperation of God too far" and go "so far as to deny action to creatures."[6]

Concurrence is *immediate* for two reasons. First, because God, though existing outside the world (as the transcendent or *supramondain* being), operates immanently and constantly within it, since everything that is real and positive in creatures and their actions emanates from him. Secondly, because his physical influence is no less great in the effect (the act committed by the creature) than in the cause (the creature itself). God does not concur with the effect (sin) merely by virtue of producing its cause (the sinner)—that is, indirectly and mediately. Rather, he does so immediately and directly by producing the effect itself in its material reality (insofar as sin contains something real from the ontological point of view).[7]

Concurrence is *special* and determined in that it is exactly proportioned to the nature and individual characteristics of the relevant creature and act. Concurrence is appropriate for its object "according to what it is and to the state wherein it is," such that "the conservation of a man standing is different from the conservation of a man seated."[8] This *proportionality* of the divine operation can be understood in two ways: from a *qualitative* and a *quantitative* point of view. From the *qualitative* point of view, divine conservation does not consist solely in causing a thing to exist, but also in determining its manner of existence, its qualities, and its accidents (insofar as they include something positive). In other words, God does not limit himself to giving the creature being and the power to act. He affects and modifies its state in accordance with the rules his wisdom has chosen and by which he governs the world (physical and moral laws[9]). From the *quantitative* point of view, it must be realized that the good man and the sinful man do not require the same quantity of divine power to remain in existence, since their moral difference is grounded in an ontological one. At the moral level, to say that one man is better than the other is to say that the one is worthy of praise and reward while the other merits blame and reprobation. At the metaphysical level, it means that the former participates in being to a greater extent than the latter. The same holds true for actions. God's physical influence is specifically differentiated by the virtuousness or viciousness of the action, the former of which contains more perfection than the latter. It is adapted to the thing (being or action), because it concerns only what is real in it.

> In acting, God concurs with the actions of things and directs them, even the evil ones, since in bad actions, too, there is some perfection, which must result from God.[10]

In concurring with sin, God only produces "that which is good in evil [*quod in malo bonum est*],"[11] that is, the portion of positive reality contained in it. However, what we might call *the evil in evil*, that in evil which is bad, comes from creatures and results originally from their natural imperfection.

Thus, within the same act it is possible to distinguish that which is owing to God and that which is owing to the creature, while still considering this act as complete and strictly indivisible at the very moment at which it occurs. Indeed, there can be no (temporal) priority between the production of the essence of a creature by God and the production of the action of that same creature. However, there is a *logical* priority or priority of nature:

> When God produces the thing, he produces it as an individual and not as a universal of logic. I grant it. However, he produces its essence before its accidents, its nature before its operations, following the priority of their nature, and *in signo anteriore rationis*. Thus we can see how the creature can be the true cause of the sin, while conservation by God does not prevent the sin. God disposes in accordance with the preceding state of the same creature, in order to follow the laws of his wisdom notwithstanding the sin, which in the first place will be produced by the creature.[12]

Consideration of this logical priority allows us to understand at what level or logical "moment" the efficacy of creatures occurs within a system that, while positing a complete and thoroughgoing divine concurrence, rejects occasionalism. Although the creature cannot concur with its own creation and conservation (otherwise it would exist prior to itself), it concurs effectively with God by its internal operation in the production of its affections and actions[13] even in the very instant at which it is produced. Its concurrence is not a creation, since it consists only in following or limiting what is received from God.[14] When we analyze (in thought) the process of conservation-operation in continuous creation—a process in which two free actions are encountered (those of God and the creature)—it is possible to identify the moment of sin and to attribute it solely to the creature, which freely restricts the perfection and grace that come from God.

By preserving the unity of the produced act, while at the same distinguishing within it what is owing to divine operation from what is owing to human limitation, the Leibnizian doctrine of concurrence avoids the reduction, favored by the occasionalists, of created substance to a cause that is inefficacious in itself. The creature is not only the author of sin from the moral point of view, by virtue of its will, but also its cause from the physical point of view, by virtue of its imperfection and resistance (as illustrated by the comparison with natural inertia of bodies). On this point, one cannot help but notice the similarity with the theses developed after 1680. However, the more complete presentation in the *Theodicy* offers additions and modifications with regard to three points. (1) It eliminates all reference to Nothingness as the "origin of origins" in favor of ideal causality and explicitly locates the principle of evil in God (6.1.2). (2) It defines evil as a privation and divides it into *metaphysical, physical,* and *moral* (6.1.3)—a division which, with regard to the notion of "metaphysical evil," raises certain difficulties (6.1.4). (3) It takes up and develops the analogy with inertial motion in order to explain concurrence and the actions of creatures, without, however, resolving certain difficulties to which the analogy gives rise (6.2).

### 6.1.2 The Ideal Origin: The Divine Understanding as Principle of Evil

In the *Dialogue on Human Freedom and the Origin of Evil* (1695), Leibniz looked beyond the natural imperfection of creatures for the origin of this origin and appealed to a "principle" of Nothingness distinct from God. In the *Theodicy*, the investigation of the origin of evil consists in identifying its *location* in the divine faculties and ultimately traces its causal origin to God's ideas. To the traditional question formulated by Boethius, "If God exists, whence evil? If he does not exist, whence good?"[15] Leibniz responds, in conformity with orthodox Christianity, by eliminating all reference to a principle other than God:

> The ancients attributed the cause of evil to *matter*, which they held to be uncreated and independent of God: but we, who derive all being from God, where shall we find the source of evil? The answer is, that it must be sought in the ideal nature of the creature, in so far as this nature is contained in the eternal truths which are in the understanding of God, independently of his will.[16]

If everything derives from God, evil itself must have its source in him, although in a way that renders him not guilty. How shall we conceive of this origin that is at once in God—in accordance with the dogma of one unique principle—*and* in the creature, even prior to its sinning, such that the sin might be imputable to it? The solution consists in locating this origin in the divine understanding, the only faculty by which God cannot be incriminated (unlike his will and power), since God is not the author of essences and eternal truths. At the same time, this origin will be closely associated with the creature, by placing it within its essence.

As we have seen, Leibniz developed a theory of moral and physical concurrence that was able to exonerate God by making sin wholly imputable to the will and action of the sinner. Leibniz now proposes an explanation of the origin of evil that can render God innocent by attributing "responsibility" (so to speak) for evil to the nature of things, over which God has no control. In this way, God is justified with regard to each of his attributes: by his *wisdom* he comprehends all possibles without being their author, by his *goodness* he only permits (but does not will) sin to become actual, and by his *omnipotence*, he causes "that which is good in evil." In each case, evil is always imputable to man (either to his nature or freedom), even though man is entirely dependent upon God, from whom he draws his being and his power to act. By nature, man is imperfect and prone to sin; by his ignorance and limited intelligence, he mistakes evil for good; by his malice or bad will, he inclines to evil; and by his inherent lack, he limits the perfection that comes from God, by committing sin.

Thus, the origin of evil is the idea of evil. This origin involves both an original and ideal *nature* (the imperfection of the creature) and a determinate *location*: "the *Region of the Eternal Truths*," which "must be substituted for matter when we are concerned with seeking out the source of things."[17] This has two consequences: (a) the possible is the ultimate cause of evil, beyond which there is no further cause to be sought; (b) the divine understanding becomes, properly speaking, the "principle" of evil.

(a) Evil arises from the creature considered in the state of pure possibility. Its origin is directly related to the status of the creature as creature. Limitation is not accidental to the creature, but constitutive of its essence, because "a being exempt from limitation would not be a creature, but God."[18] The creature, as creature, is defined by what it is not, what it lacks, what separates it from the supremely perfect being. At the same time, it is individuated by the particular way in which it limits being. The creature is "limited in this sense, that its greatness, power, knowledge, and all its other perfections are limited or restricted." Because this limitation is both inherent to the creature and insurmountable

> the foundation of evil is necessary, while its actualization is but contingent. In other words, it is necessary that evil be possible, but contingent that it be actual.[19]

The term "original" refers to the realm of the possible. Original imperfection is both logically and temporally prior to the original sin committed by Adam (which sin is the reason for the sins of his descendants) insofar as it indicates the priority of the possible to the actual and of the condition to the causally conditioned. Inscribed in the nature of things, it is, properly speaking, a condition sine qua non that is both *necessary* and *eternal*.

Let us examine this necessity more closely. It is a necessity of essence, but not a necessity of existence. Indeed, everything that is not God must carry this limitation or essential imperfection (since a perfect creature is contradictory). However, this limitation is only a possibility with regard to existence, since it is not necessary that there exist something limited (God could have decided to create nothing at all). This necessity (of imperfection) belongs to the nature of the created thing in general. However, from the point of view of essence, it implies no necessity with regard to the particular defects of any individual creature. In other words, if the imperfection of the creature is necessary, its degree of imperfection is not, since a creature can always be conceived as more or less perfect than it is. Finally, this necessity leaves intact the freedom of both the divine choice and of all human actions, since what follows from the necessary need not itself be necessary. Already in the *Confession of a Philosopher*, the distinction between the modality of the cause and the modality of the effect had made it possible to show that the necessity of the first term (God) did not prevent the contingency of events (sins) in the series that derives from it.[20] The same holds true for original imperfection. Although the reason for all evils must ultimately be sought in this natural limitation, which is the "first and most remote" cause of moral and physical evil,[21] its necessity does not render the fall necessary, nor the sins that follow inevitable.

Original imperfection is the first and necessary cause as well as the *eternal* cause of evil, since it belongs to the ideas in the divine understanding:

> Evil springs rather from the *Forms* themselves, but which are abstract, that is, from the ideas, which God has not produced by an act of his will, any more than he thus produced numbers and figures, or any more than all possible essences which one must regard as eternal and necessary; for they are in the ideal region of the possibles, that is, in the divine understanding.[22]

The origin of evil is eternal as God himself, for the idea of evil, and consequently its possibility, are in the divine understanding. *In this respect*, evil is independent of the divine will, as are numbers and essences. Just as God cannot bring it about that the sum of the angles of a triangle is not equal to two right angles, so he cannot remove evil from the nature of things, nor make it the case that evil is not contained in the best possible plan of the universe or that there is no evil (at least *metaphysical*) from the moment he decides to create something. For even a world without sin or suffering could not fail to have the defect of not being wholly perfect. The eternity of this origin lies in the metaphysical limitation that perpetually marks the creature, once it has been brought into existence, even when its virtue raises it to the perfection of the saints.

(b) This eternity and independence with respect to God (or, more exactly, with respect to his will) are characteristics that, in the *Dialogue on Human Freedom and the Origin of Evil*,[23] Leibniz attributed to Nothingness, which he elevated to the rank of a principle distinct from God. Henceforth, Leibniz attributes them to the original imperfection of possibles, which now seems to suffice without any need to recur to Nothingness as a higher level of explanation. The advantage of this solution is obvious: it allows Leibniz to avoid Manichaeism in all its forms, by locating the "dualism" within God himself:

> There are indeed two principles, but they are both in God, to wit, his understanding and his will. The understanding furnishes the principle of evil, without being sullied by it, without being evil; it represents natures as they exist in the eternal truths; it contains within it the reason why evil is permitted: but the will tends only towards good. Let us add a third principle, namely power; it precedes even understanding and will, but it operates as the one displays it and as the other requires it.[24]

In place of Manichaeism, which posits two rival entities external to one another, Leibniz substitutes a duality within God himself, or rather, a triad that exactly corresponds to the distinction among his faculties. These faculties (power, understanding, and will) can in turn be related to the Trinity (Father, Son and Holy Spirit).[25] In this way, the combat between a good and evil principle envisaged by the Manicheans is replaced by the internal relation between God's will and understanding. There is no war within God, but rather a will for the best that inevitably prevails over all other wills and chooses the most perfect universe while permitting the evil associated with it.

For Leibniz, the theoretical weakness of Manichaeism lies in a lax and overly simplistic explanation that violates the principle of parsimony by attributing evil to an express principle, a *principium maleficum*, as one might attribute cold to a *primum frigidum*. According to Leibniz, "there is nothing so easy and nothing so unimaginative."[26] Evil does not require such a principle, nor even, properly speaking, a particular principle in God. For, in reality, his understanding cannot be said to be the principle of evil without at the same time being the principle of good, insofar as it contains the ideal source of all things. In fact, the region of eternal truths is "the *ideal cause* of evil (so to speak) as well as of good."[27] To make of the divine understanding the principle of evil is only a manner of speaking, which is especially appropriate to the polemical context of Leibniz's debate with Bayle (who claims to revive the Manichean hypothesis). For, strictly speaking, there is no principle of evil, understood as a distinct principle that is really separable from the principle of good. Even when considered in its primitive source, evil is never, so to speak, "pure" and unadulterated. Leibniz shows this by calling a halt to the search for the origin of evil at the essential imperfection of creatures (that is, in God). Evil can never be conceived abstractly, separate from the being, perfection, good, or power of which it is the limit, the restriction, the vice, or the corruption.

By locating the dualism within God, Leibniz dispels the absurd specter of an evil god. There is no evil god, since evil is in God in the form of an idea—that is, of a possible. According to Leibniz, this thesis in no way calls into question God's holiness. Nevertheless, it does raise a problem within a theoretical framework according to which the possible is something more than a mere fiction or imagination. While it is certain that *to think of evil* does not mean to have evil thoughts or to be evil (otherwise omniscience would be an imperfection and would suffice to render God guilty), it is still the case that the essence of creatures is not, for Leibniz, merely a representation of the understanding: it is *realized* in God.[28] Divine intelligence is not an "external" contemplation of all ideas and essences. It knows them because it is their place ("region") of existence. Of course, they exist there not in act, but in potentiality: in potentiality to exist and even striving for existence. Their reality is not merely mental. It is founded in God; it is the reality of God himself insofar as he is indistinguishable from the nature of things.[29] What, then, of the imperfect or evil possible?

Leibniz accepts the traditional thesis that all things exist in God *eminently (eminenter)* without their limits and imperfections. However, he maintains that they are completely represented in the divine understanding with their limits and imperfections.[30] In this, he rejects the commonly held distinction between knowledge of things as they are in themselves (finite and limited) and as they are in God (without limit or imperfection). God does not know beings through the beings themselves, but rather through himself, by knowing himself. Leibniz maintains that "God's understanding is the source of the essences of created things, such as they are in him, that is, bounded."[31] As Fernand Brunner has pointed out, Leibniz had already defended this thesis against Arnauld, arguing that "the complete and comprehensive notions are represented in the divine understanding, as they are in themselves."[32] The assertion that the divine understanding is the principle of evil is evidently the direct metaphysical consequence of this epistemic position. Brunner rightly observes that this consequence is highly problematic in that it is incompatible with divine perfection, insofar as it introduces limitation and nothingness into God.[33]

The question, in my view, becomes the following. Even if nothing bad can be imputed to the divine will, which tends to the good, can God's supreme perfection be reconciled with an idea of evil (imperfection, sin, and pain in the state of mere possibles), understood not as an inert tableau or purely mental representation, but as a certain thing (*res*) existing in the divine being and striving for existence? These seem difficult to reconcile. To be sure, the striving is proportional to the perfection of the thing under consideration, so that the more imperfect a thing is, the less weight its *conatus* will have. Nevertheless, it is still in God and makes itself "felt," at least negatively, in his will. Likewise, it affects in some sense his power, understood as the common subject, the divine essence. Moreover, there is on this point an unbridgeable gap between what I have called the intellectual mechanism and the volitional mechanism (see 5.3.3). Whereas, according to the former, every possible, even if it is very imperfect (for example, a sin), must tend, however weakly, to existence; according to the latter, the will ought not to incline, even weakly, to its realization, but on the contrary ought to tend as much as possible to oppose it. The *conatus* is all the more powerful in the latter case, as it is weaker in the former.

### 6.1.3  The Privative Nature of Evil and Its Division into Metaphysical, Physical, and Moral

In eliminating all reference to Nothingness as a principle of evil, Leibniz is not content to reject all forms of dualism. He argues that evil must not be considered as a pure non-entity (even in relation to its ultimate origin), but as a *privation* of being. This amounts to the claim that evil is not extrinsic to being, but arises out of its various degrees. Why? Because it cannot be conceived independently of the subject to which it belongs (substance and its actions) and so to distinguish it from its subject would be as absurd as to conceive a limit independently of what it limits. Evil is neither a substance nor a pure negation. It is not a nothingness shorn of all attributes and qualities. It is a lack of perfection, which alters and diminishes being without destroying it.

We have already had occasion to observe the confusion on which Leibniz knowingly[34] trades between *negation* and *privation*. Doubtless, this is because he considers the distinction to be, if not irrelevant, then at least secondary. At the level of generality at which the definition of evil is to be found—a definition which must be applicable to all evils—the distinction is useless. Lack of perfection (negation) and lack of *due* perfection (privation) are equally an absence of superior perfection,[35] a non plus ultra. Whether the thing lacks this perfection by nature (as a stone lacks sight) or is accidentally deprived of what it ought to have (as a man who is blind) is a question of secondary importance. The unified understanding of evil, which Leibniz works to establish by effacing the distinction between negation and privation, is accomplished, as we shall see, through the no-tion of *metaphysical evil*.

However, notice that Leibniz clearly seems to prefer—at least in the *Theodicy*—the term privation to that of negation, as if he ultimately considered the former more adequate for defining evil. One might have thought, on the contrary, that "negation" would be more appropriate, be-cause it is less determinate insofar as it refers generally to *any* absence of being or perfection. There would seem to be two reasons for Leibniz's pref-erence. First, "negation" refers more to nonbeing, to which evil cannot be reduced. Second, the notion of privation allows him to emphasize the role of the creature, which, as a *defective* cause, restricts by its own limitation the perfection and being it receives from God. The creature "deprives it-self," so to speak, of an increase in perfection that it might have possessed had it been less limited. It can now be seen why Leibniz sometimes defines evil as that which "comes from" or "follows from" privation,[36] which itself derives from the original imperfection of creatures.[37] Privation produces evil. Privation is the effect or consequence of the original imperfection, which refers to God's ideas ("the region of the possibles"), whereas priva-tion relates most often to the nature of the thing existing in act.

From a terminological point of view, the most important innovation in the *Theodicy* is, of course, the division of evil into *metaphysical, moral,* and *physical* at §21. The distinction between evil of guilt (sin) and evil of pun-ishment (pain) had been commonplace since the time of Augustine.[38] On the other hand, the decision to treat the essential imperfection of creatures as an evil is unusual. Indeed, it is rejected by the tradition on the strength of the distinction between negation and privation. Thomas Aquinas holds that not every lack is an evil, but only the lack of good that a thing ought to have by nature (privation).[39] For Suarez, the imperfection belonging to limited being, even if it is the cause of evil, must not be considered an evil in itself, but only a negation. Otherwise, all creatures would have to be declared bad for the simple reason that they are not perfect like God.[40]

Commentators have investigated the origin of this notion of *meta-physical evil* and sought to identify the authors who might have inspired Leibniz. Grua draws an interesting parallel with Tommaso Campanella, who distinguished "relative [evil] in physical things" and "privative [evil] in moral things" from a "negative [evil] in metaphysical things."[41] William King may also have been a source of inspiration, since Leibniz says of King that "he divides [evil] as we do into metaphysical, physical and moral"[42] in chapter 2 of his *De Origine Mali* (London, 1702). However, nothing in the *Theodicy* indicates the influence of Campanella, who is cited, but only with regard to an entirely different question.[43] King, on the other hand, is explicitly invoked, and his views discussed in the *Observations on the Book Concerning the Origin of Evil published recently in England* included as an annex to the work. However, besides the fact that King speaks of evil "of imperfection"[44] and not, properly speaking, of "metaphysical" evil, the connection to Leibniz remains difficult to determine.[45]

In a recent article, Maria-Rosa Antognazza shows how the Leibnizian notion of metaphysical evil "accounts for the kind of evil that Aquinas and, especially, Suarez called natural evil."[46] Why then does Leibniz replace the traditional term "natural evil" with the new term "metaphysical evil"? According to Antognazza,

> Metaphysical evil concerns the nature of possible beings contemplated by God's intellect as constituents of possible worlds. It is at this stage of metaphysical possibility that we find the origin of what others would call natural evil. The reason for God's permission of congenital deformities and malfunctions, and, in general, natural defects or irregularities, is to be found in the natures of things which are compossible in a given world.[47]

I have likewise argued (in section 6.1.2) that the possible is the origin of evil insofar as one finds there the necessary and eternal imperfection characteristic of creatures. However, that alone does not explain the choice of the term *metaphysical*, since moral and physical evils are equally represented in the divine understanding as mere possibles and constituents of possible worlds. Yet, they are not, for all that, called "metaphysical" by Leibniz. The consideration of the metaphysical possibility at the origin of the actual world and of all the evils it contains cannot, by itself, justify the use of the term *metaphysical* to characterize one particular kind of evil in opposition to moral and physical evil. Furthermore, while the comparison with natural evil, as understood by the Scholastics, is doubtless pertinent, it must not be forgotten that the term *metaphysical evil* has for Leibniz a much broader signification than what they understood by *natural evil* (as we shall see).

Before examining what Leibniz means by "metaphysical evil" (the concept), I would like to make two remarks concerning the expression he has chosen (the word).

(1) First, contrary to what Antognazza (following Grua[48]) maintains, Leibniz is not the first to use the term "metaphysical evil." We find in the Benedictine Joseph Saenz de Aguirre, in his *Ethical Disputes on the Virtues and Vices* (Salamanca, 1677), a division of good and evil into "metaphysical, physical, moral and divine." The term "metaphysical good" designates the good in itself, insofar as it is convertible with being and so constitutes a transcendental term. According to Saenz de Aguirre, "it signifies the

essential perfection of being, of any kind whatsoever." By contrast, "metaphysical evil is that which is convertible with privation of being, since it essentially consists in the privation of good, and for this reason, cannot but be foreign to all perfection and goodness, since it excludes all perfection and goodness, as blindness [excludes] sight, and darkness, light."[49]

The book by Saenz de Aguirre, who was made cardinal in 1686, received a second edition at Rome in 1697. I do not know whether Leibniz read it, but it is certain that he was familiar with the "learned cardinal"[50] and in particular, with his *Large Collection of all the Councils of Spain and the New World* (Rome, 1693–1694).

(2) However that may be, Leibniz did not necessarily need to read the work of Saenz de Aguirre to forge the expression "metaphysical evil." For, while that term may seem unusual and novel, the term "metaphysical good," on the other hand, is more common. It can be found in Francesco Piccolomini in his *Comprehensive Philosophy of Morals*[51] (Venice, 1583) in which he divides the good into "moral, physical, metaphysical and divine." "Metaphysical" is treated as synonymous with transcendental or transcendent. This is confirmed by the definition that Scipion Dupleix provides in his *Ethics or Moral Philosophy* (Paris, 1610): "Metaphysical good is transcendent good, which receives a reciprocal conversion with being."[52] Thus, the division of good into "metaphysical, physical, moral" to which is sometimes added "divine" and "artificial" is already present in the philosophy manuals and ethical treatises prior to Leibniz. It can even be found in certain dictionaries, such as Pierre Godart's *Philosophical Lexicon*.[53] Finally, recall that Spinoza, in his *Metaphysical Thoughts* (Part I, Chapter VI, §8), published in 1663 as an appendix to the *Principles of Descartes' Philosophy*, criticized those who vainly seek a "metaphysical good" that would be absolute, that is free from any relation.

We can now see how Leibniz can assert that "good and evil are *commonly* understood in three senses: metaphysical, physical and moral."[54] It is true that the general practice was to apply the term "metaphysical" only to good and not evil (which is not a transcendental). However, it would have been easy to coin the term "metaphysical evil" with reference to its opposite. Moreover, it would seem that in Leibniz's own writings the use of the term "metaphysical good" preceded the "invention" of the expression "metaphysical evil." Annotating the *Theosophia* of Johann Christoph Sturm,[55] Leibniz pauses over the definition of perfection as a "condition that places the thing in a better state" and comments, "it would have been worthwhile to explain what is being called *good* here, for I do not think it is taken here in a moral, but in a *metaphysical*, sense."[56] Since being is convertible with good, then perfection, understood as quantity of being or essence, can be called a "good," not in the sense of a moral quality, but in the sense of a supplemental degree of reality. Considered with regard to this "metaphysical" sense of good, "metaphysical evil" would naturally designate its privation, the lack of being and imperfection.

### 6.1.4 The Problematic Notion of "Metaphysical Evil"

The similarity between Leibniz's division of good and evil and that of his predecessors is terminological rather than conceptual. This similarity should not be allowed to obscure the originality of Leibniz's conception of metaphysical evil. It should be noted in the first place that by affixing the term "metaphysical" to the notions of good and evil, Leibniz extends these notions not only beyond the realm of moral action (virtues and vices, with their physical rewards and punishments) but also beyond rational creatures, applying them to all beings. This extension poses two problems. The first relates to the definition of metaphysical evil itself, which is at once general and restricted (1). The second difficulty lies in the ambiguous relationship between metaphysical evil, on the one hand, and physical and moral evil on the other hand (2).

(1). Metaphysical evil is "that of imperfections." It "consists in simple imperfection" or in imperfection in general,[57] whatever the creature's nature (rational or not).[58] It is evil in the broadest sense of the term. This generality must be understood in two senses:

(a). In an *extensive* sense, since it is not limited to spirits but concerns all beings, rational as well as non-rational, animate as well as inanimate. Monsters, disorders in the world, and irregularities of nature are visible examples of such evil in the realm of nature.[59]

(b). In a *generic* sense, since moral and physical evil, as particular imperfections, constitute the species of metaphysical evil that belong to a certain category of substances, namely spirits.[60] Considered as a genus, metaphysical evil includes a whole variety of evil: original limitation of creatures, privation, sin (of all kinds: original, actual, habitual, venial, and mortal), suffering (whether punishment of the sinner or the trials of the just man), harmful animals, monsters, irregularities, and imperfections in nature.

This extended use of the term has been criticized by Louis Bourguet, who, doubtless relying on the Scholastic distinction between negation and privation, refuses to consider metaphysical evil as genuine evil. Rather than adhering to the general definition offered in the *Theodicy*, Leibniz responds by offering an explanation which serves to limit the meaning and extension of this evil:

> [B]ut, Sir, if you allow for Metaphysical good, the privation of this good will be a metaphysical evil. When an intelligent being loses his good sense, without suffering and without sin (and so, without physical or moral evil), do you not consider this an evil? In any case, you would do nothing but change the meanings of terms.[61]

Leibniz's explanation does not seem to be entirely satisfactory on account of the restriction introduced by his chosen example. Metaphysical evil is portrayed as the absence of a good that the being *ought to have* possessed: the loss of reason in a rational creature. Thus, there is a shift from imperfection in general to privation of due perfection, that is, to a particular kind of imperfection. What, then, shall we say of the original imperfection of creatures? Can it still be assimilated to a metaphysical evil, given that it is not the lack of a perfection that the creature *ought* to have, but the limitation inherent in its essence, the negation of everything it is not and indeed *ought* not to be in order to confirm to its nature? It is true that in offering this example, Leibniz aims not so much to explain metaphysical evil as to emphasize that it constitutes a separate kind of evil distinct from and independent of moral and physical evil (since it can occur in the absence of sin and suffering). However, the persistent confusion between negation and privation unquestionably renders the notion of metaphysical evil equivocal.

This ambiguity in the term "metaphysical evil" is reinforced by Leibniz's use of it to designate more particularly the defects of creatures that lack reason. Leaving aside the general sense, its use tends to become more specific such that it is ultimately reserved for non-rational beings. Leibniz notes that while "metaphysical good or evil is perfection or imperfection in general," "they [the terms *metaphysical good* and *metaphysical evil*] are used specifically of those goods and evils that occur to non-intelligent creatures or, so to speak, non-intelligent creatures."[62] The particular sense of the term seems to dominate when metaphysical evil is opposed to or compared with two other kinds of evil:

> [T]he moral or physical good and evil of rational creatures does not infinitely exceed the good and evil which is *simply metaphysical*, namely, that which consists in the perfection of other creatures.[63]

The distinction between moral and physical evil, on the one hand, and metaphysical evil, on the other hand, now parallels the distinction between spirits and other creatures. Metaphysical evil is thus "simple imperfection" not so much in the general sense applicable to all forms of imperfection, as in the sense of its lowest degree, its most elementary and least determinate form—namely, that which exists in the first instance in creatures without reason. To be sure, this imperfection must be found in rational creatures, since the inferior is always included in the superior. However, under the name of physical evil and moral evil, it takes on new characteristics and more complex determinations, which make it the preserve of spirits alone and distinguish it from the simple or sole "metaphysical" evil belonging to other created beings.

(2) It may be that Leibniz does not speak of metaphysical evil in the case of spirits, because moral and physical evil, which are peculiar to them, presuppose it. Indeed, moral and physical evil are always owing to a real defect residing in the being itself. An act of sin contains less reality than a good act, since the action produced is never limited to a moral relation (whence, as we have seen, the specific differentiation of God's physical concurrence). As for suffering, it is the felt indication of a substance passing to a lesser degree of ontological perfection. In this sense, all evils are "metaphysical," such that Leibniz seems right to retain, contrary Bourguet's opinion, the general notion of metaphysical evil. However, Leibniz's desire to distinguish explicitly three kinds of evil shows that, even if sin and suffering must always be traced back to an ontological foundation, they cannot be entirely reduced to it.

Such, in fact, is the principal difficulty raised by the distinction between three kinds of evil. Metaphysical good and evil consist in realities or degrees of perfection, physical good and evil in the passions (the feeling of moving from one degree to another) in conformity with justice in the case of punishment and reward. Moral good and evil consists in actions (the cause of transition from one state to another) whose signification and ends are ethical and juridical. I have already pointed out (see section 4.2.3) the difficulty that attends a global calculus of goods and evils in the universe, insofar as this calculus places on the same level (on the basis of their possible reduction to metaphysical goods and evils) perfections and imperfections that are specifically distinct and moreover belong to different creatures. Is not the unity of these three types of evil merely nominal? No. It is real once all evil is defined as an "imperfection" and so can be reduced to a metaphysical evil. However, apart from the common characteristic of being an ontological lack, does imperfection have the same meaning in the case of the natural limitation of created being as in the case of voluntary sin? The status of metaphysical evil, which is meant to ground and guarantee the unity of the concept of evil, is highly problematic:

i. In its very definition, metaphysical evil appears as both the most general expression (and in principle the most complete) of evil and as its weakest expression—the least "bad" of the evils and the one perhaps least deserving of the name (whence Bourguet's objection). It is that which is properly and fundamentally evil, the very essence of evil, while at the same time, it is that in the original imperfection of creatures, which is not sufficient to render one guilty or punishable.

ii. In its relation to moral and physical evil, it is both the *genus*, of which they are species, and their *cause*, since it is the origin of all evils, and especially of original sin, from which suffering arises as punishment. Genus, cause, species (insofar as it constitutes the evil of creatures devoid of reason), metaphysical evil also designates imperfection in the whole in contrast with the defects of the parts. Indeed, it is in terms of this part-whole relation that Leibniz sometimes seems to conceive metaphysical good, which he equates with the greatest general perfection:

> It follows that the evil that is in rational creatures happens only by concomitance, not by antecedent will but by a consequent will, as being involved in the best possible plan; and the metaphysical good *which includes everything* makes it necessary sometimes to admit physical evil and moral evil.[64]

This good "includes everything" insofar as it includes both physical and moral good (particular perfections), but also, and especially, insofar as it concerns the best harmony in the whole by producing the most beautiful universal order. In this latter sense, metaphysical good is not so much the sum total of all the particular goods of rational and non-rational creatures as the expression of the perfection of the whole, which may require, and indeed must result in, certain imperfections in the parts. It is the most perfect overall, the object of God's consequent will. Its primacy[65] over other goods, both moral and physical, as well as "metaphysical" (in the particular sense of the term) is nothing but the primacy of the whole over its parts in accordance with the "law of the best." Metaphysical evil must be understood as the privation of this *general* good—that is, as the worst of evils (disharmony, or a less perfect universe). The will to prevent it must likewise prevail over the will to prevent physical and moral evil, which concern only individual beings. In other words, metaphysical evil must be avoided as much as possible, even at the cost of those particular evils, which occur by accident or as sine qua non conditions in the best possible world.

The semantic plurality of "metaphysical evil" renders the term highly equivocal. Given its strictly ontological definition it seems incapable of explaining the ethical, juridical, and perhaps even physical (i.e., suffering) aspect of evil. At the same time, by its designation as evil, it seems inappropriate in a metaphysical context on account of the confusion between negation and privation to which it gives rise. Being equally capable of designating a particular evil (that of non-rational creatures) as of the evil in the whole, it ends up being too imprecise to be truly useful and fecund. Paradoxically, Leibniz is clearly committed to it and even undertakes to defend it against criticism, whereas in point of fact he makes very little use of the concept in the texts, abandoning it on most occasions in favor of the more accurate and less problematic term "imperfection."

## 6.2  THE INERTIAL MODEL AND ITS APPLICATION TO CREATURELY ACTIONS: FROM PECCABILITY TO MALICE

### 6.2.1  The Illustration of Divine Concurrence by the Natural Inertia of Bodies

The definition of evil as privation is traditional. Leibniz is aware of this and, on this point, explicitly identifies himself as an intellectual heir of Augustine. However, at the very moment in which he pays homage to the illustrious church father, Leibniz makes clear that Augustine's definition "is considered a subterfuge and even somewhat chimerical in the view of many people."[66] To which one is tempted to add "and in the view of Leibniz himself," at least at the time of *On the Omnipotence of God*! Has Leibniz changed his mind? No, certainly. The similarity is only apparent, since privation does not have the same sense for him as for Augustine and the Scholastics. For Leibniz, it is expressly associated with the notions of capacity and receptivity, as illustrated by the analogy with inertial motion.

As we have seen, the nature of a thing determines both its aptitude for realizing a certain quantity of perfection and a resistance to additional perfection. Positively, it is the definition of a particular reality (the created being), while negatively, it is its non plus ultra that prevents that being from acquiring any additional reality. As an effort that impedes further being, this limitation internal to the thing is compared, beginning in the years 1685–1686, to the retardation observed in bodies by Kepler and

Descartes (see 3.2.2). This physical analogy, which is taken up again and further developed in §30 of the *Theodicy*, is considered "as a perfect image and even as a *sample* of the original limitation of creatures" (emphasis added). The image becomes an example or a particular case, since the phenomenon of inertia is itself based on a property of passive force inherent in the monad.[67] Thus, evil is treated as just one case of privation among others (observable especially in physics).

Leibniz offers the example of boats variously laden with wood or stone descending a river. It is certain that they will not all travel at the same speed, presuming they are not aided by wind, or oar, or in some other way. What is the cause of the slowness of those that are most heavily laden? It is not, properly speaking, the gravity, since all the boats are descending, but rather the inertia intrinsic to matter. The inertia is greater as the mass is greater. The speed, equally impressed on the boats by the current, represents the positive reality dispensed by God to all creatures. The inertia, which is proportional to the load of the boats and the cause of the slowness of those that are heaviest, represents the original imperfection of creatures, which opposes the perfection, being, and force produced by God.

> The current is the cause of the boat's movement, but not of its retardation; God is the cause of perfection in the nature and actions of the creature, but the limitation of the receptivity of the creature is the cause of the defects in its action. Thus the Platonists, St. Augustine and the Schoolmen were right to say that God is the cause of the material element of evil which lies in the positive, and not of the formal element, which lies in privation. Even so one may say that the current is the cause of the material element of the retardation, but not of the formal: that is, it is the cause of the boat's speed without being the cause of the limits to this speed. And God is no more the cause of sin than the river's current is the cause of the retardation of the boat. Moreover, force is to matter as the spirit is to the flesh; the spirit is willing and the flesh is weak.[68]

The comparison with inertia is not merely a physical illustration of a metaphysical thesis. On the one hand, it allows Leibniz to highlight the passive power of created beings, by assimilating it to a kind of anti-*conatus*. On the other hand, it allows him to develop an explanatory model applicable at the physical, metaphysical, and even moral levels, since the power that slows the motion of a body or limits the ontological perfection of a substance is of the same kind as that which is at work in sin and the obstinacy of evil, resisting good and God's grace (see 6.2.2 and 6.2.3).

Just as matter is not indifferent to rest and motion, but "is originally inclined to retardation, or privation of speed,"[69] so the creature is not indifferent to the perfection it receives: it resists it by its very nature. Here again, there is no need to posit some distinct and external principle. For Leibniz, limited beings naturally resist being or additional being, as matter does motion. This resistance is inherent in them insofar as they are limited (and not infinite like God). It is for this reason that original imperfection (and the privation that results from it) is not simply a lack, an absence of being and perfection, but an opposition to being and perfection. Original imperfection has two aspects. First, it is that which "conserves" the thing (in the same way that inertia in the moving body perpetuates its primitive motion), preserves it as it is within the limits of its capacity (that is, within the limits of what it can receive), rejecting "surplus" being, which would threaten the integrity of its nature and risk destroying it. However, original imperfection is also that which "corrupts" the thing from the inside, by preventing its progress and complete development, to the point of producing new limitations and privations (just as motion in a body slowly exhausts itself and approaches rest tangentially). Unlike continuous creation by which God conserves the creature by continually granting it reality and perfection (positive conservation), the "conservation" at issue here is not content to maintain the created being within its narrow limits, but tends to diminish even further its receptivity (that is, a negative and restrictive conservation).

The principle of evil—though not evil itself—is thus fundamentally ambiguous. It guarantees the preservation of the nature of the thing, which is realized within the limits its nature prescribes. However, at the same time, it is the instrument of its corruption, leading it (by an inclination that is not necessary) to greater imperfection: error, bad will, and sin. However, in neither sense can it constitute a positive power nor be a source of action strictly speaking. Inertia excludes all action. Far from itself diminishing the speed it has received, matter merely "[moderates], by virtue of its receptivity, the effect of the impression when it is to receive it."[70] Retardation results from an intrinsic deficiency and not from an active, opposing force. The same holds true of the resistance peculiar to limited beings. This resistance results from a passivity that must be understood neither as a pure negation of power (otherwise nothing would oppose received perfection) nor as a positive, but an opposing force (which would no longer be passive and would therefore require a principle). Rather, it is an anti-*conatus* (and not an opposing *conatus*[71]) similar to laziness, numbness, lethargy, or torpor.

We must be careful not to attribute to passive force, which may seem to act by the resistance it opposes to change and progress, what in fact belongs only to active force. In tending to conserve the thing in its state, passive force cannot produce any action other than by accident, never by

itself: "Evil itself comes only from privation; the positive occurs only by concomitance, as the active occurs by concomitance in the cold."[72] The example
of water, which upon freezing breaks the barrel of a musket, illustrates this
point. Although the bursting of the firearm is indeed the result of a positive
action, this action is only indirectly owing to the cold, which is a remote,
defective cause. Its efficient, proximate cause is the increase in volume of
the air bubbles contained in the water, which follows upon the diminution
by cold of the "motion that separates the particles of the fluids." The action results from the inversion, provoked by the freezing, of the relation
between the force of dilation of the air (now increasing) and the water's
resistance to it (which is proportionally less). Thus, it is the dilation and
not the cold itself, which produces the rupture in the barrel: "thus it is *by
accident* that privation involves action and force." The same holds true for
evil, which "comes from privation; the positive and action spring from it by
accident, as force springs from cold."[73]

This *concomitance* of the positive and the privative, of the active and the
passive, can be understood in two ways:

1. It can be understood *consecutively*. Action results in fact from a new balance of power. It is the effect of the liberation of a force that had heretofore been contained or impeded. It is in this way that diminution of the
   motion that prevents the particles of air from aggregating leads to their
   dilation and so to the rupture of the firearm. The relation is here that of
   the remote and indirect cause to the proximate and immediate one.
2. It can be understood *simultaneously* and *concurrently*, in the action itself,
   although the matter of the effect can be attributed only to the positive,
   and its form only to the negative. Evil is a source of effects and acts, not
   by its own efficacy, but by that of the being it affects and corrupts. The
   force it uses is not its own: evil "operates" only by means of the active
   power it restrains and diverts from its good end. Here it is the direct
   cause (active power) that is corrupted, since the deficient cause alters
   the efficient cause.

Before going on to consider in the following sections (6.2.2 and 6.2.3)
the effects corresponding to this inertia at the moral level, it is worth
noting that the comparison between original imperfection and the natural
retardation of bodies presents a problem. The problem arises, in the first
instance, because, in the example of the boats, Leibniz separates what he
considers inseparable in physical concurrence: imperfection, on the one
hand, and that which it limits (namely, the nature of the thing), on the other
hand. On the physical level, Leibniz distinguishes three elements: the boat

(representing the creature), the cargo (the creature's imperfection), and the force of the current (received perfection). At the metaphysical level, he identifies only two elements: the creature's naturally limited receptivity, and the perfection continuously flowing from God. Leibniz restricts divine concurrence to the river current that carries the ships, whereas in reality, this concurrence, encompassing all that is positive, must include the ships themselves and all they contain.

Leibniz's application of the physical model to metaphysics also appears problematic in that imperfection—that is, the creature's lack of being—is paradoxically represented by the load, the excess weight (wood, stones). At the physical level, mass is a certain positive reality whose inertia is proportional to the quantity of matter: the greater the matter, the greater the resistance to motion. However, at the metaphysical level the creature contains a limited nature, whose imperfection is, by definition, inversely proportional to the quantity of being. Its greater receptivity to being and good cannot increase its power to resist them. Otherwise, one would have to hold that the more perfect a creature is, the greater its capacity for resisting, and the more imperfect it is, the less it is able to resist the good and the more it is disposed to do evil. From this it would follow that the more a spirit approaches divine perfection, the more it would be led to fall, and the greater its remove from this perfection (by its vices), the less it would be capable of evil and the less it would risk sinning![74] In fact, even at the physical level, Leibniz acknowledges that resistance is not so much a function of the quantity of matter as of "its difficulty of giving way."[75]

### 6.2.2 Inertia of the Understanding and Will

Inertia is not merely a physical and ontological property; it is also reflected at the moral level. Just as the perfection that derives from God is limited by the limited receptivity of the created being, so "all goods are due to the divine force [*vigor*]; the evils, to the torpor of the creature."[76] The dual nature of imperfection, which is at once lack and resistance, can also be seen in both the understanding and the will. Moreover, this dual nature explains both error and sin. On this point, Leibniz differs from Descartes, who locates the origin of error and evil in the disproportion between an infinite will and a limited understanding. Leibniz not only challenges the notion that the will extends beyond what the understanding represents to it (or, in other words, that one can will something of which one is ignorant)[77] but also holds that the origin of evil is to be found in these two faculties.

"Evil is therefore like darkness, and not only ignorance but also error and malice consist formally in a certain kind of privation."[78] On the intellectual level, ignorance is a lack of knowledge, which is excusable only if this lack is not owing to some fault or culpable negligence. Error is a privation, as illustrated by the classic example of the square tower that appears round from a distance. The thought that it is round "flows naturally from what I see." However, to leave things at that leads one to form a false judgment. Now,

> if I pursue the examination, if some reflection causes me to perceive that appearances deceive me, lo and behold, I abandon my error. To rest in a certain place, or not to go further, not to take account of some remark, these are privations.[79]

The content of the perception, its "matter" (the image of the round tower) cannot be false in itself, since all that is real and positive in ideas, as in things, comes from God, who cannot deceive. Error is the result of a dual restriction. The first is natural and follows from the fact that perception is limited, on account of the imperfect nature of the perceiver (the privation results from its limited receptivity). The second is voluntary, or partially voluntary, since it stems from the perceiver's failure to go beyond this sensible testimony with an additional act of reflection and attention[80] (here the privation results from laziness). Moral inertia is similar to physical inertia, although with this notable difference: physical inertia follows necessarily from created matter, whereas moral inertia merely inclines the mind, which freely chooses to yield to it by failing to go beyond the presentation of the senses. The error is owing, in the first place, to a natural defect (the limitation of perception), which is compounded by a lack of reflection that is more or less voluntary (which, for this reason, can be culpable).[81] Error is inertia and a premature cessation, by which I remain in my present state without making greater use of my understanding. The evil does not consist in seeing the round tower, but in making no effort to rectify this thought and even persevering in the error.

Such is the nature of what might be called *intellectual inertia*, which inclines the mind to cling to appearances and prejudices and which makes us act most often as mere "empirics" rather than follow reason.[82] This inertia also makes us succumb to paralogisms, to be persuaded by specious arguments, for the sake of ease and convenience, since rigorous observation of the rules of logic requires attention and effort. It is for this reason that we are often "accomplices in our errors" and even "pleased to go astray."[83] For Leibniz, the attitude of the skeptic, who on pretext of the general uncertainty of our knowledge and the need to conduct ourselves solely on the basis of appearances remains at "the surface of things," ultimately owes to this mental laziness.[84] Another result is the Lazy Sophism. Insisting on the ineluctability of fate is an easy excuse, a pretext for doing nothing and for neglecting reason and one's duties and even for committing all sorts of crimes. Acquiescence in this sophism explains superstitious practices and the consulting of fortune tellers, for people "would like shorter paths by which to arrive at happiness without difficulty"[85]—that is, to obtain the effect without bothering with the cause, to acquire the good without effort. The Lazy Sophism must be countered not only on the speculative level, by arguments that demonstrate its falsity, but also on the practical level, by struggling against this inertia of the understanding, by habitual use of attention and reflection.[86]

Corresponding to inertia of the understanding is *inertia of the will*, which likewise involves lack and resistance. In fact, it is the same fundamental inertia at issue, namely, the inertia inherent in the power or force of created substances, which manifests itself through these two faculties. The will of created spirits is imperfect by nature, since it naturally tends to the apparent good, rather than always and exclusively tending to the true good. By virtue of our imperfect freedom we are capable of choosing "evil instead of good, a greater evil instead of the lesser evil, the lesser good instead of the greater good."[87] The weakness of the human will and its lack of promptitude lead it to stop at certain goods before having attained the supreme good, the mere intellectual representation of which is not by itself sufficient to move and awaken the will. Whereas it ought to tend only to God, its supreme good, the will becomes malicious when it attaches "*through its inertia* to creatures,"[88] limits itself to sensory pleasures and inferior goods "to the detriment of greater goods, as of health, of virtue, of union with God, of felicity."[89] Malice presupposes that the sinner knows that he sins. It is, properly speaking, the will of sinning, or more exactly, the habit of sinning that resides in the will (since the will is not necessarily actual).[90]

Just as the error lies not in seeing the round tower, but in resting content with this perception in forming one's judgment, malice is not the enjoyment of sensible pleasures, but the limiting of oneself to them or the preferring them to superior goods, which alone are capable of providing true happiness. Evil consists in this stopping short, in "this privation of a further aspiration [*tendance*],"[91] which results from a lack of force and/or a culpable refusal to go further, from a resistance to the motion toward greater perfections and more solid pleasures. Even in malice, the will is not bad in itself (insofar as its object is good absolutely speaking and considered in itself), but only *relative* to the greater good it rejects. It involves evil by accident, or, rather, it tends to a good that is an evil insofar as it is an obstacle to greater goods. Thus, malice consists not in willing evil for evil's sake (which contradicts the idea of a will, which is always understood *sub ratione boni*), but in not willing the best.

### 6.2.3 From Original Imperfection to Actual and Habitual Sin

It is not enough to identify the nature and causes of ignorance, error, and malice. It must also be determined how and at what point privation, which begins as the inherent original limitation of the creature, becomes a sin. The transition from lack of perfection to obstinate resistance to the good and grace is continuous, though not necessary. It occurs in several stages, namely: *peccability, original sin*, and a *disposition* to sin that is first virtual, then actual, and finally habitual (synonymous at this point with *malice*).

(1) On account of its original imperfection, the creature is animated by two contrary motions. It is inclined to the good and perfection while at the same time being just as naturally led to stray from and resist them. God creates beings that are not only capable of disobeying him but also disposed (although not necessitated) to rebel against him. Thus, it would seem that corresponding to the natural repugnance of matter for motion (as observed in physics), there is in creatures, at the metaphysical level, if not a certain opposition, then, at the very least, a kind of fundamental reticence with regard to him from whom they receive their being. Such is the contradiction in which man finds himself. He is naturally inclined to love God (who is the supreme good) *and* to resist him, by limiting the gifts received from him (being, perfection, good, and grace). However, at this level, the limitation is evil (in the sense of metaphysical evil) without being culpable, and the inertia is all the weaker as the creature remains connected to God.

Here again, inertia cannot constitute a positive force, nor can imperfection be anything but a lack of power, a fallibility, the original weakness[92] of the creature. This natural deficiency is *peccability*. This peccability involves, on the one hand, the *possibility* of sinning, whose actualization can occur only with the concurrence of a genuinely active power. On the other hand, it refers more determinately to the *capacity* to sin,[93] or indeed (as the analogy with physical inertia suggests), to the *inclination* to sin, since "ignorance, error and malice follow one another naturally in animals made as we are."[94]

The *Theodicy* certainly places less emphasis than certain earlier texts on this original propensity for sin, this "inclination to sin, coming from the very nature of the creature," which is actualized once the creature is no longer sustained by divine grace.[95] In the *Theodicy* Leibniz clearly acknowledges that man finds himself "inclined by the original imperfection of creatures to misuse his free will and to plunge into misery," and maintains that man's "original limitation or imperfection is the source of his malice."[96] However, Leibniz seems keen to head off any misunderstanding, avoiding any formulation that might suggest the necessity of sin. Writing to Molanus, who had accused him of falling into "the Supralapsarians' unavoidable determination to positive evil," Leibniz replied in 1698:

> I had said that every creature is essentially limited, and I called this limitation or negation a privative imperfection, and I had added that this latter is the source of evil, not only of peccability, but also of sin itself. For, if creatures had had the entire degree of perfection [required], they would not have fallen.[97]

Sin was freely produced, yet it was certain and inevitable. Original limitation, together with certain circumstances, made it the case that Adam was bound to fall "actually." This limitation is a deficient cause that does not necessitate disobedience, since otherwise there would be no good angels (creatures equally stained with imperfection), only demons. For, "it must always be borne in mind that this origin of evil is only inclining and not necessitating."[98] Leibniz will emphasize this point in his correspondence with Des Bosses. In Adam there was neither an absolute (metaphysical or logical) necessity to sin nor even a moral one. There was only an inclination to sin, which gave rise to a predetermination to sin.[99] Furthermore, it must be emphasized that "Adam did not have a greater inclination to evil than to good from the beginning, that is, when he was created, but [only] at the time when he pursued sin."[100] At the moment of his creation, the inclination to good prevailed, but there were already "seeds [*semina*] of the future inclination to evil,"[101] since the present is big with the future. These "seeds" refer to the natural condition of the creature, that is, to the essential limitation and inertia which will persist even after the regeneration of man by Christ's merit. For, Christ's sacrifice can efface original sin and its effects but not that original weakness, which is the ineradicable dwelling place of evil. The source of sin remains and cannot be eliminated.[102] It will never cease to incline the mind toward sin, even if only weakly.

(2) What more is necessary for sin if original imperfection is not by itself sufficient? What is lacking is the intervention of free will and the conjunction of circumstances (that lead to temptation) described by scripture in Genesis. Leibniz does not dwell in the *Theodicy* on the reasons for the fall of the bad angels, relying for the essentials on the teaching of the sacred text. However, this does not prevent him from presenting in §18 a hypothesis based on pre-established harmony. Leibniz makes the devil the author of

sin, "the father of wickedness" and deceit.[103] The sin of Adam and Eve is portrayed as an act of transgression that was free and voluntary, albeit inspired by Satan. The fall was the result of a misuse of freedom.[104] It can be explained in keeping with the analysis of inertia discussed above (6.2.2). Malice stems from the laziness by which Eve (and then Adam) yields to the serpent's offer and constrains the motion of her will that ought to have settled on God alone, the supreme perfection. The inertia of the understanding (inattention, lack of due consideration despite God's enjoinder) conspires with that of the will, which succumbs to the sensible attraction and to pleasure.[105] From the original imperfection, we have now arrived at original sin. Mere peccability becomes culpable resistance to the divine commandments. As Leibniz writes in 1695:

> There was no positive evil in created things at the beginning, but they always lacked many perfections. Thus, because of a lack of attention, the first man was able to turn away from the supreme good and be content with some created thing, and thus, he fell into sin. That is, from an imperfection that was merely *privative* in the beginning, he fell into a *positive* evil.[106]

Original sin represents the transition from *privative* imperfection to a *positive* imperfection for two reasons:

a. Ontological limitation, which up to this point is involuntary, becomes moral when it is deliberately willed. Moral evil is a freely accepted limitation. It implies that the mind knowingly stops at an inferior good instead of turning to God. No longer does man merely suffer imperfection; he consents to it and yields to its movement which causes him to fall.

b. In sin, evil goes from the state of mere privation to the state of *possession* (so to speak), not only because what formerly existed only in potentiality is now actualized, but also because the inertia is considerably reinforced by this actualization. From imperfection there arises even more defect along with a positive inclination to sin. This "positivity" does not represent a negative quantity (according to the Kantian definition), but an excess of privation, an aggravation of the deficiency, which, being associated with active force, engenders particularly harmful effects for the sinner (Adam) and his descendants.

(3) Sin is called *original*, because it constitutes a second nature over and above original imperfection. This second nature, which is a source of new imperfections, is degraded in relation to the first nature, since

it has contracted a vicious and habitual disposition,[107] an "ordinary and perpetual inclination" to sin, sometimes referred to as "peccaminosity" (*peccaminositas*).[108]

> *Original sin* has such force [*vis*] that it renders men fragile in the body, and in the spirit dead until regeneration. It inclines the intelligence to sensible things and the will to things of the flesh. Hence we are by nature children of wrath.[109]

With the occurrence of the first sin, the initial condition of man was fundamentally altered and a habit of sinning immediately created. This alteration, in accordance with the hypothesis of pre-established harmony, concerns both body and soul.[110] Sin, which is a moral evil that follows from a metaphysical evil (original imperfection), gives rise to a new metaphysical evil: the fragility of the body, henceforth subject to illness, suffering and death, and the weakness of the soul, whose understanding, being occupied by the senses, and whose will, being the slave of the passions, are now led astray and corrupted. Thus, the relation of original sin to original imperfection is not merely that of act to potency and of sin to peccability. Original sin redoubles man's limitation by transforming what, before the fall, was only an inertia or laziness (anti-*conatus*) into a *force* that inclines toward sin, a veritable propensity for evil (understood as a kind of contrary *conatus*).

What is the nature of this contrary effort, given that everything positive comes from God? It is a power that is good by nature, given its divine origin, but which is limited and led astray so as to produce criminal actions by accident. In this sense, the "force" of evil is nothing but that of good. It resides in the perversion and abuse of power and intelligence, when these latter are put into the service of wickedness. It is for this reason that sin is more formidable and more harmful than metaphysical evils, such as natural catastrophes, when it is committed by a creature such as man, who is naturally powerful and therefore capable of causing the most terrible physical evils. "One single Caligula, one Nero, has caused more evil than an earthquake. An evil man takes pleasure in causing suffering and destruction, and for that there are only too many opportunities."[111]

Original sin has had an enduring effect on the motion of the human will, redirecting it toward inferior pleasures (the sensible and carnal) thereby limiting the efficacy of our good inclinations. However, it cannot destroy them altogether nor prevent the performance of truly good actions.[112] Men become "slow to do good, and ready to do evil."[113] Although original sin affects the entire human race, it is not by itself sufficient for damnation. Among Adam's descendants the disposition to sin must be actualized to become truly culpable. Sin must go from being *virtual* to being *actual*.[114] For this to occur, those who inherit sin must freely consent to it. It is for this reason that Leibniz cannot approve of those theologians who, following Augustine, consider infants who die before baptism to be damned, even though they have committed no actual sin (not being of an age to exercise their reason), on the grounds that they are still marked by original sin.[115] Although original sin infects our nature after the fall, for Leibniz, it can only become a cause of damnation, that is, justly imputable to us as a moral evil, once our will participates in it, and it becomes in some sense *ours*. For, according to natural law, no one can be damned for the faults of another.[116] The soul, "being once under the domination of sin" is "ready to commit sin in actual fact as soon as the man is fit to exercise reason."[117] After the fall, the soul is disposed to commit sin but is only culpable once it has effectively (that is, freely) done so. Thus, actual sin is not, in fact, a repetition of original sin—since the condition of Adam's descendants is not the same as that of Adam himself—but rather a way of approving of it, of consenting to it "performatively." Actual sin arises out of the inclination to evil acquired as a result of the fall, while at the same time rendering this inclination genuinely effective and punishable. When committed for the first time by a rational creature, the sin can itself be called *original*, since it is the source of all the creature's future sins.

The relation between original and derivative sin (which consists in the "practice [*exercitium*] of corruption"[118]) is parallel to that between original imperfection and original sin. In both cases, the inclination, which is more or less powerful, is never sufficient by itself to produce action but requires the concurrence of freedom and individual circumstances. Once produced, the act modifies in turn its cause, which goes from being a simple inclination to a propensity for evil. The disposition to sin, which at first is only virtual in souls that have not yet made use of their reason, can only be activated by an actual sin. At that point this disposition becomes almost irresistible, although not necessary, and takes the form of perseverance in sin as well as a tendency to new limitations and privations.[119] The evil endures while at the same time tending to even worse. Its *conatus* initiates a kind of spiraling motion, in which sin produces and reproduces sin, engenders new vices and inculcates bad habits, which are added on top of the disposition resulting from the sin of our first parents:

> *Habitual* sin originates in evil actions either frequently repeated or very violent, by reason of the great number or the depth of the impressions created by them. Thus malice, becoming a habit, increases the depravity which is due to original sin.[120]

*Habitual* sin constitutes a kind of third nature, a further degradation of the human condition, in addition to original imperfection and the disposition to sin resulting from the fall. It, too, becomes in a sense *original*, insofar as it is the source of particular sins.

Thus, there are four levels to be distinguished in the origin of evil: (i) the essential limitation of the creature; (ii) original sin, which was actual in Adam and becomes an original corruption that infects the entire human race and manifests itself as a disposition to sin; (iii) the disposition to sin, which first exists virtually in his descendants and then becomes actual once they commit sin (which they are not capable of doing before the use of reason); (iv) the actual disposition, which by means of actual sins, engenders habitual sin—that is, malice, a higher degree of perversity and the root of further evils. Progression from one level to the next always occurs by moral evil. Sin always results from the imperfection of the prior level, whose defect it aggravates in turn, in accordance with the perfect correspondence between the moral and the ontological realms. Metaphysical evil inclines to moral evil, which produces a new metaphysical evil, which leads to further moral evil, and so on indefinitely. Limitation gives rise to corruption, whose practice, which is first actual and then habitual, leads endlessly to ever greater corruption.

### 6.2.4 The "Naturalist" Approach to Sin and Punishment

By virtue of the perfect interaction between the (meta)physical and the moral levels, the propensity for evil, engendered in Adam and existing in the entire human race, is a *natural* consequence of original sin and not the effect of a special intervention by God. The corruption of human nature, which immediately results from the fall, is not "a mere moral relation, but a real and physical deterioration."[121] As such, it is grounded in the order and laws of nature, as is made clear by Leibniz's account of the transmission of sin and the comparison of the forbidden fruit to a poison.

The Leibnizian doctrine of the preformation of animals provides an explanation of how future human souls, which already exist in Adam's seed as "sentient or animal souls, endowed with perception and feeling, and devoid of reason," could have been infected "*physically* or in their animal nature [*animalement*] by the sin of Adam."[122] However, it is only when these souls attain to rationality, that is, at the moment of generation of the human being, that the inherited corruption of original sin "attains the force of original peccaminosity."[123] In other words, although the soul, which at this point is only sensitive, is corrupted from the moment of Adam's fall, the moral consequences of this corruption (the inclination to sin) manifest themselves only once the soul becomes rational.

The elevation to reason can be explained either naturally or by an extraordinary operation of God. Leibniz does not always take a clear stand with regard to these two possibilities. However, in certain passages, he indicates his preference for the former (which avoids having recourse to a miracle). On this hypothesis, which he presents as a kind of *traduction*, reason is already present in the sensitive soul and included in it as an *actus signatus*, prior to being "activated" in the human soul in the form of an *actus exercitus*. In Scholastic vocabulary, the *actus signatus* is the act by which a thing is signified or designated, whereas the *actus exercitus* is the act by which the thing is realized or performed. The first act is related to active power, and the second to real existence.[124] This distinction allows Leibniz to posit a natural and uninterrupted transition from the sensitive to the rational state. At the same time it helps explain why certain souls (though not all) are able to attain the rational state, namely, because they are predisposed to it, being *essentially*—that is, by their nature—different from the others.[125] This distinction also allows him to explain the deferred effect of original sin on the soul and to make the attainment of reason a precondition of actual sin. When the sensitive soul is "translated" into a rational soul at the moment of generation (at the same time that the organic body becomes a human body), original sin is "translated" into an inclination to sin. This hypothesis has the advantage of economy. It holds that the soul is already corrupted prior to being rational and that once reason is acquired sin is committed freely, instead of requiring the express creation by God of a pure rational soul that enters the body in order to be corrupted.

This "naturalist" interpretation of the transmission of Adam's sin makes of it a physical thesis, rather than a purely theological doctrine. Leibniz draws on certain hypotheses (such as those of Robert Fludd and Thomas White[126]) that interpret the forbidden fruit as a poison that insinuated itself into the first man so as to corrupt all his descendants. This idea of an infectious contagion suggests a reinterpretation of the divine interdiction recounted in Genesis. The prohibition against eating the forbidden fruit was not the result of an arbitrary and ad hoc divine decree—otherwise God would have had to intervene by a particular act so that Adam would be punished for his disobedience (since in this case there would be no natural connection between sin and punishment). Rather, the prohibition made to Adam must be seen as a notice and a warning concerning the harmful *physical* consequences of eating the fruit. On this reading, God's prohibition was made "much as one forbids knives to children." Thus, God has no need to disturb the laws of nature and to "deliberately put a corruption in the soul and body of man, by an extraordinary action, in order to punish him."[127] The punishment occurs naturally, by the order of efficient causes, as a consequence of the fault committed. God did not punish Adam, and with him his descendants, by afflicting them with an inclination to evil like some kind of anti-grace,

> this peccaminosity follows from the first fall as if by a physical nexus, just as many other sins follow from intoxication.[128]

This explanation of sin and punishment has two advantages:

(1). It provides a means of avoiding the difficulty raised by Bayle, who wondered at a punishment that, far from curing the sinner of his penchant for evil, inclines both him and his posterity even more strongly to sin.[129] For Leibniz, this inclination is not the consequence of a special decree of God, but the ordinary and inevitable result of sin (as drunkenness follows from excessive consumption of alcohol).

(2). It suggests that divine justice should be conceived as an exclusively *immanent* justice—a justice that is, properly speaking, natural, whose aim is not always to reform the guilty, but which perfectly illustrates the harmony between nature and grace. Although the propagation of sin is not a punishment resulting from a positive divine law, it shows that "the realm of nature serves that of grace; and that God as an Architect has done everything in a manner befitting God considered as a Monarch."[130] Consumption of poison is harmful for the physical constitution of man, but it is also an act of disobedience on the moral level. The physical effect is concomitant with a moral effect, although strictly speaking it belongs only to the natural order. Nature is ordered to assist grace and to fulfill what justice commands, while following nothing but its own laws.

The harmony of the two realms is manifest not only in the exact correspondence that exists between them but also in the manner in which the one is realized by the other and arises out of it, without however disturbing its laws. This makes possible a thoroughly "naturalist" interpretation of events, while still acknowledging the application of the principles of universal justice—even if this perfect application is not always apparent to us limited creatures. A parallel can be drawn here (between the physical and moral levels) with what holds true in the natural sciences (between the physical and metaphysical levels). Just as we must explain physical phenomena only by mechanism, while positing metaphysical principles as its foundation (the action of immaterial substances called monads), so we must consider peccaminosity, in the order of nature, only as the physical effect of the corruption of original sin, and nevertheless see it, according to the order of grace, as a punishment that, by rendering the sinner even guiltier, necessitates the intervention of a divine redeemer (Christ's incarnation and sacrifice).

Thus, the punishment for sin is twofold. It consists not only in physical evil (suffering) but also in the perpetuation and reinforcement of moral evil. The punishment for sin is sin itself, its strengthening and near total dominion over a soul that is ever more inclined to evil. In other words, the punishment for sin is to commit more sins, and so to incur further punishment in accordance with the spiraling motion mentioned above. This inertia, by which evil persists and even grows worse, accounts for certain spiritual states described by moral theology, such as obstinacy, hardening of the heart, resistance to grace, rebellion against God, and, of course, damnation. Such moral phenomena do not require a "kind of anti-grace" impressed on the sinner "extraordinarily." Here again, Leibniz keeps to the natural order. God is thus content "to permit that Pharaoh, for example, should be in such *circumstances* as should increase his wickedness."[131] Obstinacy arises out of an already existing disposition to evil, which events and circumstances do no more, according to the ordinary course of things, than fortify and augment. God has no need to bestow upon man a kind of anti-grace. He does not harden him by what he gives (positive reality), but by what he does not give, namely, sufficient grace to overcome man's resistance, which results from the limits of his corrupted nature.[132]

It may be wondered why God did not grant more perfection and good to Pharaoh. Absolutely speaking, this was possible. However, to do so would have required a miracle in order to overcome his resistance—that is, a miracle that would prompt him to act differently from that which his nature bears, owing to its limitation and corruption. Alternatively, it would have been necessary to create another being in place of Pharaoh, which would require modifying the whole series of existing things (given their interconnectedness) and would amount to creating a world other than ours—that is, a world other than the best (a consequence that would occur in the first hypothesis too).

"*Mas perdido, y menos arrepentido*, the more lost, the less repentant."[133] Such is the state of the rebellious and hardened mind that has become blind to its own true good, and that not only does not wish to convert, but is *ex hypothesi* no longer capable of doing so. Such a mind is subject to a kind of *unhappy necessity* which makes it persevere in evil—the exact opposite of the "happy" moral necessity, which inclines the sage infallibly to the good. As a result, the rebel is no longer capable of escaping the hopeless spiral that carries him to greater imperfection and misery.[134] This hardening makes for hopelessness in this life and for damnation in

the next. Damnation is the culmination or, rather, the perpetual continuation of this movement toward the worse, just as beatitude is the uninterrupted progress of the virtuous soul toward greater perfection and
happiness. It is for this reason that damnation does not consist merely
in the *deprivation* of supreme felicity (*punishment of loss*) and the ever
greater separation from salvation, but in positive suffering (*punishment
of sense*),[135] that is, in the "greatest physical evil."[136] Beginning with the
*Confession of a Philosopher*, Leibniz had made damnation consist in a constantly renewed and growing hatred of God, which results in repeated
and increased suffering. Similarly, beatitude consists in a perpetually
increasing love of God, which procures endless joy. The virtuous spiral
in which the blessed find themselves corresponds to the vicious spiral in
which the damned are trapped.[137]

In the *Theodicy*, Leibniz goes into less detail concerning the psychology
of the damned.[138] Instead, he stresses the notion that eternity of punishment is owing to perpetuation of the sin. There are three reasons for this:

(1). In opposition to Bayle, who insists on the uselessness of eternal
punishment, Leibniz justifies such punishment as continuing only
because the sin itself is repeated, even if this punishment serves neither to correct the guilty nor even to deter others from evil. Against
Hobbes and the Socinians, Leibniz legitimates *vindictive justice*, which
he maintains, is based on the Principle of Fitness, "which demands
a certain satisfaction for the expiation of an evil action," and whose
aim is neither to make amends nor set an example, nor even to make
reparations for the evil. Fitness is the principle of immanent justice,
which punishes every bad action and rewards every good work "in consequence of the natural sequence of things,"[139] in conformity with the
pre-established harmony between the realms of nature and of grace,
both in this life and the next. For eternal life is merely the continuation of earthly life in another "theater," such that it is the very same
"inertia" that constitutes the sinner's despair on earth that will make
him miserable in hell. Likewise, it is the same virtue that engenders
the happiness of the just man on earth that will assure his beatitude
in paradise. It is for this reason that those who sincerely love God can
consider themselves saved even in this life, whereas the rebellious and
wicked are, in a sense, already damned.

(2). If damnation is eternal because (and only because) sin is eternally
repeated, then there is no injustice in punishment nor disproportion between crime and punishment.[140] Thus, there is no need to appeal to another
reason, based on the divine majesty, to justify the perpetuity of creaturely
punishment:

[I]t was enough to say that the duration of the guilt caused the duration of the penalty. Since the damned remained wicked they could not be withdrawn from their misery; and thus one need not, in order to justify the continuation of their sufferings, assume that sin has become of infinite weight through the infinite nature of the object offended, who is God. This thesis I had not explored enough to pass judgement upon.[141]

The argument drawn from the dignity of the offended (God) is commonplace, which can be found, for example, in Anselm and Aquinas.[142] It is based on the notion that to offend God's majesty constitutes the highest crime (the crime of lèse-majesté) and carries the most severe punishment. The sin is infinitely great, since it is an offense against an infinite being. Furthermore, because the punishment must always be proportioned to the crime, the punishment itself must be infinite (in duration). The caution shown here by Leibniz, who clearly prefers not to comment on the thesis, may come from his having discerned a paralogism. The error consists in sliding from one kind of infinite (the value of the offended) to another (the value of the offense and the duration of punishment for the offender) based on a supposed affinity between them. God's infinity is actual perfection without limit. Infinity is a divine attribute, which cannot be truly applied to sin however serious it may be (except according to a pure extrinsical denomination, that is, by reference to the nature of the offended). Moreover, God's infinity is of a different nature than that of time understood as limitless duration (perpetuation). Sin is infinite insofar as it is without limit, since it is perpetually renewed. However, it is not infinite *formaliter*, that is, essentially and in itself.[143]

Leibniz is aware that this view puts him at odds with the majority of the Scholastics, for whom there can be neither merit nor demerit in the afterlife. While acknowledging that grace is no longer operative in the world to come, Leibniz reaffirms the perfect continuity between the here beyond and the here below: "God cannot change his nature; justice is essential to him; death has closed the door of grace, but not the door of justice."[144] Divine justice remains in effect always and everywhere, such that wherever sin continues, so too must its punishment. As we have seen, punishment is not extrinsic to the sin, given that sin is its own punishment, just as virtue is its own reward.

(3) Finally, Leibniz's thesis concerning the eternity of punishment by the continuation of the offense (and the eternity of beatitude by the continuation of virtue) presupposes that rational creatures always remain free. Sin is always freely committed, both in this life and in the next, despite having become almost irresistible in the mind of the depraved. It inclines

without necessitating[145] and remains voluntary, even if it results from a weakened and misguided will.

> But after this life, though one assume that the succor [of grace] ceases, there is always in the man who sins, even when he is damned, a freedom which renders him culpable, and a power, albeit remote, of recovering himself, even though it should never pass into action. And there is no reason why one may not say that this degree of freedom, exempt from necessity, but not exempt from certainty, remains in the damned as well as in the blessed.[146]

By continually sinning, the damned freely damns himself, since he retains the ability to be saved by a *remote* power,[147] even though this power is impeded by a *proximate* power (the habit of sinning) that inclines him to evil. The same holds true for the elect. By continually and freely repeating the act of love for God, the elect maintain themselves in a state of beatitude, although they retain the *remote* power of sinning (likewise impeded by their *proximate* power that leads them to the good). The happiness of the elect results from a perpetual salvation—a salvation that is contingently reaffirmed at each moment—just as the misery of the damned results from an endlessly renewed damnation.

## 6.3  REAL DEFECT OR FALSE APPEARANCE: A DUAL CONCEPTION OF EVIL

In God's physical concurrence, evil (whether metaphysical, moral, or physical) is considered an ontological defect, which is itself a source of new imperfections. By locating evil in being, Leibniz treats it as a real privation and not a pure absence (a nothingness) or a mere moral relation (failure to conform to the law in the case of sin, or the effect of a sanction in the case of pain). As a degradation of the creature in its very nature, evil is more than an appearance, an unfounded phenomenon relative to a partial and incomplete point of view. However, Leibniz's appeal to traditional arguments and comparisons, which relegate evil to the rank of shading, dissonance, or apparent irregularities, shows that this ontological interpretation of evil does not always predominate in his texts. This is especially true when evil is no longer considered in itself but in relation to good (its contrary) or to universal harmony (to the "whole"). In this sense, there is, in my view, an ambiguity and contradiction in Leibniz's thought. First, we find what might be called an "absolute" conception of good and evil coexisting with a "relative" conception that reduces evil to a degree of good

(6.3.1 and 6.3.2). Afterward, we notice that these two conceptions lead to two different and apparently incompatible, interpretations of evil in the universal harmony. According to the one, evil is a real and irreducible defect, which must nevertheless be allowed in order to secure the perfection of the universe in its entirety. According to the other, evil is merely an appearance, which is the effect of a limited perception, and which disappears from the complete view of universal harmony (6.3.2).

### 6.3.1 The Relativity of Good and Evil

Taken in its most general sense—that is, in the *metaphysical* sense—"good" means perfection. Good is positive reality, a certain quantity of essence, considered absolutely, without negation, lack, or limit.[148] However, it also designates the measure of this reality and quantity of essence. For, there are degrees of good and perfection. In this *relative* sense, good is the estimation of *absolute* good, that is, of good considered in the first sense (ontological perfection). Here it refers not to being in itself, but to a quality of being, which is determined by comparison with other real or possible beings. This quality (the relative "goodness" of the thing) is measured in two ways. A thing is said to be better or more perfect than another when it possesses more being or positive reality.[149] However, in cases where the quantity of perfection is equal, that thing is preferred that is compatible with the greatest number of other things. Thus, among equally perfect creatures, God will be led to choose "the most accommodating," that is, those that are most compatible with others.[150]

Thus, good, in its relative sense, is defined by two main criteria: the quantity of perfection of the thing, and what Leibniz calls its "harmonic properties,"[151] that is, its greater or lesser compatibility with other things. According to the comparison and relation considered, a good (understood as a determinate quantity of reality) can be judged more or less "good" to the extent that it harmonizes with other goods, or even, allows some even greater goods to be obtained. When weighed against others (that are more perfect or more "harmonious"), it can be called less good, or even a relative evil, if it represents a positive obstacle to greater goods.

This evaluation is only valid relative to a given perspective. While the gift of reason, for example, is a good in itself and the object of a divine antecedent will, it can be seen as an evil relative to its bad consequences for the human race (sin and its aftermath) and so be rejected by God's middle will. However, it can be recognized as good at an even higher level (from the perspective of the whole) and so chosen by the final will.[152] Conversely, a particular evil, initially ruled out by the divine antecedent will, could be, if not willed as a subsidiary good, then at least permitted as a condition sine qua non of a superior good: "we know, moreover, that often an evil brings forth a good to which one would not have attained without that evil. Often indeed two evils have made one great good."[153] One evil associated with another can have a salutary effect, similar to what occurs in certain chemical reactions. Furthermore, out of a single evil, a good can arise. Thus, the error of a general can unexpectedly lead to victory. The Roman Catholic Church considers original sin to be a "happy fault" (*felix culpa*) to the extent that it made possible the coming of Christ and the redemption of the whole of humanity. Thus, according to context, use, and the desired end, the same thing can be variously judged:

> It can happen that a stone, which in itself is ordinary, becomes precious, because it exactly corresponds to the location, so true it is that the value of things is not always determined by the things considered in themselves, but also by their combination or use.[154]

This relativity in no way implies that "good" and "evil" are purely extrinsic denominations, signifying nothing in the things themselves, but deriving from our relation to them or our opinion of them, as Hobbes and Spinoza had maintained.[155] Even if the characterization of things as good and evil depends on a determinate point of view (according to which the thing is considered individually or in relation to others), it still refers to the intrinsic properties of the thing (its quantity of reality and degree of compatibility). For, its essence includes all the relations in which it stands and which serve to define it. However, the fact that a particular good can be, with regard to a different relation, an evil (while still remaining in itself a good, absolutely speaking, that God wills antecedently), and conversely, the fact that a particular evil can be the means or condition of a superior good (while still remaining in itself an evil, absolutely speaking, that God does not will antecedently) shows that good and evil are relative to one another.

How is this relativity to be explained? By rejecting Manichaeism and making evil consist in privation, Leibniz showed that there is no need to posit any principle beyond being and its limits in order to account for the imperfection of creatures. It follows, by virtue of the convertibility of goodness and being, that there is also no need to consider anything other than good and its degrees in order to explain evil. One can imagine on the scale of good a continuous gradation running from worst to best, just as there is, on the scale of being, a progression in perfection from brute monads to God.[156] On this scale of goodness, which is also reminiscent of the pyramid of possible worlds, a certain number of equivalences can be posited: a lesser evil is a kind of good, just as a lesser good is a kind of evil when it prevents a greater good.[157] Evil can be an inferior good, that which prevents a good or a greater good, or it can be the means of falling into an even greater evil. Conversely, good can be a lesser evil, that which allows one to avoid an evil or a greater evil, or it can be the means of attaining a greater good.

Thus, good and evil can be taken, each in turn, as a genus or species of its contrary. This does not mean that good is only the privation of evil, as evil is the privation of good. For, the good is something positive in terms of which privation is conceived. Good is that of which one can be deprived but which does not result from a privation, except in a negative sense. Consequently, the relativity of good and evil is fundamentally asymmetrical. Good is logically prior, since it can be conceived without evil, whereas evil is logically secondary, since it can only be conceived relative to the good. The privation of good gives rise to evil, but the privation of this privation is the good itself, or a kind of "negative" good insofar as it produces the good by eliminating the obstacle that was preventing its occurrence.

This gradation in the good makes it possible to go from more to less, from better to worse, without gaps or interruptions. In light of this, it is tempting to make the following comparison with the physical. Just as, according to the law of continuity, rest is conceived as a particular case of motion and defined as "movement vanishing after having continually diminished," "as an infinitely small speed, or as an infinite retardation,"[158] so evil, considered as a species or degree of good, can be considered in the worst as a perpetually diminished good, as a good that is, so to speak, infinitely small. The greatest evil (which, in fact, does not exist) would be the continually deferred lower limit of the good, the greatest good (God) being its unsurpassable upper limit. Privation is not mere negation. It does not completely destroy the being which it limits. On the ontological level, this means that one cannot find a creature or possible world, however imperfect and evil, which does not have some, even minute, degree of perfection and goodness.

The relativity of good and evil leads us to relate and even assimilate evil to good, rather than good to evil (whence the asymmetry). By reducing evil to a degree of good, this relativity ultimately diminishes evil's effects, its unacceptable and scandalous nature. Is this reduction, which tends to minimize, if not abolish, evil, equally observable with regard to the three kinds of evil?

## 6.3.2 The Reduction of Evil to a Degree of Good and the Limits of This Reduction

In the case of metaphysical and physical evil, the reduction appears un-
questionable since Leibniz characterizes them as "subsidiary goods,"
which serves as means to an end. However, unlike metaphysical evil,
physical evil partially resists this reduction, given that pain does not consist in a lesser pleasure or in the absence of a physical good, nor is damnation merely the privation of beatitude. Both are positive afflictions.[159]
Pleasure and pain are two irreducibly antagonistic states. However,
there exists between them a multitude of intermediary states, of which
we have more or less awareness, which allow for a continuous transition
from one to the other. In the first place, there are those states that seem
to be "neutral" but in reality are not. These states, such as health, the absence of disagreement or impediment, are true goods. However, they are
only experienced as such when they are lost: "one is well enough when
one has no ill; it is a degree of wisdom to have no folly."[160] There are also
all of those affections, which Leibniz discusses in the *New Essays* and
which are ingredients of pleasure and pain or prepare the way for and
conduce to them. Such are uneasiness, the imperceptible presentiments
that precede pain and pleasure, as well as the rudiments or elements
of pain and pleasure, whose intensity and greatness vary and which by
accumulation ultimately produce a noticeable, that is apperceptible,
sensation.[161]

All of these various states number among the physical goods and evils,
which for this reason are not limited to pleasure and pain. This helps explain why Leibniz sometimes defines physical goods and evils by means
of the general terms "conveniences" or "inconveniences."[162] The "inconvenient" is anything that indisposes the mind, that importunes, afflicts, or
is noxious to it. Conversely, the "convenient" is anything that serves the
mind, that puts it in a good disposition, is suitable, favorable and agreeable to it. Each of these convenient and inconvenient states may be more
or less perceptible and more or less lively. Pleasure and pain are only species of convenience and inconvenience. They admit of degrees[163] and their
principal characteristic is to be noticeable perceptions.[164] This large extension of the notions of physical good and evil reduces the distance between
the extremes (pain and pleasure) and allows each to be defined in terms
of the other, at least up to a point. For, inconvenience can be defined as
the privation of that which is pleasing or as that which hinders, whereas
convenience can be defined as the elimination or diminution of what is
inconvenient.

The opposition between physical good and evil is further attenuated by the affinity that exists between pleasure and pain and by the mixture of good and evil that always exists in these two states. Leibniz draws attention to this in the *New Essays* by showing that joy and sadness, happiness and misery express a certain relation between good and evil in which the one is never entirely without the other but merely predominates over it. Joy is the state in which pleasure predominates over pain; sadness is that in which pain outweighs pleasure.[165] Pleasure itself is never without uneasiness. Leibniz does not conceive uneasiness as real pain—since it falls below it and is a lower degree of it—but rather as a kind of disquiet or unrest, which though unperceived by the soul, keeps it on alert and spurs it to action.

> In fact, without these semi-sufferings there would be no pleasure at all, nor any way of being aware that something is helping and relieving us by removing obstacles which stand between us and our ease. This also exhibits that affinity of pleasure with suffering which Socrates comments on in Plato's *Phaedo*, when his feet are itching. This account of tiny aids, imperceptible little escapes and releases of a thwarted endeavor, which finally generate notable pleasure, also provides a somewhat more distinct knowledge of our inevitably confused ideas of pleasure and of pain.[166]

Far from being incompatible with happiness (as Locke had maintained), uneasiness is an essential component of it.[167] Even the blessed are not without feeling this spur that incites them to new joys, nor are the damned without some small contentment, which, in making them wallow in their senseless hatred, leads them to further sin and greater suffering.[168] Thus, physical good and evil are not "pure" but always mixed, to various degrees, with their contrary. Their continual mixture, their proximity and the continuity that exists between their extremes show that, although pain and pleasure are, as such, irreducible to one another, their difference is only one of degree and not of nature.

If the reduction of physical evil to good is not entirely possible at the "psychophysical" level, it is so on the moral and metaphysical levels, where its power to expiate, ameliorate, and transform makes it a "subsidiary good." It is not because pain allegedly serves as a natural warning of danger that it is good, as the Cartesians, and especially Régis, hold (Bayle rightly criticizes the latter on this point).[169] Its utility is moral rather than physical. Pain is the punishment consequent to sin. It serves principally to amend the guilty and as an example to others. In other cases, pain always occurs in conformity with harmony. When it strikes the innocent or the good man, it is a trial that prepares them for "a greater happiness."[170] It is the step backward that better enables one to jump. Improvement occurs by way of suffering, just as germination of the planted seed occurs by way of corruption. For this reason, it may be said in general that "though afflictions are temporary evils, they are good in effect, for they are short cuts to greater perfection."[171]

Physical evil becomes a *moral* good, when used as punishment and incentive to virtue, but it also becomes a *metaphysical* good, insofar as it is the shortest path to perfection. It has the power to correct moral evil (by making reparations for sin and eliminating vice from the soul of the sinner) and to diminish, in part, metaphysical evil (ontological imperfection). The relation between metaphysical evil, moral evil, and physical evil is thus inverted. While metaphysical evil is the origin of moral evil, which is itself the cause of physical evil, physical evil can in turn eliminate moral evil and lead the creature to greater perfection, that is, reduce metaphysical evil. Notice however that physical evil can also produce the opposite effect. In the case of the desperate man or the damned, it can act to reinforce moral evil (vice) and lead to further imperfection (that is, metaphysical evil).

Suffering can provoke obstinacy and increase hatred and the desire to harm, or, on the contrary, it can lead to repentance and moral reform. Such is the function assigned to pain. However, supposing that the person who suffers is already wise and just, and that consequently his suffering is not a punishment and does not have his moral improvement as its end, how is this person's metaphysical improvement to be understood? Leibniz offers no precise explanation. He is content to invoke the image (taken from the gospel) of the grain that germinates and to recall that salvation is obtained "through many sufferings, and by bearing the cross of Jesus Christ," because "these evils serve to make the elect imitators of their master, and to increase their happiness."[172] Pain serves as a trial and also increases man's capacity for resistance, as well as his patience and endurance, both physical and moral. As experience shows, appropriate exercise frequently repeated can teach us to bear pain. By this means, one may acquire not only increased vigor and bodily strength but also great mental force and freedom of mind, which allows it to remain content even in the midst of torments.[173]

What are these greater pleasures promised to the just man who suffers? It must not be thought that the compensation promised for the afterlife will occur by the intervention of a transcendent justice. These pleasures will be produced naturally, according to the order of efficient causes, as a consequence of the creature's progress to a greater degree of perfection. How are we to explain, on the ontological level, the fact that this increase can, and indeed *must*, be preceded by a diminution in perfection (of which pain is the sensible indication)?

One plausible suggestion draws on Leibniz's frequent reference to the expression "draw back to make a better jump." The phrase suggests not so much a real loss of perfection as a retreat. The acquired perfection is not destroyed, but only temporarily impeded. Once the obstacle is removed, the perfection exerts itself with all the more force for having been previously constrained, like a spring that uncoils more violently the more it was compressed. On this reading, pain is a sign of constrained perfection, and pleasure the sign of perfection that resumes its growth once the impediment is removed. Like the uncoiling spring, perfection is not merely restored but increased, such that physical evil is the indirect cause of a physical good (greater than this evil).

Ultimately, physical evil is a true evil only for those who merit it and who, by persisting in sin, draw no benefit from their suffering. For all others, when such evil is neither beneficial nor compensated in this life, it is only temporary and is as nothing in comparison with the joys that await the just in the next life.[174] For all these reasons, and despite our natural tendency to exaggerate physical evil and to pay more attention to it than to good, physical evil is certainly, for Leibniz, the species of evil that raises the fewest difficulties for the justification of God.[175]

There remains the question of moral evil, which alone seems to escape all possible reduction to a degree of good, since it is especially with regard to it that a doctrine of permission is required. Allowed, if need be, as a condition sine qua non of the best, but never willed as a means, moral evil cannot be a good, not even a lesser or subsidiary one. Vice is neither the absence nor the privation of virtue, but the positive performance of wrong actions or the voluntary omission of duties. Just as refraining from sin is not enough to make one virtuous, so too, failure to perform any good action does not suffice to make one immoral. The love of God implies more than abstaining from evil and external respect of the moral laws and ceremonies. It requires ardor and positive actions on behalf of divine glory.[176] Likewise, hatred of God presupposes more than the corruption resulting from original sin and more than venial sins, from which even the just are not always exempt. Rather, it requires manifest dissatisfaction, rebellion, and malice.

It is possible, however, to distinguish different degrees of virtue and vice.[177] Deceit, pious fraud, dissimulation, and lies can be, in certain cases and particular circumstances, if not relative goods (insofar as they are lesser evils that make it possible to avoid a greater evil), then at least morally permissible expedients.[178] While sin cannot be attenuated in itself, it can be attenuated indirectly, by its beneficial effects—for which reason one can speak of "happy sin," [179]—and by the compensation to which it gives rise. It is only relative to the sinner that sin is a genuine evil, on account of the punishment that naturally follows from it, namely suffering and the repetition of sin. However, *absolutely* speaking, sin is part of the harmony, as Leibniz had maintained from the time of his earliest writings. Despite the disobedience it involves, sin in no way affects God.[180] It is not an evil with regard to him and from the point of view of the whole:

> Even sins are only evils for those who sin. Absolutely speaking, they increase the perfection of things, as shadows are good in a painting in order to enhance the light.[181]

### 6.3.3  Real and Apparent Evil

We have seen how evil, even when it cannot be directly reduced to a degree or species of good, is nevertheless always related to it. This is either because there is some good in the evil (imperfection does not eliminate all perfection, pain is a mixed state) or because the evil has beneficial consequences, and for this reason, can be called good or "happy" (as in the case of sin)—not, of course, in itself, but relative to its effects. The existence of evil, in all three of its kinds, is thus justified in that it contributes in one way or another, directly or indirectly, as a means or as a condition sine qua non, to the perfection of the universe. This *relative* conception of evil is not, prima facie, incompatible with the *absolute* conception of evil, according to which evil considered in itself (imperfection, pain, sin) is always a true evil. For, its relation to good and its ultimate utility within the whole do nothing to change its fundamentally "bad" nature. The fact that pain prepares the way for great happiness, that Adam's sin made possible the salvation of all of humanity by Christ, does not make pain agreeable or sin praiseworthy and just. Otherwise, Adam would have been deserving of reward rather than punishment, and Judas would number among the saints for having betrayed Christ and so made possible the Passion!

The problem is that the relative conception does more than minimize the "malignity" of evil. It tends to strip evil of its reality, ultimately reducing it to a mere appearance that is tied to our limited perception of the world, but which disappears in a comprehensive view of universal harmony. Obviously, this outcome is incompatible with the absolute conception. It is equally incompatible with the role of a means and condition assigned to evil by the relative conception. Thus, we arrive at two irreconcilable conceptions of evil.

(1) According to the first, evil is real and not merely apparent, since it is a defect that affects created being in its nature and action. This defect can be considered in two ways. (i) First, it may be seen as an irreducibly negative element of harmony, an unpleasant and inevitable consequence, which is not compensated elsewhere (in some other part). This way of considering the defect is illustrated by the comparison with architecture and gaming. (ii) Alternatively, it constitutes a positive ingredient in the harmonic dynamic, insofar as its resorption and compensation make possible a superior good in the whole. This second view is illustrated by the comparison with music.

In the first case (i), evil is not the positive means by which the best is realized, but rather one of its negative and residual effects, which could be neither prevented nor eliminated. In the same way, even a magnificent and well-built castle may include rooms that are uncomfortable, or even unhealthy, for its inhabitants.[182] Such disagreeable elements must be permitted, not because they serve to enhance the beauty of the building as whole, but because it is not possible to do otherwise without compromising the general plan. The inconvenience of "a few domestics," although regrettable in itself, is the price to be paid for the perfection of the entire work. This kind of evil is not one of those elements that contribute in itself or by itself to the best, since the universe would be all the more perfect, if it contained less of it. The castle would lose none of its perfection if the alleyways, kitchens, basements, and cellars could be healthy, beautiful, and agreeable places!

If evil is not a means here, should it be considered a condition sine qua non of the best, as is the case with sin? In one sense, it is such a condition, to the extent that its elimination would call into question the perfection of the whole. Thus, the existence of this evil is required. However, it is not required as a cause, but as a deplorable, though inevitable consequence of harmony. In this sense, it is importantly different from sin. Whereas God draws some good out of sin, and thus permits it, he does not, strictly speaking, draw anything out of this "residual" evil. Rather, he must permit it, because it is (hypothetically) impossible to eliminate. It might be objected that by this means God achieves a contrast, a source of beauty, just as the shading in a painting enhances the brilliance of the light. However, it is not at all clear, at least in the example of the castle, that the perfection of the building results from this contrast. It is difficult to imagine the lord of the manor guiding his guests through the kitchens and alleyways to better arouse their admiration when subsequently showing them the more luxurious suites!

Within the universal harmony, evil represents a kind of cost, which one would gladly forgo, were it possible, but which must be paid to attain perfection in the whole. This economic comparison is suggested by Jon Elster. Elster draws a parallel between Leibniz's God and the "instrumental rationality" typical of the capitalist mindset, which in comparing ends to the available resources (location, quality of the land, funds) adjusts costs to benefits to maximize profit.[183] On this view, evil would be the "necessary cost of production" that God must agree to pay in order to bring about the best of all possible worlds.

This interpretation strikes me as exaggerated and questionable, especially because it reduces universal perfection to a calculation of quantity (whereas it is based, in the first instance, on quality[184]) and because it reduces evil to an expense, and so to a loss, when, in fact, it is that which is leftover. However, Elster's reading has the merit of emphasizing a particular kind of evil, which is neither a means nor exactly a condition sine qua non of the best, but rather an unintended and incorrigible effect from which no good can be immediately derived and which as a result is useless in itself. To be sure, the inconvenient and unhealthy rooms in the castle have their use, but their defect (which we are here considering) results from the fact that their inconvenience and unhealthiness are without remedy and in themselves do not contribute to the perfection of the building as a whole. The character of evil as residue is illustrated by those games that involve finding the optimal disposition of tokens on a given surface (a chessboard, for example).[185] The winner is the one who succeeds in filling as many squares as possible. However, even in the best possible combination, it may happen that some squares remain empty. These squares represent things about which nothing can be done and as a consequence are irremediably sterile.

In this first case, the best possible world is best *despite* evil, for the evil it includes is an undesirable (albeit inevitable) effect, which diminishes its perfection and which must be subtracted from the global sum of goods. In the second case (ii), by contrast, the best possible world is best *on account of* evil, since evil is one of the causes of its perfection to the extent that it is a source of harmony, such that its presence increases rather than diminishes the total good. Harmony presupposes a tension between contraries (identity and diversity, unity and variety, order and disorder[186]) and resides in its dynamic resolution. The perfection of harmony and the amount of pleasure one takes in contemplating it depend on the intensity of the tension and the admiration that its resolution produces. As Leibniz indicated in the *Confession of a Philosopher*, harmony is "greatest in the case where it is a unity of the greatest number of things disordered in appearance and reduced, unexpectedly, by some wonderful ratio to the greatest symmetry."[187] The pleasure is all the greater, the more powerfully the conflict is felt (without producing true suffering, but "bordering on pain"[188]) and the more the agreement finally obtained appears unexpected and surprising.

Leibniz's preferred example in this connection is, of course, music. A talented composer is one who knows how to introduce dissonances where necessary to make the listener ill at ease and in a state of anxious anticipation of their resolution. The listener experiences pleasure at the moment of resolution, when "order is restored."[189] The comparison with music is doubly interesting. On the one hand, it shows that the defect (the dissonance) is *real* and not merely apparent and that it is precisely because it is real that its correction is required and anticipated—whence the pleasure one feels when the tension is released. On the other hand, it shows that correction of the defect is not simply a matter of restoring the situation that existed prior to the tension, as in a zero-sum game, in which the good that succeeds an evil is limited to thwarting its effects. Here, on the contrary, the correction implies a gain for the whole, the acquisition of a greater perfection of which the aesthetic pleasure is the indication. In this case, evil is the condition of a greater good that could not be attained without it. Evil makes it possible to go from good to better. It is the lack of being that leads to more being. For, as Leibniz writes to John Bernoulli,

> although evil in itself is less than nothing, yet sometimes when joined to other things, it effectively augments reality, just as shadows are useful in painting and dissonance in music.[190]

(2) Now, according to the second conception of evil, evil is not real. It is the effect of a partial and imperfect knowledge, characteristic of limited creatures like ourselves. Those things we take to be defects and disorders are, in fact, perfectly integrated into the general order. This conception of evil is especially prominent in Leibniz's explanation of metaphysical evils.[191] However, it also applies to the other kinds of evil. It is based on the idea that the world is governed by a system of laws that leaves absolutely no room for disorder. Its irregularities are only apparent, and its exceptions can only be local and relative to a particular law. If some phenomenon contradicts a law, it is because it depends on a higher law. Exceptions are not phenomena that occur outside all laws but are the result of one law limiting another, the derogation of one law by another. "Defects," or what are taken to be such, are just as well regulated as everything else, but they

occur in conformity with an unknown or more complex law. In this sense, the alleged disorders and irregularities of the world are like a line whose path appears random and disordered but for which a geometrical equation can be given, by which we discover "the reason and the fittingness of all these so-called irregularities."[192]

A pure exception, one that falls under no rule whatsoever, would violate the Principle of Sufficient Reason. Such an exception would be inexplicable and so cannot be admitted into a world created by a being who acts according to principles (God).[193] Consequently, we must not say, like Bernard of Clairvaux, simply that "it belongs to the great order that there should be some small disorder" (which would be a kind of concession that there is real disorder, even if minimal), but that "in the whole this small disorder is only *apparent*, and it is not even apparent when one considers the happiness of those who walk in the ways of order."[194] Behind any apparent irregularity there always lies a rule that provides a perfect explanation.

Here we see a shift from the *metaphysical* to the *epistemological* level. Defect no longer resides in created being, as an accepted and acknowledged characteristic of the part, an element that contributes (or not) to what is best on the whole. Rather, it is now said to reside in a limited perception, which errs in seeing imperfection where there is none. In the one case, evil is real and our awareness of it correct, whereas in the other, it is only apparent and results from a confused awareness. It no longer calls for compensation by good but requires us to move to a superior point of view from which it will vanish.

> In fact, I am of the opinion that God could not do better than he does and that all the imperfections we think we see in the world are merely the result of our ignorance. We do not yet have the correct point of view from which to judge the beauty of things.[195]

The case is similar to that of astronomy, where the motion of the planets seems confused and disordered when seen from the earth but would appear perfectly regular and uniform seen from the sun. The change in location affords a more extensive, more global vision, which allows us to see connections between things that escape us at present. It also offers a more detailed view, allowing us to further penetrate the "interior of things" in our knowledge of a particular. For, order is "so perfect that, if it were understood in detail, we would not only believe, but we would see that nothing better can be hoped for."[196]

The evils of rational creatures, their sins and their suffering, are no exception. They do not fall outside of the universal order when considered from the correct point of view, which is none other than that of God himself. Man is "a little god in his own world," "who sometimes does marvelous things," but also commits "great faults" for which he is punished. However,

> God, by a wonderful art, turns all the errors of these little worlds to the greater adornment of his great world. It is as in those devices of perspective, where certain beautiful designs look like mere confusion until one restores them to the right angle of vision or one views them by means of a certain glass or mirror. It is by placing and using them properly that one makes them serve as adornment for a room. Thus the apparent deformities of our little worlds combine to become beauties in the great world.[197]

The comparison with anamorphosis makes evil an illusion, a false appearance. The pleasure of contemplation comes when the chaotic appearance is dissipated, that is, when we move from the confused to the distinct. The spectator, who had previously seen nothing but an incoherent mass of lines and colors, frees himself from error and marvels at his clear and distinct knowledge.

The model of painting at work here stands in contrast to the earlier example of music. In the case of anamorphosis, the adequate point of view corrects the incomplete perception and shows that what we took to be defects are not really such.[198] Evil is the effect of a truncated perspective and dissipates like a mirage upon contemplating the whole—such that, as Leibniz had already observed to Magnus Wedderkopf, "nothing is to be considered absolutely evil."[199] In the case of music, on the other hand, hearing the complete work in no way alters the nature of dissonance, which, even though it contributes to the beauty of the whole, remains a real and irreducible defect. The dissonance is still dissonant; the evil is still evil, regardless of the point of view taken (total or partial).

The first conception of evil tends to inflate the effect and role of evil in harmony or, at least, to maintain that evil is inseparable from it. The second conception of evil, by contrast, tends to minimize the role of evil and even to deny it all reality. Still, might we not say that the over- and undervaluing ultimately lead to the same result? Both involve reducing evil to good, either by making it a means, a subsidiary good or a condition sine qua non, or by relegating it to the status of appearance and making it disappear in favor of good and its degrees. However, two problems remain.

a. It is not clear that moral and physical evil can be so easily reduced to apparent or illusory disorders, which will disappear once we adopt the correct point of view. As we have seen, sins and pains are still something positive, something which cannot be reduced to the privation of their contrary. The entire philosophical enterprise of justifying God by a theory of moral and physical concurrence together with the theological doctrine of redemption makes no sense unless sin is a *real* evil. Moreover, the legitimacy and effectiveness of punishment (pain) also presuppose its reality.

b. It would seem that the whole dynamic of harmony and the intensity of pleasure it procures depend on compensation for a *real* and not merely apparent evil. For, there can be no reparation or compensation where there is in reality only a combination of goods of unequal perfection.

To avoid the contradiction between these two conceptions of evil, one could maintain that they do not apply to the same level. Frédéric de Buzon suggests a distinction between the level of universal harmony, where the occurrence of dissonance produces variety and contributes to global perfection, and the level of theoretical knowledge, where the appearance of irregularity vanishes under rules and disappears in distinct perception.[200] He contrasts the beauty of the "clear-confused," which is meaningful only in art and in nature conceived as a cosmos or spectacle, with an intellectual beauty that results from the arrangement of signs or equations, where there can be no real error, disorder, or aberration. On this view, there are two kinds of beauty (and so two kinds of pleasure), corresponding respectively to a clear but confused perception and one that is perfectly distinct.

De Buzon's suggestion has the disadvantage of rendering the notion of beauty, and correlatively that of pleasure, equivocal and ultimately leads to the following contradiction. In the one case, it is asserted that true contemplation of universal harmony amounts to perfect knowledge of reasons, and consequently, recognition of the absence of real disorder and evil. In the other case, it is asserted that the pleasure derived from true contemplation of universal harmony resides, on the contrary, in the experience of dissonance and irregularities (which therefore must be considered real), albeit corrected and compensated. Is there room in the perfect knowledge of the reasons for all things, as in the knowledge of an equation (which accounts for an irregular curve), for a pleasure whose nature rests precisely in the interplay of appearances and confusions? In other words, can the beatific vision be purely and entirely rational without ceasing to be a pleasure?

Perhaps the distinction to be made is not between two types of beauty and pleasure, but between the knowledge and pleasure that belong to creatures (which even in beatitude always remain limited) and the knowledge and "pleasure" that belong to God. For the blessed, as for the sage or geometer, pleasure comes in moving from confused perception to rational discovery.[201] There is always something apparent and confused, a certain evil or, at least, some uneasiness—even in beatitude. However, no such thing is possible in the supremely perfect being, who by definition, cannot move to a greater state of perfection. His knowledge is complete and wholly adequate. It is not knowledge of a system of phenomena located in space and unfolding in time. Rather, it is an intuition of a priori reasons and pure logical relations.[202] Nor can there be in God any form of physical evil, however minimal or attenuated. "God cannot suffer either vexation, or grief or discomfort; he is always wholly content and at ease."[203] As for the effect of surprise, uneasiness and expectation (the habitual ingredients of pleasure), which depend on ignorance of the future, they are obviously incompatible with his foreknowledge. Therefore, we must believe that there exists in God some analogue of pleasure (rather than pleasure properly speaking), which, beyond the joy he takes in consideration of his own absolutely perfect nature, is the joy of seeing his work gradually come to fruition.[204]

In my view, this ineliminable equivocation in Leibniz's conception of evil results from two equally important demands. The first is that of the philosopher-mathematician, who holds that evil is like the alleged irregularities in mathematics. There is no line so irregular that a geometer cannot supply its equation, nor any sequence of numbers so disorderly that a mathematician cannot furnish the rule for its construction. The second demand is that of the theologian-jurist, who, while recognizing that sin and pain are part of the general economy of salvation, considers them according to the laws of justice, as respectively a violation of order and a well-deserved punishment of the sinner (or, failing that, as the means of improving man).

## NOTES

1. Cf. *Causa Dei*, §63.
2. T §27; GP VI, 118; Huggard, 138–139.
3. Cf. to section 3.2.2.
4. Moreover, in the *Conversation with Steno* (A VI, 4-B, 1382), Leibniz shows that it would be necessary to explain the part attributed to humans (which is an act) by God's concurrence, and so once again, to divide this part into two, then for the same reason, to divide the part attributed to man into two, and so on to infinity, and that as a result, it is better to recognize God's total concurrence from the outset.
5. Cf. section 1.2.3.
6. See T §27; GP VI, 118; Huggard, 138–139 and §381; GP VI, 342. See also section 3.2.1.

7. "the effect depends upon God not only for the reason that its cause originates in God, but also for this other reason, that God concurs no less nor more indirectly in producing this effect than in producing its cause" (*Causa Dei,* §11; GP VI, 440; S 115). See also GP III, 30.

8. T §27; GP VI, 118–119; Huggard, 139.

9. Cf. T §28.

10. GP III, 29–30.

11. *Causa Dei,* §68; GP VI, 449.

12. T §390; GP VI, 346; Huggard, 358.

13. Cf. T §391; GP VI, 347. See also §388.

14. Cf. T §395. See also GP III, 67: "modification, far from adding any perfection, [can] only be a restriction or variable limitation, and consequently, [can] not exceed the perfection of the subject."

15. Cf. Boethius, *Consolation of Philosophy*, I, Prose 4, 30.

16. T §20; GP VI, 114–115; Huggard, 135. Among the "ancients" cited by Leibniz at §379 are Plato and the Stoics.

17. T §20; GP VI, 115; Huggard, 136. See also GP III, 33.

18. *Causa Dei,* §69; GP VI, 449; S 129. See also T §31.

19. *Causa Dei,* §69; GP VI, 449; S 129.

20. CP; A VI, 3, 127–128; Sleigh, 55–57.

21. T §288; GP VI, 288. As for free will, it is "the proximate cause of evil of guilt and subsequently of evil of punishment."

22. T §335; GP VI, 313–314; Huggard 326–327. See also §380; GP VI, 341; Huggard 353: "I have already shown that this source [of evil] lies in the forms or ideas of the possibles, *for it must be eternal*, and matter is not so" (emphasis added).

23. Nothingness is "infinite, it is eternal, and it has many attributes in common with God" (Grua, 364; AG 113).

24. T §149, GP VI, 198–199, Huggard 217. The solution that consists in imputing evil to God's understanding and not to his will, so as to avoid Manichaeism is already set out in the *Confession of a Philosopher* (cf. A VI, 3, 121; Sleigh 41), though within a very different theoretical framework.

25. Cf. T §150; GP VI, 199.

26. T §152; GP VI, 200; Huggard, 218.

27. T §20; GP VI, 115; Huggard, 136.

28. *On the Radical Origination of Things*, GP VII, 305.

29. The divine understanding is constituted by the entire collection of possibles and cannot extend beyond them, since they represent all that is intelligible. However, it is distinct from possibles by virtue of its operations, that is, by the "infinitely infinite combinations" of them that it makes and that constitute the infinity of possible worlds. On this point, see T § 225; GP VI, 252.

30. Cf. Grua, 355.

31. *Dialogue on Human Freedom and the Origin of Evil*, Grua 365; AG 114–115.

32. Leibniz to Arnauld (July 14, 1686), A II, 2, 69–70.

33. Cf. Brunner, "L'optimisme leibnizien," in *Leibniz (1646–1716)*, 250.

34. Knowingly, because he is aware of the distinction (see, for example, A VI, 4-B, 1338).

35. Here I agree with the interpretation of Maria-Rosa Antognazza. See her article, "Metaphysical Evil Revisited," in *New Essays on Leibniz's Theodicy*, 127.

36. Cf. T §153 and §378.

37. Cf. GP III, 34; *Causa Dei*, §69.

38. Cf. *On Genesis in the Literal Sense* (incomplete work) I, 3; *On Free Will* I, 1. See also ST, Ia, q. 48, a. 5, and *On Evil*, q. 1, a. 4.
39. Cf. ST Ia, q. 48, a. 5.
40. Cf. *Disputationes metaphysicae*, Disp. XI, Sect. 1, §3 and Sect. 3, §§17–18.
41. Cf. JUT, 354, note 72.
42. T ob §7; GP VI, 406; Huggard, 411 (emphasis added).
43. The definition of the three divine perfections (understanding, will, and power) as three *primordials* (T §150).
44. In chapter 2 (§2, 36 of the edition of 1702) King distinguishes "evil of imperfection," "natural" evil and "moral" evil. Evil of imperfection is for him "the absence of those perfections or those conveniences [*commodorum*] to be found elsewhere or in other things."
45. Leibniz was certainly familiar with King's work, first by mediation of Pierre Bayle, who criticizes it in volume 2 of the *Reply to the Questions of a Provincial* (1704, Chapters 74 to 92). Bayle, who had not read the work, relies on a summary published by Jacques Bernard in the *News from the Republic of Letters* (May and June 1703). In volume 3 of the *Reply to the Questions of a Provincial* (1705, Chapter 162), Bayle refers to what the *Journal des Savants* reports concerning King's book. Leibniz does not specify when the *De Origine Mali* "came into his hands" (GP VI, 400), nor when he read it. In general, his references to it are limited to noting points of agreement and disagreement with his own doctrine, without indicating any genuine influence.
46. Antognazza "Metaphysical Evil Revisited." In *New Essays on Leibniz's Theodicy*, 122.
47. Ibid., 123–124.
48. Ibid., 115; cf. Grua, JUT, 368.
49. *De virtutibus et vitiis disputationes ethicae*, Dispute I, Question IV, Section 3, §35, 45.
50. Leibniz to Chauvin (1696), A I, 12, 622.
51. *Universa philosophia de moribus*, VI, Chapter 17, 348 and VIII, Chapter 3, 389.
52. *L'Ethique ou Philosophie morale*, Book I, Chapter 8, §8.
53. *Lexicon philosophicum* (Paris, 1675), 110.
54. GP III, 32 (emphasis added).
55. *Theosophiae seu agnitionis de Deo naturalis specimen*, Chapter 1, Definition 2 (Altdorf, 1689), 6.
56. Grua, 550 (emphasis added).
57. See respectively, T ob §7; GP VI, 406; T §21; GP VI, 115; Huggard, 136; GP III, 32 ("*imperfectio in universum*"). Note that in the index to the *Theodicy* the entry "imperfection" refers to "metaphysical evil" and vice versa (GP VI, 369 and 371).
58. Metaphysical good and evil taken *generally* (*generatim*) consist in the perfection and imperfection of things, including those that lack reason, whereas physical good and evil concern *specifically* (*speciatim*) rational creatures (cf. *Causa Dei*, §§30–32; GP VI, 443).
59. Cf. T §241 and §§244–245. At §246 Leibniz characterizes disorder in inanimate things as "purely metaphysical" (GP VI, 263).
60. Cf. T §263.
61. Leibniz to Bourguet (December 1714), GP III, 574. The reference to metaphysical good confirms my suggestion that metaphysical evil was first conceived in contrast to its opposite.
62. GP III, 32.

63. T §118; GP VI, 168–169; Huggard, 188 (emphasis added). See also §209; GP VI, 242; Huggard, 257–258: "perfection includes not only the *moral good* and the *physical good* of intelligent creatures, but also the good which is purely *metaphysical*, and concerns also creatures devoid of reason."

64. §209; GP VI, 242; Huggard, 257–258 (emphasis added).

65. This primacy can be seen, for example, in the case of reason. Reason is a perfection (a metaphysical good) whose end is neither uniquely nor even principally the happiness of the minds endowed with it. Despite the evils that result from its misuse, and even if it produced more moral and physical evil than good in human beings, "it might still be the case that it was more in accordance with the perfection of the universe to give reason to men, notwithstanding all the evil consequences which it might have with reference to them. Consequently, the final will or the decree of God, resulting from all the considerations he can have, would be to give it to them" (T §119; GP VI, 170; Huggard, 190).

66. T §29; GP VI, 119; Huggard, 140.

67. Cf. *Monadology*, §42, L 1051: "This *original imperfection* of creatures is noticeable in the *natural inertia* of the body"; Leibniz to Remond (February 11, 1715), GP III, 636: "As for the inertia of matter, as matter itself is only a phenomenon, though a well-founded one, resulting from monads, it is the same as with inertia, which is a property of this phenomenon."

68. T §30; GP VI, 120–121; Huggard, 141. See also §335 where Leibniz refers to the cylinder of Chrysippus; T s V; GP VI, 383–384; *Causa Dei*, §71; GP III, 34.

69. T §30, GP VI, 120.

70. Ibid.

71. Thus, I do not claim that Leibniz ascribes any kind of active nature to the origin of evil, which would lead him to adopt a kind of Manichaeism. See Newlands, "Leibniz on Privations, Limitations, and the Metaphysics of Evil," 302–303.

72. T §153; GP VI, 201; Huggard, 220.

73. Ibid.

74. Notice, however, that in a powerful being malice could have much more harmful effects than in a weak being. Nevertheless, malice does not derive from power itself.

75. *Fourth Reply to Clarke* (August 1716), §34; GP VII; 397; L 1142.

76. *Causa Dei*, §72; GP VI, 450; S 130.

77. See *Critical Thoughts on the General Part of the Principles of Descartes*, GP IV, 361 (on articles 31 and 35).

78. T §32; GP VI, 121; Huggard, 142. See also §153. Notice that ignorance, error, and malice are the three kinds of cause commonly cited to define moral fault and assess it juridically.

79. T §32; GP VI, 122; Huggard, 142.

80. The error can be explained in the same manner as an error in calculation, namely by a lack of attention or memory. See, for example, *Critical Thoughts on the General Part of the Principles of Descartes*, GP IV, 356 (on article 5) and 361 (on articles 31 and 35).

81. This lack of reflection can result from the urgency of the action (in which case it is excusable), but also from habit, the effect of certain impressions on the organs, passions, prejudices, the imagination, and memory (cf. T ob §24): "Errors are therefore, absolutely speaking, never voluntary, although the will very often contributes to them indirectly, owing to the pleasure one takes in giving oneself

up to certain thoughts, or owing to the aversion one feels for others" (T ob §25; GP VI, 430; Huggard, 435).

82. Cf. NE IV, 17, §§1–3; A VI, 6, 475; PNG §5 and *Monadology*, §28. Leibniz distinguishes the "external senses," which "properly speaking, do not deceive us" from "inner sense which often makes us go too fast" when it is based only on the senses (T pd §65; GP VI, 87; Huggard, 109).

83. T pd §30 and §31; GP VI, 68. See also T §56.

84. Cf. *Conversation du Marquis de Pianese et du Pere Emery Eremite*, A VI, 4-C, 2249.

85. Cf. T Preface, GP VI, 31–33; T s, III; GP VI, 381; Grua, 457.

86. Cf. *Critical Thoughts on the General Part of the Principles of Descartes*, GP IV, 361–362 (on articles 31–35).

87. T §319; GP VI, 306; Huggard, 319.

88. *Causa Dei*, §73; GP VI, 450; S 130 (emphasis added).

89. T §33; GP VI, 122; Huggard, 142. See also GP III, 34.

90. Cf. A VI, 3, 623.

91. T §33; GP VI, 122; Huggard, 142.

92. *Imbecillitas* (*Causa Dei*, §79, GP VI, 451), also *debilitas, infirmitas* (*Theological System*, A VI, 4-C, 2376).

93. Cf. T §156; GP VI, 203.

94. T §155; GP VI, 202; Huggard, 221.

95. Cf. A VI, 4-B, 1593. See also the variant to §30 of DM (A VI, 4-B, 1577) and A VI, 4-B, 1606.

96. T §167; GP VI, 210; Huggard 228.

97. Leibniz to Molanus (February 2, 1698?), Grua 412.

98. Leibniz to Molanus (February 22, 1698), Grua 413.

99. Leibniz to Des Bosses (February 8, 1711), GP II, 419. Leibniz prefers to reserve the term *moral necessity* for the good (GP II, 419–420).

100. Leibniz to Des Bosses (July 8, 1711), GP II, 423; LR 207.

101. Leibniz to Des Bosses (September 7, 1711), GP II, 424; LR 211.

102. Cf. *Theological System*, A VI, 4-C, 2376 and 2377.

103. Cf. T §156, §273, and §275.

104. Cf. T §273 and §277.

105. Cf. T §278. In the *Theological System*, Leibniz makes clear that unlike the angels, who fell by pride, the first man, having been seduced by the devil, fell by concupiscence, the "bestial sin" (A VI, 4-C, 2359). On the pleasure of eating the forbidden fruit, see *On Wisdom*, Grua, 584–585.

106. *Dialogue on Human Freedom and the Origin of Evil*, Grua 365; AG 114 (emphasis added).

107. Cf. A VI, 4-B, 1606; *Theological System*, A VI, 4-C, 2359.

108. Respectively, A VI, 4-B, 1593–1594; and *Causa Dei*, §80; GP VI, 451.

109. *Causa Dei*, §86, GP VI, 452; S 133–134. See also *Theological System*, A VI, 4-C, 2359.

110. Cf. Leibniz to Des Bosses (July 11, 1706), GP II, 311.

111. T §26; GP VI, 118; Huggard, 138. Cf. T ob §15; GP VI, 414.

112. Cf. T Preface; GP VI, 46; *Causa Dei*, §§94–95.

113. *Theological System*, A VI, 4-C, 2359.

114. Cf. Ibid., 2377.

115. See especially T pd §39; T §5, §§92–94, §283; T s, VI; *Causa Dei*, §87.

116. Cf. T Preface; GP VI, 36; *Theological System*, A VI, 4-C, 2360. Roman law holds that the crime or punishment of a father cannot redound to the son, since no

one can inherit the crime of another (Digest 48, 19, 26; see also Digest 50, 17, 74). With regard to canon law, see in particular Rules 22 and 23 of *Liber Sextus Decretalium*.

117. T §92; GP VI, 153; Huggard, 173.
118. *Causa Dei*, §91; GP VI, 453.
119. Cf. T §33; GP VI, 122.
120. *Causa Dei*, §93; GP VI, 453; S 135. Adam's sin can be considered to have been *habitual* from the outset, given its particularly serious and "striking" [*fortis*] nature.
121. Leibniz to Thomas Burnett (October 18, 1712), GP III, 324.
122. T §91; 152–153; Huggard, 172–173.
123. *Causa Dei*, §82; GP VI, 451–452; S 133.
124. See Goclenius, who in his *Philosophical Lexicon* (Frankfurt, 1613, 53) refers to Gabriel Biel.
125. Cf. T §397; Leibniz to Des Bosses (September 8, 1709), GP II, 389–390.
126. Cf. T §112; Grua 243. Notice that the "almost astronomical theology" presented by Leibniz at §18 of the *Theodicy* participates in this naturalizing project, by offering a physical account of the fall of the devil, of hell, and of the apocalypse.
127. T §112; GP VI, 164; Huggard, 184.
128. *Causa Dei*, §80; GP VI, 451; S 131.
129. Cf. T §112 and §126.
130. T §112; GP VI, 165; Huggard, 185. In the index to the *Theodicy*, the entry "Harmony" refers notably to "Natural Punishment" (GP VI, 369).
131. T §99; GP VI, 158; Huggard, 178; GP III, 34.
132. Cf. T s, V; GP VI, 383–384.
133. T ob §27; GP VI, 436; Huggard, 441. Leibniz comments, "which indicates a hopeless passion from which one cannot free oneself."
134. Misery is "the state of going from imperfection to imperfection, from suffering to suffering" (NE II, 21, §58; A VI, 6, 202; RB 202).
135. T §92. Contrary to what was maintained in the *Plan of Catholic Demonstrations*, A VI, 1, 499 (Ch. 50).
136. T §266; GP VI, 275. Cf. CP; A VI, 3, 119: "the greatest suffering is misery, or damnation."
137. Cf. CP; A VI, 3, 139. On the reasons for Judas's hatred, see also CP, 119, and my commentary in "L'amour: Identité et expression," *Studia Leibnitiana*, 35/1, 2003, 65–67. Leibniz to Lorenz Hertel (January 18, 1695), A I, 11, 21–22: "It is very true that there would not be an eternity of punishments if there were not an eternity of sins. For sinners damn themselves, so to speak, and keep themselves in damnation by continuing to sin. So how do we know that there aren't minds which always get worse and worse, rather than those which always get better and better and others which vary for a time before being determined one way or the other?" The suffering of the soul of the damned is sometimes assimilated to melancholy (cf. A VI, 1, 499, chap. 49). This comparison with a psychological pathology, known to doctors since antiquity, casts the damned as a sick, or even, insane person, who keeps rehearsing his disappointments and sufferings with some degree of pleasure.
138. However, Leibniz cites Jaquelot, who speaks of the reflections of the damned on their crimes, their "burning regrets" and their envy (T §268; GP VI, 276–277; Huggard, 291). Leibniz also praises King for his observations concerning the damned, whom he compares to fools who feel their misery but take pleasure in

it and perpetually increase it through their own fault and renewed errors (§270, 277–278; T ob §27; GP VI, 436).

139. See, respectively, T §73 and §74; GP VI, 141 and 142; Huggard 161 and 162. On vindictive justice, see section 7.1.4.

140. See T §133; GP VI, 186.

141. T §266; GP VI, 275; Huggard, 290.

142. Cf. Anselm, *Cur Deus Homo?* (*Why God Became a Man?*), I, 13 and 21; II, 14; Thomas Aquinas, ST, Ia IIae, q. 87, a. 4; IIIa, q. 1, a. 2.

143. Concerning the distinction between *infinitum terminative* and *infinitum formaliter*, see Grua, 251.

144. T §266; GP VI, 275; Huggard, 290. See also *Causa Dei*, §59; GP VI, 436.

145. Cf. GP III, 37: "That is why neither original sin, nor our evil dispositions render the act of sin necessary, although our inclination to sin is such that it is certain that we cannot avoid sinning, unless we are prevented from doing so by divine grace."

146. T §269; GP VI, 277; Huggard, 292.

147. Cf. T §282; GP VI, 284. On the distinction between *proximate* and *remote* power, see section 5.2.1. Concerning the point beyond which it is certain that the sinner will never repent, see T §57; GP VI, 134.

148. See, for example, Leibniz to Eckhard (Summer 1677), A II, 1, 543: "*perfection is the degree or quantity of reality or essence*"; A VI, 4-A, 556; *On the Radical Origination of Things*, GP VII, 303; *Monadology*, §41.

149. Cf. A VI, 4-A, 867.

150. T ob §22; GP VI, 425.

151. Cf. Leibniz to Wolf (May 18, 1715), GB 172.

152. Cf. T §119; GP VI, 170–171.

153. T §10; GP VI, 108; Huggard, 129.

154. Leibniz to Molanus (February 22, 1698), Grua, 415 (at issue are the reasons for election). See also T §105; *Causa Dei*, §137. Grua, 476: "It is not what is better [*melius*] in itself that is chosen, but what is most fit [*aptius*] for the end."

155. Cf. DM §2.

156. The two scales correspond on the metaphysical level, though not, of course, on the moral and physical levels, since brute monads are the most imperfect of creatures and yet are incapable of sin or suffering. On the other hand, bad rational creatures (humans and demons) are by nature more perfect, but are very imperfect morally, on account of their sins, and physically on account of the suffering they endure as punishment.

157. Cf. T §8. See also T s, VIII; GP VI, 387; NE II, 21, §§41–42; A VI, 6, 195; RB, 195: "*Good is what provides or conduces to pleasure, as evil is what conduces to pain; but when we sacrifice a greater good to a lesser one which conflicts with it, the latter can become really an evil in so far as it contributes to the pain which must result.*"

158. See, respectively, T §348; GP VI, 321; Huggard, 334; and *Letter of M.L. on a General Principle*, GP III, 52–53.

159. Cf. T §92; GP VI; 153; *Conversation with Eckhard* (April 15, 1677), A II, 1, 488: "it seems to me that one can no more say that pain is the privation of pleasure, than that pleasure is the privation of pain. Rather, pleasure as well as pain is something positive." Grua, 252: "For my part, I believe that pain, like error, is positive, but founded on privative things."

160. T §251; GP VI, 266; Huggard, 281.

161. Cf. NE II, 20, §6; A VI, 6, 165.
162. Cf. GP III, 32: "Physical good and evil are commonly understood as conveniences (*commodis*) and inconveniences (*incommodis*) of intelligent creatures, namely in so far as something agreeable or disagreeable occurs to them; and the evil of punishment is of this kind"; *Causa Dei*, §31 (see also *Conversation du Marquis de Pianese et du Pere Emery Eremite*, A VI, 4-C, 2243).
163. NE II, 21, §§41–42; A VI, 6, 194; RB 194: "I doubt that a greatest pleasure is possible; I am inclined to believe that it can increase *ad infinitum*, for we do not know how far our knowledge and our organs can be developed in the course of the eternity which lies before us."
164. Cf. NE II, 1, §11; A VI, 6, 113; II, 20, §1, 162; II, 21, §§41–42, 194.
165. Cf. NE II, 20, §7; A VI, 6, 166; II, 21, §64, 204.
166. NE II, 20, §6; A VI, 6, 165; RB 165. Cf. *Phaedo*, 60 b-c.
167. For the happiness of creatures "never consists in complete attainment, which would make them insensate and stupified, but in continual and uninterrupted progress toward greater goods. Such progress is inevitably accompanied by desire or at least by constant disquiet . . . it does not amount to discomfort, but is restricted to the elements or rudiments of suffering, which we cannot be aware of in themselves but which suffice to act as spurs and to stimulate the will. That is what a healthy man's appetite does, unless it amounts to that discomfort which unsettles us and gives us a tormenting obsession with the idea of whatever it is that we are without" (NE II, 21, §36; A VI, 6, 189; RB 189).
168. Cf. T ob §27; GP VI, 436; CP; A VI, 3, 142–143.
169. Cf. T §342.
170. T §241; GP VI, 261.
171. *On the Radical Origination of Things*, GP VII, 307; L 797. See also GP VII, 291, §24: "the evils themselves serve a greater good, and as for the pains that we observe in minds, it must be the case that they make it possible to obtain greater pleasures."
172. T §122; GP VI, 177; Huggard, 196–197; *Causa Dei*, §32, §§54–55.
173. Cf. T §257.
174. Cf. T §211; *Causa Dei*, §54.
175. Cf. T §241. Notice that the index to the *Theodicy* contains no specific entry for "pain" or "suffering." To be sure, physical evil, together with metaphysical and moral evil, is cited in the entry "evil." However, metaphysical evil and moral evil also appear respectively in the entries for "Imperfection" and "Sins." In fact, physical evil is taken up in relation to the question of justice in the entries "damnation" and "punishment."
176. Cf. T Preface; GP VI, 27–28.
177. Cf. T §105.
178. Cf. Grua 189, 702, 755, 814; NE II, 21, §37; A VI, 6, 191; IV, 19, §§1–16, 509; T §315. On the conditional nature of duty, see T §121.
179. The expression occurs in the index under the heading "Sins," GP VI, 372.
180. Cf. T §114.
181. Leibniz to Morell (September 29, 1698), Grua 138. See also Leibniz to Placcius (September 29, 1697), Dutens VI-1, 84. In his letter to Wedderkopf, Leibniz goes so far to say that sins are "good, that is, harmonious" considered together with their punishment (A II, 1, 187).
182. Cf. T §215.

183. Elster, *Leibniz et la formation de l'esprit capitaliste*, 14, and 181–189. On this reading, Leibniz was aware of the development of nascent capitalism "to the point of basing his notion of God on that of the capitalist entrepreneur" (24).

184. Cf. section 5.1.3.

185. Cf. *On the Radical Origination of Things*, GP VII, 303–304. Leibniz also uses the example of tiles to be arranged cover as much of a given surface as possible.

186. Cf. Leibniz to Wedderkopf, A II, 1, 187; Sleigh, 5: "For there is no harmony except as a result of contraries"; *Elements of Natural Law*, A VI, 1, 484; A VI, 3, 588; CP; A VI, 3, 116, 122, and 124.

187. CP; A VI, 3, 122; Sleigh, 45. See also *Elements of Natural Law*, A VI, 1, 479.

188. T §12; GP VI, 109; Huggard, 130. Thus, the poet, composer, and divine artist each must find that equilibrium and limit (which is unique on account of the uniqueness of the best) in which there are neither too many discordant elements to avoid the threat of universal disharmony, nor too few to avoid uniformity.

189. Cf. *On the Radical Origination of Things*, GP VII, 306.

190. Leibniz to Bernoulli (March 6, 1699), A III, 8, 64. See also T §216.

191. Cf. T §241 and following.

192. T §242; GP VI, 262; Huggard, 277. Leibniz also gives the example of a sequence of numbers that is irregular in appearance. See also DM §6.

193. Cf. T §207 and §337.

194. T §243; GP VI, 262; Huggard, 277 (emphasis added).

195. Leibniz to Morell (September 29, 1698), Grua 137. See also GP VII, 290 (19).

196. Leibniz to the Electress Sophia Charlotte (May 9, 1697), GP VII, 545.

197. T §147; GP VI, 197–198; Huggard, 216. Even sins increase universal perfection, cf. Leibniz to Morell (September 29, 1698), Grua,138.

198. See also, in *On the Radical Origination of Things* (GP VII, 306), the example of a painting that seems imperfect to us when we see only a small part of it and are not at a sufficient distance to appreciate it.

199. Cf. Leibniz to Wedderkopf, A II, 1, 187; Sleigh, 5.

200. "L'harmonie: Métaphysique et phénoménalité," 115.

201. Cf. CP; A VI, 3, 139. See also *On Affects*, A VI, 4-B, 1435.

202. Cf. T §192; see also §389.

203. T §114; GP VI, 166;, Huggard, 186.

204. Cf. A VI, 4-B, 1642.

# CHAPTER 7

✧

# Human Freedom and Principles
of Action

Although all things depend for their creation and continued existence on God, his moral concurrence (by virtue of his will) and physical concurrence (by virtue of his power) are limited to the permission of sin and what is positive in it (its "matter"). Evil lies within the creature and comes from it, not from God. It is at once a privation, a tendency to new privations and a resistance to being and perfection. It is that which corrupts and perverts the good. While the origin of evil lies in the divine understanding, which thinks it, it becomes actual by human will. Although God is its principle, man alone is culpable for it. For, it belongs to human beings either to acquiesce to and willingly consent to God's gifts (perfection, the good, grace) or, on the contrary, to resist them, to limit their effect or misuse them.

In this way, justification of God pushes responsibility for sin back onto human beings. Humans, who by themselves are incapable of any good movement without the aid of grace, sin by virtue of their wickedness, bad will, and abuse of free will.[1] However, Leibniz distances himself from those theologians and moralists who take pleasure in castigating human nature, endlessly denouncing its corruption, malignity, and vices.[2] Rather than heap abuse on humanity, Leibniz prefers to emphasize the "residual" freedom that remains in human beings despite sin. For Leibniz, this freedom, together with the "innate light of the understanding"[3] is a "vestige" of the image of God. For God has not neglected to provide spirits with the means of avoiding sin, resisting bad inclinations and doing good by the well-governed use of their reason and free will.

It is here that the properly anthropological and ethical wing of Theodicy begins. This wing, which is often neglected by commentators, ought not to be underestimated, especially in light of the practical implications that Leibniz would draw from his text and from science in general. Leibniz's concern with the practical is in keeping with his famous motto *Theoria cum praxi*, according to which theory and practice are inseparable. In the preface to the *Theodicy*, Leibniz declares "finally, I have endeavoured in all things to consider *edification*."[4] The practice of true piety must be the continuation of the exposition of the theory of divine justice. Knowledge is useless, if it does not move the will. We must join "ardor" to truth. Knowledge of God's attributes and the certainty that he has done everything for the best should arouse in us an enlightened and sincere love, which induces us to act well and leads to true happiness.[5] Metaphysics leads to morals, which brings perfect contentment. This perfect contentment goes beyond the imperfect virtue of the Stoics, which inspires only a "forced patience." As Leibniz had already argued in the *New Essays*:

> It should also be understood that metaphysics relates to true moral philosophy as theory to practice. That is because of the dependence on the doctrine of substances in general of that knowledge about spirits—and especially about God and the soul—which gives to justice and to virtue their proper extent. For . . . if there were neither providence nor an after-life, the wise man's practice of virtue would be more restricted, since he would refer everything only to his present satisfaction; and even that satisfaction—which has already been exemplified in Socrates, the Emperor Marcus Aurelius, Epictetus, and other ancients—would not always be as well grounded, in the absence of those broad and beautiful perspectives which are opened up to us by the order and harmony of the universe, extending to an unlimited future.[6]

By showing that God is good and has created the best possible world, Theodicy enables us to go beyond Stoic fate (*fatum stoïcum*), which emphasizes resignation in the face of the necessary order of things. Theodicy provides the means of envisaging properly Christian fate (*fatum christianum*), which consists in a voluntary and joyful adherence to a providence understood to be wise and benevolent. This ethics, which Leibniz sees as authentically Christian, is based on an original conception of freedom that is compatible with hypothetical necessity, the truth of future contingents, and divine foreknowledge (7.1). It presupposes a relation between human and divine freedom that differs according to whether one considers the ideal level (the order of possibles) or the existential level (the order of existents). Its fundamental principle is to love God above all things by striving, as much as possible, to realize his presumptive volition in the world (7.2).

## 7.1 THE LABYRINTH OF THE FREE AND THE NECESSARY AND THE PREREQUISITES OF FREEDOM

### 7.1.1 Negative Prerequisites and the Rejection of the Indifference of Equilibrium

In the *Essays of Theodicy*, the question of freedom is taken up following the examination of divine concurrence with creaturely actions (beginning at §34). It is not enough to affirm that evil is imputable to man alone. The question remains whether he is genuinely guilty and deserving of punishment, because he wills and does evil *freely*. It would appear that there is real culpability and a legitimate basis for punishment only if there is freedom. What legitimacy could there be in rewarding and punishing, assigning merit and demerit, if man were fully necessitated to do the good or evil he does?[7] Although God has been proved to be just in the sense of justice as *perfection*—that is, that his holiness is secure—it remains to be shown that he is just in the sense of justice as *law*, in his government of the republic of spirits, in that each receives his due and no one is damned except by his own fault nor saved except by his good will.

Freedom is taken to be the condition of the morality of our actions and of the application of justice. This explains why Leibniz takes up the question of freedom at precisely this point in the text. However, to grant human freedom creates problems not only for what has been said of God's nature and concurrence but also for the Principle of Sufficient Reason. How can freedom be reconciled with divine foreknowledge (God knows in advance what will happen, such that the future is certain and determined in its entirety) and his providence and omnipotence (which ensure that nothing is or occurs without his willing or permitting it and without his concurrence)? Finally, how can freedom be reconciled with determination, given that nothing can occur without a cause, and no action, however voluntary, can lack a motive or reason? In other words, how can an action be free, given that it is known by God even before it has occurred and that, consequently, it is true and certain that it will occur, and given that it is entirely determined and predetermined, since it belongs to a chain of causes that ensure it will occur without fail?

Naturally, to answer these questions, one must begin by defining freedom. At first, Leibniz defines freedom by two negative characteristics: *absence of constraint* and *absence of necessity*.[8] An agent is free if its power of acting and willing is not impeded, that is, if it is subjected neither to external constraint (e.g., when I am in chains, or when I am pushed onto a precipice) nor internal compulsion (e.g., I am under the influence of a strong passion, or when my judgment is impaired by the effects of a beverage[9]). Freedom consists in the power *to do* what one wills (physical freedom), without being forced or impeded in any way, and in the power *to will* "as one ought" (moral freedom[10]), that is, in accordance with the requirements of calm deliberation, namely, the full possession of one's faculties, which makes possible unconstrained exercise of one's reason.

Following Hobbes,[11] Leibniz acknowledges that, from a juridical and moral point of view, absence of constraint is sufficient to legitimize punishment and reward, insofar as they aim to prevent evil, incite people to good, or amend the guilty and serve as an example. Even if human beings acted by absolute necessity (which is not the case for Leibniz), praise and blame, reward and punishment would be no less "just and reasonable"[12]. They would still be *just*, because they would be the wages of virtue and vice. The judge considers the will, good or bad, without having to ask whether the defendant's actions were contingent or necessary. The latter is a philosophical question, which is not for the judge to decide, nor does it need to be considered in order to render justice correctly. Moreover, it must be recognized that there are cases where we rightly blame, or even punish, someone for actions he could not have failed to commit. Such is the case of the dangerous madman or maniac who is killed out of legitimate self-defense, just as for, reasons of safety, one might kill a savage beast or a dangerous or poisonous animal even though it is not responsible for its condition.[13] The same holds true for qualities and virtues. We admire and praise the good character of a person, the strength and vigor of a horse or the beauty of a diamond, even though these are gifts of nature. Paradoxically, the less the characteristic depends upon the will of the subject, the more it seems worthy of praise. It is for this reason that "he who said of Cato of Utica that he acted virtuously through the goodness of his nature, and that it was impossible for him to behave otherwise" did not mean to diminish his merit, but "thought to praise him all the more."[14]

Punishments and rewards, exhortations, admonitions, and reproaches would still be *reasonable* and useful, even if we were absolutely necessitated, since they serve to correct bad behavior and inspire good actions. The argument that the necessity of a crime would render all warnings and punishments vain rests on the same error as the Lazy Sophism.[15] A good or bad event, however necessitated it may be, would not occur without its causes, which would themselves be necessary. The end does not occur without the means. Now, the hope of reward and the fear of punishment figure among those causes and means that, on the determinist's view, will lead people to act well. Reward will reinforce virtue, while punishment will serve to reform the guilty. Punishment may also provoke a change in the criminal that will determine him to act justly in the future, albeit just as necessarily as before!

The mind, insofar as its judgment is not impaired, insofar as it is master of itself and the principle of its actions lies within it (and not in some other agent that compels it), has "sufficient" freedom to be rewarded or punished, whether its actions are absolutely necessary or contingent. However, for Leibniz, the mind possesses only an "imperfect freedom"[16] insofar as it has not been shown that its will is not only exempt from constraint but also unnecessitated. Perfect and entire freedom presupposes *free will*, the power to choose that belongs to the mind and by which it determines itself, not without motive, but according to the reasons that incline the most.[17] Free will does not imply that the mind is in a state of pure indifference: being free of necessity does not mean being free of all determination. The will is free when its choice is contingent (such that it could have been otherwise) and yet motivated, since choice is always made for motives and unfailingly follows from certain causes. These motives and causes, however strong and pressing they may be, are never such as to render every other choice absolutely impossible.

From Leibniz's point of view, the opposition between freedom and determination is simply meaningless, since (1) the two terms are neither contradictory nor incompatible, and (2) there can be no free act without some determining motive, unless one is willing to envisage an effect without a cause.

(1). The controversies and misunderstandings regarding freedom and necessity often result from conceptual confusions and poorly drawn distinctions. Free is not opposed to determined but rather to compelled or forced. The contrary of contingent is necessary, and the contrary of determined is undetermined or indifferent. Determination is not a modal category, as asserted by Hobbes, who treats it as synonymous with necessity.[18] In the general sense of the term, *determination* suggests a connection among things, states, or events without specifying the nature of the connection (whether necessary or contingent). More specifically, to say of a thing that it is determined is to say that it undergoes the influence of another such that it acts in a prescribed manner if nothing prevents it. Determination is that from which a certain effect follows if nothing impedes it, that is, if no contrary determination prevents it.[19] It is in itself a sufficient cause, albeit a *conditioned* one, since its effect will occur on condition of not being opposed. Consequently, it is *inclining* and not necessitating (such that its effect would be produced no matter what). In this sense, the will can be free though entirely determined, that is always inclined in its choice by prevailing motives, without that choice thereby being necessary. For there is no determination that cannot be surpassed by another more powerful one, and, because, although it is certain and infallible that the will will always follow the path to which it is most inclined, every other choice is still *logically* possible.

(2). Far from excluding determination, freedom presupposes it. Freedom could not be exercised if there were nothing to incline the will and if everything were perfectly indifferent to it. In fact, we would not be free if we were not guided by motives and inclined to certain ends, if we had no more reason to prefer one side to another, without preference for anything whatsoever. For Leibniz, indifference is chimerical and a factual impossibility. For, a situation of perfect equilibrium between the various options cannot occur in a world where everything differs and nothing is identical or equal.[20] Moreover, indifference would be useless, and even dangerous, if it could exist, since it would amount to a disregard for all considerations of good and evil. Leibniz criticizes Luis de Molina and his followers among the Jesuit theologians, who made such indifference the essence of freedom. Descartes accepts this alleged indifference, though he distinguishes between two types. The first, negative type constitutes "the lowest grade of freedom,"[21] insofar as it involves a lack of knowledge: we are indifferent to the extent that we do not know which is the right side to choose. The second type, on the other hand, involves a "positive faculty of determining oneself to one or other of two contraries,"[22] which is constitutive of the will itself. The will is fundamentally indifferent—that is, in itself independent of every motive—since it always remains free to give or withhold its consent to the solicitations and inclinations presented to it.

Cartesian freedom presupposes that motives are extrinsic to the will. Strictly speaking, the mind is not determined by anything whatsoever. It determines itself, that is, it deliberates and chooses according to present determinations (passions or reason). Leibniz cannot accept this supposed absolute power to choose independent of any motive, this abstract power that is in itself undetermined. The distinction between the will and its reasons is artificial and even illegitimate.[23] This is for two reasons. First, it is not clear how a will might be some sort of pure, naked will without any object whatsoever, instead of being a *will to something*. It would be a will that would tend to nothing and, consequently, that would not properly "will" anything. Second, it is far from clear how such a will could come to will anything after all. There would seem to be two possibilities. (1) The will might be thought to give itself its own object, without reason, by caprice. In this case, the free act is irrational and inexplicable, impossible to derive from any motive. It is, so to speak, the result of chance. (2) Alternatively, it might be held that the will determines itself according to preexisting reasons. However, in this case the distinction between the will and its motives becomes superfluous. For, if one holds that the will prefers one determination over another, choosing to consent to one rather than another *for certain reasons*, one must admit that is determined after all (by these very reasons). Furthermore, if someone should argue that the will is free with regard to these reasons themselves, it would be necessary to identify the motives that determined it to conform to these reasons. Now, by the same argument, these motives themselves will require new reasons and so on to infinity. Thus, it is better to admit from the outset that the will is not distinct from the inclination itself, whether this latter be a passion or reason.

Indifference makes it impossible to exercise freedom. If the indifference is in the object, in that all alternatives are equal, then because there would be no more inclination to one side than the other, for or against, choice and consequently action would be impossible. Such is the case of Buridan's ass, which standing at equal distance from two piles of hay, dies of hunger. If the indifference is in the subject, which is endowed with a power free of all determination and of any considerations of good and evil, choice and action are likewise impossible (since the determined cannot follow from the undetermined), or at least, incomprehensible. Indeed, "to claim that a determination comes from a complete indifference absolutely indeterminate is to claim that it comes naturally from nothing."[24] Indifference is an express violation of the Principle of Sufficient Reason and cannot exist in either God or human beings. Furthermore, the expression "free will" or "freedom of the will" must not be misinterpreted. In Leibniz's writings, they do not indicate that the will can freely give itself an object or ascribe some end to itself. The will is not under the control of the will, since the very notion of a *will to will* is absurd. There are two reasons for this.

On the one hand, it is purely redundant: to say that one wills to will something is simply to say that one wills it. One cannot will to will something unless one already wills it. On the other hand, it implies a redoubling of the will to infinity: "we will to act, strictly speaking, and we do not will to will; else we could still say that we will to have the will to will, and that would go on to infinity."[25] If in order to will, one must first will to do so, one could only will by willing to will. Now, in order to will to will, it will again be necessary to will to do so, that is, to posit a new willing and after that another upon which all the others are founded and so on. To avoid a sterile infinite regress, it must be recognized that the will cannot take itself as an object or give itself the end it wills, but that from the outset it is determined and oriented toward the good (whether it be the true good, or as in the case of created spirits, only the apparent good). The will is *determined*, yet always *contingent*.

Still, are there not cases in which the will seems to be in a state of indifference? What of those actions apparently performed "gratuitously" or without motive? Or, again, what of that interior sentiment of which Descartes speaks,[26] which is supposed to prove our independence with regard to our free acts? We believe our will indifferent, because we are not always aware of the reasons that motivate us or the causes that determine us, especially (although not solely) with regard to those actions we perform unthinkingly—as for example when we leave a room by placing the right foot in front of the left. We are often ignorant of such causes, because they go unperceived and act on us without our awareness. It must be remembered that the soul, by virtue of its faculty of expression, perceives everything that exists and everything that occurs in the universe in an essentially confused and unconscious manner. Now, this infinite and continuous flow of *petites impressions*, which ceaselessly affect the soul, does not fail to act upon it, inclining it and ensuring that it is never in a state of perfect equilibrium. Leibniz places great importance on these non-rational motives and unconscious determinations in explaining the actions and passions of the soul.[27]

Our subjective *sentiment* of independence is not a sufficient argument. It is of scarcely greater value than the feeling a compass needle might have when it takes itself to freely turn to the north, because it does not apperceive the attraction imperceptibly exerted on it by the magnetic pole![28] As for the hypothesis of acts performed without any motive or contrary to the interests of the subject, it presupposes a power that, were it to exist, would be harmful but in fact is illusory. Such a power would be harmful, indeed monstrous, since it would imply that, in the presence of a good and in full awareness of our own interest, we could neglect these considerations and deliberately choose evil (recognized and willed as evil). It is illusory, because he who seeks to act against his own good, or even without any reason whatsoever, would in reality act for motives: by caprice, or a love of contrarian behavior, or to show that he is free.[29] The desire not to follow reason, to act according to one's own pleasure or to prove one's independence is no proof of real indifference in the subject. On the contrary, it would express a very powerful inclination, capable of overpowering all consideration of one's true and acknowledged advantage.

## 7.1.2 The Positive Prerequisites (1): Intelligence

The negative prerequisites of freedom—absence of constraint and absence of necessity—allow us to identify, by way of contrast, its positive prerequisites. Constraint constitutes an obstacle to spontaneity and the perfect use of intelligence, just as absolute necessity is that which is opposed to contingency. Thus, in a positive sense, that substance is free which is endowed with intelligence, has within itself the principle of action, and whose acts are contingent. Two of these conditions of freedom will be familiar from Aristotle: spontaneity and deliberation (or choice).[30] However, these notions take on a very particular meaning within the framework of Leibnizian metaphysics. Section 288 of the *Theodicy* offers the following definition:

> [F]reedom, according to the definition required in the schools of theology, consists in intelligence, which involves a clear knowledge of the object of deliberation, in spontaneity, whereby we determine, and in contingency, that is, in the exclusion of logical or metaphysical necessity. Intelligence is, as it were, the soul of freedom, and the rest is as its body and foundation. The free substance is self-determining and that according to the motive of good perceived by the understanding, which inclines it without compelling it: and all the conditions of freedom are comprised in these few words.[31]

*Intelligence*, the first prerequisite of freedom, is equated with distinct knowledge, that is, with the knowledge that follows from right use of reason.[32] Here again, Leibniz does not distinguish the faculty from its object. Just as the will is not separate (as a distinct pure power) from its determinations and reason is nothing but a chain of truths (and not an abstract power of judging well or badly[33]), so intelligence consists of all our distinct perceptions, as opposed to the confused thoughts that come from the senses. In my view, there are three reasons why intelligence constitutes the "soul of freedom."

1. Intelligence is what distinguishes freedom (which is characteristic of spirits) from mere spontaneity, which is common to all substances, and from contingency, which characterizes the whole of nature and thus is not exclusive to the actions of rational creatures (because the laws of nature, and consequently their effects, are not grounded in absolute necessity).[34] Not everything spontaneous is free, just as not everything contingent is free, although whatever is free is spontaneous and contingent.

2. Properly speaking, intelligence is that which "animates" (is the soul of) the power to act in the sense that it is what sets it in motion (by presenting it with an end to be pursued) and ensures that the act is never the result of pure indifference, but rather of a determination that inclines without necessitating.

3. Intelligence is the measure of the degree of perfection of freedom. While a substance cannot be more or less spontaneous, nor an act more or less contingent, a spirit is more free to the extent that its knowledge is more distinct.

For Leibniz, to be free is not merely to be the principle of one's actions. It is to determine oneself according to the most distinct knowledge possible. The appeal to intelligence makes freedom a matter of degree and establishes differences between spirits. The more we are enlightened, that is the more we follow reason, the more we will be active and free. The more confused our perceptions, that is, the more we are subject to the passions, the more we will be passive and enslaved.[35]

As created beings, humans can have only limited intelligence and, for that reason, only imperfect freedom. Their freedom is further diminished by the corruption resulting from Adam's fall, which subjected them to sin. Nevertheless, there remains in us, as a mark of our likeness to God, that "light of the understanding" that includes innate ideas (and among them, the idea of the divinity), necessary truths of mathematics and logic, as well as the universal laws of justice and morality.[36] Indeed, Leibniz maintains, against Luther, that sin has not corrupted reason itself, but has merely rendered its use more difficult. For, the mind has only to turn to the light it so often neglects out of laziness and lack of attention. Our passions and our attachment to sensible things darken and obscure this light, but they cannot extinguish it. Just as human will did not become in itself evil after the fall (since it always tends to the good), although it is now attached to the sensible, so too our understanding is not corrupted, although it is dominated by the senses, which subject it to confused thoughts.

Thus, human freedom, diminished and weakened as it is (by our natural limitations, by original sin, by our confused perceptions, and our passions), can never be destroyed. Here we must distinguish freedom from its range of application. Even reduced to bondage, human beings still retain the power to choose and to act, in accordance with the state and conditions in which they find themselves:

> Yet a slave, slave as he is, nevertheless has freedom to choose according to the
> state he is in, although more often than not he is under the stern necessity

of choosing between two evils, because a superior force prevents him from attaining the goods to which he aspires. That which in a slave is effected by bonds and constraint in us is effected by passions, whose violence is sweet, but none the less pernicious. In truth we will only what pleases us: but unhappily what pleases us now is often a real evil, which would displease us if we had the eyes of the understanding open. Nevertheless that evil state of the slave, which is also our own, does not prevent us, any more than him, from making a free choice of what pleases us most, in the state to which we are reduced, in proportion to our present strength and knowledge.[37]

Limitation of our sphere of choice and action does not diminish our freedom, so much as its exercise, which is thereby confined to very narrow limits. The decisions made by the enslaved man, within the limited space defined by his oppressor, are not *in themselves* less free than those that are made when free of all external constraint. It is no different for the one who is a slave of the passions. To the extent that he does as he pleases, given his present state of knowledge—that is, determines himself according to the confused ideas he has—his choices are as free as those of the sage, who makes use of distinct notions. However, in another sense, with regard to intelligence, the choices of the man enslaved by the passions can be considered less free than those of the sage. Freedom, considered, so to speak, formally and essentially, does not admit of degrees. It is the same in the slave as in the free man, in the passionate as in the reasonable man. It is in itself absolute, for either it exists or it does not; there is no middle ground, as Hobbes had already seen.[38] However, freedom appears greater or lesser when we consider the limits within which it operates (whether or not one's freedom of acting is hindered) and the determinations that inspire it (whether one's freedom to will is guided by reason or the passions). It is in this sense, and only in this sense, that degrees of freedom are conceivable.[39]

### 7.1.3 The Positive Requisites (2): Spontaneity

The second fundamental prerequisite of freedom set out by Leibniz in §288 of the *Theodicy* is *spontaneity*. However, Leibniz's understanding of spontaneity differs somewhat from that of Aristotle and the Scholastics. For, it is not a question of distinguishing those actions that originate from within the substance (and which for this reason are characterized as spontaneous) from those that originate outside of it in external things (actions thus considered as constrained and involuntary and the cause of passions in the substance). According to the system of pre-established harmony, every substance, rational or not, is endowed with spontaneity with regard to both its actions and passions. Every substance is physically independent of the influence of all others (except God), since everything that occurs in it arises out of itself (*de son propre fonds*). It is in accordance with the law of its individual being that it unfolds the whole series of predicates that it includes and that its perceptions "spring naturally from one another, to represent the body that is allotted to it, and through its instrumentality the entire universe."[40]

Leibniz maintains that his "system" ascribes the greatest possible independence to the soul, by carrying spontaneity "beyond anything that has been conceived until now."[41] Spontaneity is not exclusive to spirits. However, in them it confers *dominion* over their actions[42] and, to a certain extent, over their thoughts and volitions. Spirits are distinguished from other substances by consciousness and reason. Thus, unlike other substances, spirits are not merely principles of their actions. They do not simply perform a series of predetermined acts without reflection. Rather, being self-aware, they act with knowledge of what they do and in accordance with the choices they make.

Consciousness and intelligence transform spontaneity into dominion. This dominion is in proportion to the degree of distinctness of knowledge, since, as we have seen, the more the spirit knows, the more it is active and free. Dominion is a power over voluntary actions, and not, strictly speaking, a power over the will that wills them. It is exercised over the chosen means and not the end: "we will to act, strictly speaking, and we do not will to will. Otherwise, we could still say that we will to have the will to will, and that would go on to infinity."[43] Thus, we do not have the power— at least, not immediately and instantaneously—to change our will, nor our inclinations, judgments, opinions, or beliefs. Just as we cannot will what we will, so we cannot desire, judge, or believe as we wish. Hence, we can see the absurdity of any commandment, whether by political or religious authority, that would obligate us to believe such and such a doctrine or dogma.[44]

Nevertheless, the mind possesses a certain *indirect* power over the understanding and will. Though it is impossible for us to act directly on present volitions and judgments (so as to change them), it is possible to act on the causes that will produce future volitions and judgments, by striving today to be in a position to will and to think otherwise tomorrow: "although it [the soul] cannot change its passions forthwith, it can work from afar towards that end with enough success, and endow itself with new passions and even habits." Furthermore, although the soul equally lacks the power to correct its opinions instantaneously, it can strive to improve its opinions for the future, or at least, to suspend judgment and postpone the decision, giving itself time to investigate. It is in this sense that

> although our opinion and our act of willing be not directly objects of our will (as I have already observed), one sometimes, takes measures nevertheless, to will and even to believe in due time, that which one does not will, or believe, now. So great is the profundity of the spirit of man.[45]

Circumstances, opportunities, company, and particular grace all play a capital role in forming our volitions and opinions. Thus, it is a matter of placing ourselves in the most propitious circumstances for effecting the desired change, by associating with good persons and following a program of reading that will gradually transform our way of thinking.[46] The action of the will on itself and on judgment is slow and indirect. It involves long preparation and exercises, but even more, it requires "artful twists" and stratagems[47] to better resist sensory impressions and promote the use of reason so far as possible. In this way, the soul can become and remain master of itself,[48] though without ever attaining complete mastery, since it will always contain confused perceptions and can never know everything within itself that determines it.

Spontaneity becomes dominion over oneself when a created substance is no longer content to be, so to speak, the "passive" source of its actions, but is able, through self-reflection, to recognize them as its own and to take responsibility for them. Spirits are not only spontaneous, like brute monads unconsciously producing everything contained within themselves, but free because they "appropriate" the internal principle with which they are identical and from which all their events and phenomena follow. Freedom consists in a reflexive and voluntary adherence to spontaneity and the greatest possible effort to master (or appropriate) it. For, it is not a question of merely approving of what happens to me, of consenting to *what I am*, but of attempting to take control of that which most escapes me, namely my will and understanding, by struggling against the passions that enslave the former and eliminating the confused perceptions that lead the latter into error. It is for this reason that

> it is important that one has good principles established to which even those who have received or taken to contrary inclinations can intrinsically adapt [*approprier*] themselves little by little, and to which they can naturally return by a carefully chosen and regulated practice, if they want to make the effort with them. For one can change even one's temperament.[49]

Here Leibniz offers an original discussion of a traditional theme in moral philosophy—self-mastery—dating back to Antiquity. His conception of self-mastery calls for two remarks and also invites an objection.

1. The power that the mind exercises indirectly, "obliquely, and not absolutely and indifferently"[50] over representations and volitions shows that the will can determine the understanding, leading it to form other thoughts and other judgments than those it currently has. Thus, the relation of the understanding to the will does not always involve the strict submission of the latter to the former, as is the case with "standard" intellectualist theories. Rather, it involves a permanent interaction between the two faculties and so leaves room for reciprocal determination. This leads Leibniz to a version of intellectualism that one might characterize as "moderate."[51] This "moderate" intellectualism offers significant advantages with regard to education and ethics in that it provides the means of reforming one faculty by acting on another.

2. This power to change oneself is a power only relatively speaking. For, it is in fact the mark of impotence. It belongs to human beings on account of their limitations, whereas God lacks such a power, since he "cannot change his nature, nor act otherwise than according to method." As Leibniz makes clear, "God's dominion, the dominion of wisdom, is that of reason. It is only God, however, who always wills what is most to be desired, and consequently he has no need of the power to change his will."[52]

   The power to modify (indirectly) one's volitions is the mark of a limited being that stands in need of correction. It is in no way an advantage or perfection. God has dominion over neither his understanding, as the defenders of the creation of the eternal truths believe, nor his will, as the defenders of voluntarism or absolute indifference maintain. This "lack" does nothing to diminish his omnipotence. On the contrary, it is a consequence of his perfection. God is perfectly free, because his ideas are all distinct. His thoughts are all true, and his volitions are all absolutely good. Therefore, he cannot change them. Or rather, he cannot do so without ceasing to be what he is, namely, the supremely perfect being. But that would be contradictory. True freedom and true power do not consist in the ability to change one's thoughts and volitions, but in the (moral) impossibility of doing other than the best distinctly perceived as such.

3. Here an objection can be raised. One might wonder whether the will can be under the control of the will, even indirectly. Leibniz claims that

one can act so as to will and judge in the future "what one *would like* [*souhaiterait*] to be able to will or judge today."[53] How are we to understand this wish? Leibniz makes clear that it is not a velleity, which is a mere will to be able.[54] Thus, the threat of an infinite regress remains, whether the object of the will is a present or future will. Consideration of time alters nothing in the case: is not willing to alter one's will, whether for today or tomorrow, still *willing to will*? Even if we were to distinguish different kinds of will or degrees of willing—from a mere wish to a complete and final will—what would determine the mind to try to change its will, if not the will itself? And what would lead it to try to correct its judgment, if not this very judgment that it has already accepted? The problem arises because (i) the will could only will what it wants by virtue of another will (and soon to infinity), and (ii) the will could only will what it wants on condition of having already willed it.

In other words, one could not change one's present or future will unless one had already changed it. Take the example of someone, who though given to vice, would like to be virtuous. To this end, he keeps company with good people, follows their advice, and engages in edifying reading in the hope of one day having a virtuous will. The point is not for him to change his will (since all actions undertaken to acquire virtue follow from it), but rather to change a habit that opposes it and to suppress the passions that impede it. The mind cannot give itself, either directly or indirectly, a will or opinion that it does not already have. How then is reformation possible for a human being without falling into the contradiction of willing to will? In my view, there are two possible solutions to this problem.

a. The first consists in considering moral transformation as the work of some third party or of circumstances. In a sense, reformation occurs unbeknownst to the concerned subject or by ruse. Leibniz observes that it is brought about by means that are usually employed "unwittingly and without set purpose."[55] Human beings must be led obliquely, by clever diversions and circumstances, to change their will over which they have no power, given that they cannot will to will. If the will can be corrected indirectly, this can be done not by the one who wills, but in spite of him, without his perceiving it, by the mediation of another (a teacher or master) and/or by the intervention of other causes: divine grace and circumstances that give rise to new motives and inclinations.

b. The second solution consists in interpreting the relation between mind and will according to the distinction between antecedent and consequent will. We cannot choose either our antecedent or consequent wills, but we can choose to favor or cause to prevail one or another particular inclination. We do not have the power to will what we will—not even for the future—since we never will anything other than what we already want, at least antecedently. All that lies within our power is to cause to prevail, by exercise and skill,[56] an antecedent will, which had heretofore been thwarted by more powerful wills and so had not yet realized its full effect in the consequent will. The "modification" of the consequent will—and the moral reformation it entails—is thus merely the result of an inversion of the relation of force between the various inclinations from which this consequent will derives.

However, there is a difficulty here. How are we to make sense of an inclination that is at once weak and strong, impeded and yet sufficiently powerful to prevail upon the mind, which attempts to act on it at the expense of all others? How is it possible that this antecedent volition should suddenly come to dominate? Of itself, the mind cannot add weight to the will, not even indirectly, since otherwise it would will prior to willing. The inclination can prevail only by means of some foreign cause, which acts either to reinforce it or to diminish the relative weight of those that oppose it. However, this leads us back to the first solution.

Ultimately, everything comes down to the grace to will. Our part is to do what is necessary to receive it:

> Grace aids all those who are willing, although not all have the grace to will. It is also true that the serious will has need of divine grace. However, it is enough that nothing is lacking to the one who is willing. Indeed, the will or the grace to will will not be lacking to anyone who does what is necessary, according to the nature of the thing, to acquire the will.[57]

Leibniz does not wish to be accused of Pelagianism or to give the impression that he makes human salvation depend solely on merit. A good will, like natural qualities, is a gift from God. Are we to say, then, that dominion over oneself is ultimately an illusion? No. For, Leibniz does not believe that God's grace (including the grace to will) is given arbitrarily and without reason. It is distributed according to reasons that are good and just, although they may be unknown to us. As the reformed theologian Ludwig Crocius observed concerning election: "the causes [of election] may be hidden, but they cannot be unjust."[58] Thus, we must believe that the merits of an individual—and the foreknowledge of his efforts to act rightly—are taken into account, but that, by themselves, they are never sufficient to obtain a good will, just as, from the point of view of salvation, they cannot constitute the ultimate reason for one's election.[59]

Self-mastery, such as Leibniz conceives it, is thus doubly limited: it is not only the mark of an imperfect and deficient creature (since God lacks this self-mastery), but it cannot truly be practiced, much less succeed, without God's grace. It is within the framework of this double limitation that the moral reform of human beings is possible and—it must not be forgotten— that the principles of Leibnizian ethics must be considered.

Here again, intelligence appears as a major prerequisite insofar as do- minion over oneself is ultimately measured by the degree to which one's knowledge is distinct. Together with spontaneity, intelligence suffices to ground moral attribution—to render humans worthy of praise or blame, reward or punishment—even if their actions were absolutely necessary. Recall that sanction is legitimate once it can be shown that the agent was under no constraint. Neither corrective justice, which aims at reparation of the wrong committed, nor "medicinal" justice (as Leibniz also calls it[60]), which seeks to amend the criminal and to ensure, by making an example of him, that the sin will not be committed in the future, requires contingency. Nevertheless, contingency is indispensable for "perfect" freedom and is the precondition for that justice that is called *vindictive*.

### 7.1.4 Positive Prerequisites (3): Contingency

*Contingency* or "non-necessity," or *indifference* (a term that Leibniz is willing to allow provided it does not indicate an absence of determination of one's choices[61]), is the third prerequisite of freedom. It presupposes that an action, however motivated it may be, is never so to such a degree that it would have been impossible to do otherwise. Contingency is compatible with certainty concerning the future or the "futurition of truths" as well as with divine foreknowledge, or the "preordination of God" and the "predis- position of things, that is, the various series of causes."[62] In other words, it is compatible with what might be considered three kinds of determina- tion: the first comes from the very nature of truth, the second from infal- lible divine foreknowledge,[63] and the third from the chain of causes. In fact, these three kinds of determination are reducible to a single one: the deter- mination of causes. For, certainty with regard to the future is nothing but the determination of causes considered as true, whereas foreknowledge is this same determination insofar as it is infallibly known by God.

How is contingency compatible with the truth of future events? "It was already true a hundred years ago that I would write today, just as it will be true one hundred years later that I have written."[64] However, the status of this action as future and certain in no way alters its fundamental contingency (Leibniz could have not written at all or written a novel instead of the *Essays of Theodicy*). Time does not enter into it: whatever is contingent remains so, whether it be considered in the present, the past, or the future. The fact that it is or is not known in advance (foreknowledge) is likewise irrelevant. That God knows what I will do tomorrow does not render my future actions necessary. Time, foreknowledge, the existence, or nonexistence of a possible thing plays no part in the definition of modality. It is true that what God foresees cannot fail to occur and is, in this sense, necessary; otherwise God would not be infallible. However, its necessity is not absolute, but merely *hypothetical*, that is relative to the state of things and the world considered.[65]

Consequently, contingency for Leibniz reduces to a kind of necessity. The contrast is not an "external" one between two modalities (contingent *versus* necessary), but is internal to necessity itself, between the absolutely necessary and the hypothetically necessary (that is, contingent). A thing is contingent insofar as there is, *in itself*, no contradiction in its being otherwise or not existing at all,[66] although it is impossible *ex hypothesi*—that is, with the universal series to which it belongs having been posited—that it fail to exist or be other than it is. Of necessity, it must occur. The contingent is that which, *considered in itself*, is not necessary according to the Principle of Non-Contradiction, but is necessary according to the Principle of Sufficient Reason *relative* to the particular universe to which it belongs. Otherwise, the effect would fail to occur, despite the existence of all its prerequisites. It would be a case of a sufficient cause that nevertheless failed to produce its effect (which contradicts the very notion of a sufficient cause) or the occurrence of an effect other than the one that ought to occur given the state of things, and which thus occurs without a sufficient cause (which is also contradictory). Thus, it must be maintained not only that the soul is always inclined, without being necessitated, to what it does but that it *always* opts for the alternative to which it is most inclined.[67]

At the moral level, the contingency of our actions implies that no inclination, not even a violent one, and no determination, however powerful it may be, is irresistible for someone who is in control of himself (absence of constraint is the precondition of freedom):

> The passion or appetite in us is never found to be so strong that our action follows from it with necessity. For as long as man has not lost his mind, he can always find some reason for arresting the impulse, however vehemently he may be swayed by wrath, thirst, or similar causes. Sometimes it suffices in such cases

that he remind himself to make the right use of his freedom and to exercise his power over his passions.[68]

As we have seen, spontaneity in conjunction with intelligence allows dominion over oneself. Contingency now adds a supplementary dimension to freedom: it shows that the force and intensity of the inclination will never change determination into absolute necessity. Under the influence of a lively passion, even the desire to prove one's freedom or the glory of being freed from the servitude of affects can act as motives[69] for abstaining or resisting. Neither original sin, nor evil inclinations, nor an acquired habit of sinning, nor even the hatred of the damned can render the act of sinning (and of continuing to sin) absolutely necessary.[70] It is always possible to act rightly and in conformity with the moral precepts that God has inscribed in the human heart. The same holds true for the assistance of grace, good inclinations, and good habits: it is always possible to resist them, to rebel, and to turn away from virtue. Even for the saints and the most virtuous, good works are free, not necessary, actions.[71]

Consideration of the contingency of our actions makes it possible to conceive of "a kind of justice and a certain sort of reward and punishment which do not appear so applicable to those who should act by an absolute necessity, if there were any."[72] This justice is called *vindictive*. The principle upon which it rests demands—in all cases and circumstances—that no fault be left unpunished and no good deed unrewarded, even if the punishment will not serve to rectify the evil, or amend the guilty, or dissuade others from sinning, nor the reward to confirm the good actions of the one who receives it, or to exhort others to follow the example. Vindictive justice is based on the Principle of Fitness (*convenance*), that is, the Principle of the Best[73] or the "Principle of Perfection and Order."[74] God always follows this principle and unfailingly observes it within the city or universal republic of spirits of which he is the monarch. However, contrary to what Grotius maintains, vindictive justice is not uniquely reserved to God, even if he takes it upon himself to exercise it "on many occasions."[75] For, temporal sovereigns must also enforce it, though on condition of using it without excess or passion, that is, without a spirit of vengeance.[76]

Vindictive justice is perhaps the sole case in Leibniz's thought in which there appears the idea of the unconditionality of the law, which distinguishes his philosophy of law and ethics from utilitarianism.[77] Vindictive justice shows the absolute character of the law, the constancy of the divine or human legislator from whom it originates and its permanent and unreserved enforcement, whatever extrinsic motives there may be to dispense with it. For, "the wise lawgiver having threatened, and having, so to speak, promised chastisement, it befits his steadfastness not to leave the action completely unpunished, even if the punishment no longer served to correct anyone."[78]

Hobbes, following the Socinians, rejects this kind of justice. He argues that the goal of law is not so much to consider the past (the crime that has been committed) as the future. The point is not to punish the criminal "for that which is past, and not to be undone," but to render both him and others just, by instilling good motives in them. In Hobbes' view, "without the good intention for the future, no past act of a delinquent could justify his killing in the sight of God."[79] Punishment, like the law itself, has no value in its own right. Its raison d'être is to be a cause of justice, that is, to introduce into the chain of causes the necessary motives (fear and hope) that will shape the will of human beings into what we would like it to be.[80] Once the punishment no longer serves this function, it loses all legitimacy and becomes indistinguishable from vengeance.

The difference between Hobbes and Leibniz on this point can be explained by their respective conceptions of justice and of systems of reward and punishment in general. Hobbes has a *positive* (or *positivist*) and exclusively *juridical* conception of justice, which he takes to be the emanation of a superior (the sovereign, God), by whose power the law is established and who ensures its application. With regard to reward and punishment, Hobbes takes a purely motivational view. For him, the function of punishment is preventive (to avoid crime), corrective (to amend the criminal once the crime has been committed), and exemplary (to dissuade others from imitating the guilty). By contrast, Leibniz holds a *natural* (or *naturalist*) conception of justice, which he takes to be based ultimately on an extra-juridical, and properly *metaphysical* principle (*fitness*). For Leibniz, justice is nothing but the expression of an uncreated universal order—harmony— that God and the sage are responsible for enforcing. In his thinking about reward and punishment, Leibniz associates, though without equating, consideration of the motives of an action (fears and hopes) with what might be called a *deontological* approach to justice, which defines obligation independently of both private and public utility. Sanctions (rewards and punishments) are therefore just, even when not useful to anyone, because they are fitting in the sense that they satisfy the general order.

For Leibniz, this principle of fitness explains and justifies the continued punishment of the damned, even though the punishment no longer serves to correct them, as well as the continued reward of the blessed, who no longer have need of such incentives to confirm them in their virtue. Punishment continues only because the damned constantly repeat their sins, just as felicity continues only because the blessed endlessly persevere in their love of God. In this way, sin *naturally* draws its punishment as does virtue its reward. Sanction occurs without disrupting the laws of nature, indeed, it is carried out by means of them. This connection between sin and its punishment and virtue and its reward is simply the expression of fitness in the physical order. It is considered by Leibniz to be "another kind of pre-established harmony" (besides that between soul and body) in accordance with the "parallelism between the two realms"[81] by virtue of which all that occurs by efficient causes also corresponds to a moral end. Vindictive justice is only a particular case of this *immanent* universal justice, whose enforcement does not require a particular intervention by God (any more than in the case of the union of soul and body), but follows the natural order. This harmony is not only internal to nature but is also the harmony of nature and grace, "between God as architect and God as monarch, in such a way that nature leads to grace, and grace perfects nature by using it."[82]

However, one question remains: Why could there be no vindictive justice, if all our actions were absolutely necessitated? Why does vindictive justice, in particular, require contingency? Leibniz responds to this question as follows:

> I have also observed . . . that, according to the celebrated Conringius, justice which punishes by means of *medicinal* penalties, so to speak, that is, in order to correct the criminal or at least to provide an example for others, could be allowed in the opinion of those who do away with the freedom that is exempt from necessity. True vindictive justice, on the other hand, which goes beyond the medicinal, assumes something more, namely, intelligence and freedom in the one who sins, because the harmony of things demands a satisfaction, or evil in the form of suffering, to make the mind feel its error after the voluntary active evil to which it has consented.[83]

The difference between corrective or "medicinal" justice and vindictive justice lies in the fact that the punishment does not have the same goal nor does it inspire the same motive. The goal of corrective justice is external and based on the motive of fear. It is an attempt to correct the guilty by punishment and to lead him and others to virtue by the fear of punishment. Subjects of corrective justice need not be free, nor endowed with distinct knowledge, since fear (a passion) will be the cause that necessitates them to act henceforth in accordance with the law. Vindictive justice, on the other hand, has no other end than itself and is based on the principle that justice must be loved for its own sake (disinterestedly). Its motive is virtue, that is, the pleasure the sage takes in contemplating the laws of order put into practice. The guilty is considered as a free being, according to the definition of perfect freedom (which excludes necessity), for he must not only feel the punishment, like any sentient creature, but he must experience it as a just sanction and *understand* it to be the consequence of the crime he committed. He must relate the punishment to his guilt, which can only be felt if he realizes that, though his actions are determined, they did and always will depend on him, since they were and always will be contingent.

Vindictive justice alone is truly worthy of the free and rational nature of human beings. It moves them neither by fear nor hope—the means by which brute animals are led—but presupposes intelligence, since it shows us that the evil we suffer corresponds to the evil we have voluntarily committed (and could have refrained from committing) and that the good we enjoy corresponds to the good that was also done contingently, and, consequently, that we alone are the authors of our own misery or happiness. In this way, the existence of vindictive justice renders illegitimate the complaints of the damned who blame God for their suffering, since it shows that it is in their power to cease to be damned and miserable. Likewise, vindictive justice renders more perfect and meritorious the virtue of the just and the blessed, who at each moment freely renew their obedience and the act of love that unites them to God. In going beyond corrective justice, vindictive justice brings together the conditions for a true reformation of the sinner, that is, for the practice of virtue for its own sake (and not by mere calculation) and for the sincere (and not merely "mercenary") love of God.

At the physical and metaphysical levels, freedom consists in the independence of every created spirit from the influence of other created substances (though not from God) and in the spontaneity of its actions. At the moral level, freedom consists in autonomy, since the spirit determines itself according to its state of knowledge (its intelligence) and the motives that most incline it. Finally, at the logical and, again, metaphysical levels, freedom implies contingency, that is, the "non-necessity" of one's actions. In my view, this latter characteristic is not the least important, nor, as Gianfranco Mormino maintains,[84] is it a feature that belongs only to finite and imperfect creatures and is absent from divine freedom. For Mormino, contingency is not a perfection inherent in free actions. Insofar as it involves a *power to do otherwise*, contingency is rather "a salient characteristic of the actions of free men, namely their fallibility."[85] This reading strikes me as problematic for three reasons:

1. Divine freedom is not more perfect than human freedom because it lacks contingency, but because the intelligence that animates it has nothing but distinct knowledge (God is Reason itself). Thus, the difference between divine and human freedom is one of degree, not of kind. To hold

the opposite view—to maintain that contingency is not a necessary pre-requisite of divine freedom—would amount to introducing an equivocal notion of freedom that is without foundation in Leibniz's texts.

2. On several occasions Leibniz invokes the contingency of the world and of the beings and events that compose it. These are said to be contingent not merely in the sense that they do not contain within themselves the reason of their existence (metaphysical reason), but because they could have not existed or been other than they are (logical reason), since "time, space and matter, united and uniform in themselves and indifferent to everything, might have received entirely other motions and shapes, and in another order."[86] The possibility of not existing or of being otherwise, based on the existence of other possible worlds, ensures that both God's choice and the act by which he creates this world rather than some other equally possible one are contingent. In other words, our world is contingent because the very choice and act of creating it are contingent.

3. It is wrong to reduce contingency to the "power to do otherwise," which is only a moral consequence of contingency, and then to re-strict this power, as Mormino does, to the ability to fail or to be mis-taken (which belongs only to creatures). For, contingency refers in the first instance to the logical modality of the possible insofar as it is the possibility of *being* otherwise or of not being at all. As for the power which contingency underwrites—that of *doing* otherwise—far from being a mark of imperfection, it is, in God, the mark of ab-solute perfection, since it is nothing other than omnipotence itself. The act of creating the world is contingent because there were an infinite number of other possible worlds, and God, as an omnipo-tent being, could have created a different one (or could have created none at all). The objection according to which it was impossible for God to have created a world other than ours (which is the best), since this would be contrary to his perfection, fails, since we are here con-sidering omnipotence independently of its relation to wisdom and goodness.[87]

Moreover, consideration of this relation (to wisdom and goodness) would in no way alter the contingency of the divine choice or of the world, since contingency is neither indetermination nor chance but, as we have seen, a particular kind of necessity: hypothetical necessity. That therefore is contingent (our world, the choice to create it), which might not have occurred, but which *ought* infallibly to occur, since God, who is supremely perfect, could not fail to choose the best.

## 7.2 FROM THE IDEAL TO THE REAL: THE EXERCISE OF FREEDOM AND THE MAXIMS OF LEIBNIZIAN ETHICS

### 7.2.1 The "Ideal Precedence" of Human Freedom

Leibniz would not have devoted so much effort to demonstrating the compatibility of freedom with the truth of future events, divine foreknowledge, and causal determination[88] if contingency were not an essential attribute of freedom. For, neither the truth of future events nor divine foreknowledge nor causal determination would put freedom in danger, if, as Mormino maintains, this freedom consisted only in intelligence and spontaneity. Arguments in favor of compatibilism would have no purpose. The point of such arguments is to protect contingency against absolute necessitarianism. In fact, the truth of future events, divine foreknowledge, and causal determination were traditionally appealed to by the partisans of absolute necessitarianism (like Hobbes) in order to undermine, not liberty (which Hobbes accepts), but contingency. Leibniz sets out to prove that these three arguments have no bearing on the modality of things. That a certain act is determined, that it is true that it will occur, and that God knows this even before it occurs, none of this can render the act absolutely necessary.

Thus, contingency belongs to the essence of freedom. This cannot be doubted, in my view. In fact, the problem lies elsewhere: it concerns the manner in which we are to understand this possibility of being and doing otherwise within the framework of Leibniz's metaphysics. For, this possibility might well seem illusory. Adam and his sin are contingent. Adam might not have existed, just as he might not have sinned. However, as I have shown elsewhere,[89] *Adam as sinner* and *Adam as non-sinner* do not refer to the same individual, understood as the subject of two possible contrary actions. In fact, they are two distinct possible individuals, one of whom acts in one way and the other in the opposite way. Adam could not have abstained from sinning without thereby ceasing to be Adam and without the world to which he belongs being completely different. Let us remember that one and the same individual cannot belong to several possible worlds, considered as so many worlds in which he performs different acts. Thus, there is not one Adam and afterward several possible Adams obtained disjunctively on the basis of their choice to sin or not sin. There are from the outset several possible individuals, who share, to be sure, certain general properties (being the first man, having been placed in a garden, having had a woman made out of his rib by God, etc.), but who are genuinely different and even have more differences than commonalities on account of their belonging to distinct worlds.

For this reason, the contingency of our actions cannot be established on the basis of consideration of counterfactual situations in which we would have acted otherwise than we in fact did (in this world). In fact, our actions are contingent, not because *we* could have done otherwise, but because God could have created a world other than ours with creatures other than us, performing actions other than those we performed. The alternative is not for some subject, $S_1$, to perform either action $A_1$ or action $A_2$ in one and the same world ($W_1$), but between a subject, $S_1$, who performs $A_1$ in world $W_1$, and a subject, $S_2$, who performs $A_2$ in world $W_2$. Consequently, the possibility of being or doing otherwise amounts to nothing else, and nothing more, than the possibility of not existing—a possibility that holds of all creatures and to which, in their cases, contingency ultimately reduces.

In what way then is the contingent distinct from the possible? In a sense, the contingent places a limitation on the possible, since it involves only the possibility of not existing, while the possible also involves the possibility of being otherwise. Whereas the possible is that whose contrary does not imply a contradiction, that is, that which is possible in a world other than the one considered (taken as a reference), the contingent is simply that whose nonexistence does not imply a contradiction. In another sense, with regard to the things God has in fact created, contingency adds an additional feature relative to the possible. Contingency concerns the possible that exists, but that might not have existed, and so, is related to a choice by God, who could have not created the things he did or created other things in their place. Contingency rests on God's freedom, and so, in part on his will, on which the possible does not at all depend, since it is based solely on his understanding.

Contingency is, so to speak, the shadow cast on that which exists by nonbeing and the nonexisting possible. It is a reminder or sign that another divine choice was possible. Still, one may wonder, given that this other choice did not occur, is not this notion of contingency very weak and of very limited significance? Once God has decreed the existence of *our* world to the exclusion of all other possible ones, the possibility of not existing becomes a purely negative property. Of course, our world, together with all of the beings and events of which it is composed could have not existed, but after all it does! Of course, other worlds with other beings and events were possible, but they do not exist, nor will they ever!

Once God has decided to create this world, it cannot be realized in any other way than in fact it has. It is bound to exist exactly as conceived by God in his understanding (as a mere possible). Everything it contains, the whole succession of beings and events, all our passions, actions, and perceptions must occur in accordance with the divine plan. What then does God do in creating but impose on me this particular destiny that he saw from all eternity would be mine, together with everything else in the world of which I am a part and which he judged to be the best on the whole? The spiritual automaton that I am—an automaton endowed with reason and reflection, to be sure, but no less determined for all that—does no more than carry out, mechanically and infallibly, all the actions of this character conceived in advance by God. Can we truly speak of freedom, after God has used his and chosen the world, if I cannot in any way change my destiny nor do anything but play the part assigned to me? Is freedom merely an illusion for those who are ignorant of their destiny, a destiny which, to be sure, could have been different in itself, but which is henceforth fixed, certain, and irrevocable once the divine choice of *this* world has been made?

The problem lies in the relation between human and divine freedom. By preceding human freedom, divine freedom seems, if not to render it completely meaningless, then at least to reduce it to a pure automatism. However, this relation must be understood differently as it is considered before the creation—from the point of view of ideal possibility—and after the creation—from the point of view of actual existence.

God does not choose the content of possibles. He is not the author of essences (which exist pre-formed in his understanding), but of the existence of a number of them, by virtue of his will to create this world rather than another. God makes no decree concerning Judas and Peter, for example, that they will sin, the former by betraying Christ, and the latter by denying him, or that grace will be denied to the former and yet bestowed upon the latter, and so forth. Their sin, together with everything that precedes it and everything that will follow from it is included in their idea or notion.[90] This idea or notion is not distinct from the idea or notion of the universe to which they belong and which God represents to himself in its entirety prior to choosing to bring it into existence. God does not create, by virtue of his will, possibles or even possible worlds, that is, those combinations of possibles compatible with one another. He merely compares all those worlds that his understanding presents to him and chooses the most perfect from among them, without being able to change anything it contains (since everything in it is interrelated) nor rectify or eliminate the least one of its events once that world has been brought into existence.[91]

The independence of the understanding from the will and the subordination of the latter to the former have the following consequence: it is not God's freedom that is exercised before that of humans, but human freedom (considered as a mere idea), which precedes that of God. Far from determining what creatures will be and do, God must on the contrary determine himself in accordance with their complete concept when he considers them in the state of mere possibles with all their actions and events. Afterward, insofar as one considers the world and the creatures it contains prior to creation (in the divine understanding) or subsequent to it (such as they actually existence), the relation between the *first cause*, God, and the *secondary cause*, man, is not the same:

> [T]he first cause is determined by the secondary cause considered ideally [*idealiter*], that is, the idea of the secondary cause, considered as it is in the divine understanding, determines the will of the first cause. However, considered actually [*actualiter*], the secondary cause is determined by the first cause, that is, every secondary cause receives its being from the first cause.[92]

Secondary causes act *ideally*—that is, as ideas—on the first cause. The creature, *qua* possible, inclines the will of God, who will decide whether to create it (together with the universe to which it belongs) in accordance with the representation he has of what it will do, or would do, were it to exist.[93] In return, the first cause physically (pre)determines, according to the doctrine of concurrence, the secondary cause, which draws from it its being and reality—since everything follows from God as from its ultimate cause. God is the origin of the series of existing things and conserves them, since it is only by virtue of his power that the world endures (conservation being a continuous creation). On the ideal level, determination comes from the essence of the thing and inclines God's will without necessitating it. On the existential level, determination comes from the divine power and providence, without, however, contradicting human freedom. In this way, the two freedoms are safeguarded and reconciled.

As represented in the divine understanding, every creature has its value, just as every action, virtue and perfection weighs in the final decision to create this world—according to the relation of antecedent wills to the consequent will. Thus, as Leibniz explains in §9 of the *Theodicy*:

> [T]he universe, whatever it may be, is all of a piece, like an ocean: the least movement extends its effect there to any distance whatsoever, even though this effect become less perceptible in proportion to the distance. Therein God has ordered all things beforehand once for all, having foreseen prayers, good and bad actions, and all the rest; and each thing *as an idea* has contributed, before its existence, to the resolution that has been made upon the existence of all things.[94]

Our freedom is at once dependent on the initial divine choice for its effectiveness and, *qua* possible, the origin of this choice. It is both determined and determinant: an actual *effect* and an *ideal* cause. Rational creatures are part of the created world in which they do not fail to bring about all that is included in their essence from eternity. In this sense, they are *conditioned*. However, they are likewise a *condition* insofar as they are those possible beings whose perfections and works (as well as efforts and prayers[95]) contributed, prior to their existence, to the divine decree to create this world rather than some other. Each of their acts is both a certain and foreseen effect, written into the framework of the universe, and, reverberating, so to speak, in the ideal and the eternal, one of the causes that led God, prior to the creation, to choose *this* series of things.

The determination of the first cause by secondary causes is clearly visible in the movement from God's antecedent to his consequent will. Man appears as the one who, by his free resistance, constitutes an obstacle to God's antecedent will, which is to render all spirits happy. Man's refusal and rebellion, which lead to unhappiness and to the damnation of some, must be integrated into the final will: "If the objectives of this will [of God's] have not always been attained, the responsibility rests with refractory human malice."[96] God does not alter human will, which he perceives to be in opposition to his antecedent will, so as to force it to conform to his plans. On the contrary, it is God who, so to speak, "alters" his will in the consequent will, by taking into account the contrariness of human beings (whose freedom is thereby respected and preserved).[97]

To say that God decides to create the world only after having consulted his understanding is to recognize the "priority" of the creature's freedom to that of the creator. I call this priority, *ideal precedence*. It establishes the freedom of creatures as co-foundational of the order of things and makes of the creation a shared work, born of the interaction of two freedoms, since God's freedom brings into existence a universe that is (at least partially and at the ideal level) pre-molded by the freedom of creatures. Does this amount to making the creator dependent upon the creature? Make no mistake: God "must not be said to be subject to things, although he accommodates himself to things."[98] Nothing, properly speaking, precedes God, just as nothing external compels him. He is subject only to himself, to his own understanding which contains all the essences. The foundation of our freedom lies in him: in his intelligence, which contemplates it, and in his will, which wills it to exist. Thus, in accommodating, so to speak, his freedom to ours, God in fact does no more than follow his understanding.

This idea of cooperation between creator and creature has important ethical implications. Rather than yield to the fatalism of the Lazy Sophism and to "Turkish fate," (*fatum mahometanum*), humans must believe that they were already present as an idea prior to the foundation of the world and that they are called upon to bring about that for which God "chose" them together with the universe to which they belong. The best possible world, considered *ideally*, will not occur without its cause, that is, without the freedom and effort of spirits *actually* applying themselves to bring it about.

### 7.2.2 Acting According to the Presumptive Will of God

It is certain that everything that is bound to exist and occur in the universe will exist and occur. Every thing, every action, *qua* existent, must be in exact conformity with what it is, *qua* possible, in the divine understanding. The realm of existence, in which God exercises his will and power, and the ideal realm, which is grounded in his omniscience and prescience, must be in perfect correspondence. However, this correspondence must not be allowed to invert the order of reasons. It must not be said that an event will occur because it has been foreseen, but on the contrary, that it has been foreseen, because it will occur—that is, because the connection between causes and effects will necessarily bring it about according to a hypothetical necessity. Divine foreknowledge is based on the order of things, such as it is—that is, foreknowledge is only true insofar as it is founded on this order—rather than the order of things being based on foreknowledge.[99]

Therefore, I must judge that it is my present efforts and actions, or my actual laziness and negligence, that will determine my future. It is what I now do or fail to do that renders me worthy of reward or punishment in the future. I act out by virtue of the motives that incline me and not by the force of some destiny that has been foreseen from all eternity, or by virtue of my essence, as contemplated by God in his understanding. My destiny is nothing but the consequence of all my free actions, passions, and perceptions, or more precisely, it is the complete representation of them in the divine understanding. A human being who sins and is damned does not sin and is not damned, because he was predestined to evil and because God has foreseen it. It is the human being who predestines himself, so to speak, to damnation by doing what leads to this, rather than acting otherwise: "as you damn yourself, so to speak, in the truth of events, so you also damn yourself in God's idea."[100] Just as it is not God's foreknowledge that makes events true, but the truth of events that founds God's foreknowledge, so it is not predestination that makes the acts I now perform lead to my salvation or damnation, but, on the contrary, it is these acts and their consequences (whose occurrence *in actuality* conforms to what they are as *possibles* in the divine understanding) that are the reason for my eternal predestination (that God alone knows).

If, at the theoretical level, it has become clear that human freedom was exercised ideally before humans themselves were brought into existence, on the practical level, the situation seems to be reversed. It is no longer the ideal that determines the actual, but in some sense the actual that determines the ideal and existence that determines essence. Human beings are the authors of their destiny and the masters of their future:

> because you are ignorant of future things or those which have been decreed, it remains for you to act according to what you know: you must be, whatever you do or do not do, the artisan of your own fortune or destiny.[101]

What sense can this injunction have in the context of a philosophical system in which essence precedes existence and not vice versa? The idea of Judas is in the divine understanding from all eternity; it is not derived from the existing Judas, but on the contrary is prior to him. The (hypothetical) necessity of his sin obtained prior to Judas's existence, such that

> when Judas deliberated whether he would betray Christ or not, it was already necessary for Judas to choose betrayal, otherwise Scripture would have been false. I mean, of course with a necessity based on a hypothesis, not based on the thing itself.[102]

Human beings do not create essences (either their own or any other) any more than God does. They are not the authors of their nature, or self-causes (*causa sui*), since otherwise they would exist prior to coming into existence. How then are we to reconcile the *ethical* point of view, according to which a free subject is the artisan of his own destiny—saves or damns himself, if he wills it to be so and acts accordingly—with the *metaphysical* point of view, according to which a created spirit cannot be the cause of its idea or notion in God, but can only act in conformity with it?

One possible response would be to understand this "voluntarist" exhortation (to be the artisan of one's destiny) as a mere manner of speaking—a rhetorical formula which does not hold in all metaphysical rigor—but whose use is permissible in ethics to counter the harmful effects of the Lazy Sophism. To one who would seek to excuse his sins and exonerate himself of all responsibility on the grounds that he was born under an unlucky star, that he was unfortunate, and that unfavorable circumstances led him to sin, it can be replied that he is not under an absolute necessity and that reform and right action are always up to him. We fulfill our destiny, not regardless of what we do, but because of what we do or do not do. Our ignorance of the future leads us to believe that it is undetermined, that it is up to us to change it or to make it this or that. However, everything is regulated in advance, and since God has chosen this world, we cannot bring about any event that is not included in God's concept of it.

It is certainly true that our conduct must be guided by our present state of knowledge and, in particular, by the fact that we do not know the future. However, ethics cannot be based on principles manifestly opposed to those defended on the theoretical level. It is difficult to believe that Leibniz could defend what until now he has expressly rejected, namely, the indeterminacy of the future, the power of human beings to change their will instantaneously and an absolute dominion over oneself. To admit such dominion would be to ignore both the decisive role of insensible inclinations on our soul and the role of grace in acquiring a good will. Might this "voluntarism" be restricted to the practical level? Might it be acceptable on account of the importance of the moral realm, an importance that would authorize certain liberties with regard to theoretical positions? That is highly doubtful, since it would have the effect of separating theory and practice and suggesting that the practical is based on different and autonomous grounds. It is clear that, for Leibniz, the practical must derive from the theoretical and that ethics must be based on the results of the metaphysical doctrine, and not on principles directly opposed to it.

In order to reconcile the language of ethics with that of metaphysics, I believe we must return to Leibniz's definition of freedom. For Leibniz, that substance is free that acts according to knowledge (freedom always presupposes intelligence). In doing our duty, we do not determine ourselves according to what we do not know (the future), but according to what we do know of the divine will. We deliberate and decide *as if* the future were not written, not because it in fact is not, but because this future cannot actually occur without doing what leads to it (see 7.2.3). In other words, the future, though determined and certain, does not yet exist. It is "written," but it cannot be realized so long as we have not done what is necessary (by acting or not acting) to bring it about.

To understand that the future is determined and known by God is of no help with regard to acting. It does nothing to clarify my choices, nor does it tell me what I ought now to do. I only know that what I will decide and what I will do, which of my projects will succeed and which will fail, are part of the series of things that, taken together, constitute the best possible universe, which God chose to bring into existence. The general knowledge, established by the doctrinal part of Theodicy, that God governs the world in the most perfect manner, encourages me to be satisfied with the past and present, even when they do not correspond to what I had initially desired. The point is not to be resigned, to accept the inevitable and adopt the "forced patience" extolled by the Stoics. Rather, it is to recognize in everything that now occurs and has occurred the mark of God's will that always tends toward the best, even if we are not always able to fathom its reasons.[103] Leibnizian ethics teaches us to be sincerely content, despite our disappointments, failures and even suffering, by taking up the universal point of view: that of the sage who considers each thing (including evils) as it ought to be, that is, according to its place in the general order.

Still, what attitude ought the sage have toward the future? However great his effort and however firm his resolution, he must always maintain tranquility of mind and be equally satisfied with whatever happens, be it success or failure. Prior to the event, the sage cannot know what God will ultimately will (or permit). He cannot conform to God's particular will, which is unknown and hidden from him—it is his consequent will that the event will reveal.[104] As a result, he must govern himself by the only thing he knows, God's general and declared will, which conveys his commandments and orders (the moral principles written in our hearts and the content of revealed teaching). This will, which is still characterized as *presumptive*,[105] is nothing other than God's antecedent will. The sage must act in accordance with what he *presumes* God will want: the good and the prevention of evil.

This presumption differs from the presumption which Leibniz discusses with regard to the logic of probability and which is a judgment that holds in the absence of proof to the contrary. For it remains true, even when circumstances seem to contradict it, by causing a good undertaking to fail. From the practical point of view, the *presumptive* is not that which is based on probabilities or on a cluster of particular indications pointing in the same direction (as is the case in jurisprudence), but that which is based on true knowledge (God's general will which tends toward the good) and which no experience can invalidate. For, the failure of my good undertaking does not prove that I was wrong to have willed as I did (provided the good I sought was real and not merely apparent), nor indeed that God contradicts himself by ordering me to seek a good that he does not bring about. When his particular and manifest consequent will fails to agree with his general and declared antecedent will (the one I followed and attempted to satisfy), it must not be thought that God wills and does not will at the same time, but rather that he wills two different, though compatible, things. On the one hand, he commands me to do as much good as possible and will reward me for my good intention and effort. On the other hand, in conformity with the relation of the antecedent to consequent,[106] God does not permit my will to achieve its end, since he considers what is best for the whole and judges that my present aim prevents a greater good or that it is inopportune to satisfy it at present. Thus, he very sincerely wills the things he orders or that he wills that we will, that is, he rewards us for what we do or at least for what we actively try to do. Nevertheless, he does not always will them with that absolute will that infallibly attains its effect. It can happen, and indeed ordinarily occurs, that God wills that I do something and that I strive to do it, although he has not decided absolutely that it shall occur or that I shall succeed, and he sometimes wills that I seek what he does not will that I obtain.[107]

God demands a good, sincere, and serious intention (that is, one accompanied by effort and which goes beyond a mere wish or velleity). However, he does not always will that this intention succeed.[108] There is no contradiction here, if we consider that these "two" volitions do not have the same object, since the end sought, in the one case, is the virtue of rational creatures, while in the other, it is the best effect on the whole. Notice that our efforts are not useless nor uselessly demanded by God, even when they are doomed to fail. For, they make it possible to obtain a good (namely, virtue) that is just as real as the one that was sought and contributes to the perfection of the universe.

The distinction between a good intention, willed by God, and its success, which is not necessarily so willed, is fundamental. It indicates what is morally just: those actions that conform to his antecedent will, though not always those actions that conform to his consequent will. The failure of our good undertakings does not prove that God did not will us to will what we did (the good), nor that he willed that we will something else, for example, that which ultimately occurred (the "best"). It is not for us, so to speak, to will the best. This is reserved for God who knows and foresees all. Similarly, the success of the wicked man does not prove that he is the beneficiary of some special favor: "in fact, [God] always rewards those who have striven to carry out his presumptive will and punishes those who have done otherwise."[109] True love of God consists in willing what God wills and not willing what he does not.[110] However, this agreement must be understood as the agreement between our will and his *antecedent* will. To act morally is not to carry out his consequent will, otherwise we should have to say that those criminals who succeed in their nefarious schemes love God and are loved by him! Success is proof of neither virtue nor justice, just as failure is no sure sign of vice or disfavor. One who has neither willed nor accomplished the good, but who brings about the "best" is no less punishable, if this "best" is sinful. God's presumptive will, which humans know and follow, remains just and obligatory even when his will as revealed by events seems contrary to it.[111]

Certainly, love of God implies being content with what has happened and therefore approving of his consequent will, once it has made itself known. The sage wishes nothing better than what has in fact occurred, and indeed would not alter it in the least were it in his power to do so. However, this does not make those sins that have been committed (and which were only permitted by God) good, nor does it justify the sinner. Otherwise, Judas must be numbered among the saints for having made possible the Passion of Christ, and by this means, the redemption of the entire human race! Nor does this contentment of the sage imply that things, as they are, ought not to be improved and reformed, when necessary. The sage, seeing that his good volitions have met with failure, accepts and consents to what has occurred only because he sees in it the manifestation of the divine will. Yet, for all that, he does not cease to will the good, nor does he spare any effort in trying to bring about for the future what was not able to occur for the past or present. The best, which has occurred, in some sense, instead of the good, is only the best with regard to the past. It is not best with regard to the future, for it is our duty to correct what is imperfect, to rectify evil, and to prevent its harmful consequences. We must refuse to allow for the future what we must be content with (or rather, *content ourselves with*) for the present. Alluding in the *Confession of a Philosopher* to the inevitable, though transitory, feeling of disappointment we experience in the face of failure,[112] Leibniz urges perseverance:

> [F]rom this it follows that if someone who loves God considers carefully some vice or evil deed—either his own or that of another, private or public, in order to remove or to correct it—he will hold as certain that it ought not to have been remedied yesterday, but he will presume that it ought to be remedied today. He will presume that, I say, until the contrary is established by his being un-successful. Nevertheless, this failure will not fatigue or crush his effort for the future, for it is not our place to prescribe the right season to God, and only those who persevere will be victorious. Hence, it is characteristic of one who loves God to be satisfied with the past and to strive to make the future the best possible.[113]

One cannot bemoan a failure for long without sinning against God. Yet, neither can one rest content with good intentions, as if success were unimportant. Leibniz's ethics combines the demand to be steadfast and persevering with a kind of detachment, or even indifference, which keeps the soul tranquil, since success is left entirely up to God. The sage is at once restless—endlessly occupied and eager to do good—and, so to speak, at peace, detached and free of all fear. He works for his own moral improvement and for that of his neighbor and for the development of virtue and harmony in human society. In this way, he contributes, insofar as he is able, to the perfection of the republic of spirits of which God is the monarch.[114] For, he loves God above all else. Fully engaged in action and in the affairs of the world, he is at the same time serene and even-tempered, whatever turn events might take, for his confidence in God's wisdom and providence is unshakable.

The duty to conform to God's presumptive will shows the true significance of the actions of a free creature. The divergence sometimes observed at the practical level between our good will and the will of God as revealed a posteriori in the event, corresponds to the one previously encountered at the theoretical level between God's antecedent and consequent will. The good is no longer simply a possible striving for existence in the divine understanding and an inclination that does not attain its full effect in his will. It is now defended and supported by human beings, who make it the object of their efforts, their prayers, and their zeal. Our good will takes up the baton on behalf of God's antecedent will, which remained unachieved. Our good will is the instrument by which God's antecedent will can be achieved in the future, that is, can prevail *consequently*. In this way, what is antecedently willed is never abandoned, even when it fails to occur, so long as humans take charge of it and work to bring it about. To make God's will one's own is to strive to bring his consequent will into conformity with his antecedent will. To realize the good is to make these two wills perfectly coincide.

Perseverance consists in never losing sight of the antecedent divine will, despite the apparent repudiation of it that God's consequent will seems to represent. The sage does not renounce the good, which present circumstances do not allow to be obtained, but treats it as merely deferred. As a result, the gap between antecedent will, which the sage makes his own, and consequent will, which is in fact accomplished, introduces a gap between historic, providential time and what might be called "ethical" time, which requires one to act against the current. For this reason it is sometimes permissible "without fault to take the side opposite to the one heaven favors, before providence has fully declared itself. And a Cato is right, when the most fortunate side is not the most just."[115] By definition, perseverance is untimely, since it requires placing oneself in an awkward position with regard to the actual state of things. The sage must judge this state of things as the best possible with regard to the immediate present, but as capable of—and even requiring—improvement for the future. At the same time, perseverance is always opportune, since the present is always a good time to act, or at least, to create the conditions that will allow the good to be realized. In this sense, it differs from obstinacy, which derives from error and a depraved will.[116]

In the context of the irenic negotiations between Lutherans and Catholics, Leibniz explains in a letter to the Landgrave von Hessen-Rheinfels the attitude that befits the persevering person. Certainly, the general political situation is unfavorable and full of obstacles to reconciliation between the churches. Nevertheless, Leibniz maintains that the moment is propitious, if the Catholic negotiator, Royas de Spinola, bishop of Tina, can prepare the way for reconciliation by obtaining from his side declarations that could be useful "at a more favorable time." Leibniz adds:

> That is why my method is to approve and to praise all good designs, for just as we say *calumniare audacter, semper aliquid haeret* [slander boldly, something always sticks], so, too, we may say *labora diligenter, semper aliquid haeret* [work diligently, something always sticks]. And Saint Paul says that in these cases we must work *opportune et importune* [opportunely and inopportunely]. Each of us must strive to do what is in our power and leave it to God to determine the outcome.[117]

It is true that "it is for [God] to know the proper hour and place for making our good designs successful."[118] However, tireless effort, even at an inopportune moment, is never fruitless, since something of value will result. Fortune and chance follow upon action; they do not incite it. To persevere is not merely to hope for better times, but to do what is necessary that such times may come.[119] One must act, as it were, unseasonably in order to be in season.

### 7.2.3 The Maxim of "As If"

Everything is determined and foreseen, since God has chosen to create the series of things that is most perfect (all the details of which he knows a priori). And yet, everything remains to be done, everything depends on our freedom and on what we will do out of virtue or fail to do neglect out of laziness. For, nothing can occur without a cause. The best cannot come to pass unless humans aspire to it and steadfastly will it. Will not the divine glory be realized, whatever humans do, even if they refuse to participate in it and fail to do their duty? Will not the Kingdom of God come, as Luther said, "without our prayers and without our efforts"?[120]

It is true that we cannot *render service* to [God], for he has need of nothing: but it is *serving him*, in our parlance, when we strive to carry out his *presumptive will*, co-operating in the good as it is known to us, wherever we can contribute to it. For we must always presume that God is prompted towards the good we know.[121]

What is this "parlance" in which it is permissible to say that we *serve* God and that we contribute to his glory and thereby, in some sense, to his felicity? Glory can be understood in two senses. On the one hand, it is the satisfaction one takes in contemplating one's own qualities and perfections. On the other hand, it is the satisfaction one receives knowing that others also admire them. In the first sense, "God possesses it always."[122] He has no need of others to possess glory in this sense, since it is the essential love that he has for himself. In the second sense, God draws his glory from intelligent substances, to whom he makes himself known and loved. This does not mean that God acquires, properly speaking, some new good, for "it is rather the rational creatures who thence derive advantage, when they apprehend aright the glory of God."[123] This second kind of glory is nothing but the first, reflected and multiplied by created spirits. It is the joint work of the creator and his creatures, since it is what they receive together by the creation: a shared felicity, this divine love that is no longer merely internal to God, but diffused beyond, bestowed upon those creatures capable of responding to it. Expression in rational substances does not consist in merely reflecting, like mirrors, God's perfections (by virtue of their representative nature), that is, of redoubling his glory. Rather, they augment his glory by the love they bear him in return. God's love is enriched by the love of his creatures, whose love is never merely contemplative, since it manifests itself by good works performed in the world.

It is with regard to glory in the second sense of the term that one can "render service" to God. Although we can have no influence on him, nor procure him any good, "nevertheless the benevolence we offer him makes us act just *as if* it were possible."[124] This maxim of acting *as if* has, in my view, a capital importance in Leibniz's ethical and religious thought. It is the maxim of the just man, who knows nothing of the future, other than that it is determined and certain, but who refuses to be taken in by the Lazy Sophism. Such a person must act as if nothing were decided, as if the contingent future were uncertain,[125] as if he were in control of things and events. In this way, what he has willed will be able to occur. For it is up to him, by his choices and actions, to bring it about that what has been decided—what is "written"—is his good, that the future is the reward for his efforts, that fortune (which "rarely forces itself on one who is sleeping") is favorable to him. As the theologian of the *Confession of a Philosopher* observes:

> [S]ince it is not evident to you whether something has been decreed in your favor or against you, act as if [*quasi*] it had been decreed in your favor or act as if nothing had been decreed, since you cannot conform your action to what is unknown to you. That is why, if you take charge of your affairs, nothing of what will come about from fate, i.e., from the harmony of things, will be held against you by God.[126]

The paradox of such a maxim is that in applying it, we are able to bring about what was initially presented as merely hypothetical and a mere manner of speaking. It is by acting *as if* fortune were favorable to me, that I draw its favors upon myself, by acting *as if* I could win my salvation and predestine myself, that I am saved. Likewise, it is by acting *as if* I enhanced divine glory, that I become the instrument of its realization. I must act *as if* I were among the elect, in order to actually be so: "whoever firmly believes himself to be elected, i.e., dear to God, he (*because he firmly loves God*) brings it about that he is elected."[127] Conversely, whoever believes himself to be hated by God damns himself. Thus, we can be predestined to salvation (or damnation), "if we will it."[128] Consequently, "he who doubts of his predestination need only do what is required for him to obtain it by the grace of God."[129]

In truth, the actual exercise of freedom can cause predestination only in the mode of *as if*, since the realm of existence cannot interfere with the realm of essence (nor with God's exact knowledge of it). The existing creature is predestined in the sense that its essence, such as it is in the divine understanding, contains the whole series of events and actions that lead to its election or reprobation. However, from another point of view, the creature is not predestined, but destines itself for eternal happiness or misery, by freely doing everything that leads to one or the other. God's idea of the creature contains *sub specie aeternitatis* the free volition to be saved or its refusal. It is this free volition that determines predestination, which therefore neither precedes this volition nor determines it, but on the contrary derives from it, taking note of and ratifying it. Thus, in the realm of existence, predestination is at once *prior* to the actions of the rational creature (from the point of view of one who contemplates its essence or complete idea), without thereby being the cause of them, and, in a sense, *subsequent* to these actions, without being so much a direct consequence of them as the confirmation by effect of what had already been known and included in the idea.

Appeal to the maxim of *as if* is not merely a convenient means of satisfying, at the ethical level, the requirement to act, given our ignorance
of the future and the need to avoid the Lazy Sophism. It is the practical
consequence of the hypothetical necessity to be found at the theoretical
level: the effect will occur only on condition that its cause is posited. Now it
is up to me to posit the cause or not, to bring it about that the effect is such
and such, and in particular, is as I want it to be. In this way, to act *as if*, is
to realize the possible that God has willed. It is also to fulfill the promise of
scripture: "true faith and true hope do not consist merely in *speaking*, nor
even merely in *thinking*, but in thinking *practically*, that is, in *acting*, as if it
were true."[130] In other words, true faith and true hope consist in acting as
if it were true what revelation teaches, that God loves man through Christ
and that if man loves him in return, "an indissoluble friendship will arise."
Actions performed as if God loves me and as if, by loving him in return,
I bring about my salvation, make his love true and my election real. Notice
that the Leibnizian *as if* has in common with the Kantian *als ob* that it
corresponds to a practical requirement (theoretico-practical for Kant in the
case of the "regulative" use of transcendental ideas), since it must determine our action. However, Leibniz's *as if* is different in that its application
actually brings about what was initially presented as a fiction. In Kantian
language, such an application no longer consists in limiting oneself to a
*problematic* way of thinking, since in acting we move from the *regulative* use
to the *constitutive* use.[131]

For Leibniz both our salvation and the future of the world are decided
here and now, even though they are completely determined by the series of
causes and are known in God's understanding. To act as if nothing were decided or certain, as if the best possible world and the glory of God could not
be realized without us, as if our election depended solely on our will, is to
do what is necessary for these things to occur and that for which God chose
our world rather than some other. In this way, the will of the creature truly
encounters that of the creator. Human beings destine themselves to what
they will, as if the actual forged the ideal. We are not the cause of our essence,
yet we must act as if we were. For, our choices and free actions, by making
our predestination possible in the divine understanding, make our predestination real in matter of fact. Human freedom is prior to divine freedom
in idea, though subsequent in existence. Human beings are authors of their
fate only with regard to this ideal precedence and are predestined only with
regard to this real subordination. God imposes upon us no character whose
role is written in advance. It is the character who freely writes his story, and
yet his least action is determined and foreseen. In condemning or saving
him, God does no more than conform to a freedom acting to bring about

its own destiny. Human beings are not rewarded or punished; they reward or punish themselves. Their predestination is the reflection in the divine understanding of the destiny they have chosen for themselves.

## NOTES

1. See especially, T §264 and §273.
2. See T §15.
3. Cf. Grua, 475; *Causa Dei*, §98: S 135.
4. T Preface; GP VI, 47; Huggard, 71 (emphasis added).
5. T Preface; GP VI, 27–28. See also T §6.
6. NE IV, 8, §9; A VI, 6, 431–432; RB 431–432.
7. Cf. T Preface; GP VI, 35; and T §2. See also T s III; GP VI, 380.
8. Cf. T §34; *Causa Dei*, §102.
9. Cf. T §34.
10. As Leibniz had already maintained in NE, II, 21, §8; A VI, 6, 175.
11. Cf. T ref §4; GP VI, 391.
12. Cf. T §67, GP VI, 139, Huggard, 159.
13. Cf. T §§68–69.
14. T §75; GP VI, 143; Huggard, 163.
15. Cf. T §71.
16. T §75; GP VI, 142. This freedom, based solely on the absence of constraint, is the only kind allowed by Hobbes.
17. Cf. NE II, XXI, §8; RB 175: Free will "consists in the view that the strongest reasons or impressions which the understanding presents to the will do not prevent the act of the will from being contingent, and do not confer upon it an absolute or (so to speak) metaphysical necessity. It is in this sense that I always say that the understanding can determine the will, in accordance with which perceptions and reasons prevail, in a manner which, although it is certain and infallible, inclines without necessitating." See also Leibniz to Bayle (undated), GP III, 58–59.
18. Cf. T ref §5; GP VI, 392 (concerning thesis 3). On the confusion between determination and necessity in Hobbes, see, for example, *Of Liberty and Necessity*, EW IV, 241 (concerning a passage from the *Numbers*) as well as 246 and 247.
19. Cf. *On Affects*, A VI, 4-B, 1426.
20. Cf. T §35, §46, §48–49.
21. *Meditations*, IV, AT, IX, 46; CSM II, 40.
22. Descartes to Father Mesland (February 9, 1645), AT, IV, 173; CSMK 245.
23. Cf. *Fifth Letter to Clarke*, August 1716, GP VII, 392; L 1136–1137 (§15): "It must also be considered that, properly speaking, motives do not act on the mind as weights do upon a balance, but it is rather the mind that acts by virtue of the motives, which are its dispositions to act." Thus, we must not separate the mind from its motives, as if they were outside of it, "as the weight is distinct from the balance and as if the mind had, besides motives, other dispositions to act by virtue of which it could reject or accept the motives. Whereas, in truth, the motives comprehend all the dispositions which the mind can have to act voluntarily, for they include not only the reasons but also the inclinations arising from passions or other preceding impressions."

24. T §320; GP VI, 306; Huggard, 319. See also §48.
25. T §51; GP VI, 130; Huggard, 151.
26. Cf. *Principles*, I, 39, AT IX, 41.
27. On this point, see in particular NE Preface; A VI, 6, 53–56; NE II, 1, §15; II, 20, §6; II, 21, §36 and §48.
28. Cf. T §50.
29. Cf. T §45. See also NE II, 21, §25.
30. Cf. Aristotle, *Nicomachean Ethics*, III, 3–4, 1111a 22–1112a 17. Aristotle is cited as early as the CP (A VI, 3, 133). On this Aristotelian origin, see in particular E. Pasini, "La doctrine de la spontanéité dans la *Théodicée*," in *Lectures et interprétations des Essais de Théodicée*, 164–165.
31. T §288; GP VI, 288; Huggard, 303.
32. Cf. T §289.
33. Cf. T pd §1, §23, §65.
34. Cf. T §34; GP VI, 122; Huggard, 143: "There is *contingency* in a thousand actions of Nature; but when there is no judgement in him who acts there is no *freedom*."
35. Cf. T §64 and §289. See also *Critical Thoughts on the General Part of the Principles of Descartes*, GP IV, 362–363 (concerning articles 37 and 39).
36. Cf. *Causa Dei*, §§99–100; GP III, 36.
37. T §289; GP VI, 289, Huggard, 303.
38. Such is the consequence of the definition of freedom that he gives at the outset of *Of Liberty and Necessity*: "For he is *free* to do a thing, that may do it if he have the will to do it, and may forbear, if he have the will to forbear" (EW IV, 240). In fact "it cannot be conceived that there is any liberty greater, than for a man to do what he will. One heat may be more intensive than another, but not one liberty than another; he that can do what he will, hath all liberty possible, and he that cannot, hath none at all" (EW IV, 263). Leibniz praises Hobbes for having clearly seen the distinction between freedom and power (T ref §4; GP VI, 391).
39. Cf. NE II, 21, §8.
40. T §291; GP VI, 289–290; Huggard, 304.
41. T Preface; GP VI, 37. See also T §59 and Leibniz to Lady Masham (September 1704), GP III, 364.
42. Cf. T §34, §59, §29, §301.
43. T §51; GP VI, 130; Huggard, 151. See also T §234 and §301; GP VI, 296; Huggard, 310: "It is true that we are not directly the masters of our will, although we are its cause; for we do not choose volitions, as we choose our actions by our volitions." See also *Conversation About Freedom and Fate*, Grua, 482.
44. Cf. A VI, 4-C, 2153: "Proposition I: Consciousness is not under our control [*in potestate*]"; "Proposition II: To believe or not believe something is not under our control"; "Proposition III: One cannot be obligated to do what is not under one's control"; p. 2154: "Proposition IV: One cannot be obligated to believe, but only to seek [the truth] with all one's strength [*summo studio*]." See also Leibniz to Landgrave von Hessen-Rheinfels (March 4–14, 1685); Grua, 193; and Leibniz to the Countess of Bellamont (July 1703), Grua, 216: "However, to believe or not believe is not voluntary. If I believe that I clearly see an error, all the authority in the world could not change my opinion, if unaccompanied by some arguments capable of satisfying my objections or overcoming them. And if the whole Church condemned the doctrine of the motion of the Earth, clever astronomers who subscribe to this doctrine could dissimulate, but it would not be within their power to agree."

45. T §64; GP VI, 137–138; Huggard, 158. See also §301 and Leibniz to Coste (December 19, 1707), GP III, 403.
46. Cf. NE II, 21, §§22–23; A VI, 6, 182. On the importance of circumstances, see T §100 and the example of the Polish twins at §101.
47. T § 327. For example, the Emperor Augustus recited the Greek alphabet "before doing anything in the heat of anger" (T §326; GP VI, 309).
48. Cf. T §328.
49. Leibniz to Electress Sophie (February 6, 1706), GP VII, 569; SLT 84.
50. T ref §4; GP VI, 391; Huggard, 396.
51. On this point see especially NE II, 21, §§17–19; Grua 211–212.
52. T §327; GP VI, 310; Huggard, 323.
53. NE II, 21, §§22–23; A VI, 6, 182 (emphasis added). Cf. T §301; GP VI, 296: "what we *would like* to will at present" (emphasis added).
54. Cf. T §404.
55. NE II, 21, §§22–23; A VI, 6, 182; RB 182.
56. Cf. NE II, 21, §40. Leibniz gives the example of a vote organized so as to favor one or another party in an assembly.
57. Grua, 254. See also CP; A VI, 3, 130; *Extract From a Letter to One of My Friends* (April 3, 1696), Grua, 375.
58. Leibniz to Spanheim (February 20, 1699), Grua, 448.
59. Cf. DM §31; Leibniz to Molanus (February 22, 1698), Grua, 414–415; Leibniz to Naudé (December 29, 1707), Grua, 502.
60. T ob §17; GP VI, 417; Huggard 422.
61. Cf. T §302; GP VI, 296. Contingency is still opposed to chance in the *Fifth Letter to Clarke*, §2, GP VII, 389.
62. Cf. *Causa Dei*, §§102–105; GP VI, 454; S 136.
63. Cf. T §37.
64. T §36; GP VI, 123; Huggard, 143.
65. Cf. T §§36–38.
66. Cf. T §44 and §53.
67. Cf. T §43.
68. *Causa Dei*, §105; GP VI, 454, S 136–137. See also T s III; GP VI, 381.
69. Thus, the hypothesis of a freedom that in some sense takes itself as an object is not an argument in favor of pure indifference (as Descartes maintained), but an argument against it.
70. Cf. GP III, 37: "neither original sin, nor our other evil dispositions render the act of sinning necessary, although our inclination to sin is such that it is certain that we cannot avoid sinning unless we are prevented from doing so by divine grace."
71. Cf. T §§279–280.
72. T §73; GP VI, 141; Huggard, 161.
73. Cf. T Preface; GP VI, 44.
74. T §345; GP VI, 319.
75. T §73; GP VI, 141.
76. Cf. Grua, 881.
77. Contrary to what has been maintained, most notably, by René Sève (in *Leibniz et l'Ecole moderne du droit naturel*) and Gianfranco Mormino (in *Determinismo e utilitarismo nella teodicea di Leibniz*).
78. T §73; GP VI, 141; Huggard, 162–163.
79. *Of Liberty and Necessity*, EW IV, 253.

80. Cf. ibid., 270. See also the definition of punishment in *Leviathan*, II, Ch. 28, EW III, 297.
81. T §74; GP VI, 142; Huggard 162.
82. PNG §15; L 1041. See also T §112 and *Monadology*, §§87–89. In this latter text, Leibniz distinguishes, perhaps more clearly than elsewhere, three pre-established harmonies: (1) that between soul and body; (2) that, in the realm of nature, between efficient and final causes; (3) that between the realm of nature and the realm of grace. Notice that punishments and rewards are sometimes related to the second kind of harmony (T §74) but are more often linked to the third (PNG and *Monadology*). It is not illegitimate to think that they can be related to both at the same time: thus, punishment is the final cause of the pain suffered and at the same time the application in nature of the principles (justice) that govern the order of grace. Nevertheless, it is important for Leibniz to maintain the distinction between these three kinds of harmony and in particular between the latter two, insofar as not all final causes necessarily correspond (at least, directly) to a moral end, as can be seen by their use in physics. In fact, it is by consideration of final causes that we can discover certain laws of nature or the reason for certain organs in animals.
83. T ob §17; GP VI, 417–418; Huggard, 422–423. See also T §74.
84. In his article "La contingence dans les *Essais de théodicée* de Leibniz," 175–189.
85. Ibid., 177.
86. T §7; GP VI, 106; Huggard, 127.
87. On this point see section 5.2.1.
88. Cf. T §§36–58; *Causa Dei*, §§102–106.
89. Cf. Rateau, "Ce qui fait un monde," 56–58.
90. Cf. Grua, 342–343.
91. Cf. T §§52–53.
92. A VI, 4-B, 1458.
93. Cf. A VI, 4-B, 1592.
94. T §9; GP VI, 107–108; Huggard, 128. See also §54; *Conversation About Freedom and Fate*, Grua, 485.
95. Cf. T §54; T s III; GP VI, 381; *Causa Dei*, §44.
96. *Causa Dei*, §123; GP VI, 457; S 140.
97. Cf. *Causa Dei*, §§124–126.
98. Grua, 475.
99. Cf. T §38. *Conversation About Freedom and Fate*, Grua, 481: "And the understanding or foreknowledge of God corresponds to the nature of things."
100. *Conversation About Freedom and Fate*, Grua, 481.
101. Grua 459. The expression "to be the artisan of fortune" (also employed in the *Conversation About Freedom and Fate*, Grua, 481) is an allusion to a famous saying attributed to the consul Appius Claudius Caecus (*Faber est suae quisque fortunae*). Cf. Pseudo-Sallust, *Letters to the Elder Caesar Concerning the Affairs of State* (Letter I, 1, 1).
102. *Conversation with Steno* (November 27, 1677), A VI, 4-B, 1377; Sleigh, 117.
103. Cf. T Preface; GP VI, 30–31. See also *Fifth Letter to Clarke* (August 1716), GP VII, 391 (§13).
104. On the distinction between this particular will and the known, general, and declared will, see A VI, 4-C, 2893; *Conversation About Freedom and Fate*, Grua, 484, *Monadology*, §90.

105. Cf. T §58.
106. Assimilation of the presumptive to the antecedent and of the secret to the consequent is made explicit at *Monadology*, §90.
107. A VI, 4-C, 2893. See also Grua, 254.
108. Cf. DM §4. One must at least strive to do good, "for God, who knows intentions, takes a genuine will for the effect itself" (*On Generosity*, 1686–1687?, A VI, 4-C, 2721; SLT 159).
109. A VI, 4-C, 2893.
110. Cf. DM §4: "Idem velle et idem nolle vera amicitia est." This dictum is attributed to Catiline by Sallust in the *Conspiracy of Catiline*, 20, 4. See also Cicero, *On Friendship*, 20: "Friendship is nothing other than agreement [*consensio*] on all things, both divine and human, accompanied by benevolence and affection [*cum benevolentia et caritate*]."
111. Cf. T §122; GP VI, 177; Huggard, 196–197: "God is not lacking [in good will], he could do the good that we would desire; he even wishes it, taking it separately, but he must not do it in preference to other greater goods which are opposed to it."
112. In fact, we have two reasons for being satisfied. On the one hand, we should be pleased with ourselves for having steadfastly willed the good, and on the other hand, we should be happy, despite our failure, that the best has occurred thanks to God (who knows better than do we what is fitting at such and such time and place).
113. CP; Sleigh, 91 (A VI, 3, 142). See also Leibniz to Arnauld (March 23, 1690), A II, 2, 312–313, and Leibniz to Morell (October 1, 1697), Grua, 114.
114. Cf. *Dialogue Between Theophile and Polidore* (Summer–Autumn, 1679?), A VI, 4-C, 2238–2240. See also T Preface; GP VI, 27–28.
115. Leibniz to Queen Sophie-Charlotte, GP VI, 527.
116. How can I know whether my conduct is the result of perseverance or obstinacy? "However, perseverance is wrong when one despises the warnings of reason, especially when the subject is important enough to be examined carefully; but when the thought of change is unpleasant, one readily averts one's attention from it, and that is the way which most frequently leads to stubbornness" (T ob §25; GP VI, 430; Huggard, 436).
117. Leibniz to the Landgrave von Hessen-Rheinfels (March 4–14, 1685), Grua, 190. Cf. 2 Timothy 4:2: "Preach the word. Be prepared whether the time is favorable or not. Patiently correct, rebuke, and encourage your people with good teaching" (*New Living Translation*).
118. DM §4; A VI, 4-B, 1536; L 468. Cf. Acts 1:7: "It is not for you to know the times or dates the Father has set by his own authority" (*New Living Translation*).
119. Cf. CP; A VI, 3, 129–130.
120. Leibniz to Morell (October 1, 1697), Grua, 114. *Memoir for Enlightened Persons of Good Intention* (circa 1692), A IV, 4, 615: "It is true that God has no need of us and that when we neglect our duty things will still turn out perfectly well." If we do not work for the common good, "the general order or harmony of things *will lose nothing*, rather it is us who will be losers, since we will have less relation to it" (Grua, 92; emphasis added).
121. T §58; GP VI, 134; Huggard, 154–155.
122. T §109; GP VI; 163, Huggard, 183.
123. T §109; GP VI; 163, Huggard, 183.
124. Leibniz to the Electress Sophie, GP VII, 548; SLT 178 (emphasis added).

125. Cf. A VI, 4-C, 2310: "Moreover, God's knowledge and providence certainly ex-
    clude the uncertainty of things, for what will occur will occur in conformity with
    the truth, or in other words, is certain given the way things are, but they do not
    undermine freedom, since we are in fact ignorant of what will happen, just as we
    choose *as if the truth of future contingents were not certain*" (emphasis added).
126. CP; Sleigh, 61 (A VI, 3, 129–130).
127. CP; Sleigh, 37 (A VI, 3, 119). Emphasis added. However, it is not sufficient to
    believe oneself to be among the elect in order to be so. The belief only produces
    election because it is the result of an authentic love of God.
128. CP; Sleigh, 61 (A VI, 3, 130).
129. T §55; GP VI, 133; Huggard, 153. Here Leibniz alludes to a saying tradition-
    ally attributed to Augustine: "If you are not predestined, endeavour to be
    predestined."
130. *Plan de création d'une Société des Arts et des Sciences en Allemagne*, §4, trans.
    J. Baruzi, in *Leibniz. Avec de nombreux textes inédits*, 369.
131. Cf. Kant, *Critique of Pure Reason*, "Transcendental Dialectic," Appendix, "Of the
    Regulative Employment of the Ideas of Pure Reason"; AK III, 427–428, and "Of
    the Ultimate End of the Natural Dialectic of Human Reason," AK III, 456.

# Conclusion

From the time of Leibniz's earliest writings, the question of evil was closely related to that of justice, since the cause of evil is sought from the perspective of determining human and divine responsibility. The explanation of evil—whose existence is undeniable—falls within the domain of theology as well as law. On the one hand, it is based on knowledge of the nature and attributes of God (considered as the origin of all things) and, on the other hand, on the principles of universal justice to which all rational beings, without exception or restriction, are subject. The explanation of evil is part of an attempt, begun in 1667 (see chapter 1) to establish a rational theology that would demonstrate the existence of a supremely wise and good God (in opposition to atheism and skepticism) and a unified jurisprudence that would align positive law with natural law (in opposition to every form of juridical relativism as endorsed by Hobbes) and reconcile individual utility with general interest. The unity of this philosophical project, whose aim is at once moral and religious (true piety and reconciliation of the churches), is based on the conviction that there is a perfect continuity and complementarity between theology and law. Their continuity is evident insofar as theology is defined as a species of jurisprudence. Their complementarity is equally manifest, in that the proofs of the existence of God and the immortality of the soul that theology provides allow for a more extensive and complete application of natural law and also because love of God sits atop the hierarchy of the degrees of law. On this score, Leibniz breaks with those modern jurisconsults who would separate conformity to the law as required of us in this life from reward and punishment after death.

The ambitious goal of the *Catholic Demonstrations* (1668–1671), whose aim is to apply the rigor of demonstrative reasoning to the Christian mysteries (and so to establish their possibility), runs up against certain limits in *On the Omnipotence and Omniscience of God and the Freedom of Man* with regard to the cause and imputation of evil. The casting into syllogistic form of the "sophism" that seeks to make God the author of sin does not provide an adequate solution. On the contrary, it leads to a severe criticism of traditional solutions to the problem of evil that are based on the division of God's physical concurrence and the reduction of evil to nothingness. On this point, there is a clear similarity with Luther, who makes God the cause of evil and rejects the terminology and distinctions of the Scholastics. The similarity with Hobbes is also apparent, even if Leibniz rejects all forms of voluntarism and any suggestion of equivocity with regard to the notions of justice, good, and evil, opting instead for a kind of necessitarianism according to which the divine will is absolutely determined to the best (cf. Leibniz to Magnus Wedderkopf, May 1671).

*The Confession of a Philosopher* (1673) is only partially successful in responding to the difficulties raised in *On the Omnipotence of God*[1] (see chapter 2). Nevertheless, the *Confession* is Leibniz's first genuinely complete work on divine justice. Divine justice is defined as a love that is universal, though one that admits of degrees according to the nature and qualities of the object considered. Despite a sort of rehabilitation of the two kinds of necessity (*per se/ex hypothesi*), Leibniz defends a specific form of necessitarianism according to which God is the first link in the chain of beings that constitute the world, yet absolves him of all responsibility for sin based on a distinction between *reason* and *author*. The consequence of this justificatory strategy is a very restrictive conception of the role of the divine will and the reduction of permission to mere knowledge. The years that follow (beginning in 1675 and especially from the late 1670s onward) are marked by important changes and revisions at the theoretical level. Leibniz is obviously concerned to distinguish more clearly his views from Spinozism and from the strict necessitarianism to which his own conception of God was tending. For, although subject to the necessity of the best, the God of Leibniz was still at risk of being assimilated to nature or fate.

This evolution of Leibnizian doctrine leads to three major theoretical innovations (see chapter 3). First, on the theological level, the personhood of God (his being endowed with understanding and will) is more vigorously affirmed, and his relation to the world is no longer conceived on the logical model of modus ponens. The divine will acquires a more positive role in bringing the world into existence, thereby avoiding the notion of God-fate or a mechanistic God (*Deus mechanicus*). Second, the possible acquires a new characteristic: the "pretension" (*pretention*) to existence. This striving (*effort*) of the possible, which is proportional to its degree of perfection, is not only in God's understanding (the theater of the "conflict" of possibles) but is also exerted in his will in the form of motives and inclinations. As a result, understanding and will are treated as two different expressions of one and the same activity, or *conatus*. This *conatus* is nothing other than force in created substance and omnipotence in God. Third, God's physical and moral concurrence with evil is likewise revisited. The notion of an original imperfection in creatures provides an explanation of the origin of evil and a means of absolving God of sin without calling into question the idea of a complete physical divine concurrence. At the level of moral imputation, the permission of sin becomes part of a "more general, more comprehensive" volition regarding the series of things as a whole. In other words, the doctrine of permission is integrated into the thesis of a unique and global divine decree. Sin is inseparable from the world to which it belongs. For this reason, it must be considered from the point of view of the whole and, to the extent that it contributes to the best system, accepted as a condition sine qua non (though not as a positive means).

It is within this new theoretical framework that the project of Theodicy begins to take shape during the years 1695–1697 (see chapter 4). At first glance, it can seem difficult to determine the object and limits of this project, since the original working title, "Theodicies," suggests a collection of reflections at the intersection of natural theology and jurisprudence. The controversy that arose in the wake of Bayle's writings should not be seen as the direct and unique cause of the composition of the *Essays of Theodicy* (which would appear in 1710). Nevertheless, it led Leibniz to revisit not only the limits but even the very form of his initial project. It showed the need to extend the discussion to problems of revealed theology, to establish the conformity of faith and reason, and to develop a true art of disputation, by establishing the rules of philosophical debate and clearly defining the respective rights and obligations of the defender and objector. The originality of the work is owing to the composite character (which in no way threatens its global coherence) of its argumentation, which combines "demonstration" with proofs drawn from experience and of various degrees of probability. These proofs are both admissible and sufficient in the context of the dispute. Thus, we can distinguish three kinds of discourse. The *refutational* discourse includes (1) the "negative" defense or defense in the strict sense (based on two main arguments: presumption and ignorance of detail) and (2) the "positive" or supererogatory defense, which aims to answer the adversary's objections (notably by appeal to a posteriori evidence of a universal order and of the general prevalence of good over evil in the world).

To this we must add the properly *doctrinal* exposition (3), which aspires to demonstration. This latter consists of two parts, one theological, which concerns "God's conduct" (and considers moral concurrence, physical concurrence, and the origin and nature of evil), and the other anthropological, which concerns human freedom and the moral principles of human action.

If the positive defense does not succeed in developing truly conclusive proofs (which, in any case, is not its aim), the doctrine, which Leibniz characterizes as "so to speak, a kind of science" cannot consist of demonstrations in the strict sense of the term, since it is impossible to *demonstrate* that God chooses the best and that the actual world is the most perfect of all possible worlds (see chapter 5). The thesis of the best of all possible worlds is established on the basis of both a priori and a posteriori considerations. It involves conceiving of our world in its totality—taking into account all times, all places, all creatures, and all events—as the most determinate form in comparison with other possible worlds. It is for this reason that there is only one best world. The proposition that God has chosen the best, although certain and a priori, is nevertheless contingent. Its certainty is infallible, though not absolute, and is based on consideration of *moral* necessity. In the explanation of God's moral concurrence, this moral necessity justifies the permission of sin, which becomes an indispensable obligation that must be satisfied on pain of wrongdoing. In this connection, Leibniz's appeal to the Scholastic distinction between antecedent and consequent will is of capital importance, since it characterizes permission as the effect, in the final volition, of the concourse of particular and incompatible antecedent volitions.

As for God's physical concurrence, Leibniz affirms that it must be complete, continuous, immediate, and special without, for all that, making God responsible for sin (see chapter 6). The origin of evil is rooted in the original imperfection of creatures, who limit, by their very nature, the perfection they receive from God. The model of inertia, despite the difficulties it raises, helps explain certain phenomena, especially moral phenomena, such as resistance to the good and to grace, the inclination to evil, peccaminosity, habitual sin, and obstination in sin. Evil is not merely a defect or a lack but also a tendency (a sort of anti-*conatus*[2]) to further imperfections. For repetition of sin is the wages of sin, its "natural" punishment.

This conception of physical concurrence and the comparison to bodily inertia tend to make evil a "real" ontological deficiency and not a mere moral relation (non-conformity to the law) nor an unfounded phenomenon relative to our particular, incomplete point of view. At the same time, however, evil undergoes a twofold reduction: insofar as it is reduced to a kind or degree of good (an inferior, lesser, or subsidiary good) and insofar as it is considered to be illusory with regard to the universal order that excludes all irregularity and genuine exceptions. As a result, one finds in Leibniz two opposing conceptions of evil, the one *absolute* (according to which evil is a real defect, which must be compensated in the universal harmony) and the other *relative* (according to which evil is the effect of confused perception).

This justification of God places the responsibility for sin squarely on human beings. Must they be free in order to be rightly punished (see chapter 7)? With regard to *corrective* justice, absence of constraint suffices to make reward and punishment legitimate. However, perfect freedom requires in addition absence of necessity. Such freedom justifies the punishments of *vindictive* justice, which go beyond reparation, amendment, and example. Freedom consists in understanding together with spontaneity and contingency.[3] It admits of degrees, since it is based on our understanding—that is, on the distinctness of our knowledge. Spontaneity makes possible a kind of self-mastery, and contingency is compatible with determination, the truth of future contingents, and divine foreknowledge. Although predetermined at the level of existence (*actualiter*), human freedom determines and "precedes" divine freedom at the ideal level (*idealiter*), since the actions foreseen by God number among the reasons that inclined him to create this world rather than some other. The certainty (established by doctrine) that God always acts for the best is the foundation of our confidence in him and provides satisfaction with regard to the past. However, it ought also lead us to act *as if* the future were undetermined and *as if* our salvation and God's glory were uncertain and depended on our present efforts and perseverance. In this way, the divine will will be realized (when human freedom aligns with divine freedom) and the best possible world and the happiness promised to those who love God with a sincere love will be brought about in a completely determinate but wholly contingent manner.[4]

For Leibniz, "Theodicy" is more than simply the title of a book. It is "so to speak, a kind of science." It cannot be a full-fledged science, on account of the different kinds of discourse and argument it involves—negative defense, positive defense, arguments based on possibility, probability and presumption, and a priori arguments that are not strictly demonstrations. Nevertheless, it is a product of reason, which transcends the bounds of a mere controversy with Bayle, a legal plea, or an apologetic discourse on behalf of God's justice. For, it aspires to arrive at certain knowledge of God and of human beings. However, the natural light is incapable of completely satisfying finite creatures like ourselves. It provides the means to resolve difficulties *in general*, "to the extent necessary."[5] However, it cannot provide a *detailed* explanation of the existence of particular evils. There remains a certain gap between infallible certainty of the best and our individual experience, as also between *believing* or *knowing* and *seeing*.[6] As a result, the just person ought to be confident yet prudent in interpreting things and events. If, in this life, explanation of evil is possible and even sufficient to meet objections to God's providence and goodness, it cannot be complete and entirely satisfactory. In this regard, human reason (understood as the collection of truths accessible to our finite minds without the aid of revelation) must recognize its limits. However, its ignorance is not de jure, but de facto and results from its inability to comprehend distinctly the infinite. It is here that Theodicy leads to faith. Nevertheless, this faith must not be thought of as external to reason, but on the contrary, as anticipating an enlarged reason. It is the hope of attaining ever greater knowledge and of grasping a larger and larger proportion of the chain of truths that extends to infinity (and which constitutes universal Reason). Nevertheless, absolute and complete knowledge is unattainable for creatures; it belongs to God alone. Even the blessed who contemplate universal harmony will never cease to grow in knowledge, to penetrate further into the detail of things, and to encounter new reasons for loving divine wisdom.[7] Consequently, even for them, evil will always retain something impenetrable and enigmatic.

## NOTES

1. As can be seen from the opuscule, *The Author of Sin* (1673; in A VI, 3, 150–151), which repeats the critique of God's partial concurrence with sin.
2. Nevertheless, this anti-*conatus* is not a "negative magnitude" in the Kantian sense of the term
3. Cf. T §288; GP VI, 288.
4. To act *as if* is to make real what is conceived as merely hypothetical. It is likewise to bring about what to that point had been in a state of mere possibility and had been among the reasons that determined God to create this universe.
5. T §265; GP VI, 274.
6. Cf. T pd §44 and §82, "here on earth we see apparent injustice, and we believe and even know the truth of the hidden justice of God; but we shall see that justice when at last the Sun of Justice shall show himself as he is" (GP VI, 98; Huggard, 120).
7. Cf. PNG §18.

# BIBLIOGRAPHY

The bibliography does not include Leibniz's works or other primary sources on the list of abbreviations.

## PRIMARY SOURCES

Aguirre, Joseph Saenz de. *De virtutibus et vitiis disputationes ethicae*. Salamanca, 1677.

Anselm of Canterbury. *S. Anselmi Cantuariensis Archiepiscopi opera omnia*. Edited by Franciscus Salesius Schmitt. 6 vols. Rome and Edinburgh: Thomas Nelson and Sons, 1940–1961.

Augustine of Hippo. *Bibliothèque Augustinienne, Œuvres de Saint Augustin*. Paris: Desclée de Brouwer, 1939–.

Bayle, Pierre. *Dictionnaire Historique et Critique*. 5th ed. 4 vols. Amsterdam, 1740.

Bayle, Pierre. *Historical and Critical Dictionary: Selections*. Edited and translated by Richard H. Popkin. Indianapolis: Hackett, 1991.

Boethius. *Consolation of Philosophy*. Translated by Joel C. Relihan. Indianapolis: Hackett, 2001.

Boethius. *De consolatione Philosophiae. Opuscula Sacra*. Edited by Claudio Moreschini. Rev. ed. Munich/Leipzig: K.G. Saur, 2005.

Cicero. *On Friendship*. Translated by W. A. Falconer. In vol. 20. Cambridge, MA: Harvard University Press; London: William Heinemann, Loeb Classical Library, 1923.

Cicero. *On Fate*. Translated by H. Rackham. In vol. 4. Cambridge, MA: Harvard University Press; London: William Heinemann Ltd., Loeb Classical Library, 1942.

Duns Scotus, John. *Opera Omnia*. Lyon, 1639; repr. Hildesheim: Georg Olms, 1968.

Dupleix, Scipion. *L'Ethique ou philosophie morale*. Paris, 1610.

Durandus of Saint-Pourçain. *In Sententias theologicas Petri Lombardi commentariorum libri quatuor*. Lyon, 1556.

Erasmus. Desiderius. *De libero arbitrio diatribe sive collatio*. Basel, 1524.

Erasmus. *Collected Works of Erasmus*. Toronto: University of Toronto Press, 1974–.

Goclenius, Rudolph. *Lexicon philosophicum*. Frankfurt, 1613.

Godart, Pierre. *Lexicon philosophicum*. Paris, 1675.

Jaquelot, Isaac. *Conformité de la foi avec la raison; ou Défense de la religion contre les principales difficultés répandues dans le* Dictionnaire historique et critique *de Mr. Bayle*. Amsterdam: H. Desbordes and D. Pain, 1705.

John of Damascus. *An Exact Exposition of the Orthodox Faith*. Edited by Philip Schaff and Henry Wace. Nicene and Post-Nicene Fathers, Second Series. Vol. 9. Buffalo, NY: Christian Literature, 1899.

Kant, Immanuel. *Kant's gesammelte Schriften*. Edited by Prussian (then German) Academy of Sciences. Berlin and Leipzig: Georg Reimer (later Walter De Gruyter), 1900– (Abbrev. AK).

King, William. *De Origine Mali*. London: B. Tooke, 1702.

Leibniz, Gottfried Wilhelm. *Leibniz. Avec de nombreux textes inédits*. Edited by Jean Baruzi. Paris: Bloud, 1909.

Leibniz, Gottfried Wilhelm. *Confessio Philosophi. La Profession de foi du Philosophephilosophe*. Edited and translated by Yvon Belaval. Paris: Vrin, 1970; 1993.

Leibniz, Gottfried Wilhelm. *Leibniz-Thomasius. Correspondance 1663–1672*. Edited and translated by Richard Bodéüs. Paris: Vrin, 1993.

Leibniz, Gottfried Wilhelm. *Protogaea*. Edited and translated by Claudine Cohen and Andre Wakefield. Chicago: University of Chicago Press, 2008.

Leibniz, Gottfried Wilhelm. *Opuscules philosophiques choisis*. Edited and translated by Paul Schrecker. Paris: Vrin, 1959.

Luther, Martin. *On the Bondage of the Will*. In *Luther and Erasmus: Free Will and Salvation*. Edited and translated by Philip S. Watson and B. Drewery. Vol. 17. Library of Christian Classics. Philadelphia: Westminster Press, 1969.

Malebranche, Nicolas. *Œuvres completes*. Edited by André Robinet. 20 vols. Paris: CNRS/Vrin, 1958–1984.

Malebranche, Nicolas. *Treatise of Nature and Grace*. Translated by Patrick Riley. Oxford: Clarendon Press, 1992.

Molina, Luis de. *Concordia liberi arbitrii cum gratiae donis, divina praescientia, providentia, praedestinatione et reprobatione*. Paris: P. Lethielleux, 1876.

Ockham, William of. *Opera philosophica et theologica*. 17 vols. St. Bonaventure, NY: The Franciscan Institute, 1967–1988.

Piccolomini, Francesco. *Universa philosophia de moribus*. Venice, 1583.

Pufendorf, Samuel von. *De officio hominis et civis juxta legem naturalem libri duo*. Lund, 1673.

Pufendorf, Samuel von. *On the Duty of Man and Citizen According to Natural Law*. Edited by J. Tully. Translated by M. Silverthorne. Cambridge: Cambridge University Press, 1991.

Ricœur, Paul. *Le mal. Un défi à la philosophie et à la théologie*. Geneva: Labor et Fides, 1996.

Scaliger, Julius Caesar. *De causis linguae latinae libri XIII*. Lyon, 1540.

Spinoza, Baruch. *Opera*. Edited by Carl Gebhardt. 4 Vols. Heidelberg: Carl Winters, 1925.

Sturm, Johann Christoph. *Theosophiae seu agnitionis de Deo naturalis specimen*. Altdorf, 1689.

Suarez, Francisco. *Opera omnia*. Edited by M. André and C. Berton. 28 vols. Paris: Louis Vivès, 1856–1878.

Suarez, Francisco. *Disputationes metaphysicae*. 2 vols. Paris: 1866; repr. Hildesheim: Georg Olms, 1965.

Thomasius, Christian. *Institutionum Jurisprudentiae divinae libri tres*. First published in 1688, 7th ed. Halle 1730; repr. Aalen: Scientia, 1963.

Toland, John. *Christianity not Mysterious: or, a Treatise Shewing, That there is nothing in the Gospel Contrary to Reason, Nor Above it: And that no Christian Doctrine can be properly call'd a Mystery*. London: S. Buckley, 1696.

Valla, Lorenzo. *Dialogue on Free Will*. Translated by C. Trinkaus. In *The Renaissance Philosophy of Man*, edited by E. Cassirer et al. Chicago: University of Chicago Press, 1948.

Vattel, Emer de. *The Law of Nations, or, Principles of the Law of Nature, Applied to the Conduct and Affairs of Nations and Sovereigns*. Translated by Joseph Chitty. Philadelphia: T. and J. W. Johnson, 1883.

## SECONDARY SOURCES

Adams, Robert M. "Presumption and the Necessary Existence of God." *Noŭs* (22/1), 1988.

Adams, Robert M. *Leibniz: Determinist, Theist, Idealist*. New-York: Oxford University Press, 1994.

Adams, Robert M. "Leibniz's *Examination of the Christian Religion*." *Faith and Philosophy* (11/4), 1994.

Allen, Diogenes. "The Theological Relevance of Leibniz's Theodicy." *Akten des II. Internationalen Leibniz-Kongresses. Studia Leibnitiana.* Supplementa 14. Wiesbaden, Franz Steiner Verlag, 1975.

Anderson, Joseph M. "Leibniz and Bayle on Divine Permission." In *Leibniz et Bayle: Confrontation et dialogue*, edited by Christian Leduc, Paul Rateau, and Jean-Luc Solère. *Studia Leibnitiana. Sonderheft* 43. Stuttgart: Franz Steiner Verlag, 2015.

Anfray, Jean-Pascal. "Leibniz, le choix du meilleur et la nécessité morale." In *Lectures et interprétations des* Essais de théodicée *de G. W. Leibniz*, edited by Paul Rateau. *Studia Leibnitiana. Sonderheft* 40. Stuttgart: Franz Steiner Verlag, 2011.

Antognazza, Maria Rosa. *Leibniz: An Intellectual Biography*. Cambridge: Cambridge University Press, 2008.

Antognazza, Maria Rosa. "Metaphysical Evil Revisited." In *New Essays on Leibniz's Theodicy*, edited by Larry M. Jorgensen and Samuel Newlands. Oxford: Oxford University Press, 2014.

Baruzi, Jean. *Leibniz et l'organisation religieuse de la terre, d'après des documents inédits*. Paris: Alcan, 1907.

Baruzi, Jean. "Du *Discours de métaphysique* à la *Théodicée*." *Revue philosophique de la France et de l'Étranger* (136/10–12), 1946.

Belaval, Yvon. *Leibniz critique de Descartes*. Paris: Gallimard, 1960.

Belaval, Yvon. *Leibniz. Initiation à sa philosophie*. Paris: Vrin, 1962.

Belaval, Yvon. *Études leibniziennes. De Leibniz à Hegel*. Paris: Gallimard, 1976.

Blumenfeld, David. "Leibniz's Theory of the Striving Possibles." *Studia Leibnitiana* (5/2). Wiesbaden: Franz Steiner Verlag, 1973.

Blumenfeld, David. "Perfection and Happiness in the Best Possible World." In *The Cambridge Companion to Leibniz*, edited by Nicholas Jolley. Cambridge: Cambridge University Press, 1995.

Bouveresse, Jacques. "Leibniz et le problème de la *science moyenne*." *Revue internationale de philosophie* (48), 1994.

Brogi, Stefano. "*Le dualisme caché et l'ars disputandi: Leibniz, Bayle et les manichéens*." In *Leibniz et Bayle: Confrontation et dialogue*, edited by Christian Leduc, Paul Rateau, and Jean-Luc Solère. *Studia Leibnitiana. Sonderheft* 43. Stuttgart: Franz Steiner Verlag, 2015.

Brown, Gregory. "Leibniz's Theodicy and the Confluence of Worldly Goods." *Journal of the History of Philosophy* (26/4), Johns Hopkins University Press, 1988.

Brown, Gregory. "Does the Best of All Possible Worlds Contain the (Absolute) Most?". In *Einheit in der Vielheit*. VIII. Internationaler Leibniz-Kongress. Hanover: Gottfried-Wilhelm-Leibniz-Gesellschaft, 2006.

Brunner, Fernand. "L'optimisme leibnizien." In *Leibniz (1646–1716), Aspects de l'homme et de l'œuvre*. Paris: Aubier-Montaigne, 1968.

Burgelin, Pierre. "Dieu comme architecte et Dieu comme monarque." In *Leibniz (1646–1716), Aspects de l'homme et de l'œuvre*. Paris: Aubier-Montaigne, 1968.

Buzon, Frédéric de. "L'harmonie: métaphysique et phénoménalité." *Revue de métaphysique et de morale* (100/1), 1995.

Celada Ballanti, Roberto. *Erudizione e teodicea. Saggio sulla concezione della storia di G. W. Leibniz*. Naples: Liguori, 2004.

Couturat, Louis. *La logique de Leibniz d'après des documents inédits*. Paris: Alcan, 1901.

Dagron, Tristan. *Leibniz et Toland: l'invention du néo-spinozisme*. Paris: Vrin, 2009.

Dascal, Marcelo. "Nihil sine ratione. *Blandior ratio*." In *Nihil sine ratione*. VII. Internationaler Leibniz-Kongress. Hanover: Gottfried-Wilhelm-Leibniz-Gesellschaft, 2001.

Deleuze, Gilles. *Le pli. Leibniz et le baroque*. Paris: Éditions de Minuit, 1988.

Echavarría, Agustín. *Metafísica leibniziana de la permisión del mal*. Pamplona: EUNSA, 2011.

Echavarría, Agustín. "Leibniz's Concept of God's Permissive Will." In *Lectures et interprétations des* Essais de théodicée *de G. W. Leibniz*, edited by Paul Rateau. *Studia Leibnitiana. Sonderheft* 40. Stuttgart: Franz Steiner Verlag, 2011.

Echavarría, Agustín."Leibniz's Dilemma on Predestination." In *New Essays on Leibniz's Theodicy*, edited by Larry M. Jorgensen and Samuel Newlands. Oxford: Oxford University Press, 2014.

Elster, Jon. *Leibniz et la formation de l'esprit capitaliste*. Paris: Aubier-Montaigne, 1975.

Fichant, Michel. *La réforme de la dynamique. Textes inédits*. Paris: Vrin, 1994.

Fichant, Michel. *Science et métaphysique dans Descartes et Leibniz*. Paris: PUF, 1998.

Fichant, Michel. "L'invention métaphysique." In *Discours de métaphysique, suivi de Monadologie et autres textes*. Paris: Gallimard, Folio/Essais, 2004.

Fichant, Michel. "La constitution du concept de monade." In *Les cahiers philosophiques de Strasbourg*. Strasbourg: Université Marc Bloch, Vol. 18. 2004.

Foucher de Careil, Louis-Alexandre. *Mémoire sur la philosophie de Leibniz*. Paris: F. R. de Rudeval, 1905.

Gaiada, Griselda. *Deo volente. El estatus de la voluntad divina en la teodicea de Leibniz*. Granada: Editorial Comares, Nova Leibniz, 2015.

Gale, George. "On What God Chose: Perfection and God's Freedom." *Studia Leibnitiana* (8/1), Wiesbaden: Franz Steiner Verlag, 1976.

Gaudemar, Martine de. "Éthique et morale chez Leibniz." *Philosophie* (39), Paris: Éditions de Minuit, 1993.

Gaudemar, Martine de. *Leibniz. De la puissance au sujet*. Paris: Vrin, 1994.

Gil, Fernando. "Du droit à la théodicée: Leibniz et la charge de la preuve dans les controverses." *Revue de synthèse* (3/118–119), 1985.

Grua, Gaston. "Optimisme et piété leibnizienne avant 1686, avec des textes inédits." *Revue philosophique de la France et de l'Étranger* (136/10–12), 1946.

Grua, Gaston. *Jurisprudence universelle et théodicée selon Leibniz*. Paris: PUF, 1953 (Abbrev. JUT).

Grua, Gaston. *La justice humaine selon Leibniz*. Paris: PUF, 1956 (Abbrev. JH).

Gueroult, Martial. *Leibniz, Dynamique et métaphysique*. Paris: Aubier-Montaigne, 1967.

Heinekamp, Albert. "Zu den Begriffen Realitas, Perfectum und bonum metaphysicum." *Studia Leibnitiana. Supplementa* 1. Wiesbaden: Franz Steiner Verlag, 1968.

Heinekamp, Albert. *Das Problem des Guten bei Leibniz*. Bonn: H. Bouvier, 1969.

Hildebrandt, Kurt. *Leibniz und das Reich der Gnade*. The Hague: M. Nijhoff, 1953.

Hostler, John. "Some Remarks on 'omne possibile exigit existere.'" *Studia Leibnitiana* (5/2). Wiesbaden: Franz Steiner Verlag, 1973.

Hübener, Wolfgang. "Sinn und Grenzen des leibnizischen Optimismus." *Studia Leibnitiana* (10/2). Wiesbaden: Franz Steiner Verlag, 1978.

Ishiguro, Hidé. "Contingent Truths and Possible Worlds." In *Leibniz: Metaphysics and Philosophy of Science*, edited by R. S. Woolhouse. Oxford: Oxford University Press, 1981.

Jalabert, Jacques. *Le Dieu de Leibniz*. Paris: PUF, 1960.

Jesseph, Douglas M. "Leibniz, Hobbes and Bramhall on Free Will and Divine Justice." In *Nihil sine ratione*. VII. Internationaler Leibniz-Kongress. Hanover: Gottfried-Wilhelm-Leibniz-Gesellschaft, 2001.

Johns, Christopher. *The Science of Right in Leibniz's Moral and Political Philosophy*. London, New Delhi, New York, and Sydney: Bloomsbury, 2013.

Jolley, Nicholas. *Leibniz*. London and New York: Routledge, 2005.

Jolley, Nicholas. "Is Leibniz's Theodicy a Variation on a Theme by Malebranche?" In *New Essays on Leibniz's Theodicy*, edited by Larry M. Jorgensen and Samuel Newlands. Oxford: Oxford University Press, 2014.

Knebel, Sven K. "Necessitas moralis ad Optimum. Zum historischen Hintergrund der Wahl der besten aller möglichen Welten." *Studia Leibnitiana* (23/1). Stuttgart: Franz Steiner Verlag, 1991.

Knecht, Herbert H. *La logique chez Leibniz. Essai sur le rationalisme baroque*. Lausanne: L'Age d'Homme, 1981.

Knobloch, Eberhard. "La détermination mathématique du meilleur." In *Leibniz: Le meilleur des mondes. Studia Leibnitiana. Sonderheft* 21. Stuttgart: Franz Steiner Verlag, 1992.

Kulstad, Mark A. *Leibniz on Apperception, Consciousness and Reflection*. Munich: Philosophia Verlag, 1991.

Latour-Derrien, Annik. *Logique du probable et épistémologie théologique dans les* Essais de Théodicée *de Leibniz*. Doctoral dissertation. University Paris IV–Sorbonne and University of Montreal, 2004.

Latzer, Michael. "The Nature of Evil: Leibniz and His Medieval Background." *The Modern Schoolman* (71/1), 1993.

Latzer, Michael. "Leibniz's Conception of Metaphysical Evil." *Journal of the History of Ideas* (55/1), 1994.

Lærke, Mogens. *Leibniz lecteur de Spinoza. La genèse d'une opposition complexe*. Paris: Honoré Champion, 2008.

Lee, Sukjae. "Leibniz on Divine Concurrence." *The Philosophical Review* (113/2), 2004.

Lorenz, Stefan. *De Mundo Optimo. Studien zu Leibniz'Theodizee und ihrer Rezeption in Deutschland (1710–1791). Studia Leibnitiana. Supplementa* 31. Stuttgart: Franz Steiner Verlag, 1997.

Mates, Benson. *The Philosophy of Leibniz: Metaphysics and Language*. Oxford: Oxford University Press, 1986.

McDonough, Jeffrey. "Leibniz: Creation and Conservation and Concurrence." *The Leibniz Review* (17), 2007.

Mormino, Gianfranco. "Optimisme a posteriori et lois du mouvement dans les *Essais de Théodicée*." In *Nihil sine ratione*. VII. Internationaler Leibniz-Kongress. Hanover: Gottfried-Wilhelm-Leibniz-Gesellschaft, 2001.

Mormino, Gianfranco. "La limitation originaire des créatures chez Leibniz." In *La Monadologie de Leibniz: genèse et contexte*, edited by Enrico Pasini. Paris and Milan: Mimesis, 2005.

Mormino, Gianfranco. *Determinismo e utilitarismo nella Teodicea di Leibniz*. Milan: Franco Angeli, 2005.

Mormino, Gianfranco. "Peines humaines et peines divines. Théodicée et droit de punir dans la pensée de Leibniz." In *L'idée de théodicée de Leibniz à Kant: Héritage, transformations, critiques*, edited by Paul Rateau. *Studia Leibnitiana. Sonderheft* 36. Stuttgart: Franz Steiner Verlag, 2009.

Mormino, Gianfranco. "La contingence dans les *Essais de Théodicée* de Leibniz: Un réquisit de la liberté?" In *Lectures et interprétations des* Essais de théodicée *de G. W. Leibniz*, edited by Paul Rateau. *Studia Leibnitiana. Sonderheft* 40. Stuttgart: Franz Steiner Verlag, 2011.

Murray, Michael J. "Leibniz on Divine Foreknowledge of Future Contingents and Human Freedom." *Philosophy and Phenomenological Research* (55/1), 1995.

Murray, Michael J. "Intellect, Will, and Freedom: Leibniz and His Precursors." *Leibniz Review* (6), 1996.

Murray, Michael J. "Spontaneity and Freedom in Leibniz." In *Nihil sine ratione*. VII. Internationaler Leibniz-Kongress. Hanover: Gottfried-Wilhelm-Leibniz-Gesellschaft, 2001.

Murray, Michael J. "Pre-Leibnizian Moral Necessity." *The Leibniz Review* (14), 2004.

Murray, Michael J. "*Vindicatio Dei*: Evil as a Result of God's Free Choice of the Best." In *New Essays on Leibniz's* Theodicy, edited by Larry M. Jorgensen and Samuel Newlands. Oxford: Oxford University Press, 2014.

Nadler, Steven. *The Best of All Possible Worlds: A Story of Philosophers, God, and Evil*. Farrar, Straus and Giroux, 2008; Princeton University Press, 2010.

Naërt, Émilienne. *Leibniz et la Querelle du pur amour*. Paris: Vrin, 1959.

Naërt, Émilienne. *Mémoire et conscience de soi selon Leibniz*. Paris: Vrin, 1961.

Newlands, Samuel. "Leibniz on Privations, Limitations, and the Metaphysics of Evil." *Journal of the History of Philosophy* (52/2), 2014.

Nicolás, Juan Antonio. "La rationalité morale du monde chez Leibniz." In *Leibniz: Le meilleur des mondes. Studia Leibnitiana. Sonderheft* 21. Stuttgart: Franz Steiner Verlag, 1992.

Parkinson, G. H. R. *Logic and Reality in Leibniz's Metaphysics*. New York: Oxford University Press, 1965.

Pasini, Enrico. "La doctrine de la spontanéité dans la *Théodicée*." In *Lectures et interprétations des* Essais de Théodicée *de G.-W. Leibniz*, edited by P. Rateau. *Studia Leibnitiana. Sonderheft* 40. Stuttgart: Franz Steiner Verlag, 2011.

Piro, Francesco. *Varietas identitate compensata. Studio sulla formazione della metafisica di Leibniz*. Naples: Bibliopolis, 1990.

Piro, Francesco. "L'action des créatures et le concours de Dieu chez Leibniz: Entre trans-créationnistes et durandiens." In *Lectures et interprétations des* Essais de théodicée *de G. W. Leibniz*, edited by Paul Rateau. *Studia Leibnitiana. Sonderheft* 40. Stuttgart: Franz Steiner Verlag, 2011.

Poser, Hans. *Zur Theorie der Modalbegriffe bei G. W. Leibniz. Studia Leibnitiana. Supplementa* 6. Wiesbaden: Franz Steiner Verlag, 1969.

Poser, Hans. "Wahrheit, Möglichkeit, Kompossibilität. Die komplexe Basis der Theodizee-Argumentation." In *Lectures et interprétations des* Essais de théodicée *de G. W. Leibniz*, edited by Paul Rateau. *Studia Leibnitiana. Sonderheft* 40. Stuttgart: Franz Steiner Verlag, 2011.

Rateau, Paul. "Art et fiction chez Leibniz." In *Les Cahiers philosophiques de Strasbourg* (18), 2004.

Rateau, Paul. "Le problème du calcul des biens et des maux dans l'harmonie universelle, dans les *Essais de Théodicée*." In *Einheit in der Vielheit*. VIII. Internationaler Leibniz-Kongress. Hanover: Gottfried-Wilhelm-Leibniz-Gesellschaft, 2006.

Rateau, Paul. *La question du mal chez Leibniz. Fondements et élaboration de la Théodicée.* Paris: Honoré Champion, 2008.

Rateau, Paul. "L'essai leibnizien de théodicée et la critique de Kant." In *L'idée de théodicée de Leibniz à Kant: Héritage, transformations, critiques*, edited by Paul Rateau. *Studia Leibnitiana. Sonderheft* 36. Stuttgart: Franz Steiner Verlag, 2009.

Rateau, Paul. "Ce qui fait un monde: Compossibilité, perfection et harmonie." In *Lectures et interprétations des* Essais de Théodicée *de G. W. Leibniz*, edited by Paul Rateau. *Studia Leibnitiana. Sonderheft* 40. Stuttgart: Franz Steiner Verlag, 2011.

Rateau, Paul. "The Theoretical Foundations of the Leibnizian Theodicy and Its Apologetic Aim." In *New Essays on Leibniz's* Theodicy, edited by Larry M. Jorgensen and Samuel Newlands. Oxford: Oxford University Press, 2014.

Rateau, Paul. "Leibniz, Bayle et la figure de l'athée vertueux." In *Leibniz et Bayle: Confrontation et dialogue*, edited by Christian Leduc, Paul Rateau, and Jean-Luc Solère. *Studia Leibnitiana. Sonderheft* 43. Stuttgart: Franz Steiner Verlag, 2015.

Rateau, Paul. *Leibniz et le meilleur des mondes possibles*. Paris: Classiques Garnier, 2015.

Rescher, Nicholas. *Leibniz's Metaphysics of Nature*. Dordrecht: D. Reidel, 1981.

Riley, Patrick. *Leibniz's Universal Jurisprudence: Justice as the Charity of the Wise.* Cambridge, MA: Harvard University Press, 1996.

Robinet, André. "Les Destinées du mythe de Sextus dans la *Théodicée*." *Les Études philosophiques* (1), 1982.

Robinet, André. *Architectonique disjonctive, automates systémiques et idéalité transcendantale dans l'œuvre de G. W. Leibniz*. Paris: Vrin, 1986.

Robinet, André. *G. W. Leibniz: Le meilleur des mondes par la balance de l'Europe.* Paris: PUF, 1994.

Rösler-Le Van, Claire. Negotium Irenicum. *L'union des Églises protestantes selon G. W. Leibniz et D. E. Jablonski*. Paris: Classiques Garnier, 2013.

Russell, Bertrand. *A Critical Exposition of the Philosophy of Leibniz*. Cambridge: Cambridge University Press, 1900.

Rutherford, Donald. *Leibniz and the Rational Order of Nature*. Cambridge: Cambridge University Press, 1995.

Rutherford, Donald. "Justice and Circumstances: Theodicy as Universal Religion." In *New Essays on Leibniz's* Theodicy, edited by Larry M. Jorgensen and Samuel Newlands. Oxford: Oxford University Press, 2014.

Schmaltz, Tad M. "Malebranche and Leibniz on the Best of All Possible Worlds." *Southern Journal of Philosophy* (48/1), 2010.

Schmaltz, Tad M. "Moral Evil and Divine Concurrence in the *Theodicy*". In *New Essays on Leibniz's* Theodicy, edited by Larry M. Jorgensen and Samuel Newlands. Oxford: Oxford University Press, 2014.

Scribano, Emanuela. "False Enemies: Malebranche, Leibniz, and the Best of All Possible Worlds." *Oxford Studies in Early Modern Philosophy* (1), 2003.

Sève, René. *Leibniz et l'École moderne du droit naturel*. Paris: PUF, 1989.

Shields, Christopher J. "Leibniz's Doctrine of the Striving Possibles." *Journal of the History of Philosophy* (24/3), 1986.

Sleigh, Robert, Jr. "Remarks on Leibniz's Treatment of the Problem of Evil." In *The Problem of Evil in Modern Philosophy*, edited by Elmar J. Kremer and Michael Latzer. Toronto: University of Toronto Press, 2001.

Solère, Jean-Luc. "Création continuelle, concours divin et théodicée dans le débat Bayle-Jacquelot-Leibniz." In *Leibniz et Bayle: Confrontation et dialogue*, edited by Christian Leduc, Paul Rateau, and Jean-Luc Solère. *Studia Leibnitiana. Sonderheft* 43. Stuttgart: Franz Steiner Verlag, 2015.

Wilson, Catherine. "Leibnizian Optimism." *Journal of Philosophy* (80/11), 1983.

Wilson, Catherine. *Leibniz's Metaphysics: A Historical and Comparative Study*. Princeton: Princeton University Press, 1990.

Wilson, Catherine. "Plenitude and Compossibility in Leibniz." *The Leibniz Review* (10), 2000.

Yakira, Elhanan. *Contrainte, nécessité, choix. La métaphysique de la liberté chez Spinoza et chez Leibniz*. Zurich: Éditions du Grand Midi, 1989.

# INDEX